IT WAS A LONG TIME AGO,
AND IT NEVER HAPPENED ANYWAY

It Was a Long Time Ago, and It Never Happened Anyway

Russia and the Communist Past

■

David Satter

Yale

UNIVERSITY PRESS

New Haven & London

Yale University Press books may be purchased in quantity for educational,
business, or promotional use. For information, please e-mail
sales.press@yale.edu (U.S. office) or sales@yaleup.co.uk (U.K. office).

Set in Galliard Oldstyle type by Keystone Typesetting, Inc.
Printed in the United States of America.

Library of Congress Cataloging-in-Publication Data
Satter, David, 1947–
It was a long time ago, and it never happened anyway :
Russia and the communist past / David Satter.
p.   cm.
Includes bibliographical references and index.
ISBN 978-0-300-11145-3 (cloth : alk. paper)
1. Soviet Union — History — 1925–1953. 2. Atrocities — Soviet Union —
History. 3. Atrocities — Soviet Union — Public opinion. 4. Communism —
Soviet Union — History. 5. Communism — Soviet Union — Public opinion.
6. Public opinion — Russia (Federation) 7. Kommunisticheskaia partiia
Sovetskogo Soiuza — History. 8. Soviet Union. Narodnyi komissariat
vnutrennikh del — History. 9. Soviet Union. Komitet gosudarstvennoi
bezopasnosti — History. 10. Stalin, Joseph, 1879–1953. I. Title.
DK267.S24   2012
947.084′2 — dc23
2011022685

A catalogue record for this book is available from the British Library.

This paper meets the requirements of ANSI/NISO Z39.48-1992 (Permanence
of Paper).

10 9 8 7 6 5 4 3 2 1

For Raphael, Claire, and Mark

Хотелось бы всех поиммено назвать,
Да отняли список, и негде искать

—*Анна Ахматова, "Реквием"*

I would have wanted to recall them all
   by name
But they took the list and there's
   nowhere to find it

—*Anna Akhmatova, "Requiem"*
(translation by the author)

CONTENTS

■

CONTENTS

ACKNOWLEDGMENTS

■

I owe a debt of gratitude to a number of institutions that provided me with support: the Sarah Scaife Foundation, the Smith Richardson Foundation, the Kathryn W. Davis Foundation (now the Diana Davis Spencer Foundation), the William H. Donner Foundation, and the Earhart Foundation. In addition, I received support from the Hoover Institution, where I was a research fellow from 2003 to 2008. I would like to express my personal thanks to Daniel McMichael, Michael Gleba, Nadia Schadlow, Marin Strmeki, Diana Davis Spencer, Abby Moffat, Curt Winsor, Ingrid Gregg, and John Raisian. This book could not have been written without this timely and generous assistance.

I am currently affiliated with the Hudson Institute and the Johns Hopkins University School of Advanced International Studies (SAIS). I would like to thank Kenneth Weinstein, the president of Hudson, and Amir Pasic, the director of the Foreign Policy Institute at SAIS, for their encouragement and help.

In Moscow I benefited greatly from the assistance of the Memorial Society, in particular Arseny Roginsky, Yelena Zhemkova, Irina Flige, Boris Belenkin, Alexander Daniel, Leonid Novak, Nikitia Petrov, Alexei Korotaev, and Marina Grant.

The staff of the Slavic Reference Service at the University of Illinois, Urbana-Champaign, helped me to find needed materials both when I was a visiting professor at the university in 2008 and after my return to Washington. I am also grateful to the research staff of the Hoover Institution Archives for their help.

ACKNOWLEDGMENTS

Andrew Nagorski, Gershon Braun, my sister Beryl Satter, and my sons Raphael and Mark read early versions of the manuscript and provided helpful suggestions and comments. Olga Printseva took time from a busy schedule to help me with the bibliography and notes.

ABBREVIATIONS AND
ADMINISTRATIVE DELINEATIONS

■

Cheka	All Russian Extraordinary Commission for Combating Counter Revolution and Sabotage
FSB	Federal Security Service
GAI	State Automobile Inspection
GIBDD	State Inspectorate for the Security of Automobile Traffic, successor in 1988 to GAI
KGB	Committee for State Security
MChS	Ministry for Extraordinary Situations
MVD	Ministry of Internal Affairs
NKVD	People's Commissariat of Internal Affairs
OGPU	Joint State Political Directorate, successor to the Cheka
RSFSR	Russian Soviet Federative Socialist Republic, the Russian "republic" of the Soviet Union
SVR	Foreign Intelligence Service
Sovnarkom	Council of People's Commissars, the first Soviet government
Voenkomat	Military Commissariat
Krai	Best translated as "province" or "territory," a krai is a territorial subdivision that generally encompasses a large area, such as Primoriye in the Far East or the Krasnoyarsk region in Siberia.

Oblast   Often similar in size to an American state, an oblast is a territorial subdivision of the Russian Federation. Since 2004 the governors of oblasts, as well as the mayors of Moscow and St. Petersburg, which are also considered "subjects of the federation," have been appointed by the president.

Raion   A raion is a subdivision of an oblast or city and is responsible for most local administration, including the police and the courts.

Okrug   An okrug is an administrative subdivision of Moscow. The Moscow okrugs were created in the mid-1990s as a result of the consolidation of groups of raions. An okrug can also be a Russian military district, for example, the North Caucasus military okrug.

IT WAS A LONG TIME AGO,
AND IT NEVER HAPPENED ANYWAY

Introduction

■

In spring 1989 a group of students from the Memorial Society entered a pine forest near Barnaul in western Siberia carrying shovels and tarpaulin bags. They were seeking the site of a mass burial ground of Stalin's victims. There had long been rumors about burial pits in the area. But before perestroika, few had the courage to search for them.

It was a cool, windy day. The students ascended a steep incline near the walls of the old city prison. In the winter, the forest is blanketed with snow, but the spring reveals depressions in the earth created as bodies buried just beneath the surface decompose. The students reached an area of sparse trees. There were several dozen such pits, twenty-five to thirty-five feet in diameter and about one and a half feet deep. They chose a pit in the center and began to dig. The shovels soon hit bones. The members of the group, which included Vladimir Ryzhkov, a future liberal member of the State Duma, opened a mass grave containing the remains of ten to twelve persons and the rotting remnants of shoes and clothes. In the back of the skulls were visible the holes from bullets. There were several Soviet coins from the 1930s. Some of the victims were barefoot.

According to longtime residents of Barnaul, victims were shot at night in the basement of the oblast NKVD building on the corner of Lenin Prospect and Polzunovskaya Street. There are traces of bullets in the old bricks. The building today is still being used as a prison. The internal courtyard, which dates from the 1930s, is used as an exercise yard by the current detainees.

The students did not open the remaining pits. It was already clear what they contained. The city council and the mayor's office put up a memorial plaque. But the site was never fully investigated. Like many others, it still has no official status. In fact, there is no federal registry of such burial grounds, of which there are hundreds if not thousands all over Russia. As a result, many Russian families still do not know where their relatives are buried.

Ryzhkov was deeply moved by what he saw. The task of registering the sites, he wrote, "is work first of all for ourselves. If we don't do this, no one will do it. . . . I know as one who stood at the edge of that cold pit that a person who sees this, forever becomes different."[1]

Russia as a country has not been willing to face the full truth about Communism. Some people insist that the scale of the crimes has been exaggerated or that they were a product of necessity in a unique historical situation. Some say that there were comparable crimes in the West. Many argue that the Soviet system had redeeming features, that it brought literacy to millions of people and modernized the country. In fact, the failure to condemn Communism unreservedly — as Nazism was condemned in Germany — is now taken for granted in Russia.

During the period 1929 to 1953, eighteen million persons passed through the Soviet labor camp system. The artificial famine of 1932–33 took seven million lives. Nearly a million persons were shot during the Great Terror of 1937–38. In all, the number of persons who died in peacetime as a result of the actions of the Communist authorities is estimated at twenty million. If one considers the demographic impact on three generations (1917–53), it can be estimated that the total population loss — those killed and those who were never born — comes to 100 million persons.[2]

Despite this, there is no will in Russia to understand the moral significance of what took place. Vyacheslav Nikonov, a political scientist and the grandson of Stalin's prime minister, Vyacheslav Molotov, said, "People are not interested in the past. Any attempt to dig into the past evokes only irritation."[3] But this attitude is not without risk. Communism built on the authoritarian instincts of a historically enslaved population. Left unexamined, these instincts now threaten Russia's future.[4]

The situation in Russia bears some resemblance to that of Germany after World War II. The German philosopher Karl Jaspers at that time wrote, "All of us have somehow lost the ground under our feet. Only a transcendent . . . religious or philosophical faith can maintain itself through all these disasters. . . . We are sorely deficient in talking to each other and listening to each other. We lack mobility, criticism and self-criticism. We incline to doctrinism. What makes it worse is that so many people do not want to think. They want only slogans and obedience. They ask no questions and they give no answers, except by repeating drilled in phrases."[5]

Russia has neither a national monument to the victims of Communist terror nor a national museum. In 2008, on the territory of Russia, there were 627 memorials and memorial plaques dedicated to the victims. This is fewer than the number of labor camps.[6] The majority are not in central locations, and almost all were created by private citizens, not the government. (Exceptions are a few monuments erected by local Russian governments during perestroika and the monuments in Katyn and Mednoe to the Polish victims of the Katyn massacre, created by the Polish government with Russian cooperation.)

At the same time, sites that are critical to the memory of what happened in Russia during the Communist terror may be destroyed. One such place, the building of the Military Collegium of the Supreme Court of the USSR at 23 Nikolskaya Street, where thirty-five thousand persons were sentenced to death in two years, has been purchased by a bank close to the government of Moscow. It will be renovated and used as part of a trade and entertainment complex.[7]

A visitor strolling through Moscow finds little to remind him that the city was the scene of mass terror, yet a "Topography of Terror" prepared by the Memorial Society lists hundreds of sites. On April 4, 2007, a group of deputies in the State Duma, acting at the request of Memorial, appealed to the country's leadership to return to the idea, first raised during perestroika, of creating a national museum and monument dedicated to the victims of Communist terror. One of the places that would unquestionably be part of the memorial, the authors said, was the building of the Military Collegium on Nikolskaya Street. There has been no response.[8]

Reminders of the Stalinist terror are visible everywhere. Bolshoi Uspensky Street, which in 1922 was renamed Potapovsky Lane, begins with a three-story building on the corner of Arkhangelsky Lane in which Viktor Abakumov, Stalin's minister of security, had his apartment. It ends at Pokrovka Street, once the site of the Uspeniya Bogoroditsa church, which was built at the end of the seventeenth century and was considered the most beautiful church in Moscow after St. Basil's.[9] According to legend, Napoleon in 1812 liked the church so much that he wanted to transport it to Paris.[10] More than a century later, on November 28, 1935, the Moscow city council ordered the church destroyed. The reason was the "urgent necessity of broadening the thoroughfare on Pokrovka Street."[11]

Immediately next to the empty square where the church once stood is an apartment building that today houses an art gallery. During the Great Terror, the bodies of executed "enemies of the people" were buried in its basement and in an underground passageway that led under Potapovsky Lane to Sverchkov Lane.

This activity was known to the residents of Potapovsky Lane, but no one spoke of it during the terror. People from every building on the lane were taken to be shot. Twenty-two persons were taken from building number 9, three from building 6, and one each from buildings 4, 5, and 7. Four persons were taken from building 10, two from house number 12, and one from number 16. In all, thirty-five residents of the quiet side street, which is 283 paces from beginning to end, were executed during the Great Terror. More than a hundred others were arrested and sent to labor camps or exile. Similar figures exist for nearly every street in Moscow.[12]

Besides the lack of a national monument to the victims of Communist terror, there has been a failure to punish the guilty. Instead, the Soviet Union's most criminal leaders, particularly Stalin, have been tacitly rehabilitated.

In 1998 the number of Russians approving Stalin's activities, according to public opinion polls, was 19 percent. By 2002–3, with Vladimir Putin as president, the percentage had risen to 53 percent and was still at that level in 2008.[13] In August 2009 an inscription honoring Stalin — "We were raised by Stalin on loyalty to the people . . . " — was unveiled in the restored Kursk metro station in Moscow, and serious consideration was given to displaying posters of Stalin in Moscow and St. Petersburg in connection with the sixty-fifth anniversary of the Soviet victory in the Second World War.[14] In the end, the idea was dropped, but Stalin's portrait appeared as an advertisement on a bus that ran along the main street in St. Petersburg, Nevsky Prospect.[15]

The support for Stalin is sometimes attributed to a sense of national inferiority in the wake of the collapse of the Soviet Union. But its roots are deeper. It derives from the fact that criticism of Stalin in Russia did not touch on the core principle of the Soviet system of power, the disregard for the individual in the face of the need to realize the tasks of the state. This is one reason why the "young reformers" in post-Communist Russia also did not hesitate to resort to brutal social engineering to achieve their goals.[16] They were creating capitalism instead of communism, but their actions legitimized the notion, associated most of all with Stalin, that the transformation of society justifies any human cost.

In this situation, there has been no genuine act of repentance on the part of the Russian government directed toward the millions who suffered under Communism. The rehabilitation process consisted of the government removing the guilt of those who were falsely convicted. The state reserved the right to judge; it was not judged. Insofar as Russia is the legal heir to the Soviet Union, it left the question of the Soviet state's guilt unresolved.

Jaspers argued that only a nation that acknowledges its guilt can overcome the spiritual disaster wrought by totalitarianism. He identified three types of guilt that apply to the individual: criminal guilt, which is susceptible to objective proof; political guilt, which involves the deeds of statesmen; and moral guilt, which involves basic principles and can be applied even to one who is carrying out military or political orders. But there is also, he argues, a fourth type of guilt, which applies to the community as a whole and may accrue even in the absence of specific criminal acts. This is "metaphysical guilt," which affects all those who were touched by atrocious crimes, whether as participants or not.[17]

"There exists a solidarity among men as human beings that makes each co-responsible for every wrong and every injustice in the world, especially for crimes committed in his presence or with his knowledge," Jaspers wrote. "If I fail to do whatever I can to prevent them, I too am guilty. If I was present at the murder of others without risking my life to prevent it, I feel guilty in a way not adequately conceivable either legally, politically or morally. That I live after such a thing has happened, weighs upon me as indelible guilt." For Jaspers, metaphysical guilt, the lack of absolute solidarity with the human being as such, makes a claim beyond "morally meaningful duty."[18] It is a characteristic of the world today that Germans, as a people, accepted this metaphysical guilt and the Russians did not.[19]

In Russia, the idea that tragic history can be absorbed and made part of the national consciousness has not been acknowledged. In place of national memory, a new national myth has replaced the myths of Communism. It says: "We are a country with a great past. There were bad things in our history. No one justifies terror and repression. But we were great in the past and we will be great in the future." Talk of terror interferes with the return of historical pride.[20]

Putin, in a speech given in April 2008, demonstrated how little importance Russia's leaders attach to the fate of the individual. He said that "maintaining the governance of a vast territory, preserving a unique commonwealth of peoples while occupying a major place in world affairs calls . . . for enormous sacrifices and privations on the part of our people. Such has been Russia's thousand-year history. Such is the way in which it has retained its place as a mighty nation. We do not have the right to forget this."[21] In other words, the Russian people, at the cost of "enormous sacrifices and privations," should support the regime's ambitions until the end of time. "The elite's view of the people . . . as God fearing riff-raff, as colonial natives, raw material for national stunts of one kind or another," wrote the Russian publicist Andrei Piontkovsky, "led us equally to the catastrophe of 1917 and to the catastrophe of 1991. It will lead us to a third if our elite, bloated and reckless as never before, does not abandon its centuries old enthusiasm for sacrifice and privations inflicted on a people whose mission is the accomplishment of great tasks."[22]

The failure to memorialize the victims of Communist terror has contributed to the moral corrosion of Russian society. Disregard for human life exists in many countries, but in Russia it is unsurprising to see it carried to grim extremes. In January 2002 a victim of this attitude was Taras Shugaev, a twenty-five-year-old billiard player. His story stunned even the normally complacent Russian capital.

Sometime between 5:30 and 6 A.M. on January 9, Shugaev left the billiard hall in the Moscow Palace of Youth. He had been drinking, but he was not dead drunk. Nonetheless, he lost consciousness on the street, and a person or persons put him in a garbage bin that was emptied into the back of a garbage truck. When Shugaev came to, he was in complete darkness inches away from showers of garbage being pulverized by the blades of the truck. For the next twenty-three minutes, he was on his cell phone to the Rescue Service, begging for help to escape. The following are excerpts from Shugaev's desperate last conversations. At 6:20 A.M. there is a call from Khamovnichesky Val:

"Operator 23, Moscow Rescue Service, I'm listening to you."

"Hello! Is this the rescue service?"

"Yes. Yes."

"I am in a garbage truck."

"What are you doing there?"

"I don't know. I simply had too much to drink. My acquaintances, friends. I don't even know who put me here. I am being turned around but I'm still alive, please call to the police or GAI so that they stop the garbage truck!"

"And where are you going?"

"I left from the Frunzenskaya metro station."

"In what direction?"

"I think in the direction away from Moscow on Prospect Vernadsky or maybe toward the center. Please call the GAI."

"But different branches of the GIBDD serve this area."

"I can't call the GAI, understand that my life depends on this — please call!"

At 6:21 A.M. there is another call from Khamovnichesky Val.

"Rescue service . . . hello!"

"I am calling you. I am in a garbage truck!"

"Yes. Where did you turn up?"

"How am I supposed to know?! I'm in complete darkness inside a truck."

"Well in what region did you end up in there?"

"Hello!"

There is the sound of garbage being pulverized.

"Hello! Can you give a sign or somehow knock so that the driver stops the truck?"

Commotion.

"Hello, young man, can you do something so that the driver stops the truck and helps you to get out. Do you have something with which to knock? Where is the driver located?"

"He doesn't hear me. I already know that he doesn't hear me!"

"Well, what do you know? Have you tried to knock? Take off one of your boots!"

"He doesn't hear me! I know this!"

"I understand that he doesn't hear you right now. But how can we find you? Should we stop every garbage truck in Frunzenskaya and check them? Do you understand?"

There is interference with the line.

"How did you end up there?"

At 6:31 A.M. there is a third call, this time from Bolshaya Pirogovskaya Street:

"Hello (practically crying). I am from the garbage truck."

"Are you in the container or where the press is located?"

"Inside the container or where the press is I don't know. I've already been struck."

"You've been struck? Yes? Can you use something to knock on the walls of the truck?"

"I knock and scream but no one hears me."

"It's not necessary to scream. You need something metallic. Is there something there? Take off your boots. Find anything that comes to hand. Knock on the walls."

"I don't have anything. I've already been hit."

"I understand that your hands are free. You've dialed this number. Find something in the garbage. There must be a lot around you."

"I don't have free hands!"

"Well, find something. How did you end up in this truck?"

"I don't know. I drank too much. I don't know what happened next. This truck is modern. It mills the garbage. I've already been struck. Do you understand! What's going on with you? I called you a half an hour ago. You couldn't call the GAI?"

"We called the GAI but they can't find you."

[Sergei Nikitin, who was on duty that morning in the 5th department of GIBDD of the central administrative okrug of Moscow, which has responsibility for Komsomolsky Prospect, was later contacted by a reporter for *Novaya Gazeta*. He said that there was no call regarding a garbage truck and there is no notation of such a call in the logbook.]

The operator continued:

"You understand that to search for every garbage truck and examine each one of them inside. You yourself understand. . . . You have to make yourself known. Knock constantly. Get to the wall of the truck."

There is the sound of garbage being pulverized.

"Hello, hello. Young man, who were you with? Hello! Hello! Young man! Hello! Young man! (There are sighs. The operator is clearly tired.) Hello! Young man! Young man! Say something please, take the receiver."

There are horrible screams.

"Hey, driver!!! Driver!!!"

"Young man, pick up the telephone!"

"Driver!!"

"Young man, pick up the telephone! Oh akh! Young man, do you hear me?"

The connection is interrupted.

Finally, at 6:35 A.M., there is one last call. Shugaev would remain on the line until 6:43 A.M., but he was able to get out only a few words. The call came from Pogodinskaya Street.

"Hello! Hello! Operator!"

"Hello! Young man! Is that you in the garbage truck? That's you, isn't it? Who were you with? Do you have their telephone numbers?"

"I'm already choking."

"Hello!"

"I'm choking"

"Who played this kind of trick on you? Were you with friends? Who were you with?"

"That's it. I think I'm choking, that's all . . . "

"If you can remember the telephone number of your friends . . . "

This was Shugaev's last conversation with the Rescue Service. According to the information obtained by *Novaya Gazeta*, neither the traffic police nor the regular police in the region had any idea of what had happened on their territory until Shugaev's parents reported his disappearance. Once an investigation was opened, the police checked with Shugaev's mobile phone company and learned that the last calls from his cell phone were made to the Rescue Service.

Reporters from *Novaya Gazeta* spoke to representatives of the police and traffic police, who insisted that if they had been notified that a person was trapped inside a garbage truck, the truck could have been stopped and identified within fifteen minutes. Shugaev spoke on the phone with the Rescue Service, urgently asking for help, for twenty-three minutes. The routes of the garbage trucks are well known to the beat officers. The truck in Shugaev's case would have been particularly easy to identify: the territory of the central region had only two new garbage trucks equipped to grind up garbage.[23]

The fate of Shugaev and the transcript of his calls to the Rescue Service were widely reported in Moscow, and on the morning of January 21 the Salaryevo dump outside Moscow, which receives garbage from the central Moscow okrug where Shugaev disappeared, was cordoned off by Russian internal troops. The troops were ordered to use shovels and poles to check all of the garbage that had collected there over the previous three days. A section of some four thousand square feet was dug up with the help of two excavators and a treaded tractor. The garbage was fifteen feet deep. The new garbage trucks of the type in which Shugaev was imprisoned cut garbage into fragments no more than eight inches in length. Local vagrants told reporters from *Novaya Gazeta* that six corpses had been found in the dump in recent years. One of them had been cut into pieces and had come out of one of the modern trucks. But despite the intense search, no trace of the former billiard player was ever found.[24]

His loss is a reflection, among countless others in Russia, of an absence of "absolute solidarity with the human being as such."

CHAPTER 1

The Statue of Dzerzhinsky

■

On September 13, 2002, Yuri Luzhkov, the mayor of Moscow, stunned Russians and the world by calling for the return of the monument of Felix Dzerzhinsky, the first head of the Soviet secret police, to Lubyanskaya Square. The call was surprising because a few years earlier, he had sharply opposed a call for the return of the monument from the Communist-dominated State Duma. It was also unexpected because his arguments were not so much political as architectural. He said that the statue was irreproachable as a piece of sculpture, and it gave the square a finished appearance.

As for Dzerzhinsky, Luzhkov said that some people associate him with the KGB but others associate him "with the struggle to solve the problem of homeless children, resurrect the railroads, and restore the economy." He said that people unfairly blame Dzerzhinsky for the Great Terror of 1937, but Dzerzhinsky was not alive at that time, and if he had been, he would have been one of the first victims.[1]

On the face of it, there should be nothing appealing about Dzerzhinsky or his legacy. In 1918–19, ten thousand persons were shot on the basis of decisions that Dzerzhinsky signed personally, and the lists are far from complete.[2] S. P. Melgunov wrote in *Red Terror in Russia* that mass shootings took place at night, barges filled with hostages were sunk. "The oral instructions of one person [Dzerzhinsky] doomed to immediate death thousands of people."[3]

Martyn Latsis, one of Dzerzhinsky's chief lieutenants, explained the philosophy of the Cheka in his advice to interrogators on November 1,

11

1918. "We are not waging war against individuals," he wrote. "We are exterminating the bourgeoisie as a class. During investigation, do not look for evidence that the accused acted in word or deed against Soviet power. The first questions that you ought to put are: To what class does he belong? What is his origin? What is his education or profession? And it is these questions that ought to determine the fate of the accused."[4]

It was this legacy that a crowd of thousands of demonstrators had in mind on the night of August 22, 1991, when, after the failure of a coup by hardliners who tried to save the Soviet Union, they demanded the removal of the statue of Dzerzhinsky from Lubyanskaya Square. Today, the place of the statue is taken by a grassy knoll in a vivid demonstration that on one fateful night an antitotalitarian crowd ruled the streets in Moscow, and a symbol of repression in the country was deposed.

Lubyanskaya Square contains only two reminders of the suffering that was inflicted from there. The first is the Solovetsky stone, a gray boulder from the Solovetsky Islands, the site of the first Soviet camps for political prisoners, which is a monument to the victims of repression. The second and more telling reminder is the grassy knoll. Nikolai Kharitonov, a deputy in the State Duma aligned with the Communists, indirectly acknowledged the role of the grassy knoll as a symbol of the defeat of totalitarianism in an interview on the radio station Ekho Moskvy. He called for returning the monument of Dzerzhinsky to the square because without it, "Lubyanskaya Square is defenseless and the agents of the KGB and FSB are defenseless."[5]

By the same token, if the statue were returned to its former location, nothing about the square would hint at the crimes of the Soviet regime except the Solovetsky stone, barely noticeable in the shadow of the headquarters of state security.

Luzhkov's proposal provoked a major controversy. There was an immediate negative reaction in the Russian press. It focused, however, less on Dzerzhinsky than on Luzhkov's perceived hypocrisy. Most newspapers did not believe that he was motivated by respect for Dzerzhinsky's supposed role in aiding homeless children or by a concern for the aesthetics of Lubyanskaya Square.[6] The latter explanation was found especially ridiculous, given that Luzhkov had no artistic education and was not distin-

guished for his good taste. In the opinion of a number of newspapers (*Moskovsky Komsomolets, Vremya-MN, Vremya Novostei,* and others), Luzhkov was simply trying to curry favor with a new regime that, "for well-known reasons," had a positive attitude toward the return of the monument to the "first Chekist."[7]

Human rights organizations raised the issue of Dzerzhinsky's crimes. On September 16, at a meeting held at the Solovetsky stone and organized by the Union of Right Forces (SPS) party, Boris Nemtsov, the party leader, described Dzerzhinsky as "a hangman who destroyed several million of his fellow countrymen."[8] Protestors from Memorial said that a monument to Dzerzhinsky in Russia was "the same as a monument to Himmler in Germany."[9] The Union of Orthodox Citizens also opposed the return of the statue. The organization said that believers greeted with "bewilderment" Luzhkov's proposal to return to the square the statue of "one of the organizers of the genocide of the Russian Orthodox Church and the Russian people."[10]

The general public, however, favored returning the monument. A poll conducted by the organization Public Opinion showed that 56 percent of Russians supported the idea of returning the monument to the square and 14 percent were opposed; 30 percent found it hard to answer. In Moscow, the figures were 53 percent in favor and 35 percent opposed.[11]

The reason so many Russians supported the return of the monument of the founder of the Soviet secret police to one of Moscow's central squares was that, despite his role in the deaths of thousands, they viewed him as a legitimate Russian historical figure, not as an embodiment of radical evil.[12] Leftists and Communists made clear that they supported the return of the statue. The chairman of the Duma, Gennady Seleznyev, said the monument "was removed in a wave of emotion [after the collapse of the August 1991 coup]." He said that he did not see "any catastrophe" in its restoration to the center of Moscow.[13]

More significant, even many liberal Russian political commentators, without calling for the return of the monument, implicitly supported it by arguing that Dzerzhinsky was a part of Russian history that should not be denied. Alexei Pankin, the editor of *Sreda,* a magazine for journalists, wrote in the *Moscow Times,* "When a frenzied crowd of victorious 'democrats' brought down the Dzerzhinsky monument in August 1991, my reaction was similar to what the non-Christian intelligentsia of the early

1920s felt when churches were wantonly destroyed. . . . They viewed this destruction as vandalism."[14] Boris Kagarlitsky, a sociologist, also writing in the *Moscow Times,* said that the squares of Europe were filled with monuments to bloodthirsty villains. "You can tear down statues but that won't annul an entire era. History should be comprehended, not cursed."[15]

Gavril Popov, the former mayor of Moscow, wrote in *Moskovsky Komsomolets* that the past lives "in every cell of each of us." Popov quoted Chekhov's remark that he had to "squeeze the slave out of himself drop by drop." Any monument from the past, including those from the Communist period, Popov said, aids in this process of "squeezing out the slave."[16] He did not make clear why monuments to a slavish past helped to emancipate a people from slavery.

Reacting to the controversy, Luzhkov insisted that the sculpture was a "powerful work of art" and that "if one put on the scales everything that Dzerzhinsky did, the good would outweigh the bad."[17] Since the one hundredth birthday of the sculptor, Evgeny Vuchetich, would be celebrated in 2008, the return of the sculpture to the square was entirely appropriate. "We should be ashamed," he said, "before this great sculptor who was undeservedly insulted."[18]

On September 19, however, Vladislav Surkov, the deputy head of the presidential administration, broke the silence of the Kremlin and indicated that, in the interest of social peace, the statue should not be returned to the square. "It's important to be very accurate with symbols," he said. "Today some call for the return of the monument of Dzerzhinsky, tomorrow others will demand the removal of the body of Lenin from the mausoleum. Both are untimely and not acceptable for a large part of the citizens of our country. . . . It is unacceptable to insult the feelings and memory of people."[19] On the following day, Patriarch Alexei II also told reporters that the statue should not be returned because this "would undermine the fragile accord in Russian society." Like Surkov, he felt that it would also be unwise to remove the body of Lenin from its mausoleum.[20]

Dzerzhinsky was born in 1877 into a family of Polish landowners. A fervent Catholic until the age of sixteen, he even planned to be a priest or monk. Once, his older brother, Cazimir, asked him how he imagined God. He replied, "God is in my heart! And if I were ever to come to the conclusion, like you, that there is no God. I would shoot myself. I couldn't live without God."[21] In the end, Dzerzhinsky forsook his love of God and substituted for it an ardent love for the revolution.

Dzerzhinsky spent eleven years in tsarist jails, exile, and penal servitude. In his first year as head of the Cheka, he lived in his office on Lubyanskaya Square, working, sleeping, and taking meals there. He refused any privilege denied to other Chekists and was totally incorruptible. "My strength," he said, "comes from never sparing myself." He was also disinclined to spare anyone else, particularly those whom he identified as "class enemies." In a speech on December 20, 1917, the night when the Sovnarkom authorized the creation of the Cheka, Dzerzhinsky said, "It is war now — face to face, a fight to the finish. Life or death! I propose, I demand an organ for the revolutionary settling of accounts with counterrevolutionaries." Within a month of the creation of the Cheka, summary executions began in Moscow.[22]

Yakov Peters, Dzerzhinsky's closest associate, described Dzerzhinsky's work habits in those years:

> It is in this building in the plainest, smallest room . . . that Comrade Dzerzhinsky lived during the first years of the revolution. In this room, he worked, slept, received guests. A simple desk, an old screen hiding a narrow iron bed: such was the setting of Comrade Dzerzhinsky's personal life. He never went home to his family except on holidays. He worked round the clock, often conducting the interrogations himself. Wrung out with exhaustion, wearing high hunting boots and old threadbare tunic, he took his meals at the same table as all the other Chekists.[23]

At first, there was some opposition to the terror. I. Steinberg, the commissar for justice and one of the few Left Social Revolutionaries who remained in the government, tried to subordinate Dzerzhinsky's Cheka to the courts. Following an order in February 1918 calling for the summary execution of all "profiteers, hooligans and counter-revolutionaries," he protested to Lenin, "Then why do we bother with a Commissariat of Justice at all? Let's call it frankly the 'Commissariat for Social Extermination' and be done with it!" According to his account, Lenin brightened and said, "Well put, that's exactly what it should be; but we can't say that."[24]

Nemtsov uncovered documents in the state archives showing that, in a meeting in 1919 about the peasant rebellion in Tambov, Dzerzhinsky had included "terror" in a list of recommendations that also included bread and fuel. Nemtsov said, "This meant, according to Peters, that everyone over eighteen, regardless of whether they were women, pregnant, or old people, would be shot until the rebels ceased their resistance." Dzerzhinsky's fanaticism was such that in January 1921, when the resistance of the Whites was already broken, he insisted that "in regards to the bourgeoisie, it is necessary to intensify the repression."[25]

One of those who met with Dzerzhinsky in those years was Nikolai Berdyaev, the Russian religious philosopher, who was arrested in February 1920 in connection with the case of the "Tactical Center," one of the innumerable anti-Soviet conspiracies that the Cheka was supposedly uncovering and destroying. Berdyaev, perhaps the best-known Russian thinker of his time, was the only person involved in this case to be interrogated personally by Dzerzhinsky. Berdyaev described what happened in his philosophical autobiography, *Self-Knowledge*.

At midnight, Berdyaev, who was being held in the internal prison of the main Cheka building on Lubyanskaya Square, was called for interrogation. As he described it:

> They led me down an endless number of gloomy corridors and stairways. At last, we ended up in a cleaner and more well-lit corridor with a rug and entered a large office that was brightly lit and had the skin of a white polar bear on the floor. On the left side, near the desk, stood a person I did not know in a military uniform with a red star. This was a blond with a straggly pointed beard, with gray, cloudy, and melancholy eyes; in his manner, there was something soft and one felt a certain breeding and politeness. He invited me to sit down and said, "My name is Dzerzhinsky."[26]

The interrogation had a ceremonial character. Lev Kamenev, the head of the government, arrived to take part, as well as Vyacheslav Menzhinsky, the deputy head of the Cheka, whom Berdyaev had known in the past in St. Petersburg as an aspiring and unsuccessful novelist.

Berdyaev reacted to the danger he was in by taking the offensive. "Bear in mind," he said, "I consider that it is part of my dignity as a thinker and writer to say exactly what I think."

"We expect this of you," said Dzerzhinsky.

Berdyaev then explained on what basis—religious, philosophical, and moral—he was an opponent of communism, although not a political person.

Dzerzhinsky listened carefully and only occasionally interjected a comment, for example, the following significant phrase: "Is it possible to be a materialist in theory and an idealist in life and, the opposite, an idealist in theory and a materialist in life?"

Berdyaev's speech went on for forty-five minutes. It seemed to him in retrospect that its frankness had appealed to Dzerzhinsky. After it was over, Dzerzhinsky nonetheless tried to ask a few questions connected with specific persons. Berdyaev refused to answer any questions about individuals. At the end of the interrogation, Dzerzhinsky suddenly said, "I'm going to let you go but you cannot leave Moscow without permission." He then turned to Menzhinsky and said, "It's already late and there is a lot of banditism. Perhaps you can give Citizen Berdyaev a ride home in an automobile?" No automobile was available, but a motorcycle was found, and Berdyaev was driven from the internal prison in the Lubyanka to his home.

Vitaly Shentalinsky, in an article about the philosophers of the Silver Age, wrote, "What saved Berdyaev? Determination and stubbornness? Or was Dzerzhinsky convinced that Berdyaev was not really guilty of anything and that he landed in the hands of the Cheka by mistake? And that he hovers so high that he is harmless on Earth? Or perhaps the fanatic of revolution was attracted by the same selfless fanaticism but in the service of a different faith?"[27]

Berdyaev wrote that "Dzerzhinsky gave the impression of a person who was completely convinced and sincere. He was a fanatic. There was something terrible in him. . . . In the past, he wanted to become a Catholic monk, and he transferred his fanatical faith to Communism."[28]

Another person who encountered Dzerzhinsky in those years was Leon G. Turrou, who in 1922 served as the interpreter to Col. William N. Haskell, then the head of the Russian Unit of the American Relief Administration. Turrou was moved to put down his recollections on learning of the death of Dzerzhinsky, the man he described as "the most sinister, the most feared, the most Herod-like figure that semi-barbaric Soviet Russia has produced in its nine years of reign."[29]

The Soviet Union was in the grip of a deadly famine, and scores of shiploads of American wheat and other food and medical supplies were pouring into Russia in an ultimately successful effort to save millions of lives. It was not hard to unload the supplies at Soviet ports and ship them to Moscow. But to get them from Moscow to provincial cities for further distribution to remote towns and villages was extremely difficult, because the Soviet railway system was in complete disarray. Turrou recalled that one day Haskell received a telegram from an A.R.A. representative named Darragh in Balashov, a major rail junction, saying that a large number of trains were being held up there and that when he protested, he had been arrested. Haskell demanded a meeting with Dzerzhinsky and Kamenev. The meeting took place at the railways ministry, which was also under Dzerzhinsky. Haskell said that if the shipments did not go through, it would mean another year of famine for Russia. He also said that the arrest and detention of Darragh was a violation of the Riga Agreement and could not be tolerated.

Dzerzhinsky said that he was aware of the facts but that the shortage of locomotives was acute and he did not have the power, physically or officially, to move the trains out of Balashov. He suggested that the grain be unloaded and stored until the rail congestion had cleared.

Turrou described what happened next in his memoir:

Colonel Haskell rose suddenly to his feet. "Turrou," he said, controlling the anger that smoldered within him, "tell them this — and don't be afraid to be strong about it. Tell them the American people did not contribute money to buy food for shipment to Russia only to have it sidetracked at a desolate way station. Tell them we bought it to save the millions of Russians who are in daily danger of death by starvation. Tell them that we intend to get it to those millions and that I don't give a damn for nor want their excuses. I want those trains moved immediately if they have to stop all the traffic in Russia, if they have to send the last locomotive in the country down to Balashov. Tell them that furthermore if this is not done, I will immediately cable to America ordering all further shipments stopped. And if this comes to pass, it is the Soviet government only who will be responsible for what may follow."

Haskell's statement was greeted by dead silence. Turrou recalled that Dzerzhinsky seemed to be in the grip of tremendous emotion. Turrou assumed that Dzerzhinsky would refuse, since moments before he had seemed to rebuke Kamenev for whispering what Turrou thought was a conciliatory suggestion. Finally, Dzerzhinsky rose and said he would need fifteen minutes to come to a decision.

He left the room with his and Kamenev's subordinates, as well as other Soviet officials, and when he returned, he was accompanied by only two of his subordinates. He asked Turrou to repeat Haskell's demands. Turrou did so and Dzerzhinsky, ignoring the Americans, turned to his aides. "With not a trace of emotion on his death mask face," he said, " 'I have told you of the limited time you have in which to carry out the details. The trains will move—and, if you fail, the supreme punishment is awaiting you. That is all; you may go.' " Shortly after that, the trains did move and Haskell received word that the American representative had been released from detention.[30]

Dzerzhinsky died in 1926 after giving a speech in which he furiously denounced the Trotskyites. The regime needed saints, and the cult of Dzerzhinsky began to develop immediately. An effigy of Dzerzhinsky, in uniform and incorporating death masks of his face and hands, was placed in a glass coffin in the OGPU officers' club and became an object of veneration.[31] Vladimir Mayakovsky, a Futurist poet and one of the few writers to throw in his lot with the Bolsheviks, wrote a poem in which he urged young people to emulate Dzerzhinsky. It read:

To a young lad
      Plunged
           Into meditation
After whom
      To model his life,
           Just commencing
I would say
      Without hesitation
Model it
      On Comrade Dzerzhinsky[32]

In 1929 Edward Bagritsky devoted a poem to Dzerzhinsky in which Dzerzhinsky's ghost appears at the bedside of a tubercular poet. Sitting down at the poet's bedside, Dzerzhinsky teaches him to overcome all personal afflictions and rise to the demands of the century. Speaking to the poet in the voice of the century, he says:

> The century lies in wait by the roadway,
> Staring fixedly like a sentinel.
> Don't be afraid, go stand beside him.
> Your solitude is no different.
> You look around: enemies lurk;
> You reach out: no friends come;
> But if he says: "Lie," you will lie,
> But if he says: "Kill," you will kill.[33]

In 1936 the executive committee of Moscow's central raion decided to put up a monument to Dzerzhinsky in Lubyanskaya Square, which by then had been renamed Dzerzhinsky Square. (The name was changed back after the fall of the Soviet Union.) A competition was announced for the best design for the monument, but plans were canceled by the outbreak of war.

The cult of Dzerzhinsky waned in the 1940s as the Stalin cult reached its zenith. In the wake of Khrushchev's denunciation of Stalin, however, there was a need for a Soviet leader who was not implicated in Stalin's crimes—which, according to Khrushchev, were the only Soviet crimes. This led to the revival of the cult of Dzerzhinsky. Plans were again made to erect a monument to Dzerzhinsky in Dzerzhinsky Square. This time, the design was entrusted to Vuchetich, a favorite of Khrushchev's. His design depicted Dzerzhinsky in a long coat with his right hand in his pocket and with a self-confident expression. One variant had Dzerzhinsky with a waist belt and a pistol attached to his side, but in the end these details were discarded. The finished monument, almost twenty feet tall and cast from fourteen tons of bronze, was dedicated on December 20, 1958.[34]

The dedication of the monument inspired a new wave of idealization. It was said that Dzerzhinsky had defended the young Soviet state, that he had acted on behalf of the party and persecuted only genuine counter-revolutionaries. Yuri German, a well-known Soviet writer, published a collection of short stories, *Tales about Dzerzhinsky*. The stories described how Dzerzhinsky, though severe toward the enemies of the young Soviet state, cared about honest people and helped them to become the "masters" of their country.[35]

The idealization of Dzerzhinsky was particularly strong in the KGB.

The men who succeeded him, Genrikh Yagoda, Nikolai Yezhov, and Lavrenty Beria, besides their role in the Stalinist terror, were unsavory personalities. Yagoda collected pornography, Yezhov was a promiscuous homosexual, Beria a serial rapist. Dzerzhinsky, although a murderous fanatic, was relatively "normal." Perhaps for this reason, KGB officers looked with gratitude to a former leader who at least was not a degenerate. The effigy of Dzerzhinsky apparently was discarded but now his portrait was hung in KGB offices. In the First Chief Directorate (FCD), responsible for foreign intelligence, a bust of Dzerzhinsky was put on a pedestal and constantly surrounded with fresh flowers. All of the young officers in the FCD, at some point in their early careers, had to lay flowers or wreaths before the bust and stand silently for a moment with head bowed.[36]

The heroic image of Dzerzhinsky could be preserved as long as the regime controlled access to information. Once glasnost began, however, facts became available. In the case of Dzerzhinsky, a figure who had been idolized was shown to have been an indiscriminate executioner. Particularly important was the publication of Melgunov's *Red Terror in Russia,* which was based in part on the findings of the Denikin commission on the crimes of the Bolsheviks and was soon available in virtually every street kiosk in the center of Moscow.[37]

Melgunov described the reprisals after Fanny Kaplan's attempt on the life of Lenin in which thousands of completely innocent persons were rounded up and killed, including officers in Petrograd who were bound together with barbed wire on two barges that were subsequently sunk. He recounted the practice of taking wives as hostages and shooting children in front of their parents and parents in front of their children. Melgunov himself had been arrested several times by the Cheka, barely escaping death. This, in addition to his literary talent, gave his descriptions a particular immediacy.

> Those who were imprisoned in the Butyrki Prison in those torturous days [after the attempt on the life of Lenin], when there were arrested thousands of people from the most varied strata of society, will never forget their spiritual anguish. This was a period called by one witness, "the wild bacchanalia of red terror." It was frightening and terrible at night to hear and sometimes to be present when they took

dozens of people to be shot. An automobile arrived and took away the victims, and the whole prison did not sleep and trembled with the sound of every automobile horn. . . . I was a prisoner during these days and myself endured all of these horrible nightmares.[38]

Melgunov also quoted the testimony of other witnesses. One described the following scene:

A group of officers, five persons . . . are called to the "shower room." Several of them were picked up by accident in a roundup on the street. . . . White as a sheet, they gather their things. But one of them cannot be found. The fifth person doesn't answer, doesn't respond. The escort leaves and comes back with the head of the cellblock and several Chekists. They begin calling everyone by name. They discover the fifth person. He is hiding under a cot. They pull him out by the legs and the terrified sounds of his voice fill the entire corridor. He flails, screaming, "What for?" "I don't want to die!" But they yank him out of the cell and disappear . . . and then he again appears in the yard. . . . But there are no more sounds, a rag has been stuffed in his mouth.[39]

In the wake of revelations like these, there was a wave of revulsion in the country toward the Old Bolsheviks, Dzerzhinsky, the KGB, and the whole Soviet regime. On the night of August 22, 1991, the day after the collapse of the coup, a crowd of about fifteen thousand formed around the statue and mottos were scrawled on the pedestal: "antichrist," "bloody executioner," and "shit in a leather coat." Some persons wanted to storm the KGB building. Gavril Popov, the mayor of Moscow, agreed to remove the statue to avoid violence. He feared that in the event of a successful storm, some of the protestors would find the home addresses of KGB agents and begin to hunt them down, as had happened in Budapest in 1956. KGB agents in the building were also armed. If there was a storm, they might open fire on the crowd. In the end, the statue was lifted from its pedestal by a crane, put on a flatbed truck, and taken to the courtyard of the House of Artists, where it remains with statues of other Soviet leaders.[40]

In the first years after the fall of the Soviet Union, there was little sentiment in favor of restoring the monument of Dzerzhinsky to Lubyanskaya

Square except among KGB nostalgics. As the economic crisis continued, however, many Russians began to view the Soviet period more favorably and to regret Russia's lost power. The knoll in the middle of Lubyanskaya Square became to many a kind of antisymbol, testifying to the new Russia's weakness and insignificance. For years it had been a point of pride for Soviet citizens that the Soviet Union was not only respected but *feared*. But who could fear a country where in the place of a statue of the first head of the secret police there was now only a grassy knoll?

On December 2, 1998, four months after the Russian default and financial crash, the State Duma passed its resolution calling on the government of Moscow to return the statue of Dzerzhinsky to Lubyanskaya Square. The official argument for returning the statue was Dzerzhinsky's supposed battle with crime. Public opinion polls at the time showed that only 27 percent of the population supported the return of the monument, whereas 56 percent were opposed. Luzhkov strongly rejected the Duma vote.[41] In the summer of 2000, however, Kharitonov again raised the question of the return of the monument, and by this time, public sentiment had begun to change. According to one poll, 38 percent of Russians favored the return of the monument and 35 percent were opposed.[42]

In an article in *Moskovsky Komsomolets,* at the height of the discussion of Luzhkov's call to restore the statue, Popov gave several reasons for the shift in public sentiment. In the first place, many Russians, like the KGB, gave Dzerzhinsky credit for being more honest and principled than the secret police chiefs who came after him. At the same time, the people were exposed to so many examples of corruption and hypocrisy on the part of people calling themselves "democrats" that they reduced their demands on the leaders of the past. "The ordinary citizen," Popov wrote, reasons as follows: "'How is it that they [the leaders of the Soviet period] are obliged to be saints and for the present leaders everything is permitted?'"[43]

In August 1999 Vladimir Putin, the head of the FSB, was named prime minister. This was followed by unmistakable moves to raise the status of the KGB. One of Putin's first official acts was to restore a plaque commemorating former KGB head Yuri Andropov to the wall of the former KGB headquarters. He named former KGB officers to high positions, and they in turn hired their erstwhile colleagues. Soon veterans of the "force ministries" came to dominate the new government. During a visit to Dzerzhinsky's native region in Belarus in 2002, Nikolai Patrushev, the head of the

FSB, reportedly promised that the statue of Dzerzhinsky would be returned to Lubyanskaya Square. At the same time, Luzhkov appeared to be vulnerable in the upcoming mayoral elections. Most Moscow political observers believe that he floated the idea of restoring the statue to improve his electoral prospects and ingratiate himself with Putin.[44]

In the end, the statue of Dzerzhinsky was not returned to Lubyanskaya Square. The final decision was taken by the monument committee of the city Duma, which, reflecting Kremlin disapproval, ruled on January 21, 2003, that the statue would not be restored.[45] The square, nonetheless, preserves the spirit of the secret police, and everything is in place psychologically for the statue's return.

A three-story green building covered with the dirt of decades at the corner of Bolshaya Lubyanka Street and Varsonofevsky Lane, a short distance from the square, is barely noticed by passersby. The double-glazed windows set in half-moon casements on the first floor are barred and have drawn curtains. On the façade is a plaque with the head of Dzerzhinsky in profile; the legend on the plaque states that he worked in the building from April 1918 until December 1920. There is nothing to indicate that from 1920 until at least 1941, the basement was used for mass executions.

By 1920 the Cheka had established an entire network of buildings around Lubyanskaya Square with prisons and execution chambers. Few of these places have been identified, but the building at 11 Varsonofevsky Lane is an exception, perhaps because it was in use for so long. Muscovites referred to it as the "ship of death." The building now belongs to the FSB and is still in use.[46] There are air conditioners in the windows, and through the gap in a drawn curtain a photocopier is visible in one of the rooms. At the corner there is a guard post, but there is no indication of what is being guarded or why. There is nothing to prevent society from insisting that the building be marked in some way. But this has not been done. Instead, the building looks like many nineteenth-century structures in Moscow, with its friezes depicting Greek gods and goddesses, but one that, for some reason, was not restored.

Not far from the former "ship of death" and on the same street are the fashionable Central Beer Restaurant, the Seventh Continent grocery store, which is well stocked with foreign delicacies and is a favorite of members of the security services, and most remarkably, the Shield and Sword restaurant, dedicated to the present and past of the Russian intelligence services.

Upon entering the Shield and Sword, one first notices a white bust of Yuri Andropov, surrounded by flowers and red Soviet flags. In the main dining room there is a statue of Dzerzhinsky, a scale model of the one that was removed from Lubyanskaya Square in 1991. On one wall of the dining room is a painting of a revolutionary scene, with Lenin in the lead and Stalin, holding a pipe, directly behind him. The other early Bolsheviks are also depicted, including Lev Trotsky, who is off to one side. On the adjoining wall are portraits of former leaders of the Soviet secret police, including Yezhov and Beria, who directed the terror in which millions of Soviet citizens were murdered, including many of those shot in the basement only two doors away.

One night when I visited the Shield and Sword, I spoke to Anatoly, one of the managers. He said that he had worked as the administrator of the buffet on the sixth floor of the Kremlin Palace of Congresses. He recalled seeing Party General Secretary Leonid Brezhnev and the other members of the politburo at the receptions that were held after the November 7 Revolution Day ceremonies in Red Square. He said that Brezhnev was very sociable and friendly. As for the restaurant, he said people came to relax and have a good time. "We celebrate weddings, birthdays. People dance. There is a small band and, as you see, there is enough space for a dance floor."

I asked him whether anyone was offended by the pictures of Yezhov and Beria.

"No," he said, "this is history."

"But Yezhov was the organizer of the Great Terror."

"People today condemn what happened, but they did not live in that time. It was a different time, different people. You cannot deny history."

Dominating the neighborhood at 2 Lubyanskaya Square is the FSB building itself, a sandstone-colored, rectangular nine-story building with rows of windows set on alternate floors in square frames and arches, separated by heavy cornices and pillars. There are air conditioners in some of the windows and, as dusk falls, a faint light is visible inside. The clock at the top of the building is cloaked in shadows under an illuminated hammer and sickle. FSB officials insist that executions were not carried out in the building itself. This is impossible to check. The FSB has every reason to deny that killings took place in what is now its main headquarters, if only to head off demands for a plaque or other memorial on its walls. The only concession to history on the exterior of the building is the plaque depicting Yuri Andropov. It states that from 1967 to 1982, "the outstanding statesman of the USSR," hero of socialist labor, and general of the army worked in the building as chairman of the KGB.

On the other side of Lubyanskaya Square is 23 Nikolsky Street. This is the former building of the Military Collegium of the Supreme Court where thousands of death sentences were handed out to members of the party or military elite. The three-story beige building (a two-story annex was added later) has rows of frosted double-glazed windows and, until recently, was the headquarters of the Moscow military commissariat, where draftees reported for induction. The area is prime real estate, and the former court building is surrounded by an Ermengildo Zegna clothing store and Bentley, Ferrari, and Maserati dealerships on one side, and the Nautilus shopping center on the other. A sign on the building still identifies it as the headquarters of the voenkomat and gives the hours of operation. There is nothing to indicate the building's historical significance. For twenty years, social groups, including relatives of the victims, called for turning the building into a museum dedicated to the victims of repression. But those plans were never realized, even though the fates of Marshal Tukhachevsky, Marshal Yegorov, and members of the party nomenklatura from all over the country were sealed there.[47]

Leonid Novak, a historian with the Memorial Society, collected evidence confirming that death sentences were carried out in the basement of the building and that there was an underground passageway leading to the NKVD headquarters. Despite this, the building has been purchased by the Sibneftegas energy company, which plans to tear it down, construct underground parking, and rebuild it as a commercial and entertainment complex.[48]

On a balmy September night, a breeze rustles the leaves in the small park on the east side of the square. Floodlights attached to the cornices illumine the lower floors of the FSB building. Streams of traffic enter the square from three directions, circulating around the grassy knoll. A floodlit banner over Teatralny Proezd, one of the main arteries, advertises a special model of Jaguar automobiles for $59,000. The commercial part of the square is ablaze, dominated by the Nautilus shopping center, where mannequins and jewelry glitter in glass display cases visible in the tall windows.

Under the trees, young men sit on the back of a bench drinking beer, their empty bottles accumulating on the sidewalk nearby. At the end of the park, the remains of flowers as well as food wrappers and bottle tops clutter the granite base of the Solovetsky stone. At 9 P.M. an elderly couple approach the stone. The woman places four roses on the marble base. Curious, I walk up to them and ask whom they are honoring. The woman says that she and her son are marking the anniversary of the death of her brother, an engineer who was shot for "wrecking" on September 27, 1938. I ask the woman her name, but she refuses to say. I tell them that I am writing about the Solovetsky stone, but she still refuses to give her name. Finally, I ask her, "What can they do to you that they haven't already done?"

This logic seems to persuade her.

Her name is Margarita Elsgolt, and she is eighty-nine years old. She worked for many years as a teacher. Her older brother was Fyodor Elsgolt. He worked in the People's Commissariat of Heavy Industry and was condemned to death by the Military Collegium of the Supreme Court in a trial that lasted fifteen minutes. At the trial, he renounced his testimony, which was undoubtedly given under torture, but he was sentenced nonetheless. In 1956 he was rehabilitated.

After the fall of the Soviet Union, Margarita was able to read the file of her brother's case. She learned the date of her brother's execution but not where he was buried. It was then that she began to come every year on the anniversary of his death to the Solovetsky stone.

I ask Margarita and her son, Rogdai Zaitsev, what they think about Luzhkov's proposal to return the statue of Dzerzhinsky to Lubyanskaya Square. "Such a suggestion is possible," Rogdai says, "because the most progressive and active people were killed, and the persons who survived were informers and their children."

On the morning of November 8, 2005, an event about a mile away from Lubyanskaya Square showed the durability of the Dzerzhinsky cult. A bronze bust of Dzerzhinsky that was also removed from its pedestal on the night that his statue in Lubyanskaya Square was toppled was returned to the center of the courtyard of the building at 38 Petrovka Street, the headquarters of the Moscow police. The bust now dominates the courtyard and is clearly visible through the bars of the fence. The reason for restoring it was not announced. One officer told Irina Vlasova, a reporter for *Noviye Izvetiya,* "Of course, we were all surprised, but, as you know, the decisions of the bosses are not discussed."[49]

Human rights groups appealed to the government to remove the bust, but since this was not public property, their protests had no effect. On November 9, 2005, a reporter for the *Los Angeles Times* witnessed a man placing flowers at the foot of the bust, then standing back and quietly saluting it. The man said his name was Alexander Nikolaev and that he was a sixty-year-old retired police colonel. The reporter asked him the reason for his gesture. "Dzerzhinsky was my teacher," he said. "I built my life according to his ideology. . . . The flowers are a tribute to those who brought him back."[50]

CHAPTER 2

Efforts to Remember

■

In the fall of 1990 Moscow was suffused with an unmistakable atmosphere of *fin de régime*. The food stores were all but bare, a sign that the distribution system had broken down. On October 30, thousands of persons, including hundreds of former political prisoners, gathered at the Sretenskiye Gates and began walking slowly, in a steady stream, down Dzerzhinsky Street to Dzerzhinsky Square. Led by Orthodox priests, they carried candles, portraits of murdered relatives, and banners with the names of Stalin-era labor camps—Karlag, BAMlag, ALZHIR. As they walked, a woman pronounced the names of victims of the Great Terror over a loudspeaker and, after each name, the word *shot*. The smell of incense mixed with the odor of urban soot. Finally, the marchers entered Dzerzhinsky Square, walked past the statue of Dzerzhinsky, and gathered in front of the Polytechnic Museum around the Solovetsky stone. Hundreds of people waited to lay flowers. Those who could not reach the stone put burning candles around the trees. It was already dark. The small park in front of the museum was filled with people, and the ground was covered with a carpet of flowers.[1]

The marchers had come to dedicate the Solovetsky stone, the capital's only memorial to the millions murdered by the Soviet regime. Two elderly survivors of the Stalinist camps, Zoya Marchenko and Oleg Volkov, were asked to come forward. The crowd waited as Marchenko and Volkov, both of whom could barely walk, stepped up to the base of the monument. They then pulled the covering off the gray boulder.

Marchenko later wrote:

I cannot express my worry. I had to sum up the suffering of several decades, and around me were others like me, full of sorrow and recollections, wives, daughters, sisters, parents. . . . I said that for decades, we lived, not daring to show photographs, show a letter, in general to mention our departed loved ones. And now we can come here, show to our children and grandchildren this stone and tell them that their grandfather or father was not an enemy of the people, that it is necessary not to be ashamed but to be proud of him.[2]

In his speech, Mikhail Bulgakov, the chairman of the Moscow Commission on the Victims of Political Repression, said, "There is not a single law where it is possible to read clearly the repentance of the government before millions of tormented people."[3]

Soviet President Mikhail Gorbachev was invited to attend the ceremony but did not. Yuri Prokofiev, the head of the Moscow party, did attend and left a bouquet of red carnations at the stone. A delegation from the KGB laid a wreath at the stone with the words, "To the Victims of Stalinist Repression from the KGB."[4]

The dedication of the Solovetsky stone gave to millions of survivors and family members a symbolic monument for their murdered loved ones and friends. It was seen by many as an important first step. As events unfolded, however, it became clear that it was not the beginning of an effort to honor the memory of the victims in a manner commensurate to the tragedy that had befallen them, but rather the end.

Russia had witnessed merciless regimes before, but nothing like what was ushered in by the successful coup d'état of November 1917. The terror unleashed by the Bolsheviks was waged not on behalf of a person or group but for the benefit of an idea that both obsessed and devalued its most committed adherents. In the end, it annihilated not only opposition but unwavering support. As Hannah Arendt wrote in *The Origins of Totalitarianism,* the Soviet regime was absolutely loyal to its "idea," which it held to be the source of law:

It is the monstrous yet seemingly unanswerable claim of totalitarian rule that far from being lawless, it goes to the sources of authority from which positive laws received their ultimate sanction, that far from being arbitrary, it is more obedient to these suprahuman forces than any government ever was before, and that far from wielding its power in the interest of one man, it is quite prepared to sacrifice everybody's vital immediate interests to the execution of what it assumes to be the law of History.[5]

Grigory Zinoviev, a Bolshevik leader who was later murdered by Stalin, declared in September 1918: "We will have to create our own socialist terror. For this, we will have to train 90 million of the 100 million Russians and have them all on our side. We have nothing to say to the other 10 million; we'll have to get rid of them." Trotsky, who was also executed by the Soviet regime, warned in December 1918, "Not only prison awaits our enemies but the guillotine, that remarkable invention of the French Revolution which has the capacity to make a man a whole head shorter."[6]

The purpose of the terror was to force individuals to live and react as if the precepts of the ruling idea actually reflected reality. In this sense, the Soviet terror can be seen as the attempt of political actors, on the scale of a vast nation, to liquidate the truth.

Under the tsarist regime, between 1825 and 1917, 3,932 persons were executed for their political beliefs or activities. The overwhelming majority of these (3,741) were executed between 1906 and 1910, when the regime was fighting revolutionary terror. Once in power, the Bolsheviks exceeded this figure in four months. That was only the beginning. On September 3, 1918, with the Bolsheviks threatened by White armies, peasant revolts, and urban insurrection, the regime introduced the Red Terror, which was based on hostage taking and liquidation according to class. In the next two months, the Cheka killed between 10,000 and 15,000 persons.[7]

With the outbreak of the Russian Civil War, the Red Terror was answered by White Terror. The wave of anti-Jewish pogroms in Ukraine in 1919 claimed 150,000 lives. The Red Terror, however, "was more systematic and better organized and it targeted entire social classes." When the Bolsheviks took over cities, they executed thousands who belonged to the "possessing class." In the Crimea, after the White forces fled, more than 50,000 people were shot or hanged. Sevastopol became known as the "City of the Hanged."[8]

The end of the Civil War did not cause an end to the bloodletting. Almost immediately after seizing power, the Bolsheviks tried to create a socialist economy. In March 1918 they imposed a state monopoly on the food trade, and in 1920 they tried to replace money with state rationing. The policy of "War Communism," however, provoked open rebellion. In 1920, in the wake of a bad harvest, rural areas revolted against grain requisitioning. To suppress the uprising, the Bolsheviks in the Tambov region, the center of the resistance, shot the eldest son in any family holding arms or giving shelter to the insurgents and attacked the rebels in the forests with poison gas. It was the first use of poison gas by a country against its own population. The rural insurrection was suppressed, but the price of the crisis in the countryside was famine in large parts of Russia and Ukraine. At least five million persons starved to death in 1921 and 1922.[9]

Meanwhile, in the cities, industrial workers were reduced to rightless servitude. If production quotas were not met, their rations were cut and they could be imprisoned or even shot. In the winter of 1920–21, plagued by disruptions in the transportation network, the government cut bread rations for major cities by 33 percent. This provoked a revolt by the sailors of the Kronstadt Naval Base that was crushed by Marshal Mikhail Tukha-chevsky, who also directed the suppression of the Tambov revolt at a cost of thousands of lives.[10]

In 1921, under the pressure of the peasant uprising and the Kronstadt revolt, the regime instituted the New Economic Policy (NEP), which restored market relations in the countryside and allowed small-scale private manufacturing. NEP made it possible to relieve food shortages, and the Soviet Union began to recover. At the same time, however, the first labor camps were set up in the Solovetsky Islands. By the end of 1923 they held more than four thousand prisoners. Five years later there were nearly thirty-eight thousand. The purpose of the camps was "reeducation," but camp administrators soon concluded production contracts with state organizations, giving birth to the Soviet system of forced labor. It would undergo tremendous expansion after 1929.[11]

NEP allowed an exhausted country to recover, but it left most of the economy in private hands. For the Soviet Communist rulers this was politically and ideologically unacceptable, and in June 1929 capitalism in the countryside came to an abrupt end. The government began the process of forced collectivization. More than 2 million peasants were deported as "kulaks" or wealthy peasants. Approximately 300,000 died of cold, hunger, and disease.[12]

The purpose of dekulakization was to break all resistance to collectivization, and in its wake a fragile collective farm system was established in the rural areas. The regime, however, was determined to exploit the countryside in order to finance industrialization. In 1930 the state took 30 to 38 percent of the harvest (compared with 15 to 20 percent sold by peasants during NEP). In 1931, with the harvest considerably smaller, the state took 39.5 percent to 47 percent. In 1932 the collection target was 32 percent higher than in 1931. Unable to feed themselves, the peasants turned to theft in order to survive. The Communist leadership then decided to starve them into submission. The peasants were restricted to their villages, "shock brigades" were sent in from the cities, and the rural areas were emptied of grain. The famine of 1932–33 claimed an estimated five million to seven million lives. It was a criminal regime's greatest crime.[13]

At first, life in the urban centers seemed little affected by the horror in the countryside, but history soon took its revenge on many of the perpetrators. In 1937 Stalin launched a drive to wipe out all real or potential opposition. The result was the Great Terror, whose victims included almost the entire hierarchy of the party. Every Soviet region received quotas for executions and arrests. To meet these quotas, innocent persons were implicated in an ever-expanding web of invented plots. By November 16, 1938, when the terror finally abated, 681,692 persons had been shot, according to official Soviet figures. Another 663,308 had been sent to labor camps, where almost all of them died.[14]

After mass executions subsided, arrests continued. The Soviet Union had become dependent on slave labor. By 1941 there were almost 2 million prisoners in the camps. During the war, nearly 3.3 million members of nationalities suspected of disloyalty—Soviet Germans, Chechens, Kalmyks, Ingushi, Crimean Tatars, and others—were deported. Many were sent to the camps. After the war, Soviet prisoners of war and citizens who had been forced laborers in Germany were sent to the Gulag. By 1945 the Soviet camps and prisons held nearly 5.5 million inmates.[15] It was only with Stalin's death that millions of prisoners began to be liberated and the apparatus of terror was partially dismantled.

In the thirty-six years from its creation to the death of Stalin, the Soviet regime executed, starved, or worked to death some 20 million persons, not including 4 million killed during the Civil War and 5 million who died as a result of the 1921–23 famine, which were consequences of the Bolshevik

33

seizure of power.[16] No other regime in history has ever inflicted such an inferno on its own people.

With the end of the Stalin era, Soviet society entered its period of "normalcy." Fear of arbitrary arrest abated, but there was also almost no public opposition. Those who disagreed did so quietly, in their "kitchens," with trusted friends. The situation began to change only in 1965 with the trial of Sinyavsky and Daniel for publishing their work abroad. The medieval spectacle of writers being put on trial for their work led to the first political protests and gave rise to the Soviet dissident movement. The invasion of Czechoslovakia in 1968 created more dissidents. In 1975 the Soviet Union signed the Helsinki Accords, in which it pledged to respect human rights, a promise it never intended to keep. This gave an even greater impetus to dissent, as dissidents formed groups to monitor Soviet compliance. Dissenters were arrested and sent to labor camps and mental hospitals, leading to a new generation of political prisoners. The persecution came to an end only with the decision by Gorbachev to liberalize Soviet society and, in 1987, to release political prisoners from the camps.

Repression conditioned millions of Soviet citizens to think and react according to the rules of the imaginary world of communist ideology. For more than seventy years, Soviet citizens had performed their obligatory roles—acting out the part of members of a classless society who, guided by infallible rulers, were creating heaven on earth at home and striving to bring the benefits of their paradise to the outside world.

Connected with this deluded view of reality were assumptions about human nature that sprang from the experience of mass murder for utopian purposes by history's most "progressive, and humane regime." The first of these was that a person is a means, not an end. He has no inherent value. This was nowhere better expressed than by Stalin in his famous toast after the end of the Second World War to Soviet citizens, whom he described as "screws in the great machine of the state."[17] The second assumption was that nothing is sacred but the objectives of the state. This conviction was reflected in the standard justifications for Soviet crimes, such as the invocation of "the difficult birth of a new society" or the explanation that, of course, "you can't make an omelette . . . "

These assumptions deformed the moral sensibility of Russian society. The regime treated individuals as expendable, and, even worse, Russians treated their own lives and the lives of others the same way. This is why, when the Soviet Union fell, it was vital to remember the victims of Soviet terror: not only to honor their memories but also to counteract the moral consequences of Soviet mass crimes on those who survived. In fact, a struggle to memorialize the victims began as soon as repression in the Soviet Union started to wane, but its progress was uneven, and even after the Soviet collapse its success was far from assured.

The most important question was whether there would be a national monument to the victims in Moscow. The struggle to create it began with the first stirrings of change in the Soviet Union. But the national symbol of repentance was never built, a failure that casts a long shadow over Russia today.

With the beginning of glasnost in the Soviet Union, long-silent Soviet citizens, to the amazement of the world, began to talk. In order to support Gorbachev's reform policies, the regime allowed the creation of "informal organizations," the first ones not controlled by the state. One was a discussion group, the Perestroika Club, organized under the auspices of the Central Econometrics Institute. Moscow intellectuals came to meetings to discuss such previously forbidden topics as "Is it possible to have socialism with a human face?" and "Was Lenin a criminal?" Two of the participants were Yuri Samodurov, a young geologist, and Yelena Zhemkova, a mathematician from Odessa who was studying in Moscow. Samodurov had grown up with persons, including his great aunt, the writer Olga Adamova-Sliozberg, who had suffered in the repression, and he found it hard to accept that their lives had been ruined and no one had been held to account. Zhemkova had little knowledge of the Stalinist terror while growing up in Odessa. It was only after she came to Moscow that she read Alexander Solzhenitsyn's *The Gulag Archipelago*, which made a huge impression on her. In a speech to the Perestroika Club in June 1987, Samodurov proposed creating a monument to the victims of the terror. Shortly afterward, he, Zhemkova, and five other persons formed a group to work for this goal. The group called itself "To Keep Alive the Memory of the Victims of Repression." It was later renamed Memorial.

Gorbachev's policy of glasnost was exposing Soviet citizens to facts about their society that they once could only have imagined. On November 2, 1987, in a speech commemorating the seventieth anniversary of the October Revolution, Gorbachev referred to "thousands" of party and nonparty members who had suffered repression under Stalin. The absurdly understated figure shocked liberals, but after years of silence, the subject of Stalin's victims had at least been officially reopened. Several days later, Samodurov, Zhemkova, and other members of the group set up a table in front of the Vakhtangova Theater on the Old Arbat, a street in the center of Moscow, to collect signatures on a petition to the Supreme Soviet demanding a monument to the victims of Stalinism.

The group asked not only for signatures but also for addresses, which led many people to refuse to sign. Some said that they wanted to sign but were afraid that the KGB would come to their homes and arrest them. In any case, shortly after the table was set up, the police arrived. They said that the action was not permitted. This was followed by five minutes of discussion. Reinforcements then arrived and took the activists to a police station and then to court. They were given small fines. The activists returned several times, and each time, they were arrested. But each time, people signed.

The members of the group began collecting signatures at their places of work. Zhemkova asked for signatures in the Institute of the Food Industry, where she was a graduate student. This led to angry confrontations. The situation was disorienting for ordinary Soviet citizens, whose opinion was being asked for the first time. Some insisted that no one in their family had suffered. Others became aggressive and refused to talk to Yelena. Many simply said they were afraid. The climate, however, was changing. Branches of Memorial were being organized spontaneously all over the country.

In Moscow on March 5, 1988, the thirty-fifth anniversary of Stalin's death, a six hundred–person silent march to commemorate Stalin's victims was broken up by the police. After this incident, however, harassment ceased and activists redoubled their efforts. By June they had collected fifty thousand signatures. At a news conference that month on the eve of the 19th Party Conference, Samodurov presented a plan for a memorial in Moscow with a monument, library, archives, and museum. At a rally on June 25, demonstrators called for the KGB headquarters on Lubyanskaya Square to be used for the memorial. When the party conference opened three days later, Yuri Afanasyev, the rector of the Historical-Archives Institute and a delegate, presented the petitions to the conference.

The petition campaign appeared to have an effect. In his closing remarks at the conference, Gorbachev said a monument to the victims of repression would be built in Moscow and that this was the party's "political and moral duty." He did not mention Memorial, and it appeared to many that he was trying to appropriate the idea. But his remarks testified to how much the atmosphere had changed.

After the party conference, the Cinematographers' Union gave Memorial a small room near the Aeroport metro station to use as its first headquarters. The room was open from 10 A.M. to 9 P.M. six days a week, and persons who had been affected by the terror began arriving in a steady stream. Lines sometimes stretched out of the office, down the steps of the building, and out onto the street. Some came to look for lost relatives, others to find witnesses who could tell how a relative met his or her death. Children of "enemies of the people" who had been raised in orphanages and had their last names changed wanted to learn the identity of their parents. As they told their stories, people often fainted or cried uncontrollably. The walls were soon plastered with appeals for information: "Who knew my father . . . ?" "Who knew my husband . . . ?" "Has anyone seen . . . ?"

On July 27, 1988, the writers' union weekly, *Literaturnaya Gazeta,* opened an account at the USSR Social Bank on behalf of Memorial for donations for a monument. Although the Soviet Union was slipping into a deep economic crisis, 1.5 million rubles ($2.1 million) in private donations was eventually collected. The magazine *Ogonyok* called on the public to submit proposals for a design.

At the end of October, Memorial, which now had branches in 110 cities, held its first conference in the theater of the Cinematographers' Union. It chose an advisory board that included Sakharov, Yeltsin, Afanasyev, the poet Yevgeny Yevtushenko, the director of the Soviet cultural foundation, Dmitri Likhachev, the poet and bard Bulat Okudzhava, and the historian Roy Medvedev, among others. Additionally, a group was formed to organize work in Moscow.

The authorities, however, began to fear that Memorial could become the base of an alternative political party. At the end of the year, they acted to take the drive for a monument out of Memorial's hands. The newspaper *Sovetskaya Kultura* announced a competition sponsored by the Ministry of Culture for a design for a monument. The ministry then laid claim to the money that *Literaturnaya Gazeta* had raised for Memorial. The money properly belonged to Memorial, but as long as Memorial was not officially registered and had no bank account, it could not touch the funds. It also could not rent space at a time when its need for an adequate place to conduct its business was becoming critical.

The stage was now set for the founding conference of Memorial, which was held in the Moscow Aviation Institute on January 28, 1989. The policy of glasnost, intended to overcome resistance in the party to liberalization, had made history an urgent political issue. Memorial was also, for a time, the only vehicle in the country for expressing political opposition other than the Democratic Union, a small, self-proclaimed political party. The political potential of Memorial was becoming obvious. The flow of activists into Memorial, however, led to a split between those who wanted to focus on the creation of a monument and those who wanted to build a mass movement. Samodurov feared that if Memorial became a political movement, the goal of honoring the memory of the victims of repression might be lost.

The founding conference was attended by a thousand delegates and by Soviet and foreign journalists. The draft resolution and charter, prepared by the Memorial central editorial commission, said that the chief goal of the organization was the memorial complex. Nonetheless, each branch of Memorial came to the conference with its own charter, and the delegates proposed twenty-three additional resolutions, twenty-two of which contained political demands. Samodurov's attempts to insist on Memorial's original mission led to shouts that he was a KGB agent and provocateur. When other leaders of Memorial did not back him, he left the conference and then resigned.

In the end, the conference adopted a charter that, besides pledging Memorial to fight for a monument to the victims of totalitarianism, called for restoration of Solzhenitsyn's citizenship, publication in the Soviet Union of *The Gulag Archipelago,* and the freeing of the small group of Soviet political prisoners who were still being held despite a far-reaching amnesty. The additional causes were almost universally acknowledged to be worthy. But their adoption identified Memorial as a political organization.

On October 30, 1989, the wave of anti-Stalinism reached a symbolic peak. Fifteen hundred demonstrators with candles formed a human chain around KGB headquarters on Lubyanskaya Square for thirty minutes distributing leaflets. They called for turning the building into a museum dedicated to the victims of political terror. In the past, Soviet citizens had avoided even walking past the KGB building.

Memorial, however, had no power to create a monument on its own, and registration, which would give the organization legal rights, was not forthcoming. After the founding conference, Memorial made another attempt to register, but the authorities refused, explaining that it would be better to wait for the new, elected Supreme Soviet. When the new parliament convened in June, registration was again denied, this time because there was no law on public organizations. Andrei Sakharov died of a heart attack on December 14. After his death, Gorbachev met Sakharov's widow, Yelena Bonner, and suggested several possible ways to honor Sakharov's memory. Bonner told him that the best way would be to register Memorial. Memorial, however, was not registered until the autumn of 1991, shortly before the fall of the Soviet Union.

In the meantime, many elderly Gulag survivors were dying. The feeling was widespread that there was a need to do something to commemorate the victims while some were still alive. This led to the dedication of the Solovetsky stone, which was as close to a monument to the victims of repression as Moscow would come.

In June 1989 a stone was dedicated as a monument to the victims of the Gulag in the village of Solovetsk in the Solovetsky Islands. It was the first monument in the Soviet Union to the victims of repression. Inspired by this example, two members of Moscow Memorial, Lev Ponomaryev and Sergei Krivenko, suggested putting up a similar monument in Moscow. In spring 1990 newly elected liberal deputies took control of the Moscow city council. They made clear that in the matter of a memorial, they were ready to act on their own, disregarding the opinion of the higher Soviet authorities and the party's Central Committee. A boulder from the islands was transported by ship from Arkhangelsk and then by train to Moscow, and a joint commission of Memorial and the city council agreed to locate the stone in the small park in front of the Polytechnic Museum, diagonally across Dzerzhinsky Square from the KGB headquarters. The KGB asked the city council to find any other spot and promised assistance. But the request was refused, and the monument was set up next to the KGB building.

The stone was seen as a temporary measure, a monument to symbolize a nation's grief until a memorial could be erected that corresponded to the scale of the tragedy. The dedication of the stone, however, coincided with the descent of the Soviet Union into its terminal political crisis. Distracted by the final confrontation between democrats and hard-line Communists, the country would not return to the subject of the innocent victims of Communist rule.

The Moscow city council, having supported the placement of the Solovetsky stone, took no further action. Alexander Milchakov, a journalist for *Vechernyaya Moskva* who actively investigated Stalin era execution sites, proposed creating an eternal flame in honor of the victims of Communist terror in the Alexandrov Gardens in front of the Kremlin wall.[18] He also suggested turning the former building of the Military Collegium of the Supreme Court into a museum. These ideas were well received, but no action was taken.[19]

The last year of the Soviet Union was subsumed by politics as the population deserted Communism en masse and the dying Soviet regime tried desperately to prolong its existence. With the possibility of bloody mass repression hanging in the air, a demonstration in March 1991 in support of Yeltsin in Moscow drew 500,000 persons. Finally, in August, pro-Communist hard-liners seized power and prepared to eliminate the country's democratic gains. The coup failed after three days when military and KGB units refused to carry out orders, and the fate of the Soviet Union was sealed. In the resulting euphoria, enthusiasm for a monument to the Soviet system's victims all but disappeared.

The fall of the Soviet Union opened a new era in Russian history. On January 2, 1992, the "young reformers" who were put in charge of post-Soviet Russia began to transform the country, and Russians whose world had been turned upside down by perestroika and the fall of the USSR were subjected to new shocks as they made their acquaintance with capitalism. The first thing that happened was that prices were freed, leading to runaway inflation and wiping out the life savings of the vast majority of the population. Russians, left for the first time to fend for themselves without the social guarantees of the Communist system, became fixated on what was happening at the moment. The determination to honor the memory of Communist victims left center stage once and for all.

In late 1992 Yeltsin issued a decree that called for memorializing those who had suffered at the hands of the Communist regime. The decree, however, was nonbinding and had little effect. The only act with real consequence was the decision to grant Memorial a headquarters on Maly Karetny Street in the center of Moscow, where it could receive visitors and house its voluminous archives.

Bonner, Sergei Kovalyev (the only Soviet-era dissident to serve in the Russian parliament), and Samodurov, who became the director of a fund to memorialize Sakharov, wrote to Yeltsin calling for the creation in Lubyanskaya Square of a monument to the victims of Communism but received no reply. An international group including Elie Wiesel, Helmut Schmidt, and Adam Michnik also appealed to Yeltsin to create a memorial, but they too received no answer. Memorial organized groups of well-known Russians such as Yevtushenko, Afanasyev, and Okudjava to meet with representatives of the federal and Moscow governments to press their case. But these meetings had no result. The officials usually conceded that a monument was needed, but in light of the dire economic situation, they felt that finding money for such a project would be impossible. At the same time, there was little pressure for a memorial from Russian society. By the mid-1990s Russians no longer reacted emotionally to information about Soviet crimes, and as the economic collapse deepened, many were overwhelmed by the daily struggle to survive.

Samodurov tried to raise money for a museum on the Stalinist terror from private donors. Finally, in 1993, a deputy in the Tagansky raion local council suggested a house on the Yauza River as a site. It was out of the way, but Samodurov and Bonner decided to accept the offer. The building became the Sakharov Center. It had a library and meeting rooms on the first floor, and a hall on the second floor divided between exhibits dedicated to Sakharov and those dedicated to the history of political repression. With this, the effort to create a national museum came to an end. The Solovetsky stone, which had been seen as a temporary expedient, and a few exhibits on the second floor of the Sakharov Center were all there were in Moscow, the former epicenter of the terror, to commemorate the Soviet regime's war against its own people.

While the struggle to erect a monument was going on in Moscow, similar efforts were being made in the provinces. Before and after the Soviet collapse, plaques, plinths, and pedestals were dedicated in provincial cities to mark the sites of future monuments. The monuments were usually planned at newly discovered burial grounds, but in most places they were never built. All that was left was the pedestal and the promise.

In the few places where monuments were erected, their significance was diminished by the same dulling of empathy that characterized Moscow, as well as by their location far from the major centers of population and power.

During the 1990s one of the principal memorials to the victims of the Soviet regime outside Moscow was a small museum in the basement of the former NKVD investigative prison in Tomsk. It was unusual because it consisted of a cell and the office of an interrogator still preserved from the period of the Great Terror. The cell is a small room with one fold-out bed. Its door has a spyglass and an iron bolt lock. At the height of the terror, it held fifteen to twenty inmates. Down a corridor is the office of an interrogator. It has a table, a lamp, two chairs, an inkwell, and a portrait of Dzerzhinsky on the wall. On the table are the documents of a case.

The Tomsk museum was created in 1989. In the wave of anti-Stalinism then sweeping the country, the Communist city government approved the creation of the museum in a single day. The local branch of Memorial received documents, photographs, and personal items from relatives of victims, and these became the basis of the exhibits. At first, the museum attracted visitors from all over the country and abroad. Its special status, however, was short-lived. In spring 2004 Tomsk needed funds to celebrate the four hundredth anniversary of the city's founding, so it began transferring municipal property into private hands. The museum had been given its location "indefinitely," but after a series of opaque maneuvers, the building in which it was located was handed over to Igor Skorobogatov, a successful local businessman who expelled the old residents and opened a casino on the floor above the museum.[20]

The center of Tomsk took on a strange appearance. Opposite the mayoralty was a "Stone of Sorrow" commemorating the victims of terror, the museum, and, in the same building, a casino and entertainment center doing an active business despite a campaign against gambling in the oblast legislature and the local press.

Skorobogatov displayed a friendly attitude toward the museum. He acted as its sponsor, a fact that was noted in a sign outside the building. He carried out extensive renovations. While communications were being replaced, an underground passage was discovered. It was apparently the route along which prisoners were led to their deaths. The passageway was filled with debris, and it was not excavated. Instead, a black metal plaque was placed at the entrance, commemorating those who were executed with a bas-relief depicting a man's body disappearing into nothingness. Boris Trenin, the head of Tomsk Memorial, said that the current municipal leaders were indifferent to the museum. "I have the impression," he said, "that now there are two people to whom this museum is necessary, me and the director, Vasily Khanevich. If I leave the post of chairman of Memorial, that will be the end of the museum."[21]

The most imposing monument in Russia to the victims of the Gulag is the Mask of Sorrow in Magadan, the gateway to the Kolyma gold mining region. The work of the Russian sculptor Ernst Neizvestny, it was completed in 1996. It is a 60-foot-high cement head at the top of the Krutaya Hill, 650 feet above sea level. It is located next to the site of a former transit camp for prisoners on their way to the Kolyma labor camps.

According to documents of the Magadan oblast ministry of internal affairs, 740,434 prisoners were transported to Kolyma by ship between 1932 and 1953 from Vladivostok and other Far East ports.[22] An unknown number of additional prisoners were brought to Kolyma by ship through the northern, Arctic route. It is officially estimated that 120,000 persons died in the Kolyma camps from overwork, starvation, murder at the hands of criminals, and executions. Other estimates, however, put the number at as high as half a million.[23]

The left eye of the mask weeps sculpted stone tears, each drop a human face. The right eye has the form of a barred window. A stairway leads into the interior of the monument to an isolation cell. This gives way to an open-air chapel with a cross and the figure of a young girl crying for those who died. Large boulders in the area are marked with religious symbols to represent the beliefs of the victims, including a hammer and sickle for orthodox Communists.

The monument was proposed in 1989, at the height of the anti-Stalin campaign. Neizvestny, who emigrated in 1976, returned to the Soviet Union in 1989, and while there he received an invitation from Magadan to design the monument. In 1990, when the contract was signed, 90 percent of the Magadan residents surveyed favored the monument. The top of the

Krutaya hill was selected as the site so that the monument would be visible from all parts of the city.[24]

The project began with widespread support because all who lived in Magadan were aware of region's terrible history. But as work began in the early 1990s, after the fall of the Soviet Union, grants from the city and federal budgets and from private donations were wiped out by inflation. At the same time, living standards in Magadan collapsed. By January 1995, with the monument two-thirds finished and $200,000 still needed, there began to be opposition to spending any more money on the memorial. In an interview in *Literaturnaya Gazeta,* Neizvestny argued that despite the hardships that people in Magadan faced, not to put up the monument was "spiritually dangerous."[25] A public campaign began and it had an effect. Money was allocated by the government to finish it—in part because the monument would be useful to Yeltsin in his reelection campaign in the face of a challenge from a resurgent Communist Party.

On June 12, 1996, four days before the presidential elections, tens of thousands of persons braved freezing, windy weather under overcast skies to attend the dedication of Russia's most important monument to the victims of Stalinism. Funereal music was played, and a knell sounded in memory of the dead. Neizvestny said that the monument showed "that the person is not destructible." Alexander Yakovlev, a former Soviet politburo member and the head of the commission on rehabilitation, said, "We must acknowledge the past and ask forgiveness of the still living survivors of the camps."[26]

But then the dedication began to resemble a Yeltsin campaign rally. Sergei Filatov, the head of the campaign, and Alexander Zaverukha, a deputy prime minister, called on those present to vote for Yeltsin in the upcoming election. They cautioned that voting for Gennady Zyuganov, the Communist candidate, would result in a return to terror. As the crowd shivered, the political content of the speeches led to anger and heckling.[27] Later, the NTV news program carried a report that concluded: "Whether there will be monuments or [labor] camps will be clear on Sunday."[28]

After the monument was dedicated, it became one of the region's principal landmarks, frequently visited by officials and foreigners. The attitude of Magadan's residents, however, began to change. Most had come to Magadan in the post-Stalin era, attracted by high wages and the chance to "conquer the North." These willing migrants did not dwell on how the region had been developed. Their attitude was very different from that of the former prisoners, who had stayed in Magadan because, after years in the camps, they had formed close bonds with one another and had nowhere else to go.

The economic hardships of the 1990s deepened the split between the newcomers and the camp survivors. The new Russian government recognized that the remote northern cities were uneconomical and discussed ways to eliminate them. This led many who viewed themselves as "heroes of the North" to feel that they were being abandoned. Many people in Magadan lost tolerance for attention to the Stalin era, which they associated with indifference to their contribution.[29]

When foreign nongovernmental organizations and religious groups argued that the region needed to be saved from its past, these residents frequently answered that the past should be consigned to history and not form part of Kolyma's contemporary identity. John Round, a British authority on Magadan, found that by the early 2000s the Mask of Sorrow was widely disliked. Many persons said that the monument was "watching over them" and was imposed on the region, adding that it was funded by "Jewish money" and designed by a "Russian who left."[30]

Perhaps the best-known monument outside of Moscow is the former Perm 36 labor camp, which held the Soviet Union's leading dissidents and is now a museum. It is located in the Perm oblast, a region of rolling hills, swamps, and unbroken forests seven hundred miles east of Moscow. The region is the watershed between Europe and Asia. Winds constantly change direction, causing fierce headaches. Winter temperatures drop to 45 below zero. The hundreds of prisoners who passed through Perm 36, Perm 35, and Perm 37 years later recalled the isolation, the silence, unbroken except for the sound of sparrows and thrushes, the beautiful sunsets, and the guards in green uniforms who manned the watchtowers. For inmates, the camps of the "Perm triangle" were torture chambers at the end of the world.[31]

I visited the Perm 36 museum on a bright, cold morning in April 2006. The area in front of the camp was deserted except for a few patients from a nearby psychiatric clinic, who loitered nearby trying to strike up conversations. Snow-covered fields glittered in the sun. A former political prisoner, Yevhen Sverstiuk, was skeptical that any museum could simulate the atmosphere of the camp. "To recreate daily life in the zone," he wrote, "where demons of various ranks waited for you, where half of the year is bitter winter, with the ever present smells of drying wet boots and prison jackets; where, locked up in isolation, a *zek* [prisoner] is deprived even of a jacket, that would be impossible to recreate even in my dreams."[32]

At 10 A.M., a cheerful, middle-aged woman guide from the nearby village of Kuchino arrived and unlocked the gates of the strict-regime section, the largest part of the camp. It was a Saturday morning and Alexander Kalikh and Mikhail Cherepanov, two members of the Perm Memorial, and I were the only visitors.

The strict-regime zone is only partly restored. In one room of the barrack, where prisoners slept fifty to a room, is an exhibit about four prisoners — Yuri Litvin, Valery Marchenko, Vasil Stus, and Olexa Tikhy — who died from torture and medical neglect in 1984 and 1985.[33] In the other room are exhibits about the Gulag, including the camps in Kolyma. Beyond the barrack are the blackened ruins of the dining hall and medical unit, which were set on fire when it was learned that the camp would be turned into a museum. The administration building is now a movie hall, and behind it is the internal prison. Beyond a wooden fence is the camp workshop. Prisoners were taken there under guard and spent eight hours a day producing details for laundry irons.

After several hours, we left the strict-regime camp and walked fifteen hundred feet to the "special zone," for "dangerous recidivists." The prisoners there were allowed out of their cells only to work in tiny cubicles stamping details. For the slightest offense, one would be put in a punishment cell, a concrete box where one starved and froze. The barrack was surrounded by a high wooden fence, making it impossible to see outside. A prisoner's only human contact was with the guards and a cellmate chosen for his incompatibility. As a result, prisoners stopped talking, and what many remember best about the special zone was the unending silence.

The idea of turning Perm 36 into a museum arose in 1992, during a conference sponsored by Memorial to mark the twentieth anniversary of the arrival of the first political prisoners in the Perm oblast from camps in Mordovia. Perm 35 and Perm 37 had been turned into labor camps for ordinary criminals. Perm 36, however, was being used as a shelter for some of the patients at a nearby psychiatric clinic. Viktor Shmyrov, a leader of Memorial, suggested turning it into a museum.[34]

The Perm oblast government, which hoped that a museum would attract tourists and business to the area, gave the project its support. The ministry of culture also approved the project, as did several local factories. Later, funding came from Western foundations, and in 2005 the museum received a grant from the U.S. embassy.[35]

When work began, the strict-regime zone was dilapidated but intact. The special zone was in ruins. In 1989, after Ukrainian and Estonian movie crews had filmed there, local police and selected criminals had torn up the roof, floor, plumbing, and electrical fixtures, leaving a hollow shell. Many persons in the area either were former prison guards or had family members who had worked in the camps, and they were angry about being negatively depicted.[36]

In light of the destruction, the leaders of Memorial decided to make restoration of the special zone their first priority. In places where the original security installations were not restored, mockups were constructed and the camp gradually took on its former appearance. There were watch-towers at each of the four corners of the wooden fence, and inside the fence, barbed wire and a control strip of plowed earth six feet wide to detect footprints. This was followed by a second fence, another control strip, a path for the guards, and more barbed wire, with a sign stating that the guards had the right to fire without warning at anyone approaching the fence.

The museum opened officially on August 29, 1998. Its creation was hailed in the West as a triumph of historical memory. In Russia, however, the reaction was muted. There were very few visitors. The September 1998 financial crash wiped out the country's nascent middle class. Meanwhile, the trip to Perm took four hours over bad roads. In the 2000s the economic situation improved, and a new road cut the journey to two hours. Members of the intelligentsia from Moscow and St. Petersburg and children of victims started to visit the museum. By 2006 there were about five thousand visitors a year — still a very modest response in light of the effort made in creating the museum.

"The attendance is still not much for a museum of this type," said

Kalikh one night in Perm, "but we work for the future. This is not for contemporary Russians. I have an acquaintance who is an ardent Communist even though his father was shot. I asked him how he could continue to believe in a system that killed his father. He said that if his father was shot, it meant that it was necessary.

"For many years, I said that we should not expect immediate results. We simply have to work . . . and attract the youth."

CHAPTER 3

Butovo and Kommunarka

■

On the Kaluga Highway, two and a half miles beyond the Moscow city limits, a large sign with an Orthodox cross indicates the site of the Kommunarka state farm, a mass burial ground for Stalin-era victims. Clearly visible to drivers in both directions on the heavily traveled highway, it is the most prominent acknowledgment of Stalin-era crimes in the Moscow area.

Just beyond the sign, a narrow road turns off the highway. It leads to the gates of what is now a branch of the Svyato-Yekaterininskogo Monastery. During the Great Terror, long columns of trucks turned off the highway onto that road carrying victims to their final destination. Today, a visitor entering the road on foot leaves the noise of heavy trucks and traffic behind and is quickly surrounded by a peaceful world of chirping birds and singing crickets, moss-covered birch trees, ferns, saplings, and weeds. In some places, grass breaks through the asphalt, endowing the road with a center strip that leads to the monastery gates.

The gates are locked, and visits are by appointment. The reason is that the monks are alone in the vast territory and feel their physical vulnerability. Until 1991 the authorities did not encourage curiosity about the site. There was a "dead end" sign at the entrance to the road, and the grounds were patrolled by armed "mushroom pickers" provided by the KGB. Once the guard was withdrawn, however, would-be grave robbers entered the territory and began digging in the burial trenches, looking for valuables.

Inside the gates, a gravel road runs between two rows of tall pine trees.

At the head of the road is a small wooden gazebo with an Orthodox cross and next to it, two monuments — to the Mongolian victims of the terror and the victims from Yakutia — that were intended to form part of a row of monuments leading to the burial sites. The monument to the Mongolian victims is a piece of black marble with a blue ribbon engraved on its polished surface. It commemorates thirty-five ministers — the entire government of Mongolia — who were summoned to Moscow on Stalin's orders and then shot and buried in Kommunarka. The leaders of the Soviet Republic of Yakutia were also shot en masse during the purges and are buried here. By agreement with the monastery, the Mongolian monument is one day to be moved to make room for a general Russian monument, but the years have passed and no Russian monument has been built. Nor are there monuments to other Soviet national groups.

Deeper in the woods is the refectory of the monastery, a long one-story building of green-painted logs with a rusting tin roof. Opposite it is a newly constructed church. The site is isolated, and there is no drinking water for the monks. The electricity is unreliable and the lights frequently go out. But the monks are at home here. They receive visitors and pray for the victims.

The main burial ground is located in a birch grove near a pond. There are small hollows with standing rusty water and rotting leaves where the earth has settled. These are the burial pits, scattered in a disorderly fashion. The distance between them is not great, and they have various shapes — round, almost square, one even resembling a diamond. There are also grass-covered mounds, created by the earth dug from the holes. Willows hang diagonally over several of the pits, a sign that at one time the trees were undermined by digging. Against the gray sky, they resemble mourners. The Orthodox Church has declared February 7 "the day of the new martyrs" in honor of those who were killed by the Soviet regime, and a special liturgy is served at the burial site on that day, attended by the victims' surviving relatives.[1]

The other mass burial site in the Moscow area is the former Butovo firing range, south of the city. From the Boulevard Dmitri Donskoi metro station, the last stop on the gray line, a bus to the site goes through a former rural area, now dotted with garbage dumps, metal sheds, the ruins of old log houses, and modern concrete apartment blocks. The bus operates only eight times a day, with the last one returning at 8:31 P.M. Clearly, there was no expectation of a large flow of visitors.

On a cold, gray Saturday afternoon in January 2005, the Butovo firing range is covered with a blanket of snow. A log church with a wooden cupola and Orthodox cross and a nearby bell tower are the only buildings of significance. The rest is a vast, open field dotted with stands of bare trees. Next to the church, a wooden wall with plaques bears the names, birth dates, and dates of death of 907 representatives of the church who were murdered at Butovo. None of the thousands of other victims are mentioned.

Beyond the bell tower are concrete poles with strands of rusted barbed wire still attached, the remains of a fence that encircled the barracks where prisoners were held before being shot. There are pine trees where the barracks once stood. Not far away, in the open field, are birch and oak trees with multiple trunks. The trees were chopped down to give the executioners a better view of the territory, and new trunks grew back from the roots and later fused. In the distance are a forest and a fence, beyond which are dachas that belonged to NKVD officers. Some now belong to the officers' descendants. Because many of the burial ravines extend beyond the fence, some of the dachas are undoubtedly built on bones. About four thousand persons a year visit the former firing range. On this Saturday, however, there are no visitors. The paths are covered by snow and the ropes delineating the burial trenches are partly drifted over. The only activity is the preparation for a christening that is to take place in the church.

The year was 1937. Spanish children, refugees from the Spanish Civil War, started arriving in Moscow. They were soon noticeable, speaking Spanish, in the courtyards and schools of the city. Muscovites wept as newsreels showed distraught Spanish parents parting with their children as they boarded ships for the safety of the Soviet Union. Stalin said that it was necessary to treat each person with the tenderness that a gardener shows to a delicate plant. On fences and the walls of buildings, signs appeared calling on citizens to liquidate illiteracy or engage in sports. "Women, don't be fools, engage in sports!" There were also posters offering advice, "Syphilis is not a disgrace but a misfortune."[2]

The city was the scene of constant celebrations. Russians celebrated the new constitution, the opening of the first line of the new metro, and the landing of a Soviet expedition at the North Pole. Officially, "life was getting happier, life was getting gayer." Unofficially, arrests of "enemies of the people" took place every night, and the city fell into a state of absolute terror.

On July 2 the politburo ordered local party secretaries to arrest and shoot "the most hostile anti-Soviet elements." Shortly afterward, Nikolai Yezhov, the head of the NKVD, said to a meeting of regional heads of that organization, "I warn that I will arrest and execute all, irrespective of rank or level, who dare to interfere with the battle with enemies of the people." On July 30 he presented order no. 00447 to the politburo, according to which each krai and oblast was to receive a quota of "enemies of the people" to be shot and arrested. He proposed that a total of 72,950 be shot and 259,450 arrested. The politburo confirmed the order the next day. These quotas, however, were soon exceeded, and local branches of the NKVD and party demanded that their targets be raised. By the time the terror abated on November 16, 1938, almost 700,000 persons had been shot and roughly as many sentenced to slave labor. In Moscow more than 40,000 persons were shot.

The newspapers leveled fantastic accusations against former Soviet leaders. A lead editorial in *Izvestiya* accused Lev Trotsky, Nikolai Bukharin, and Alexei Rykov of being "hirelings of fascist special services." It said that the "black trio was always united." Veteran Bolsheviks denounced their former comrades. "There should be no mercy. Mercilessly destroy the contemptible killers and traitors." Andrei Vyshinsky, the prosecutor of the USSR, said: "I demand that the crazed dogs be shot — every single one."[3]

A stranger's unexplained gesture — for example, someone sketching in a station restaurant — could give rise to panic. So might an unexpected phone call or knock at the door. Many, desperate to save themselves, rushed to denounce their neighbors. The slightest contact with a foreigner could be grounds for arrest, and when an American woman in Moscow approached Soviet citizens on the street, they "scattered like mice."[4] Some tried to flee the capital to remote areas, only to find that party committees in rural villages were also vigilantly searching for counterrevolutionaries — although some persons did save themselves in this way. For many of those who remained, particularly if they held responsible posts or were of foreign origin, the terror was inescapable.

On June 26, 1938, Mark Rafalov was thirteen years old. It was a bright, sunny day. Mark's father, Mikhail, left on foot for his job as a senior economist in the Soyuzzrivprom trust, which was located near the family's apartment. Shortly after noon, two NKVD officers arrived at the trust and arrested him. They put Rafalov in a car and drove him away. Mark never saw his father again. Other NKVD officers then began a search of Rafalov's apartment. They took away the complete works of Plekhanov and the camera that Mark had received from his father as a gift.

In desperation, Mark's mother, Vera, dialed the number of her husband's brother.

Her brother-in-law picked up the phone. "I'm listening," he said quietly.

Vera described what had happened. There was a brief pause and Mark's uncle said, "Vera, I ask you, please, don't call this number again."

This was followed by a series of short signals that indicated that the other party had hung up.[5]

The night they came for her father, Stanislaw, a postal official, Nellie Tachko woke up from the sound of furniture being moved around.

"Papa parted with us, hugged, kissed. He took all his money out of a purse and gave it to Mama." The NKVD officer took as evidence a pair of large field binoculars and several "suspicious" books.

"At the door, I asked as always, '*Papochka,* are you coming back soon?'"

"I don't know, *dochenka.*"

"Those were his last words. We never saw or heard from him again."[6]

Valery Bronshtein, a great-nephew of Lev Trotsky, was twelve years old when his father, Boris Bronshtein, a civil aviation official, was arrested.

It was the summer of 1937, I prepared to go with my grandmother to the village of Ternovka, somewhere in the Tambov oblast, where her close acquaintances were living. . . . I went to grandmother's house to spend the night, and early that morning mother arrived and I heard how she quietly asked grandmother if I was sleeping. After getting a positive answer, she . . . said, "During the night, they arrested Boris." A lump came in my throat and my heart beat wildly, and burying my head in my pillow I tried to hold back tears. I didn't tell my mother or grandmother that I knew about father's arrest. I hid this until autumn.

When I returned to Moscow from the country, I was a different child . . . unsociable and gloomy. My mother, meeting me, busily began preparing dinner. Sitting at the table, I said, "Mama, I know everything. We will live together just the two of us." But I was mistaken. They came for her in the middle of the night when I slept. . . . I woke up from the light going on. A strange woman came into the room and began a repeat search in the apartment.

As Valery's mother was being led away, she asked the NKVD officers to take Valery to his grandmother's apartment. One of them nodded, and after forty minutes a car arrived. Valery was driven through the sleeping city to an unfamiliar area. The car stopped at the gate in a crenellated stone wall. "Where have you taken me?" he asked. "To the Kremlin," answered one of the NKVD officers. "In this way, I ended up in the famous Danilovsky reception center for juvenile delinquents and the children of 'enemies of the people.'"[7]

Once arrested, victims entered a world they could have barely imagined. The charges against the arrestees were almost always pure fiction, but the authorities wanted confessions to give delusion the appearance of reality. Confessions were obtained with the help of a reliable method — torture.

N. I. Kazartsev, a former interrogator, described a scene in which he participated.

"[L. M.] Zakovsky [the deputy people's commissar of internal affairs] suddenly appeared in the interrogation room accompanied by Grigory Yakubovich [the head of the Moscow NKVD]. The accused at this time stood against the wall. Zakovsky started screaming and swearing at me. 'What are you agitating him for?' He then kicked the accused in the stomach and said, 'That's how you're supposed to interrogate and not persuade him.'"[8]

Aino Kuusinen, a Finnish woman who worked in the Comintern, described the methods applied to a young Latvian woman charged with espionage, who shared a cell with her in the Butyrki prison: "From the moment they brought her to Butyrki," Kuusinen wrote,

> they treated her with exceptional cruelty. She had hardly had time to wash in the prison, her long hair had not dried, and they came for her. She did not return for an entire week. Then they pushed her

into the cell. We were all experienced people and we had seen every-thing, but we looked at her and shuddered. The appearance of this woman had completely changed. Her face was deformed by big, black bags under her eyes, her body and face were swollen. She eventually came to and she described for us how these perverts had treated her. In the penalty isolator, she sat cross-legged on a small round table with water dripping on her head twenty-four hours a day. In the morning, they gave her a piece of black bread and a glass of cold water. At the end of the second day, her temperature rose and she lost consciousness. When she came to, they tied her naked to a bench and began to beat her with rubber hoses until she again lost consciousness. They poured hot starch on her naked body and tor-mented her day and night. When I was sent again to Lefortovo, she was still in Butyrki. But I don't doubt that she was shot.[9]

Officers of the NKVD suffered the same fate when their turns came. A. D. Rakitin, the deputy head of the third department of the Moscow NKVD, who refused to admit his guilt, was beaten to death.[10]

Once the prisoners had "confessed," they were sentenced. The sentenc-ing was carried out in two different ways depending on whether the prisoner was an ordinary citizen, and thus treated by the authorities as one of the "terrorist rank and file," or a member of the party and military elite. The cases of the persons who fell into the first category were handled by the Moscow NKVD, and once confessions were extracted, they were sen-tenced by extrajudicial organs — a *troika* consisting of representatives of the NKVD, the prosecutor, and the party, or occasionally, a *dvoika,* made up only of representatives of the NKVD and the prosecutor. The troika and dvoika examined the case files and passed sentence without seeing the accused.

At the height of the terror, there were three troikas operating in Mos-cow — under the chairmanship of Zakovsky, Stanislaw Redens (until he was replaced on January 20, 1938, as head of the Moscow NKVD and chairman of the troika by Grigory Yakubovich), and Mikhail Semyonov, the head of the Moscow police. The dvoika consisted of Yezhov and Vyshinsky. Isaiah Berg, who worked with Semyonov and was himself later sentenced and shot, described what took place:

The cases were examined at a rate of about two cases a minute. . . . In the speed of examination of cases, Semyonov [who was a member of the troika headed by Yakubovich as well as chairman of his own] competed with Yakubovich. . . . After the meeting, Semyonov always came to Yakubovich in his office and took pride that in the same period as Yakubovich, he examined fifty more cases, and they both laughed over how rapidly, without examining the cases, they condemned the accused.[11]

When the arrested person was a member of the party elite, the case was handled by the central NKVD and the accused was given something resembling a trial. In the vast majority of cases, the prisoner was tried by the Military Collegium of the Supreme Court, the highest organ of military justice. "Persons who had been tortured, who had been brought here from many prisons, milled around in a side room," wrote Alexander Milchakov, whose father, Alexander Ivanovich Milchakov, the former head of the Komsomol, was sentenced to death in that building. "They hoped and waited their turn in court but their fate had already been decided."[12]

According to protocols of the trials, the chairman asked the accused whether he knew the charges against him and whether he considered himself guilty. The chairman then asked a few questions. The accused was allowed a last word. In many cases, the accused used the opportunity to renounce a confession given under torture. But this had no effect on the outcome of the case. The judges left the room to confer and then returned with a verdict of guilty. The "trial" usually lasted from ten to fifteen minutes.[13]

In 1937 and 1938 the court often handed down more than a hundred death sentences a day, so it is possible that the judges did not always confer and read out sentences; court documentation that they did may not be accurate. But whether or not the protocols are trustworthy, the trials were meaningless. The lists of persons who were to be tried before the Military Collegium and for whom the NKVD had recommended the death penalty were shown to Stalin in advance. He and other politburo members invariably approved the executions, so the sentences of the court only confirmed decisions already made.[14]

As huge numbers of people were sentenced to death, the regime carried out mass executions. The first executions under the Soviet regime had taken place in cellars near Lubyanskaya Square, particularly in the building at 11 Varsonofevsky Lane. Later, executions began at the Butyrki Prison and, apparently, the Lefortovo Prison. In December 1934 an execution chamber was opened in the Moscow City Court on Kalanchevskaya Street. There were also executions in the building of the Military Collegium of the Supreme Court after the passing of sentences, for which it earned the sobriquet, "shooting house."[15] These facilities, however, were not adequate for the Great Terror.

A. V. Sadovsky was the head of the administrative-economic department of the Moscow NKVD from January through October 1937. In that capacity, he was responsible for compiling execution lists and determining the places and times of executions. In 1990 he was located by a KGB search group that had been formed to find someone with a direct connection to the killings during the Great Terror. The agents went through thousands of personal and investigative files in the KGB archives before they found him. Sadovsky met with them and, after initial hesitation, agreed to tell them what he knew.[16]

"In the fall of 1936," he said,

all of the execution chambers in Moscow were working at full capacity. Yet there were more and more people to shoot. It became difficult to remove the bodies of those who had been executed without being noticed by people in the area. There began to be bad rumors and the executioners, meanwhile, were pushed to the limit. What went on! What went on! There was no time to wash away the blood in the basements. There were brains on the walls. . . . But people kept coming and coming and it seemed like the shooting would never end. I did not know where to send the corpses, everything was filled . . . everything.[17]

Finally, two new sites were created for mass executions and burials. These were the Butovo firing range, eleven miles out on the Old Warsaw Highway, and the territory of the former dacha of Yagoda on the land of the Kommunarka state farm, fifteen miles away on the Old Kaluga Highway. The Moscow NKVD used Butovo as its execution site and burial ground, whereas the central NKVD used Kommunarka in some cases for executions and burials and sometimes only for burials. Executions continued at 11 Varsonofevsky Lane, and some of the victims of the central NKVD apparently were still being cremated in the Donskoi crematorium.[18]

Of the two locations, the more important was Butovo, which became the principal execution site for the Moscow area during the Great Terror. Ninety-one persons were shot on its first day of operation, August 8, 1937, and thereafter it was a rare day when fewer than one hundred were executed. Some days, three hundred or four hundred people were shot. Four hundred seventy-four persons were shot on December 8, 1937; 502 were shot on February 17, 1938, and 562 on February 28, 1938.[19]

At first, the local people did not pay much attention to the shots from the Butovo firing range. They assumed that exercises were being conducted. Soon, however, an atmosphere of fear settled over the area. People on their way home were passed by black prison vans. They began to hear strange sounds. A muffled woman's voice shouted, "Don't do it . . . don't touch me, I have children . . . " Sometimes there were distant screams. There was the singing of the Internationale interrupted by shots. Cars raced down neglected forest roads, sometimes a dozen at a time. People stopped speaking about their forebodings, even to one another. Children were forbidden to walk past the firing range, which was surrounded by barbed wire.[20]

Sadovsky was asked whether any of the local residents took an interest in the reason for the shots.

"Not a single person," he said, laughing, "I'd like to lay eyes on someone brave enough to do that . . . and at that time."[21]

According to Sadovsky, the condemned prisoners were taken to Butovo in special trucks that held up to fifty persons and generally arrived between 1 and 2 A.M. The prisoners were not told why they were being brought there. The area, at first, was surrounded by barbed wire, but this was soon replaced by a wooden fence. The trucks stopped at the watchtower in front of the gates, and the prisoners were led out and taken to a wooden barracks about 250 feet long, supposedly for hygienic checks. The guards then meticulously verified each prisoner's name and place of birth, and compared him to his photograph. This went on for several hours. If there were any inconsistencies, or if a prisoner's photograph was missing, he was sent back to Moscow or placed in temporary detention. Once all the papers were in order, he was taken to be shot.[22]

Despite these efforts, mistakes occurred. Persons were shot who had been sentenced to labor camp terms, and persons sentenced to death were sometimes dispatched to slave labor. There were cases in the 1950s where a person listed as shot miraculously appeared and asked for rehabilitation. This meant that in 1937 or 1938, someone else had been shot in his place.[23]

After the victims were led out of the barracks, their hands were tied behind their backs and they were read their sentence. The executioners, who had been waiting in a stone house nearby, appeared, and each led a victim deep into the firing range, to the edge of a ravine. The victim was forced to his knees and shot in the back of the head. The body was then pushed into the ravine, and the executioner returned for a fresh victim. Some prisoners were beaten before being killed. Sometimes this was done to ensure their silence before execution. There were cases of prisoners shouting "Long live Comrade Stalin," and it was feared that this could create doubt in the minds of the executioners as to whether those being killed were really enemies.[24] After the day's executions were complete, a local employee used a bulldozer to spread a thin layer of dirt over the corpses. The next day, everything began again.

The execution squads normally consisted of four persons, although when there was a mass execution the number increased. In all, the Moscow execution brigade consisted of twelve people. An NKVD driver in garage number 1, next door to the building on Varsonofevsky Lane, said that he often saw the executioners passing their free time playing checkers in the courtyard.[25]

The executioners were party members with little education. Several were described as taciturn, but they gave the impression of being dedicated to their work. Nonetheless, there is evidence that their role in thousands of murders had an effect on them. According to their personnel records, not one lived to old age. One shot himself, another hanged himself, one went out of his mind. Ernst Mach, who was an executioner for twenty-six years and received several decorations for his work, was fired on "psychological grounds." Others became alcoholics, including Pyotr Maggo, who began working as an executioner in 1918 and achieved fame from the accounts of Russian emigrants who miraculously escaped execution in the cellars of the Cheka. He participated in the executions at Butovo and died shortly before the war.[26]

At Butovo, steps were taken to facilitate the executioners' labors. A barrel of vodka was provided, and the executioners were allowed to drink as much as they wanted. There was also a large container of eau de cologne; after the killings, the executioners rinsed themselves with it to kill the odor of death. The smell of powder and blood was so overwhelming, however, that, in the words of one executioner, "even dogs recoiled from us." With the night's executions complete, the executioners went to the commandant's office, where they filled out various forms and signed the certificates of execution. Once this was done, they had dinner and were taken back to Moscow, usually in a drunken stupor.[27]

In addition to the normal executioners, high-ranking NKVD officers also took part in the shooting of prisoners, although in keeping with their rank, they were not obliged to do so. This was called "having a shoot" and was apparently done for relaxation. One of those who relaxed in this manner was General Vasily Blokhin, one of the few high-ranking officers to survive into the 1950s.[28]

The case of Blokhin is particularly illustrative of the way NKVD officers viewed their victims as enemies who were completely without humanity. In addition to shooting prisoners for sport, he was a central figure in many liquidations, including the murder of thousands of Polish prisoners of war in Kalinin. He also executed Tukhachevsky, the writer Isaac Babel, and the director Vsevolod Meyerhold. When he participated in large-scale liquidations, he donned his own uniform — a rubber apron, leggings, and boots. Yet despite his participation in hundreds if not thousands of murders, he was extremely popular in the NKVD "for his simplicity, cheerfulness and readiness to help anyone in a difficult situation."[29]

The execution site at Kommunarka appeared slightly later than the one at Butovo. Less is known about Kommunarka than about Butovo because the authorities did not succeed in finding anyone from the NKVD with direct knowledge of the executions there. In the 1990s, however, the FSB determined that the former dacha of Yagoda, which burned down after the war and was replaced by the building that now serves as the monastery's refectory, was used not for executions but as a gathering place for the prisoners and for the filling out of documents.

At about the same time, Leonid Novak, a historian affiliated with Memorial, received permission from the FSB to visit the site. He saw that the remains of rusted barbed wire scattered around Kommunarka appeared to mark off some kind of zone. Novak went from tree to tree, following the rusted pieces of barbed wire still attached to nails in the trees, and plotted out a barrier. On the inside of the barrier was the area where the victims were buried. "At some point, there was an entrance," Novak wrote. "Here, after the final checks, the condemned person was [brought into the zone] . . . and on the edge of a pit, executed. Apparently, that's how it was. They didn't put up the barbed wire for dead persons."[30]

As the killings intensified, the punitive organs had to deal with the question of burials. The flow of corpses of the regime's victims threatened to overwhelm the cemeteries. The most important task was to make sure that the victims of the Stalinist terror disappeared forever. An instruction issued on October 14, 1922, in the first years of the Soviet regime, stated that the bodies of the victims "should not be handed over to anyone and should be buried without any formalities . . . at the place where the sentence was carried out or in some other deserted place . . . so that there will be no trace of a grave."[31]

Between 1920 and 1926 victims were buried in the cemetery of the Yauzskaya Hospital. From 1926 to 1936 they were buried in the Vagankovskoye cemetery, and from 1935 until 1953 they were burned in the crematorium at the Donskoi cemetery or buried on the grounds. There is evidence of burials in other Moscow cemeteries, sometimes in unused parts of the cemeteries, sometimes in existing graves, with the exception of the Danilovsky and the Preobrazhenskoye.

At first, the prisoners executed in Butovo were buried in holes that were dug as needed by a local resident with a small bulldozer. But the number of bodies soon became so great that procedures had to be changed. The authorities brought in a huge excavator to dig out enormous trenches twelve feet deep, ten to sixteen feet wide, and hundreds of yards long. Hundreds of bodies were thrown each night into these prepared trenches.[32]

There is no information about burial procedures in Kommunarka, but in the early 1990s the Russian Ministry of Security carried out a survey of the territory that identified many of the ravines and pits in which the victims were buried. There is no indication of the order in which these pits were dug or who is buried where, but Kommunarka is the burial site of persons who were once the Soviet Union's rulers. The body of Nikolai Bukharin is there, along with those of dozens of people's commissars. The husband of Marina Tsvetaeva, Sergei Andreev-Ephron, is buried there, as are the commanders of the Soviet Union's military districts and fleets. Kommunarka is also the resting place of the NKVD officers who fell victim to the terror within their own ranks.[33]

For fifty years, the locations of the Butovo and Kommunarka burial grounds were known to only a handful of people. As far as the family members of the victims were concerned, their loved ones had disappeared from the face of the earth, and finding their graves was an unrealizable dream. With the advent of glasnost, however, what had long been unrealistic suddenly became possible. There was renewed attention to the fate of the victims of the Great Terror. If the regime that went to such lengths to murder the victims was willing to make a commensurate effort to locate their remains, the burial sites might be discovered.

In December 1988, at a meeting of the politburo, it was decided to rehabilitate persons repressed under article 58 (counterrevolutionary activity) of the Russian criminal code, and the question was raised of finding the places of mass burial. The KGB assigned a group of officers to work on rehabilitation and a separate group to search for information about the burial grounds. In the meantime, people began to come to Memorial with information about possible sites. Milchakov, who was on the board of Memorial, started his own investigation. In late 1988, appearing on the television program *Up to and after Midnight,* he stated that he had information that victims were buried in the Kalitnikovskoye and Donskoi cemeteries. He appealed to the KGB to help in locating other places of mass burial in the Moscow area but received no response.[34]

In the following months, in addition to the Kalitnikovskoye and Donskoi cemeteries, Milchakov received the first reports about Butovo and Kommunarka. In late 1989 he informed the KGB about these burial grounds and said that confirmation of their existence could be found in the archives of the central KGB. He even specified the location—fund no. 7, collection 1. The only reaction from the KGB was that officers in the central apparatus of the KGB and the Moscow directorate had searched for fund no. 7 and could not find it.[35]

As the revelations of glasnost led to a wave of anti-Communist feeling in the Soviet Union, Milchakov tried to bring public pressure to bear on the KGB. In interviews with *Vechernyaya Moskva* in April and May 1990, under the headlines "Duel: Alexander Milchakov against the KGB" and "The Duel Continues," Milchakov said that despite an effort to appear "open," the KGB was in fact failing to cooperate with his efforts to find mass burial grounds, citing a supposed absence of documents. He called on the KGB to search its archives and suggested that its officers interview retired NKVD officers and the drivers who had transported the victims to the burial and execution grounds. The interviews inspired a large number of letters and calls, including letters with additional information about Butovo.

Milchakov now wanted to investigate the Butovo firing range himself. To avoid complications, he asked the local branch of the KGB for assistance. On July 15, 1990, he was invited to central KGB headquarters. He was received there by Gen. Maj. Alexander Karbayinov, the head of the center for ties with society, and an officer of the investigative directorate, A. F. Krayushkin. They told Milchakov that the head of the KGB, Vladimir Kryuchkov, attached great importance to the effort to find the mass burial grounds. But when Milchakov stressed the need to search for documents concerning the mass executions in the KGB's own archives, Karbayinov said, "I give you my honest party word that those archives were not preserved." He nonetheless admitted that the KGB also had information that there was a burial ground at Butovo.[36]

In fact, the locations of Butovo and Kommunarka had not been a complete secret to the KGB. In those years, the fenced perimeter of Butovo had been guarded twenty-four hours a day. The young officers on the detail had no idea what they were protecting, but someone was paying their salaries and organizing their shifts. As later became clear, the sites were the responsibility of a curator within the KGB. Information about the sites was restricted, but the curator was known to the KGB leadership.[37]

On July 18, 1990, Karbayinov called Milchakov and said that a test of the soil had confirmed that Butovo was a place of mass burial. That night, the KGB broke its silence on the burial grounds of Stalin-era victims in the Moscow area. A short bulletin was read on the nightly news. It said that the KGB had recently received information about the location of burial grounds on the territory of the Vagankovskoye and Donskoi cemeteries and in the area of Butovo, and that it supported the search for burial sites and would question local residents and its former employees. The bulletin was printed the next morning in all the newspapers.[38] A month later, on August 17, 1990, the KGB announced that a burial site had been discovered in the area of the Kommunarka state farm.

The KGB statement only increased the demand for information. Milchakov continued to receive reports about Stalin-era burial grounds, including one located near the Rechnoi Vokzal metro station containing the remains of prisoners who died building the Moscow-Volga Canal. In an interview in *Vechernyaya Moskva* in October 20, he said that the KGB had released only information about burial grounds that had already been uncovered by his investigation, and he repeated that there was more information in the KGB's own archives.[39]

A short time after Milchakov's October 20 article, the KGB announced that fund no. 7 had been found in the archives of its central apparatus. According to the story it gave to Milchakov, a single employee had known where fund no. 7 was located but had blocked access to it. The documents in the fund included execution orders, acts certifying that executions had been carried out, instructions for burial or cremation, and certificates of burial or cremation. They concerned two groups of victims: persons buried until 1936 in the Vagankovskoye cemetery, and persons cremated in the Donskoi crematorium or buried in the nearby cemetery from 1935 to 1953.[40]

Once the KGB acknowledged the existence of fund no. 7, it agreed to provide lists of victims with their biographical data and photographs to *Vechernyaya Moskva,* which, on December 6, 1990, began to publish them.

"First in the list published in your newspaper, December 6, was my father, Komarov, Sergei Nikolaevich," wrote R. Parshinova. "At the time of his arrest, I was four years old and I hardly remember him. I remember only that he was kind and affectionate. I missed him for my whole life, and mother could not understand how it was possible to imprison and shoot such a completely honest and decent man. Please tell me where in the Vagankovskoye cemetery he is buried. I would like to go there and lay flowers. My elderly mother, my son and grandsons will be grateful to you."[41]

Another victim was Dmitri Baratinsky, the great-grandson of the Russian poet Yevgeny Baratinsky. He worked as a staff photographer for the Institute of Timber. The employees of the Baratinsky museum-estate asked for a copy of the photo taken of him in prison for an exhibit at the museum. The publication of the photograph and news of the tragic fate of the poet's great-grandson shocked many members of Moscow literary society.[42]

It was already known, however, that the Donskoi crematorium and cemetery and the Vagankovskoye cemetery were not the main places of burial. As the search for information in the KGB archives continued, Milchakov and his associates tried to gather information in the village of Butovo.

In the early 1990s Butovo was a depressing sight. The main avenue, Jubilee Street, consisted of several dilapidated brick and log buildings. The residents, almost all elderly, avoided contact with outsiders. Questions about life in the village during the Stalinist period were cut off in the sharpest manner. The reason was that the villagers lived in fear that the terror would return, and nothing could convince them otherwise. When they were shown that information about Butovo had already been published, they said, "No one knows what will happen in five years. If everything returns to the way it was, we'll be the first ones that they'll take."[43]

Only gradually were some contacts made. One of them was with a resident of the neighboring village of Bobrovo who had been a driver for the NKVD. He recalled that he had driven prisoners to the Sukhanovskaya Prison, a notorious torture center, and to the Butovo firing range. He confirmed that Butovo had been used for mass executions. With tears in his eyes, he said he would never forget how a young woman gave birth while he was driving her to Sukhanovskaya. The guards delivered the baby boy, cutting the umbilical cord with an army knife before handing him over to the prison authorities.[44] Local residents and another driver for the NKVD also confirmed that Butovo had been used for executions and burials. They also mentioned Kommunarka. In the meantime, investigators searching the archives found indirect confirmation of Kommunarka as an execution site in the form of a note from Yezhov to Stalin reading, "Yagoda's dacha—for the chekists."[45]

It rapidly became obvious that there were divisions within the KGB. The officers assigned to search the archives for information about the mass killings often worked intensively and conscientiously, but they met strong resistance from their own organization. KGB veterans were frequently uncooperative, and the investigators found it difficult to locate documents even confirming the fact of executions in 1937 and 1938, let alone the places of burial.

The KGB was also unwilling to let relatives see the case files of those who had been killed. In November 1990 Milchakov called for giving these files to relatives and turning over prison photographs. Soviet officials, however, argued that the files needed to stay closed because children would be ashamed to see that their parents had given testimony incriminating themselves and others. Milchakov replied that the whole world knew how this testimony was extracted.[46]

Whoever blocked access to fund no. 7 (if, indeed, this is what happened) may have been motivated by sheer recalcitrance. In an interview in *Vechernyaya Moskva,* Milchakov said, "Under Stalin . . . persons having a certain amount of power were not only executors of an alien will but in their area of authority, they were all powerful. . . . This acted like a narcotic. . . . I think that the bacteria of Stalinism infected that person . . . who deliberately hid these archives." In the same issue of *Vechernyaya Moskva,* Milchakov made a point that would have continued relevance. The search for the mass burial grounds, he noted, should be the job not of volunteers but of the government.[47]

In 1991 the KGB made its most important discovery. Eighteen bound volumes containing certificates of execution for 20,675 persons were finally found in the archive of the Moscow KGB. They had not been listed in any inventory. The tomes contained acts of execution for persons shot between August 8, 1937, and October 19, 1938. But even in the "execution books," there was no indication where the victims were buried. This discovery, however, made it possible to acquire definitive information from the one person directly connected with the executions that the KGB was able to locate, Sadovsky.[48]

The members of the KGB search group met with Sadovsky on December 6 and December 20, 1990. The meetings took place in a semiconspiratorial atmosphere. Sadovsky was not eager to speak even to representatives of the KGB. The officers, for their part, were afraid of jeopardizing his cooperation. By the third meeting, however, on July 30, 1991, the Soviet Union was disintegrating and the execution books had been found. The KGB officers showed the execution books to Sadovsky.

On the basis of the signatures of the executioners, Sadovsky confirmed that the shootings took place in Butovo.[49]

With this confirmation, there were calls to recognize Butovo and Kommunarka as historical sites. Beginning in 1991 a commission on the victims of Stalin-era repression began to operate under the Moscow city council. The chairman, M. B. Mindlin, had spent more than fifteen years in prisons and labor camps. In June 1992 members of the commission began compiling a card index based on the execution books found in the archive of the Moscow KGB. The index became the basis of memorial books for Butovo, published annually from 1997 until 2004, that included the names, biographies, and photographs of the victims.[50]

After the fall of the Soviet Union, the atmosphere surrounding the issue of Stalin-era atrocities began to change. With no contemporary political motive for focusing attention on these crimes, many who had campaigned for historical justice turned to other concerns, of which there were many. Those who remained committed were too few to put pressure on government institutions, including the successors to the KGB.

Butovo remained a closed site, guarded by the FSK, a successor organization to the KGB. There was not even an effort to preserve the grounds. Over the years, the earth had settled above where victims were buried, and to conceal the depressions, the KGB filled them with garbage. As a result, the firing range came to resemble a huge weed-choked garbage dump, filled with bricks and broken concrete, wooden frames, metal waste, and everything from children's galoshes to couch springs. To establish legally that Butovo was the burial ground of thousands of people, it was necessary to open a trench to confirm the presence of human remains. The FSK officers who dealt with the issue of victims of repression asked the prosecutor to conduct a partial exhumation and open a criminal case within whose framework it would be easiest to carry out necessary investigations, such as determining the exact boundaries of the burial sites. The prosecutor, however, had no desire to begin this process and refused to take any action.[51]

At the same time, however, the commission established by the Moscow city council on the victims of Stalin-era repression began to press for access to the firing range. Finally, permission was given to visit Butovo, and on June 7, 1993, a group of relatives and commission members entered the territory, along with representatives of state security, the Moscow government, and the commission on rehabilitation. It was the first time the territory had been opened to outsiders, although the existence of the site had been widely known for at least three years. Five months after the visit, a memorial stone was dedicated in the southern part of the firing range. On it was engraved: "In this zone of the Butovo firing range in 1937–53 were secretly shot many thousands of victims of political repression. To their eternal memory."[52]

The formal opening of the firing range to visitation, however, did little to mitigate the policy of neglect. Members of Memorial tried with no success to persuade the government to build a memorial complex for the whole country at Butovo. It often seemed to Memorial activists that Russian officials simply wanted the question to disappear. Leonid Novak said, "Sometimes when I talked to officials of the need to create a memorial, they looked at me as if I was unbalanced." Reflecting the attitude of those who wanted to commemorate the places of mass burial, Milchakov said in the February 18, 1992, issue of *Vechernyaya Moskva*, "In Butovo, it is necessary to preserve everything as it was. If we act differently, our descendants will never forgive us." The newspaper received more than a thousand letters in response to Milchakov's interviews, all supporting the creation of a memorial complex. A better indication of the new spirit of the times, however, was the decision by the Ministry of Security to offer tours of the KGB headquarters, including the Lubyanka internal prison, for thirty dollars per person.[53]

The indifference of the government did not extend to the Russian Orthodox Church. The persons working on the first volume of the Butovo memorial book quickly noticed that among the victims were a large number of church representatives. A list of 250 clergymen and laymen who were shot at Butovo was presented to the Patriarch Alexei II, and with his blessing, the church erected a large Orthodox cross deep in the territory of the firing range.[54] A plaque affixed to the foundation promised that on that spot a church would be built in honor of the "new martyrs" who died for their faith. At the end of 1994 a congregation composed of relatives of those killed at Butovo was formed, and construction of a log church began shortly afterward. The first service of the Church of the Holy New Martyrs and Confessors of Russia took place a year later.

In 1995 several residential buildings in Butovo belonging to the FSB were given to the new congregation and then, without discussion, the entire firing range was transferred to the church. From that point on, all commemoration and all work connected with guarding and reclaiming the territory became the church's responsibility. At first, Catholic, Muslim, and Jewish clergymen attended memorial services at Butovo, but, apparently discouraged by the exclusively Orthodox orientation, they soon stopped coming. The congregation of the new Church of the Holy New Martyrs, in the meantime, began to observe a full church calendar, celebrating holidays, baptisms, and weddings.

The attention of the church saved the burial ground at Butovo from total neglect but raised a number of questions that remain unresolved. In the first place, the ancestral faith of many of those buried at Butovo was not Orthodoxy but Roman Catholicism, Islam, or Judaism. At the same time, a large percentage of the victims, whatever their origins, were Communists who regarded themselves as atheists and arguably would not have wanted their deaths commemorated by any religious denomination.

It was, in fact, the responsibility of the government, acting on behalf of the entire people, to honor the memory of those murdered at Butovo. This was all the more true since the victims had been killed at the behest of the Russian state, for which the memorialization would constitute an act of repentance. The government, however, having shown no inclination throughout the 1990s to memorialize those shot and buried at Butovo, found in the interest of the church a convenient way of avoiding its responsibilities.

Until 1997 there was no effort to open the burial trenches. In August of that year, however, with the blessing of Alexei II but with no government authorization, a team of archeologists and forensic scientists excavated one of the ravines. At a depth of five feet the investigators found piles of clothing that had apparently belonged to the victims, as well as five rubber gloves with their fingers turned inside out, apparently thrown in the trench by the executioners immediately after the executions. A little deeper, the excavators found human remains chaotically jumbled together. Lydia Golovkova, a witness and a principal compiler of the Butovo memorial books, wrote that among the tangled remains "were persons who died for their faith and militant atheists, illiterate peasants and the most educated people of their time." Perhaps, she wrote, among the bodies were "geniuses whose discoveries and works would have glorified and enlightened the world." The bodies had been shoved into the pits as in a graveyard for cattle, and those who witnessed the opening of the burial trench were united in the conviction that the victims "have not been laid to rest to this day."[55]

Members of the church began to restore the site. They removed truckloads of garbage and demarcated many of the burial trenches with poles and ropes. They laid roads and planted some trees while removing others, draining an area that had become a swamp. Slowly, Butovo again became an open field. Between the log church and the bell tower they erected the memorial board with the names of the representatives of the church.

The number of worshipers grew until, by 2001, the church on the territory of the firing range could no longer accommodate them, especially on holidays. Work began on a massive red brick church directly opposite the firing range. If the original log church was rather modest, the new one is the size of a cathedral. Together, they create the overwhelming impression that Butovo is a Russian Orthodox shrine, particularly as no other religion is represented. Of the 958 murdered priests and laymen who are buried at Butovo, 344 have been canonized, making Butovo also a place of pilgrimage.[56]

While efforts were being made in the 1990s to decide the fate of Butovo, similar discussions took place concerning Kommunarka. In the case of Kommunarka, however, very little was done. Two architects, I. I. Barinov and N. T. Buzikova, who were among the early visitors to Kommunarka, produced a design for a memorial that sought to preserve the site to the maximum extent possible. The Moscow city government accepted the proposal, but after several meetings, the idea was quietly dropped. There was no decision even on access to Kommunarka. The FSB refused to relinquish the site, and it remained guarded and closed to visitors.[57]

In the spring of 1999, however, the authorities finally took action. Kommunarka was transferred from the FSB to the Moscow eparchy of the Russian Orthodox Church. It became a part of the Svyato-Yekaterininskogo monastery. According to some reports, the church felt compelled to take over Kommunarka in 1999 because otherwise the FSB was prepared to give it to a businessman for the construction of dachas. Several months after the transfer, relatives of those who were killed could finally visit Kommunarka, and on November 14, 1999, a metal plaque was put up by Memorial on the gate stating that this was a burial site for thousands of victims of political terror.[58]

Thus the Butovo and Kommunarka sites are both in the hands of the Orthodox Church, which takes the position that the best way to commemorate the dead is to pray for them. In an appeal for support, the senior priest and monks of the Church of the New Martyrs and Confessors of Russia in Kommunarka wrote: "Where there is prayer, there is compassion, even to those who themselves did not know compassion."[59] The priests and monks stress that they pray for all the victims, whether or nor they were Orthodox or even believers. In response to the question of why the Russian Orthodox Church should be in charge of burial sites where the victims are representatives of various religions as well as atheists, including, in the case of Kommunarka, virtually the entire government of the Stalin-era Soviet Union, the answer is generally, "This is Russia, and the religion of Russia is Orthodoxy."

Few, of course, would deny the right of Orthodox priests to pray for the dead whatever their denomination. But the transfer of execution and burial sites of the Great Terror, which affected the entire nation, to the Orthodox Church has a number of important consequences for the way in which Russia understands its past. In the first place, putting these sites in the hands of the church frees the government, in the case of Butovo and Kommunarka, of the need to make a symbolic act of restitution. The crimes committed by the Russian state are not addressed by the Russian state, and in this respect, the state's responsibility is not acknowledged.

At the same time, turning the burial grounds over to the church precludes any serious effort to honor the victims as individuals. The resources of the church are limited. They sufficed to put up memorial boards with the names of the 907 church representatives murdered at Butovo, but they were apparently not enough to create memorial tablets with the names of all of the 20,675 persons, at a minimum, who were murdered and buried there, although it was promised that this would be done when the memorial board honoring the religious victims was erected. The church's funds are certainly insufficient to cover the cost of a truly appropriate gesture of national repentance — such as the exhumation of the bodies, their identification with the help of DNA technology, and their reburial in individual caskets. It could be argued that this, and an expression of grief and horror over their fate, is the least that the Russian government owes the victims of state terror. At the same time, a detailed examination of the mass burial grounds by forensic medical experts could lead to information that is important for history. There may be documents in the pockets of the victims and evidence of when and how they met their deaths. The relatives of those who were killed may want to know how their loved ones spent their last moments. Clues to the fates of thousands are still buried at Butovo. But no forensic examination was undertaken, and there is no prospect of any being done in the future.

The conversion of the sites into a Russian Orthodox shrine, finally, makes it possible for the Russian government, with the church's cooperation, to misrepresent the nature of the tragedy. On May 27, 2000, at the first open-air service at Butovo, Alexei II called Butovo the "Russian Calvary." It has been described this way by the church ever since. The attempt to treat Butovo as a scene of religious martyrdom was evident during the ceremony. Worshipers were brought to Butovo in buses bearing the names of Moscow churches and monasteries in a line that stretched for miles. Eight church hierarchs and two hundred priests took part in the service. The choir was from the Orthodox Svyato-Tikhonovskogo theological institute. The service was attended by thirty-five hundred worshipers. According to Lydia Golovkova, "it appeared that all of Orthodox Moscow was in attendance."[60]

But the depiction of Butovo as the "Russian Calvary" is a misrepresentation. Even those victims who had been christened in the Orthodox Church did not, in most cases, die for their faith. Only the representatives of the church buried at Butovo can be regarded as having died for religious reasons, and they are but a small percentage of the known victims. The overwhelming majority of Stalin's victims were no more religious martyrs than they were terrorists and spies. They were the random victims of political terror that was initiated in order to guarantee the absolute domination of a totalitarian regime.

The notion of Butovo as the "Russian Calvary" also suggests that the tragedy was a Russian tragedy, and that the fate of Russians was different from and more tragic than the fate of other Soviet nationalities. There is no reason to believe Russians suffered more than others. About 30 percent of the victims at Butovo were non-Russians.[61] Some nationalities were singled out for persecution by the Communist regime: Latvians, Germans, and Poles during the Great Terror and, during the war, Germans, Chechens, Igushi, Kalmyks, Crimean Tatars, and others, who were deported en masse. There was never any persecution directed specifically against Russians. On the contrary, as Stalin made clear in his speech in November, 1941, Russians were considered the backbone of the regime.[62]

Some, including Alexander Solzhenitsyn, have argued that the Communist regime was "anti-Russian." This was true only to the extent that it was antinational in general. The Soviet Union was based on a supposedly "internationalist" ideology, so it persecuted all forms of nationalism, including Russian, as a threat to the new Soviet identity that the regime sought to impose. But it did not persecute Russians who identified with the new ideology. They participated fully in the life of the society. Russians, besides being victims, were well represented among the regime's executioners.

The idea that the terror was directed specifically against Russians also suggests that Russians were the victims of a force that was somehow external to them: Western ideas, the Russian Empire's minority nationalities, international finance. It is a short step from this to absolving the Russian state from historical responsibility altogether.

On October 30, 2007, the day of political prisoners in Russia, Putin attended a service at the Butovo firing range marking the seventieth anniversary of the Great Terror. Although he regularly observed the "Day of the Chekists," December 20, this was his first visit to Butovo in seven years in office, and the first by any Russian leader ever. The government television station First Channel reported that human rights defenders described the visit as "symbolic," omitting the rest of the phrase, "independent of the motives for Putin's trip."[63]

At the entrance to the Church of the New Martyrs, Putin was met by Patriarch Alexei II and the senior priest of the church, Kirill. After the service, Putin spoke to the assembled journalists. He made no effort to suggest that the Russian state bore any responsibility for what happened at Butovo and made no reference to the need for repentance on the part of society. He said that Stalin-era repression showed that political dispute was "crucial for a country's development." But he cautioned that political battles should be "constructive, not destructive," and should not go outside a "cultural and educational framework."[64]

The real point of Putin's visit may be seen in a statement released by the Orthodox Church on the same day. It said that the crimes of the Communist era should be commemorated with prayer and not political meetings. In an interview with the news agency Interfax, Metropolitan Kirill said that "requiem services are the proper form of remembering the departed and killed." Of course, he acknowledged, people have the right to organize political meetings around the memorial of the victims of repression, but "from a Christian point of view, this is an improper memorial." In keeping with Christian tradition, "the proper form of memorialization" is observed when "people without any meetings and demonstrations go to the places of execution or other places of memory and take part in collective prayer."[65]

CHAPTER 4

St. Petersburg

■

On an autumn day in 1996, Natalya Kruk entered the headquarters of the St. Petersburg FSB at Liteiny 4 and was taken by an FSB officer to a small room, where she was seated at a table with three other persons. She was then handed the file on her father, Semyon Kruk, a military engineer arrested in September 1937, and shot four months later. The file had a gray cardboard cover printed with the words "USSR, NKVD, director- ate, Leningrad oblast." Under that, in ornate handwriting, was "case no. 30174-37 in the matter of Kruk, Semyon Petrovich, begun September 28, 1937, and ended January 25, 1938."

Natalya began to turn the fragile pages, and for the next four hours, in a state of extreme agitation, she read the details of her father's fate. A docu- ment certifying his arrest on September 28, 1937, "for Trotskyite activity" stated that he had been a participant in a counterrevolutionary "wrecking" group in military construction. The file contained the protocol of the search that was carried out in the communal apartment where the family lived, on Khalturina Street in the center of the city. A questionnaire filled out by another person said Kruk was excluded from the party the day after his arrest for ties with the "wrecker Fashinsky." A protocol of a party meeting at his place of work stated that he had denied the charges, and that the party organization had voted unanimously to exclude him for participating in a wrecking group with Fashinsky and Vurovtsev.

On December 10, 1937, according to the documents, Kruk admitted his wrecking activity. He also gave the names of those he said assisted him. During an interrogation on December 12, he first denied espionage and then admitted it. The neatly typed record of the interrogation gave no indication of the reason for Kruk's change of heart, but in the period between the time he denied espionage and the time he admitted it, he was almost certainly tortured. Natalya noticed that, as the months passed, her father's signature degraded. By December 12 he signed the record of his interrogation with his first name and patronymic, "Semyon Petrovich," leaving off his last name. For some reason, he then wrote his initials. His signature was badly distorted, and it suggested that he already was not in his right mind.

A typed conclusion stated that Kruk had admitted guilt to fully having engaged in counterrevolutionary espionage work in favor of Poland. A postcard in the file specified that he had been sentenced to the "highest measure of punishment," and a certificate revealed that he had been executed on January 25, 1938. It was signed by the commandant of the NKVD for the Leningrad oblast, A. Polikarpov. There was no indication of where Kruk was shot or where he was buried.

As Natalya read the file, her hands shook. The hours allotted to her flew by. The other three persons reading at the table showed no obvious reactions. Each was lost in his own thoughts. From the file, Natalya learned for the first time that her father had been born in an area of Poland that later became part of Western Ukraine, that he had five brothers, and that before he married Natalya's mother, he had had another family and children. She also learned his nationality and, as a consequence, her own. Documents in the file said that although he was registered as Russian, he was really Polish.

She left the building in shock. It would be months before she could calmly recollect the experience of peering into the maw of the madness that had claimed her father's life.

Natalya was only a year old when her father was arrested, and throughout her childhood there was a curtain of silence around his execution and arrest. At first, her mother, Lydia, was told that he had been sentenced to ten years without the right of correspondence. When the war began, Natalya and her mother were evacuated to the Kirov oblast. After the war they returned to Leningrad, and Lydia went to Liteiny 4, where her husband was taken after his arrest. An official repeated to her that her husband had been exiled for ten years without the right of correspondence.

The years passed and Semyon Kruk did not return to his family. Natalya's mother tried to think of reasons why his release might have been delayed; but there also began to be rumors that a sentence of "ten years without the right to correspondence" was a euphemism: it meant that a person had been shot.

In 1954 Natalya entered Leningrad University and, for the first time, filled out an official questionnaire seeking information about her father. Anxious to conceal his arrest, she wrote that he had died in the Finnish War. After Khrushchev's speech exposing Stalin in 1956, the KGB began to respond to questions about persons who had been arrested. Natalya's mother asked for information and applied for her husband's rehabilitation. In 1958 she received a letter stating that he had been rehabilitated, and a death certificate which said that he died in 1944 from cardiovascular disease. She died without knowing his true fate.

Although many persons began to be rehabilitated, the attitude in Russia was that if someone had been arrested, there must have been a reason. So for the next twenty years, whenever Natalya had to fill out a questionnaire, she wrote that her father died in the war with Finland. "People didn't like those unsuccessful persons who landed in prison," she said. "This was a matter of mentality. People didn't say anything to your face, but at all stages of life you encountered obstacles. No one said that we won't take you because your father was repressed, but it was a subtext."

This attitude began to change only with the start of perestroika, as revelations about the scale of the Stalin-era repression began to appear in the press. In 1988 Natalya, who was working as a librarian in the Academy of Sciences, joined Memorial and began to participate in the first efforts to collect information about the Great Terror. It was not until 1995, however, that she wrote to the FSB and asked to see her father's file. She received a call and was given a date and time to read the case file.

Several months after reading her father's case, Natalya wrote to the FSB asking for the location of her father's grave. The FSB answered that persons executed in those years were probably interred in the Levashovo burial ground outside the city. By then, however, Memorial's own investigation had uncovered evidence that thousands of victims of the terror were buried on the territory of the Rzhevsky firing range near the village of Toksovo, twenty miles from St. Petersburg. There were also rumors that the bodies of many victims had simply been thrown in the Neva

River. The confusion plunged her into renewed despondency. It meant that her father's story is unfinished, as are the stories of millions of others who perished in the Great Terror.

The feared knock on the door usually came after midnight, and the knowledge that the NKVD could come at 2 or 3 in the morning deprived the entire city of sleep. Lyubov Shaporina, the founder of the Leningrad puppet theater, described the atmosphere in her diary. In an entry dated November 22, 1937, she wrote, "I wake up in the morning and automatically think: thank God, I wasn't arrested last night. They don't arrest people during the day, but what will happen tonight no one knows. It's like Lafontaine's lamb—every single person has enough against him to justify arrest and exile to parts unknown. I'm lucky, I am completely calm; I simply don't care. But the majority of people are living in absolute terror."[1]

The arrests were accompanied by heartbreaking scenes. Yelena Klein was asleep when the NKVD came to arrest her father, Evgeny Klein, on October 2, 1937. "I don't know when they came or whether there was a search," she recalled. "When they were ready to leave, Mama woke me up and said, 'Get up and part with your father.'"[2] Shaporina described the arrest of her neighbor, Veta Dmitrieva. "They came at 7 in the morning, locked them in their room and conducted a search. . . . Veta said goodbye to [her four-year-old daughter] Tanechka. 'When I come back,' she said, 'you'll be all grown up.'"[3]

The NKVD were usually led by a building custodian to the right apartment, and the arrest was preceded by a search. Lyudmilla Gordeeva was scarred for life by the arrest of her father. "I was five years old when they arrested father," she wrote.

> A black maria pulled up at the old iron fence of our yard a little after midnight and three men in NKVD uniforms got out. Their boots clattered on the flagstones in the yard and they appeared in the room where our family lived; Papa, Mama and three daughters. If I saw those people today, I would recognize each of them, they were so burned into my memory. Father was ordered to sit in a chair and not move and they forbade him to smoke. A search began. . . . Everything in the room was overturned. My terrified mother stood at the stove. . . . The two more aggressive of the NKVD men dug around

in the writing table. My older sisters cried. They were twelve and fourteen years old. Finally, the search came to an end. They took some antique objects, silver, the Gospels. They ordered father to get dressed—he put on his winter coat. From the window we saw how in the nighttime silence, father was led away in a convoy—never to return.[4]

For many, the arrests were totally unexpected. In 1937 Andrei Khodalsky was a translator from German for the Okhtinsky Chemical Combine. The combine achieved outstanding results and, in honor of this event, a banquet was held that was attended by the leaders of the factory, specialists from Germany, and Khodalsky. The day after the banquet, Khodalsky was arrested. Shortly afterward, his name appeared in the newspaper in a list of "enemies of the people" who had been shot. His wife, Galina, fainted when she saw his name in the list. She wrote to Stalin insisting on her husband's innocence. Shortly afterward, she was arrested as well.[5]

A signals operator on the railroad with a blind son was arrested in 1937 and disappeared. When the six-year-old boy asked his mother, "Where is Papa?" she replied, "Leave me alone. Don't think about it. . . . There is nothing we can change."[6]

To justify the arrests, the NKVD needed accusations. One charge was "wrecking."

In Leningrad, there was a case of poisoning caused by tainted cream in the Café Sever. It was followed by mass arrests. A packed trolleybus smashed through a barrier and fell into the Fontanka Canal. This, too, was followed by mass arrests.[7] After an accident with a high-voltage transformer in Leningrad, Stefan Shevtsov, an electrician, was arrested for supposedly pouring "defective oil" into the transformer. When the NKVD came for him, his wife urged him to take warm things, but he said, "I'll leave them for our son." The child was one year old.[8]

Besides wrecking, there were accusations of spying and counterrevolutionary activity. If someone had a Polish relative, he was charged with spying for Poland. If he had studied in Germany, he was a German spy. Someone who had once been to Japan was working for the Japanese. A man in the Shpalery Prison who was encountered by Yakov Efrussi, an inventor, was charged with espionage on behalf of Poland, for which purpose he supposedly had arrived in the Soviet Union illegally. In fact, although his mother had been born in Poland, he had never left the USSR. Another inmate was arrested because there was an order to arrest his neighbor, who had the same last name. The first inmate was forced to confess to spying, by which time his neighbor had also been arrested.[9]

Shooting took place in the basements of the city's prisons, and trucks left the prisons at night loaded with dead bodies.[10] Other trucks carried live prisoners to the forests to be shot.[11] In Leningrad it was taken for granted that people simply disappeared. Vladimir Brailovsky recalled his teacher, Vaclav Obukhovsky.

> He began teaching in our school in September 1936 and wrote his first name, patronymic, and last name — Vaclav Lutsianovich Obukhovsky — on the blackboard so that we would remember it and pronounce it properly. I recall that he was tight with grades. I received a commendation from him only once, for a proof of the theorem of Pythagoras not by the textbook. He never became my favorite teacher or perhaps he did not have time to be: a year later in class, in place of him, appeared another mathematician. And Vaclav Lutsianovich disappeared, we did not know where. And here fifty-five years later, a newspaper, publishing his name in the list of victims of Stalinism, finally made clear where.[12]

Shaporina wrote that the terror deadened the moral instincts of the population, creating a new normality.

> The nausea rises to my throat when I hear how calmly people can say it: He was shot, someone else was shot, shot, shot. The word is always in the air, it resonates through the air. People pronounce the words completely calmly, as though they were saying, "He went to the theater." I think that the real meaning of the word does not reach our consciousness — all we hear is the sound. We don't have a mental image of those people actually dying under the bullets.

Shaporina told her diary: "the words 'shot' and 'arrested' don't make the slightest impact on young people." The faces of ordinary people standing in long lines are "dull faced, embittered, haggard." "It is unbearable," she wrote, "to live in the middle of it all. It's like walking around a slaughterhouse, with the air saturated with the smell of blood and carrion."[13]

The meat grinder of arrests and executions was fed by denunciations. Persons afraid for their own lives inundated the authorities with false reports of wrecking, spying, and sabotage. At every workplace, there were meetings to denounce Trotskyites, wreckers, and counterrevolutionaries. Anyone staying away risked being accused of being a coconspirator or, at the very least, could expect a midnight call demanding that his "voice be heard" as part of the chorus of denunciation.

By the time the Great Terror was over, more than forty thousand persons had been murdered in the Leningrad oblast, which at the time included the territory of the current Pskov, Novgorod, and Murmansk oblasts, as well as part of the Vologda oblast. Originally, the NKVD planned to shoot four thousand persons and send ten thousand to labor camps. But prisoners under torture named others, including relatives, friends and coworkers. The NKVD then demanded that the quotas be raised. As a result, the number killed exceeded by many times the initial plan.

In the wake of the Great Terror, there was little possibility of memorializing the victims. Shootings continued, though on a reduced scale, and the stigma attached to those who were labeled as "enemies of the people" was such that family members were afraid to speak of them. Out of fear, children often destroyed the photographs of arrested parents.

The reaction to terror was, in part, the natural response of helpless individuals to pitiless force. But in Leningrad another factor also tended to destroy the memory of the Great Terror's victims. This was the city's experience during the Second World War. The entire Soviet Union suffered during the war, but the fate of Leningrad was exceptional. The Nazis laid siege to the city for nine hundred days. There was soon no heat, water, or electricity, and almost no food. In the bitterly cold winter of 1941–42, the food ration reached one quarter-pound of bread a day. It was impossible to survive on that, and the flood of death was overwhelming.

In a gruesome way, the Great Terror primed Leningrad for the mass slaughter that was to come. During 1937–38, the city suffered at the hands of its own rulers. During the war it was besieged by a foreign enemy. But the murder of tens of thousands of selected individuals during the Terror prepared the people of the city to be sacrificed in the hundreds of thousands in the interests of the Soviet state. The principle had been established that the objectives of the state, justified or not, were the highest objectives of all.

Soviet officials said that the citizens of Leningrad were united in its defense. This is doubtful in light of the high number of persons arrested in the besieged city for sabotage and espionage. But they were treated as if victory in the war was their fervent objective and their lives could have no other goal.

The conditions in Leningrad during the winter of 1941–42 defied imagination. As people died in droves, the dead from the Kuibyshev, Dzerzhinsky, Red Guard, and Vyborg sections were transported to the Piskaryevsky cemetery, where steam shovels dug trenches amid thousands of corpses. A Leningrader wrote, "There were on both sides of the road such enormous piles of bodies that two cars could not pass. A car could go only on one side and was unable to turn around. Through this narrow passage amidst the corpses, lying in the greatest disorder, we made our way to the cemetery." Many of the corpses were eventually placed in common graves. More than 650 common graves were dug in Leningrad in the winter of 1941–42.[14]

To compound the horror, the city was stalked by cannibals. Relatives bringing corpses to the cemeteries were revolted to see that the bodies lying around in piles had the fleshy parts cut away. In the Haymarket, starving people did not inquire too closely about the nature of the cutlets offered for sale. "In the worst period of the siege," a survivor told Harrison Salisbury, "Leningrad was in the power of the cannibals. God alone knows what terrible scenes went on behind the walls of the apartments."[15]

In some ways the fate of the city was epitomized by the experience of Tanya Savicheva, an eleven-year-old schoolgirl, who described what happened to her family during the blockade in a school notebook that had a letter of the alphabet on each page. Tanya's entries, in a child's hand, under the appropriate letters, were:

- Z — Zhenya died 28 December, 12:30 in the morning, 1941
- B — Babushka died 25 January, 3 o'clock, 1942
- L — Leka died 17 March, 5 o'clock in the morning, 1942
- D — Dedya Vasya died 13 April, 2 o'clock at night, 1942
- D — Dedya Lesha, 10 May, 4 o'clock in the afternoon, 1942
- M — Mama, 13 May, 7:30 A.M., 1942
- S — Savichevs died. All died. Only Tanya remains.

Tanya was evacuated from Leningrad in the spring of 1942 and sent to Children's Home no. 48 in the village of Shakhty near Gorky (now Nizhny

Novgorod), suffering from chronic dysentery. She died there in the summer of 1943.[16]

The number who died in the siege of Leningrad is unknown, but it is generally thought that 1 million persons died of hunger and that the overall military and civilian death toll was between 1.3 and 1.5 million. Nothing on this scale had ever happened in a modern city.[17]

The experience of mass death in Leningrad during the siege all but destroyed the already weakened moral fabric of the population. Leningraders, having been terrorized by the NKVD and then having endured starvation, cannibalism, and the loss of loved ones during the siege, were often little prepared to think in moral categories. Two decades earlier, in 1922, in the wake of war, civil war, and famine, there had already been indications that the Russian population had become unhinged mentally. The Russian psychiatrist Petr Gannushkin told Lenin that half of Russia's population was suffering from some form of mental illness. It is reasonable to assume that something similar took place among the survivors of Leningrad in 1942. After nearly seven years during which an individual had no control over this fate and his life counted for absolutely nothing, many came to accept the idea that it was normal to sacrifice people for the ends of the state. Even the deaths of children were seen as a contribution to the victory over Nazi Germany, giving them the aura of a necessary sacrifice.

The attitude toward human life was reflected in the way the victims of the blockade were memorialized. The Piskarevsky cemetery, at the end of the Avenue of the Unvanquished, is the largest burial ground for victims of the siege. It is believed that at least 500,000 victims are buried there. At the head of two rows of raised mass graves is an eighteen-foot bronze statue of a woman called *The Motherland*. The woman stands proudly upright and offers a garland of oak leaves, as though conferring laurels on those who died for their native land. Such a statue takes no notice of the children who died in the siege and who could not have made a mature decision to sacrifice themselves, or of those who, having survived the Stalinist terror, felt no love for the Soviet Union but were doomed to die in its defense.

At the same time, many other places of interment were ignored. One was the brick factory in the Moskovsky raion, where an estimated 117,000 bodies of siege victims were burned in 1942, in furnaces that worked around the clock.[18] The ashes were shoveled into canisters and dumped in the adjacent pond, or buried in trenches. After the war the Soviet authorities, instead of erecting a memorial, created a park on the site to commemorate the victory over Germany. Victory Park became a popular place of relaxation, with carousels and boating on the pond where the ashes of thousands of people were deposited.

The idea that it was normal to die for the state affected Leningraders for years. In 1995 a group of survivors succeeded in getting a memorial to the victims erected on the site of the brick factory. It was dedicated in late January. After the ceremony, a group of cold-weather swimmers appeared and announced that they wanted to do a demonstration for the crowd. They went onto a small wooden bridge over the pond, lowered themselves to a place where the ice was broken, and began swimming in the freezing water. Some of those who had arrived for the ceremony were disgusted by the swimmers' insensitivity, but many saw nothing out of place and watched the demonstration with interest.

After Stalin's death, the Soviet government freed millions of labor camp inmates, who began to return home. The regime spoke constantly of the heroism of those who had perished in the defense of Leningrad during the siege. But it remained silent about those who died in the Great Terror.

In 1985, however, the accession of Gorbachev opened up new possibilities. As long as the Soviet state punished any reference to its crimes, most Soviet citizens treated them as if they did not exist. But once it became possible to discuss events that had long been denied, the floodgates of memory began to open. Individuals began to insist on the importance of the state's war against its own people and the fates of the victims themselves.

Inspired by the more liberal atmosphere, labor camp survivors and relatives of those who were killed began to meet in the summer of 1987 in the Usupov Garden, in the center of Leningrad. In 1988 they founded the Leningrad branch of Memorial.

At the early meetings of Memorial, people came with photographs, biographies, and questions about the fates of missing relatives. They remembered some details but not others. They recalled neighbors who had lived alone and been arrested, as well as friends and acquaintances. There was a desire to name those who had disappeared and to find out where they were buried. One of the leaders of Memorial, Veniamin Ioffe, a former political prisoner, prepared a questionnaire for the relatives and survivors about their experiences. For three years, Irina Flige, who later became Ioffe's wife, processed up to one hundred questionnaires a week, entering the information into a card catalogue and trying to prioritize it.

Besides compiling personal histories, the group also began to search for the burial places of the terror's victims.[19] The children who had witnessed the arrests of their parents were now elderly, but many had not lost hope that they would one day learn where their parents were buried. As articles about the Stalin-era repressions started to appear in the press, Memorial began receiving reports of the locations of the burial sites. Killings were said to have taken place on the territory of the Rzhevsky firing range in the area between the Kovalyevo and Berngardovka stations two and a half miles outside Leningrad and bodies were said to be buried near the village of Levashovo. There were also rumors of a major execution site twenty miles from Leningrad near Toksovo. The place mentioned most often was Levashovo.[20]

Leningrad Memorial organized a search group under Valentin Murav-sky, whose father was killed in 1937. In the spring of 1989, at Leningrad Memorial's founding conference, Ioffe appealed to the KGB to reveal the location of the mass graves. The KGB did not respond. By this time, however, the search group believed that it had enough information to find the site near Levashovo on its own. As soon as the snow melted, a group of Memorial members and reporters went to an area of forest surrounded by a six-foot wooden fence and guarded by soldiers with dogs. Muravsky asked the soldiers what they were guarding. They said, "We ourselves don't know." They refused to let anyone enter the area, but people in the village confirmed that behind the fence was a burial ground.

After this discovery, two of the reporters in the group, Elizaveta Bo-goslovskaya and Sergei Chesnokov, both from *Leningradskaya Pravda,* were summoned to the Leningrad party committee and banned from publishing anything about the site. The ban on publication, however, did not last. The political situation in the Soviet Union was changing rapidly, and as glasnost became official policy, local party officials felt the ground shifting under their feet. A month after Memorial discovered Levashovo, the Leningrad city government reacted to demands for further details by forming a committee to search for Stalin-era burial sites itself. The local authorities eased access to Levashovo, and articles about the site started to appear in the Leningrad press.[21] On July 18, 1989, Levashovo was recognized as a memorial cemetery for the victims of political repression. In October the KGB formally acknowledged the NKVD's role, and on June 1, 1990, it transferred possession of the site to the city. Relatives of victims began to put photographs, signs, and tablets on the trees.

On an afternoon in September 2005, sunlight filters through the birch and pine trees and dapples the ground of the Levashovo cemetery. The wind rustles the upper branches of the trees. Visitors enter through the heavy wooden gates that admitted trucks bearing the bodies of those killed, and walk past the former guardhouse, now a museum.

A path leads into the forest. Soon raised earth indicates graves, and metal crosses and ceramic photos adorn the trees. On one Orthodox cross is a photo of a man in a white collarless shirt and a worker's cap. Under it is written, "Ivan Semyonovich Zavadsky, born 1893, shot September 20, 1937; We remember, love, and grieve—children, grandchildren." Nearby is a monument to two brothers, Ain and Toivo Lotto, killed in 1937 and 1945, both in the prime of life.

The forest path leads to a crossroads and a tall, wooden Orthodox cross with an attached icon and a small glass box for candles. Beyond it, in the fading light of day, the faces of the dead stare out from every tree in the dark pine forest. On one tree is a photo of a young man with a waxed mustache and military uniform and the words, "For Yefim Alekseevich Yershov, born 1891, medical assistant, arrested March 7, 1938, shot, rehabilitated posthumously November 2, 1959." On some trees are the faces of women. A plaque with a picture of Evgeniya Antonovna Stankewicz, born in 1903 and shot in 1938, is screwed to a tree along with a holder filled with red plastic flowers.

Deeper in the forest, rays of sunlight only intermittently break through the cathedral-like darkness. Depressions in the forest floor indicate the ravines where victims were buried. Moss-covered tree stumps are decorated with artificial flowers, and wooden and metal grave markers, attached to the trees by relatives, friends, and even strangers, are visible as far as the eye can see.

Levashovo is the official burial site of the victims of the Great Terror in Leningrad, but it is at the heart of a mystery that no official in St. Petersburg wants to unfold. Almost from the beginning, it was clear that

Levashovo was not the only burial site. The KGB said that forty thousand persons were killed in the Leningrad oblast during the Great Terror. An internal KGB inquiry, carried out in 1965 but not released until 1990, showed that during the Terror only eight thousand were buried in Levashovo. The KGB arrived at this figure by interviewing the truck drivers who delivered bodies there in 1937 and 1938 and multiplying the number of trips by the capacity of the trucks.[22]

The KGB study also confirmed that Levashovo was not a place of execution. The persons buried there were shot in the NKVD prisons, including at Liteiny 4, or died under torture or from disease. There were also victims during the Second World War. During the siege, spymania led to thousands of arrests, and the arrestees starved to death en masse in the prisons. These victims were also buried in Levashovo, and probably constitute the majority of those interred there. The total number of persons buried at Levashovo, according to KGB estimates, is 19,450.[23] Despite this, the KGB has continued to state that all 40,000 acknowledged victims of the Great Terror are buried in Levashovo. But if only 8,000 of the persons killed in the oblast during the Great Terror were buried at Levashovo, at least 32,000 victims were buried elsewhere. Where are their remains?

What is striking is that the government did not consider it important to try to find out. The KGB and, later, the FSB recognized Levashovo as a burial site since it was difficult to do otherwise after it was discovered so close to St. Petersburg by civilian volunteers. But they discouraged people from searching for other places of execution and burial in and around Leningrad. When family members of victims asked where their loved ones were buried, they were told, "the documents were not preserved but in the period 1937–38, those who were shot were buried in the Levashovo cemetery." Many people had waited for this answer for sixty years, and in fact it was not false. The KGB did not say that *all* of the victims were buried in Levashovo. But it falsely gave that impression. As a result, thousands of people mistakenly think that their relatives are buried in Levashovo. Any victim who was transported alive to an execution site, shot, and then buried on the spot definitely was not buried in Levashovo.

In 1989, after the discovery of Levashovo, Memorial began efforts to find the other burial sites. In 1990 and 1991 people came to Memorial with information. The most reliable and important reports came from ethnic Finns who had lived in the Leningrad oblast before the war and had been subjected to massive repression. The Finns said that they witnessed shootings in a heather-covered field they called Koirangakangas, Finnish for "dog's wasteland," between the former villages of Kiurumyaki and Konkkolovo, just east of Toksovo and just inside the territory of the Rzhevsky firing range. The village of Kiurumyaki was situated on top of a hill and offered a clear view of the field where, the Finns said, thousands of victims of political terror were executed and buried.

Despite the evasions of the authorities, the elderly Finns had no doubt about what had happened on their native territory. "On the hill we had a club," said David Pelganen, who grew up in Kiurumyaki and was interviewed by Memorial.

> We used to go there for dances and the elders socialized. When it was dark, cars arrived and there were shots. When it was finished, they turned around and left.
>
> We went [to investigate]. . . . We came back and said to my father, we found people killed and buried. Their heads were visible. They [the adults] took shovels and went to dig out what was there. They discovered everything. They went to the guard for the firing range and told him what they had seen. The guard picked up the phone and called Porokhovie [a nearby town]. They told him: "Get out of there and don't set foot in that place or you'll end up there yourself."
>
> After that, we began to be afraid. . . . At home, they said that we should not open our mouths on this theme.[24]

"I remember that we walked through the sand looking for berries," said Alonas Khyuza, another witness interviewed by Memorial. "There were graves there. The wolves had torn them apart. Everyone knew that they were shooting. They came at night. The lights were visible and the road was nearby. They dug the holes themselves . . . but who they shot there — God knows. . . . We walked along and they [the bodies] lay around everywhere."[25]

Ivan Fyodorov, another villager, said, "I remember very well how we ran to look at the bodies of persons who had been shot. 'They've again brought the bourgeoisie,' said the kids who had been taught that the only thing that kept us from the good life were 'bourgeoisie' with gold teeth."[26]

The witnesses who came to Memorial had endured their own traumatic experiences. During the 1930s life in the villages of Kiurumyaki and Konkkolov went on against the background of these nighttime shootings and the lights of convoys bringing doomed victims to the execution site. But there were waves of arrests in the villages themselves. Two-thirds of the men in Kiurumyaki were arrested. On March 20, 1942, the military council of the Leningrad Front decided to exile all Finns from the area. On March 26 the village of Kiurumyaki was liquidated. The residents were driven out into the frost and allowed to take with them seventy-five pounds of belongings. They were told by the guards, "You're not leaving in order to live but to die." Very few returned.[27]

One of those who did return was Pelganen. He succeeded in escaping from exile, and after the war came back to the region. Not a single house was left standing in the former village of Kiurumyaki; the only traces were a few foundations and an old well. But Pelganen wanted to be close to the place where he spent his childhood, and he settled in a village nearby.

By the 1990s the heather field had become a forest. Memorial activists studied aerial photos of the area taken by German intelligence in 1943. An obvious violation of the earth was visible. In 1997 they went to the area indicated in the photos. The area where the shooting took place covered between two and three square miles — a much larger area than Memorial had the manpower to search. In the course of a summer, only two to three members of Memorial were available two times a week. The activists, however, were encouraged by their recent success in finding a burial site near the Karelian village of Sandormokh.

The annals of the Great Terror are replete with enigmatic disappearances, but one of the most haunting is the story of the Solovetsky transport, a group of 1,116 prisoners held in a labor camp on the Solovetsky Islands who were let out and put on a boat, only to disappear without a trace. What made the transport particularly notable was that it contained some of the Soviet Union's most distinguished men, including the father of the religious philosopher Pavel Florensky; two Ukrainian ministers, A. Krushelnitsky of independent Ukraine and M. Poloz of Soviet Ukraine; A. Bobrishchev-Pushkin, the lawyer who defended Menahem Mendel Beilis in a famous Kiev ritual murder trial; A. Vangengeim, the founder of the Soviet weather service; and Father P. Veigel, who had been sent by the Vatican to investigate the persecution of believers in the Soviet Union.[28]

From the memoirs of former inmates, it was known that the prisoners had been transported from the Solovetsky Islands in several stages to Kem, a port on the White Sea. But for decades, nothing further was known about them. In 1993, however, a copy of an execution list with the names of the victims was found in the archives of the Archangelsk KGB by Antonina Soshina, who worked in the Solovetsky Museum documenting the islands' history. Two years later, Ivan Chukhin, a member of Memorial, discovered the case of Captain Mikhail Matveev, who had carried out the executions, in the KGB archives in Petrozavodsk. In an example of the Soviet period's extraordinary pseudolegality, Matveev had been prosecuted for mistreating prisoners because, before they were shot, he and his assistants allegedly beat and humiliated them. In July, a group from St. Petersburg Memorial was given access to the case file by the head of the Karelian FSB.

During his interrogation, Matveev had testified that the prisoners were taken from Kem by rail to Medvezhye Gora (now Medvezhegorsk), where they were placed in the investigative prison of Belbaltlag, the labor camp complex for workers on the White Sea Canal. They were then stripped naked and beaten unconscious with clubs before being loaded into trucks, covered with tarpaulin and driven to the execution site in the forest outside the city. There, Matveev shot the prisoners with his revolver. Every day, he shot 200 to 250 persons. At one point in his interrogation, Matveev said, "How could we not beat them? For nineteen kilometers [twelve miles] we went through a populated area." He told of a truck breaking down near the village of Pindushi. From this testimony, the investigators knew how far the execution site was from Medvezhegorsk, and in what direction.

In 1997 Ioffe, Flige, and several others from St. Petersburg Memorial traveled to Karelia. They entered the forest in the area indicated by Matveev and saw depressions in the earth. The group began to dig and immediately found bones. For decades, no one had known the final resting place of the prisoners in that transport. But on October 27, 1997, Memorial was able to mark the sixtieth anniversary of the execution with sixty children of the victims, at the place where it occurred.

After Sandormokh, the staff at Memorial returned to the search for the killing ground at Koirangakangas. But serious problems soon became obvious. There was high groundwater in the area. This meant that the depth of the burial pits had to be no more than six feet, with the bodies only three feet below the surface. The depressions were only slightly visible. The second complication was that because of constant shooting on the firing range, the earth was disturbed. There were craters, metal refuse from military maneuvers, and even shells.

Ioffe met with the supervisors of the firing range in 1998 and asked for their help, but the range bosses insisted that if Memorial wanted to enter the territory, it had to give them the names and passport data of the searchers months in advance — a condition that, for a social organization like Memorial, was impossible to meet. Unable to reach agreement with the leadership of the firing range, the searchers decided that they would enter the territory at their own risk. A checkpoint on the main road prevented them from taking the most direct route to the site. They began to use a dirt road instead, until the military began to dump heaps of earth on the road, rendering it impassable. The volunteers were forced to bring their bicycles from St. Petersburg on the electric train and then cycle from Toksovo to the search area. They stored their shovels and prods in the woods.

In 1998 Pelganen led a group of searchers to a place he said was the execution site and burial ground. Mikhail Pushnitsky, a member of Memorial and the most active searcher, returned with Ioffe and Flige to the area, and the three of them searched extensively using shovels and metal prods. They found nothing and assumed that Pelganen had been mistaken. In 1999 a group went to see Anna Arikanen, another witness. She described a place a mile and a quarter from the site identified by Pelganen. The activists searched that spot too, also without success.

In 2001 Memorial wrote to the prosecutor requesting that he conduct an investigation of Koirangakangas. There was no response. It became obvious that neither the military nor the judicial authorities wanted Memorial to prove that thirty thousand bodies were buried on the territory of the firing range. If such a discovery were made, there could be pressure to construct a memorial complex and possibly close the firing range.

Despite the risk of working in the firing range without permission, Memorial continued to search for the burial site. Pushnitsky worked a twenty-four-hour shift as a stoker in a St. Petersburg bathhouse followed by several days off. As a result, he had more opportunity than most of the activists to search the site. By 2002 he had been searching in the forest outside Toksovo on and off for more than four years. On August 20 he was working alone about three miles from Toksovo, testing the ground with a metal rod, probing for places where there was less resistance, indicating that at some point the ground had been broken. It was getting late, but at the last minute, his attention was attracted by a depression that he had not tested. He probed with his rod and realized he was hitting something. He took a small shovel and began digging. He found a human pelvic bone. He dug further and he found other bones. Clearing away the earth, he saw two skeletons, one lying crosswise atop the other, and also shoes. He returned to St. Petersburg to inform his colleagues.

On August 31 an expedition organized by Memorial arrived at the spot and began digging. They found bones in dozens of holes. In two of the holes eight skeletons buried one on top of the other. Eight skulls and several rib bones were removed for analysis. According to Andrei Dybovsky, a pathologist who did the analysis for Memorial, the skull of "person no. 5" from the "second excavation" belonged to a woman between the ages of twenty-five and thirty-two who had been shot twice in the back of the head, once with a .38-caliber firearm and once with a .45-caliber firearm. In the 1930s such pistols were used mainly by the NKVD. The body had been buried for fifty to eighty years. By the end of September searchers from Memorial had located more than fifty pits with human remains, occupying an area of more than three thousand square feet. There now was little doubt that Koirangakangas had been a mass burial ground of victims of political terror in the 1930s.[29]

The discovery meant that Memorial had found the final resting place of the majority of the Leningrad victims of the Great Terror. Many of these people had living relatives in St. Petersburg. But there was little public reaction. What press interest there was came mostly from foreign correspondents. The government took no steps to explore the site, just as it had done nothing to help discover it. Memorial asked the FSB for additional information about execution sites and burial grounds in the 1930s, but the FSB repeated its previous assertion that its archives contained nothing about any mass burial site except the grounds in Levashovo.

Memorial, on the basis of its discovery, petitioned the prosecutor for the Leningrad oblast to open an investigation. This would have permitted exhumations and a detailed examination of the site. But the prosecutor declined to help. It was clear that any further work would have to be carried out by Memorial itself. Memorial, however, lacked both the means and the manpower to carry out a major excavation. As a result, the exploration of the Koirangakangas site ended almost as soon as it began. The only change to the site is a wooden sign, put up by Memorial at the entrance to the road leading to the burial pits, that reads, "In this place, in the 1930s were shot thousands of people; don't disturb their graves."

On an overcast afternoon in January 2005, an unearthly silence reigned in the forest three miles from Toksovo. Two guides from Memorial, a local reporter, and I formed a melancholy procession as we looked for the burial pits that Memorial had partially excavated. They proved hard to find in the trackless forest.

A gray light lit the moss and branches. The woods looked the same in every direction—the narrow trunks of the birches and pines resembled rows of poles against a screen of saplings and bushes. As we walked through the mud, grass, and matted leaves of the forest floor, I saw a shattered birch tree, a rusted shell, and depressions in the earth the size of shell craters, all reminders that the area was also an artillery range.

I asked Miron Muzhdaba, one of the guides, whether the forest had been there at the time of the Terror. He said no, it had grown up in the past fifty years. Ilya Yershov, the other guide, pointed to a tall fir tree. "That one probably was here," he said. It had spreading branches and was slightly bent over. In the ground at the base of the tree was a large hole surrounded by raspberry bushes. It was the excavation we were seeking. At the bottom of the hole, which was filled with branches and leaves, I noticed bones dyed green by the moss. "Could these be the bones of the victims?" asked Valery Beresnev, the journalist. "The very ones," said Muzhdaba. He leaned over, picked up a jaw bone, and held it in his hand. I was reminded of the skull of Yorick. "Here hung those lips that I have kissed I know not how oft." But who knew the name of the person to whom this jaw belonged, and was anyone alive who still remembered him?

The FSB refuses to acknowledge that Koirangakangas is a burial ground for victims of the Great Terror. Valery Kuznetsov, the press secretary of the St. Petersburg FSB, challenged Valery Beresnev, "What relation do we [the FSB] have to the Toksovo firing range? Who proved that the human remains found there belong to the victims of political repression? Until this is established, we will hardly deal with this question."[30] In fact, the only way to establish what happened at Koirangakangas is through major excavation. It is likely that the site contains between thirty thousand and forty thousand bodies and covers almost half a square mile. To study it properly requires a well-equipped expedition able to spend months in the forest. It also requires official forensic examinations of the bodies, not unofficial examinations carried out by volunteers.

The Levashovo cemetery was dedicated when interest in the Stalin repressions was at its height. The authorities today do not want to call attention to a second and much larger site. At the same time, there is no public pressure to memorialize Koirangakangas. The result is that the burial ground is quietly neglected. The evidence that it was a mass execution site serves to remind the victims' relatives that they do not know where their family members are buried — in Levashovo, Koirangakangas, or some third, as yet unknown, location. To find out more would require the excavation of Koirangakangas, the dating of remains, and the matching of findings from the grave sites with information in the FSB archives. This is unlikely to happen. But when children don't know the burial site of their parents, it also troubles the grandchildren. In this way, the terror in Leningrad continues to claim victims.[31]

CHAPTER 5

The Appeal of Communism

■

"Life in our town was pretty interesting," said Yuri Zhigalkin, a New York–based correspondent for Radio Liberty, of his native Korsakov, a town of thirty-eight thousand on Sakhalin Island, during the 1970s. "We had a small amateur theater that people attended regularly. The local party bosses were very accessible. If you had a problem you could go to them and ask for support. The idea of just socialism was ingrained and party officials helped people. For many Russians, the late Brezhnev years were the happiest years of their lives."

I asked him to elaborate. "For most of the people," he said, "life was basically fair. People felt that the major problems in life were taken care of. There was a communal spirit. It was all right to knock at the door of a stranger and ask for help. The people had a sense of supporting each other. There were warm relationships. We were all together building socialism. At the same time, the outside world was seen as hostile and threatening. Russia was a fortress in a hostile world, always threatened, always the target of missiles."

"But did people feel that they were being prevented from expressing themselves?" I asked.

"Maybe to some extent, but most people did not feel a need to express themselves politically because they did not feel injustice. They might complain about bad service, but not about politics."

"Did people live in fear of the KGB?"

"I never encountered fear of the KGB. I don't even remember where the KGB headquarters in Korsakov was."

I asked Yuri about the foreign radio stations. "Did they have any effect in providing balanced information?"

"You could catch the Voice of America in town. But few people listened to it. The Soviet Union was a huge country, an entire continent. To fly from Yuzhno-Sakhalinsk "[the administrative center for Sakhalin Island] to Moscow took ten hours. The outside world was not on the radar screen of those who lived in Korsaskov. The propaganda worked extremely well, as it does today. Most people got their news from television, and it was completely controlled by the regime."

"Did anyone talk about the Stalin-era terror?"

"I didn't hear about it except from my mother. The attitude was that there was no point in discussing it. There was the 'Cult of Personality.' During the Cult of Personality there were certain abuses. That was it. Nobody knew the extent of the repression because nobody had read Solzhenitsyn at that time."

"Did people fear the 'evils' of capitalism?" I asked. "Did they feel they were lucky to live under socialism?"

"I think you should realize that on a primitive level life is the same everywhere. When an average person goes to work, he or she is dealing with the same set of problems. You have your boss. You have your colleagues. Life there was real life. It wasn't cartoonish."

"What the regime was telling its people and telling the world was cartoonish, but within that cartoon, people were living a normal life?"

"Exactly. That's why some people miss that kind of life. At that time, their life was based on primitive things."

Yuri Zhigalkin's memories of Korsakov, a closed city less than a hundred miles from Japan, were typical of those of many Russians who grew up during the Brezhnev years. The Soviet totalitarian system was the creation of terror, but the terror abated, and by the 1970s little in the Soviet Union was terrifying for most of the population. Soviet citizens benefited from cradle-to-grave security and did not miss the freedom they had never had. The ability of people in the Soviet Union to adapt to a caged existence was described by the Russian writer Alexander Zinoviev in his book *The Reality of Communism.*

The nub of the matter is that people in communist society, because of their education and the obvious conditions of their personal fate, have to accept whatever limitations apply to their behavioral free-dom or unfreedom as something natural and self evident. They are brought up to live within these limits and grow accustomed to them from childhood. They accept the form of life that is foisted upon them, having no other choice, and they themselves foist it on others.[1]

Russians not only accepted their lack of freedom but reconciled them-selves to the violence through which the system was created. Even rela-tives of victims found it difficult to confront the state over its atrocities. In speaking about the Stalin period, the typical remark heard from survivors and ordinary citizens was that the years of mass killings were "terrible times," a valid observation but one that implied that the terror was some-thing unavoidable, like the weather, and beyond any individual's control.

Westerners often assumed that Soviet citizens suffered from their lack of freedom and yearned for the collapse of the Communist regime. This perception is not accurate. It was born of contact with a minority of Soviet citizens who held democratic values, and of the assumption that Soviet citizens could not but be appalled by the regime's crimes. In fact, although discontent existed in the Soviet Union, those who actively opposed the regime were a tiny minority. Not until perestroika, after the revelations of glasnost and under conditions of unprecedented freedom, could the polit-ical values of this minority become a force in millions of people's lives.

Communism appealed to Russians for several reasons. First, it pro-vided security, minimizing the individual's need to worry about his own fate. It also provided a universal idea that gave Soviet citizens a feeling of mission and filled a basic spiritual need. Finally, it appealed to the chauvin-ism of the ordinary man, who compensated for his personal impotence by identifying with a powerful state.

The security of life under Communism was not a myth. A Soviet citizen was guaranteed a job (it mattered little that, in many cases, this "job" required no real work), medical care, an education, and a pension. All of this led Soviet citizens to boast that, unlike the citizens of the West, they had "no fear for the morrow." By the time Leonid Brezhnev became the Soviet leader in 1964, the upheavals of Stalinism and the revolutionary period were well in the past. In fact, Soviet society gave the impression of extraordinary stability. With a few exceptions, everyone lived, looked, dressed, and thought alike. Disparities in wealth existed but were not strikingly evident. Tranquility was valued, and anyone who disturbed the peace was quickly suppressed. In a restaurant, café, or other public place, a diminutive babushka could impose her authority on a potential trouble-maker because she knew and he knew that she could call on the full force of a repressive society at the first hint of resistance to her demands.

Maria Rakitina is a dispatcher for a group of apartment buildings in central Moscow. I was introduced to her by Felix Serebrov, a one-time Soviet dissident who had played a key part in fighting psychiatric repres-sion under the Soviet regime.[2] The new Russia had little use for former dissidents, and Felix was working as an electrician to support his large family. He had met Maria through his work and regarded her as a kind person despite her pro-Communist sympathies. Maria worked a twenty-four-hour shift, sleeping when she could on a cot in a back room, and then spending three days at home. During her shift, little usually happened, leaving her time to talk.

I met her in the dispatcher's office on an overcast Sunday afternoon in late March. She boiled water for tea on a hot plate and recalled the sense of security she had felt when there was a Soviet Union. "I remember that period as kinder, quieter, more generous, and more stable," she said.

People had a future. After the Soviet Union collapsed, people be-came lonely.

Before, everyone helped each other. People were friendly. Now we all have different passports, different money. Earlier we all lived harmoniously, but after the breakup of the country, I brought my mother here from Kirghizia. The Kirghiz began to drive us out. "When are you leaving?" they asked us. Now they cry because they drove out the Russians.

I used to send my twelve-year-old son in the summer to his grand-mother. He spent three days on the train to Kirghizia and I was calm. I knew that nothing would happen to him. Now he is thirty-two and I worry every day that he is in danger. There are constant explosions and disorders.

In the Soviet period, after a person finished school, he would go to the institute, and then after the institute, he would be assigned work as a young specialist and given a free apartment. A person had a future. The collective was everywhere. There were political information sessions. People took an interest in politics. If a person needed to go to a sanatorium, the trade union helped, and they helped in tragic situations. When my brother died in 1977, I lived in Kirghizia in the Osh oblast. I worked as an accountant, and the collective helped me. They gave me money and a car and helped to organize the funeral. My brother worked in a traveling construction brigade. His bosses could not help. But in my collective, people could count on help from the director's fund, and this help was given to me.

Each collective looked after its members. It could refuse a drunk his pay and insist that his wife receive his salary. There was the comrades' court to punish violations. Now there is no collective, there are no trade unions, and there is nowhere to turn for help.

Later, I met with Maria again, along with several of her friends: Nikolai, a major in the internal forces; Valery Grushnin, a subway conductor; and his wife, Svetlana Kuznetsova.

All of them expressed nostalgia for the security of the Soviet Union.

"Earlier," said Svetlana, "we paid five kopecks for the metro and two kopecks for a kilowatt of electricity for a heating plate."

"Most important," said Nikolai, "there was no unemployment. Every person was defended by the party organization. He could not be fired, even if he was lazy."

"In the Soviet times," said Grushnin, "any family could receive a free education, independent of religion, income, or profession. My mother raised me alone. She worked at low-paying jobs. But I went to musical school, completed college, and gave my children an education."

"Money didn't matter," Maria said. "Now you need money for everything. What does a simple person need? He needs a roof over his head, work where he knows they won't fire him tomorrow, money for the education of his family. In the Soviet period, this was all accessible."

At this point, I asked Maria and her friends whether they had suffered from the lack of freedom in the Soviet Union.

"Absolute freedom does not exist anywhere," said Grushnin. "Journalists do not have the right to write what they want in any country. The journalist does not write what is not wanted by the chief editor, and the chief editor does not allow what is not wanted by the owner."

"Well, what about the repression in the Soviet Union?"

"There was no illegal repression," Grushnin responded.

Arrests were carried out according to the law that existed at that time. In the United States, all of the Japanese were put in concentration camps. We know that there are more than just black spots in the history of the U.S. It's the same here. I think the repression in the Soviet Union is exaggerated. In 1937 my mother and others were in Crimea. She worked in an ordinary sewing factory. But because she worked well, she was given this free trip. I have photos of her relaxing with the other people in the sanatorium. Even today, if you ask people how many people in their family were repressed, the numbers are not that great. I am from the Ryazan oblast. I have a large family and not a single person was repressed.

"In Abkhazia, there were none among my close relatives," said Maria.

"You can't compare the numbers to the number that died in the war," said Grushnin. "Two of my mother's brothers and her first husband were killed in the war."

"I have a very positive attitude toward Stalin," Maria said. "My mother lived in the Tambov oblast. She was a leading collective farmer. She heard Stalin at the Congress of Collective Farmers. Someone said, 'Comrade Stalin, we'll die but we'll work.' He said, 'It's not necessary to die, just work.' Churchill said he found Russia with a wooden plough and left it with the atom bomb. I listen to Radio Liberty and Ekho Moskvy. There is such slander. They all benefited from Soviet power. Why do they hate it so?"

Western visitors were often appalled by the miserable housing in the Soviet Union, the tiny apartments, and the long lines in the stores for low-quality goods. But what they did not see was the absence of competition and the freedom to avoid work. If the minimal exertion required of Soviet citizens was taken into account, one could argue that they were actually paid better than people in the West. One of the persons convinced of this was Zinoviev:

If x is the quantity of work in terms of input and y the size of remuneration, the relation between y and x is the coefficient of remuneration. In communist society, the quantity y is lower than in the

West [but] the quantity x is lower still, so that the coefficient of remuneration y/x is significantly higher than in the West. This is why the workers in communist society almost always prefer the conditions of life under communism to those in the West. Of course, they dream of good food, clothes, flats and cars. But they would scarcely be prepared to pay the price for them that Western workers pay.[3]

Besides security, Communism gave Russians a sense that their lives had meaning. The relation between man and God was replaced with the relation between man and the regime. The result was the elimination of a sense of universal values which depend on a supramundane source. But Russians received in exchange Marxism's "class values" and a regime that treated itself as a single generator of absolute truth.

Communism proved to be particularly well suited for Russia. Work is the main source of social participation for the majority of people in any society, and the Soviet regime, which treated labor as having sacred significance, was able to convince people that their apparently pointless existence actually had a higher purpose. This was particularly important for a nation that traditionally searched for holiness in life and longed to combine theory and practice.

Russians were tied to Communist ideology with the help of collective ceremonies. At the age of nine, Russian children joined the Pioneers, where they were taught about Lenin's life and ideas, basic principles of Marxism-Leninism, and the horrors of life in the West, and they were given some initial military training. At fourteen, almost all young Russians became members of the Komsomol, which inculcated the current line of the party. University students were required to take courses in the history of the Communist Party, scientific atheism, and dialectical and historical materialism.

The imprint of this ideological conditioning was so profound that when the Soviet Union fell, many Russians found themselves spiritually and emotionally adrift, with no system of explanation to support and guide them.

In his first years in office, Boris Yeltsin received many letters from Russians describing their spiritual and political confusion, and after his victory in 1996 over the Communist candidate, Gennady Zyuganov, he convened a panel under an aide, Georgy Satarov, to search for a new national idea. The group came up with nothing beyond what they called "social advertising." These were cartoons intended to boost people's spirits by assuring them that life was not so terrible and that much depended on them. There was no indication that the cartoons had the desired effect.

Russian newspapers also joined the search for a new national idea. In 1997, *Rossiskaya Gazeta* awarded five million rubles ($830) to an official from Vologda, north of Moscow, for recommending that the national idea be found in "concern for the Fatherland" and the rejection of the "money-oriented mentality of the West." Another suggestion came from Vitaly Tretyakov, the editor of *Nezavisimaya Gazeta*. He suggested combining two slogans, "Get rich!" and "Survive!" for a new national idea, "Get rich to survive!"[4]

With the accession of Putin, the search for a new national idea became more focused. But post-Soviet Russian society was not in a condition to base itself on the values that Communism had destroyed. Instead, the new attempts at a national idea bore an eerie resemblance to the Marxism-Leninism that Russians had so recently left behind.

One such attempt was the theory of "Eurasianism," which posited a mortal opposition between a united Eurasia and a transatlantic West. The most prominent exponent of this theory was Alexander Dugin, a nationalist writer. Dugin gained a significant following in Russian military and political circles with his book *Foundations of Geopolitics: The Geopolitical Future of Russia*, which calls for Russian domination of the Eurasian land mass based on alliances with Germany, Iran, and Japan.

The Eurasian movement enunciates a number of principles, chiefly the "priority of the public over the individual" and "a positive reevaluation of the archaic," in which it resembles Nazism. According to the movement's manifesto, Eurasianism is an answer to the decadence of modern civilization. It supports "the strong, passionate, healthy and beautiful man . . . a celebration of physical and spiritual health, force and worthiness, faith and honor."[5]

In an interview with the newspaper *Arguments and Facts,* Dugin contrasted Eurasianism to "liberal democracy," which he described as based on the individual and emphasizing his "economic and bodily needs." Eurasianism, he said, derives from the "principle of brotherhood" and regards the people "as a living organism that cannot be split up into atoms . . . a unified community rooted in history." The best kind of democracy for

Russia is, accordingly, "the democracy of brotherhood . . . participation by the entire people in their own fate."[6]

In 1998 Dugin became an adviser to the speaker of the State Duma, Gennady Seleznyev, and in 1999 he became chairman of the geopolitical section of the Duma's Advisory Council on National Security. Nikolai Klokotov, the head of the Russian general staff, wrote the preface for Dugin's book, and Colonel General Leonid Ivashov, a former high-ranking defense official, served as a consultant.[7] "In Russia it so happened," wrote the journalist Nikita Kaledin, that "the first people to feel the need of a national idea were the members of the defense industry. For them, it was necessary urgently to find an enemy in order to unite, rearm, and expand. . . . Their imperial ideas coincided precisely with Dugin's Eurasian ideas."[8]

The Eurasianist movement is opposed to the transatlantic world (particularly the United States), which it says seeks to destroy "spiritual, intellectual, and material variety" on the planet in order to build a world order subordinated to the political-financial oligarchies of the West. "Eurasists," on the contrary, supposedly support the right of all peoples to choose their own paths of historical development.

According to the Eurasist platform, Eurasists and Atlantists "defend two different, alternative, mutually excluding images of the world and its future. It is the opposition between the Eurasists and Atlantists which defines the historical outline of the twenty-first century."[9] Dugin's theory thus resurrects communist ideology. It suggests a bipolar world to replace the division between the West and the Soviet bloc, and the "principle of brotherhood," a new justification for the domination of the individual by the state to replace the subordination of the individual to his economic class in Marxism-Leninism.[10]

Another attempt to invent a new national idea was the effort to create an "ideology of morality." In October 2005 the search for such an ideology became official with the creation in St. Petersburg of a new State Institute of Morality.

The new institute was established within the Institute for Adult Education of the Russian Academy of Education. The director, Pyotr Yunatzkevich, said that he was invited (he did not say by whom) to develop a new state ideology following Putin's reference to the need for morality in his

2005 message to the Federal Assembly. The effort was undertaken even though article 13 of the Russian Constitution explicitly bans the creation of any state ideology.[11]

Yunatzkevich came to the Institute of Adult Education with his brother Rostislav, who became the institute's head of administration. Both brothers previously worked in real estate. In various interviews, Yunatzkevich said that the work of the Institute of Morality was voluntary, but the Institute of Adult Education is a state-run institution, and there was speculation in the press that the Institute of Morality was financed out of the state budget.

According to Yunatzkevich, the ideology being developed in the Institute of Morality is based on three premises: a person should not harm himself; he should not harm his friends and family; and he should not harm society. He believes that these premises are a "global ecological principle" that is "scientifically verified" and should be the basis of the state. There is no danger in the government adopting this new ideology of morality, since by definition it cannot be immoral. At the same time, a legitimate opposition to the suggested moral path, according to Yunatzkevich, "cannot exist in principle."[12]

Yunatzkevich and his colleague Viktor Chigirev developed a project called Smolny-2 to reorganize the government of St. Petersburg. The idea was to have a council of experts evaluate all strategically important decisions of the St. Petersburg government and parliament from the point of view of morality. If the council deemed a particular project to be immoral, it would announce this to the media. For bureaucrats who persisted in their immoral behavior, the next step was a public hearing leading to the possible removal of the offender from his position and assignment to manual labor.

For a time, the project existed only on paper. In March 2006, however, the leadership of the Institute of Morality announced the creation of a council of experts in St. Petersburg consisting of 240 persons. The purpose of the group was to assure the "triumph of justice" in the city. In addition to the council, the Institute proposed other measures to assure the victory of morality in St. Petersburg and in Russia. The most important of these was the creation of departments of morality in the police and a morality court. Immoral bureaucrats would be subject to reeducation by the morality police and to public condemnation by the morality court on the basis of denunciations provided by the public. A special form for making denunciations was printed in the newspaper *Zemlya Russkaya*. The newspaper advised readers to send their denunciations to the Institute of Adult Education or call a special telephone line.[13]

Intrigued by the Orwellian implications of the project and eager to know who stood behind it, Valery Beresnev, a correspondent for the St. Petersburg weekly *Tainii Sovetnik*, decided to call the number. A woman at the other end of the line was obviously confused. "Where are you calling?" she asked with irritation. "Isn't this the morality police?" Beresnev asked. "This is the Vasileostrov division of the party United Russia," she said and hung up the phone.[14]

In addition to providing security and fulfilling a real spiritual need, Communism made it possible for Russians to compensate for personal inadequacy and lack of freedom by identifying with a powerful state. During the 1960s and 1970s, many Soviet citizens were aware that they had less freedom than people in the West, but they took pride in being citizens of a great power that was building socialism. Soviet collective farmers, condemned to poverty and deprived of the right to leave their collective farms, worried about the condition of peasants in El Salvador and blacks in the United States. According to *The Soviet People,* a volume published in Moscow in 1974, "there is nothing that does not concern him [the Soviet citizen], be it an event of global significance or simply the life of his neighbors on the same landing."[15]

Identification with the state led Soviet citizens to appreciate much that was connected with the state's power and military glory, particularly the armed forces and the intelligence services. Soviet citizens seemed to have a nearly insatiable appetite for books, films, and lectures about military victories and the successes of Soviet spies, which were treated as events of almost religious significance.

After the collapse of the Soviet Union, there was a brief respite in the adulation of the Soviet Union's force structures as society absorbed new information about the role of the NKVD and KGB in mass repression. But after only a few years, the adulation began again and even intensified.

With the accession of Putin, the commemoration of the victory in the Second World War regained its Soviet-era importance. In a speech at the Victory Day ceremonies in 2004, Putin described the war as "the pinnacle of our glory."[16] A year later, on the sixtieth anniversary of the victory, official commentaries hailing the victory drew no distinction between Russia and the Soviet Union. The RIA Novosti press agency quoted an essay on the anniversary by Vera Shuvalova, a thirteen-year-old school-girl from Nizhnevartovsk. "Our people have probably never loved their Motherland as sincerely and deeply as they did during the Great Patriotic War," she wrote. "They say that in order to appreciate the value of something, we have to imagine it disappearing. The Nazis wanted to take away our Motherland, and so everyone rushed to defend it."[17]

On December 11, 2004, ten years after Yeltsin signed a decree calling for the restoration of "constitutional legality" in the Chechen Republic, a commemoration of the anniversary was broadcast on NTV, the Russian television network. The purpose was to honor those who fought in the Chechen war, and this was done by referring to the tradition of World War II. "Veterans of the Great Patriotic War are looking at you," said the presenter, addressing the veterans in the hall, "because only to you they could entrust the country that they saved from fascism, along with the banner of the victory which they carried throughout the Great Patriotic War . . . the banner that was raised on the top of the Imperial Chancellery in Berlin on May 2, 1945." The second host of the evening said the veterans had done everything they could to ensure that "our country would regain its previous dignity and grandeur." Video footage of the Russian flag raised in Chechnya was carefully preceded by archival shots of the Soviet flag flying over the Reichstag in Berlin.[18]

There were similar developments in regard to the security services. In 1995 Yeltsin named December 20, the anniversary of the founding of the Cheka, the day of the security services. Two years later he celebrated the eightieth anniversary of the secret police in a radio address that referred to the FSB as "our chekists."[19] When Putin, the former head of the FSB, became president, he unveiled a plaque dedicated to Andropov on the wall of the FSB headquarters. On December 19, 2007, the eve of the ninetieth birthday of the Cheka, Nikolai Patrushev, the head of the FSB, told a group of Russian editors that there was a strong link between the FSB and the Cheka. The FSB, he said, was working tirelessly against foreign agents and protecting against terrorism. The theme of the KGB-FSB as the protectors of the nation was also developed in awards created for the best works of literature and art dedicated to the activities of the security services. One of the laureates was Vadim Shmelev, the director of the film *Code of the Apocalypse,* about a plot by a wealthy banker to detonate four atomic bombs in major cities that is foiled by the FSB.

In 2002 glorification of the FSB reached a new level with the dedication of a church to the agency, the Saint Sophia Wisdom of God church on Lubyanskaya Square. The FSB, the move suggested, was responsible for guarding not only the physical security of the Russian state but also its spiritual security. But the contradiction inherent in having a church that propagates moral rules confer legitimacy on an organization that is accustomed to operating without them became apparent as early as the consecration ceremony.

The service took place on March 6, 2002, and was led by the Orthodox patriarch and attended by Patrushev and other high-ranking FSB officers. At the point in the service where all present, including the patriarch, were to kneel and ask for God's blessing for the new church, the leaders of the FSB all remained on their feet, neither praying nor crossing themselves but simply watching the patriarch at the altar. There was not a single reference during the service to the millions of people who had suffered at the hands of the NKVD and the KGB. At the end of the ceremony, with the patriarch still standing at the altar, Patrushev turned and left, accompanied by the entire leadership of the FSB. The church immediately emptied. "It turned out," said Andrei Zubov, a theologian and historian who attended the service, "that those who wanted to restore the church actually did not need it. The first liturgy is a great ceremony for the restoration of a church . . . but they all left. I felt that for this organization, this church was nothing more than an expensive toy. . . . This is not the fruit of repentance, and this organization has something to repent for."[20]

One night in March 2005, Pavel Kanygin, a reporter for *Novaya Gazeta,* stepped out of the Children's World department store for a smoke and was surprised to hear singing coming from a church next to FSB headquarters across the street. "That's a service for the FSB," explained a police sentry.[21] Intrigued, Kanygin went to the church the following evening to have a look. He found it closed, and for the next fifteen minutes he stood on the sidewalk outside, his movements followed by a closed-circuit television camera. Suddenly, out of the corner of his eye, he saw two men running toward him, a traffic policeman and someone in plainclothes.

"Hey pal," said the traffic policeman, "what do you need here?"

Kanygin gave the policeman his press identification. The officer turned it over in his hands for a long time. He then gave it to the plainclothesman, who frowned and handed it back to Kanygin, advising him that it was better not to be out so late without a passport. It was 7:30 P.M.

The next day, Kanygin went again to the church. This time it was open. He walked in and encountered a woman, a small boy, and a bearded man named Maxim, who Kanygin gathered was an assistant to the priest. Soon the priest appeared. He was short and, from his build, Kanygin guessed that he practiced martial arts.

"Maxim, get some water," the priest said, speaking very quickly.

"I didn't understand the task, Your Holiness."

"What, are you deaf?"

"No, not at all."

"I said get some water." He then threw a coat over his robes, took his briefcase and disappeared behind a closed door.

Kanygin told Maxim that he wanted to write an article about the church and about the defense of the monuments of Moscow's past, and put it on the *Novaya Gazeta* website.

Maxim stroked his beard, looked to one side and said, "That, of course, is good. But to write something you need the permission of the Patriarchy." He then added, "And . . .," and made a gesture in the direction of the FSB headquarters.

Kanygin said, "I don't understand."

"Well, our church is official. It's part of the FSB. Why make problems for yourself?"

"But I thought . . . "

"It's harmful to think. And in general it would be better if you didn't show up here anymore." He then made a gesture as if he was talking to himself, took a canister, and left.

Kanygin ignored Maxim's warning and returned to the church the following night. This time, neither Maxim nor the priest was present. Instead he saw two men dressed in black, carrying briefcases. One of them stood at the counter where an elderly woman sold icons, candles, incense, and other religious items. The candles sold for 3.50 rubles each, and the man at the counter bought several of them. He paid with a 500-ruble note and did not take any change.

After the men left, Kanygin asked, "Grandmother, when is the senior priest Alexander coming?"

"Oy, I don't know. They are already building a second church."

"The FSB is probably helping," suggested Kanygin.

"Yes, yes, they're helping. How is it possible without them?" With the mention of the FSB, the woman became agitated and started to chew on her tongue.

"Do people often pay 500 rubles for candles?" Kanygin asked.

"What kind of strange questions you ask, dear one."

It was obvious to Kanygin that she was becoming very nervous, and he decided not to prolong the conversation. He left the church. A traffic policeman was waiting for him at the exit, but not the one who had stopped him on the first night.

"It was explained to you in plain Russian, shitass, don't come here!"

This was followed by more abuse as he walked out onto the street.

The fall of Communism left a gap in the psychology of Russians. A system that submerged the individual in the collective while encouraging him to identify with the overwhelming power of the state proved as capable of inspiring loyalty as Western democracy. The Soviet system denied the existence of universal morality and introduced a radical deprivation of freedom, but it appealed to instincts, in particular the desire for security and authority, that are no less deeply rooted and probably more basic than the drive of each person to realize himself as an individual.

To resist the power of the totalitarian regime a person needed, in the words of Jung, to be "as well organized in his individuality as the mass itself."[22] After seventy-three years of Communist rule, very few persons in Russia met that criterion.

The new regime that replaced the Soviet regime set about introducing democratic capitalism. For the transition from Communism to a democratic political system to be successful, however, it was necessary to replace the Communist notion of the person as a cog in a machine with a system that enshrined respect for the individual. Only such a complete transition could provide the environment for the rejection of the mass psychology that had grown up within the confines of the totalitarian system. This never took place.

The new regime was run by former Soviet cogs who respected neither themselves nor others. As a result, it engaged in the largest peaceful transfer of property in history without the benefit of the rule of law. This led, in the words of former finance minister Boris Fyodorov, to "the biggest robbery of the century, perhaps even the biggest in human history."[23] National production fell by half, the population declined precipitously (demographers in the 1990s registered six million "surplus deaths"), and a small group of corrupt oligarchs took control over a huge share of the nation's wealth.[24] This process was accompanied by elections, but taking place in a society without law, they could not create the conditions for genuinely democratic practices. Instead, they helped to discredit "democracy," leading to nostalgia for the Soviet Union's social guarantees, strict punishments, and absence of private property.

In 1999, in the wake of the mysterious bombings of Russian apartment buildings, Russia launched a new invasion of Chechnya, which distracted Russians from their anger over the pillaging of the country during privatization.[25] Putin directed the military campaign and, on the strength of its initial successes, was elected to succeed Yeltsin. He immediately began to restore symbols such as the Soviet anthem and to glorify the military and the security services. Communism was gone, but Russians were now to submit to the supererogatory claims of a deideologized Russian state. Once again, they were denied the possibility of living in a society based on higher values and moral choice.

In its long confrontation with Communism, the West tried to win over the peoples of the East with the help of facts. It was pointed out that Americans and other Westerners had more freedom than the citizens of the Soviet Union and could create more wealth. This reasoning, however, usually had little effect. On the contrary, it frequently inspired Russians to insist that in light of Soviet social policies, their way of life was superior to that of the West.

There was an argument against Communism that was not based on material comparisons and was potentially persuasive to Russians. This was that there is no such thing as "class values," that values are not a function of economic interests but are eternal and universal and emanate from a transcendent source. But making such an argument was not easy. In the first place, an appreciation of ethical transcendence is a matter of moral intuition. There is no way to "prove" that values come from a supramundane source. At the same time, refuting the pseudo-rationality of articulate

Communist ideologues, although possible, is not within the capacity of everyone.

The result was that although Russians needed intellectual support if they were to defend universal values against the onslaught of a class-based ideology, no answer to Communism was forthcoming from the West that went beyond a reiteration of the obvious fact that the system destroys freedom. The West proved powerless to offer Russians moral criteria for condemning their previous society.

Russia today has many of the characteristics of the Soviet Union, with a permanent leadership and a president for life (Putin). The socialist economy is gone, but the conception of the individual as raw material and the conviction that nothing is higher than the goals of the state continues to prevail. This made it inevitable that the moral lessons of the Soviet experience would not be learned and that Soviet habits would continue to influence the Russian population.

CHAPTER 6

The Responsibility of the State

■

Although she was only nine years old when he was arrested, Nadezhda Rodina, the daughter of Mikhail Rodin, an official who was shot by Stalin, said that she will never forget her father. "He was kind and loved children," she said. "We hoped for years that he was alive. Mother dreamed that he saved himself and was living in a distant collective farm and had a new family."

Nadia and I were talking in a café located on the first floor of the building in central Moscow that was the setting for Mikhail Bulgakov's novel *The Master and Margarita*. The young patrons chatting over coffee or puffing on water pipes paid little attention to the timid, bespectacled old woman as she told her story, halting to recall details and retrieving weathered documents from a cloth bag.

Rodin was arrested on May 11, 1938. He was a deputy people's commissar of the timber industry and number 100 of 138 Soviet leaders who were executed on Stalin's orders in the largest single massacre of the top Soviet leadership during the Great Terror.[1] On the night of his arrest, Rodin had left the dacha in Bakovka outside of Moscow where he and his family were staying in order to attend a meeting. Anna Fyodorovna, his wife, put Nadia and her brother and sister to bed. When the children awoke, the house was full of men in uniform. Anna and the children were ordered to vacate the dacha immediately.

Only ten days before his arrest, Rodin, Nadia, and her brother had occupied a place of honor next to the mausoleum during the May Day parade in Red Square. Her father had pointed to Stalin on the reviewing stand with Budenny, Voroshilov, and Kaganovich.[2] Nadia recalled that it began to rain and Stalin stared up at the sky with a dissatisfied expression.

After Rodin's arrest, his wife lived in terror. She photographed her children and snipped locks of their hair. The NKVD was arresting parents and sending children to orphanages, and she feared losing her children and not being able to find them. She went regularly to the NKVD reception center on Kuznetsky Most to seek information about her husband. During one such visit, an NKVD officer told her, "Get out while you still can." She decided to leave Moscow to live with her sister in Rodniki, a town in the Ivanovo oblast. It was probably this that saved her from arrest.

Nadia grew up in Rodniki. Her mother said that her father was on a business trip. One day, however, her teacher told her to stand up before the class. "Nadia Rodina," he said. "Why did you lie? You said your father is on a business trip. In fact, he is an enemy of the people and you are the daughter of an enemy of the people." Nadia burst into tears and ran out of class. She stayed away for a week. Later, the teacher made a tacit apology. "Nadia," he said, "You have to go to school."

Nadia's father was privileged and powerful until he was declared an enemy and shot. He was then supposed to disappear forever. Even after Nadia received confirmation in 1956 that he was dead, there was no indication where he was buried. She learned his likely place of burial only in 2002, sixty-four years after he was killed.

I asked Nadia whether, in light of her father's fate, she felt any hostility to the Soviet regime.

"No," she said, "I did not become bitter. I considered myself a loyal citizen of the country. Now I feel gratitude to the new government. [Putin] was in the KGB, but he is a deeply religious person. He doesn't chatter like Gorbachev. He isn't a disgrace like Yeltsin. He does a lot and we should judge by deeds. He has good relations with [Patriarch] Alexei. This is a great happiness. Except for gratitude to the new government, I don't feel anything."

Nadia's attitude is not unusual. For decades, Russians have found it very difficult to hold the state responsible for its crimes. One factor was their magnitude: the victims numbered in the millions, giving the crimes an impersonal quality. They were carried out by the bureaucracy of the state, which made them seem "official." They were also ostensibly under-taken to defend communism. Since many Russians accepted the ideology and its emphasis on class struggle, it was hard for them to regard what was going on as totally unjustified. Finally, it was accepted in Russia that the state exercises absolute authority. It was not thought that the state was beholden to citizens or could be judged by them.

After the death of Stalin, Russians experienced the Khrushchev "thaw," the years of stability (retrospectively termed stagnation) under Brezhnev, Gorbachev's perestroika, and the birth of a non-Communist Russia under Yeltsin. In each of those periods, situations arose that demanded that society pass judgment on the actions of the state.

But this reckoning with history never took place. The upheaval that destroyed millions of lives never received a historical shape. It existed in the Russian consciousness as a primordial social explosion, an orgy of violence that propelled the nation into the modern era and that, although now in the past, could occur again regardless of the will of individuals.

Russia's most important opportunity to acknowledge the Soviet crimes and settle with history was the process of rehabilitation. Rehabilitation was understood as the return of "the unblemished name and dignity" of an innocent person, the removal of legal limitations on him, and compensa-tion for confiscated property. Potentially, it was owed to millions of peo-ple. Until the late 1980s, however, the number of persons whose guilt was expunged was limited. Rehabilitation was granted grudgingly and for political reasons. At the same time, it was carried out within the frame of reference of the regime, a pattern that was to be preserved even when the number of persons rehabilitated was greatly expanded. There was no blan-ket pardon extended to persons convicted under political articles of the criminal code. A person could be rehabilitated only if it could be shown that an accusation of engaging in "counterrevolutionary activities" was false. In this way, the process cleared individuals but upheld the Stalinist system.

If the Russian Empire was the "prison of nations," its successor state, the Soviet Union, was often just a prison. On January 1, 1953, there were 2.5 million prisoners in Soviet labor camps. Of these, more than 500,000 were political prisoners.[3] If we add the inmates of prisons and corrective labor colonies and forced exiles, the number of people deprived of liberty was between 4 and 5 million.[4] Lavrenty Beria, the minister of internal affairs, ruled this empire, and in the months after Stalin's death, he dominated the leadership. But his position was far from secure. Beria was a serial rapist who supervised mass executions and personally executed prisoners. To prevent his rivals from uniting against him under the banner of anti-Stalinism, he took steps after Stalin's death to mitigate his murderous reputation. He banned torture and announced that the Doctors' Plot, in which Jewish doctors had been arrested for conspiring to kill Stalin, had been fabricated. He said that the famous Jewish actor Solomon Mikhoels, the head of the Jewish Anti-Fascist Committee, had been murdered on Stalin's orders, and he proposed transferring many enterprises that were under the authority of the Ministry of Internal Affairs to economic ministries and shutting down projects carried out with forced labor. He also approved an amnesty that led to the release of 1,181,264 nonpolitical prisoners. The vast majority of these were common criminals, who unleashed a crime wave as soon as they were freed. Their mass release, however, was the first major break in the Gulag system.[5]

Despite these efforts, Beria was arrested in a palace coup, as a result of a conspiracy organized by Khrushchev, and then shot. Khrushchev emerged as the undisputed leader. Like Beria, he realized that the country needed relief from constant terror, and he immediately began to use the issue of repression to his political advantage. He reopened the "Leningrad case," in which nearly the entire leadership of the Leningrad party was shot, and thus compromised Georgi Malenkov, his main remaining rival and one of the men responsible for the deaths of the leading figures in the case.[6] The victims' rehabilitation, which was given wide publicity in the party, greatly strengthened Khrushchev's position.

Raising the question of the repressions was risky for Khrushchev because he too had participated in the purges. According to materials in the KGB archives, in 1936–37, when he was the head of the Moscow party organization, the NKVD in Moscow and the Moscow oblast were responsible for the arrest of 55,741 persons. Under Khrushchev's leadership in Ukraine, 106,119 persons were arrested in 1938, another 12,000 in 1939, and approximately 50,000 in 1940.[7] Despite this, Khrushchev apparently calculated that if he took the lead in exposing the Stalinist crimes, his personal guilt would be overlooked and the positions of his political opponents would be undermined.

The liberation of political prisoners began slowly. Those who were known to the leadership had the best chance of being freed. In other cases, the review of appeals took months and usually ended with a refusal. Of 237,412 appeals officially reviewed in the twenty-eight months ending in April 1955, no more than 4 percent were approved. In 1953, however, there were mass revolts in the labor camps of Norilsk and Vorkuta, and, in spring 1954, in Kengir in Central Asia. The uprisings unnerved the leadership. By the end of 1955, 195,353 persons had been freed.[8]

On December 31, 1955, Khrushchev created a commission chaired by Pyotr Pospelov, a former editor of *Pravda,* to look into "violations of socialist legality" under Stalin. Pospelov was an arch-Stalinist who, according to Khrushchev's account, had cried so uncontrollably when Stalin died that Beria had shaken him, saying, "What's the matter with you. Cut it out." Khrushchev thought that this orthodoxy would create confidence in Pospelov's report. In the meantime, the presidium called in Boris Rodos, the former deputy head of the NKVD for "especially important investigations," to give his account of the Stalinist terror. Khrushchev would soon describe him as a "good for nothing with the brain of a chicken." Rodos, who had beaten confessions out of high-ranking party leaders, described what he had done and said that he had acted on orders not just from Beria but also from Stalin.[9]

Several days later, the Pospelov commission issued a seventy-page report that Pospelov himself found so horrifying that his voice shook at times while reading it aloud, and he once broke down in sobs. Between 1935 and 1940, according to the report, 1,920,635 persons had been arrested and 688,503 shot. The alleged plots and conspiracies had all been fabricated. The revelations were used by Khrushchev to place the question of the repressions on the agenda of the upcoming 20th Party Congress.[10] On February 13, 1956, a day before the opening of the congress, he proposed giving a speech on "the Cult of Personality" and its consequences. "If we don't tell the truth at the congress," he said, "we'll be forced to do it at some time in the future. But we won't be the speech makers. No, then we'll be the people under investigation."[11] The speech was approved over the objections of Molotov, Voroshilov, and Kaganovich.[12]

The speech, given shortly after midnight on February 25, 1956, took four hours to deliver. For the first time in Soviet history, some facts were made public about the massive repression that had swept the country. Many in the audience fainted. The effect of the speech was described by Alexander Yakovlev, who as a liberal member of Gorbachev's politburo was later to play a critical role in dismantling the totalitarian system:

> I sat in the balcony and very well remember the feeling of deep distress, if not desperation that seized me after all that was said by Khrushchev. In the hall, there was deep silence. There was not the scraping of chairs, not a cough. No one looked at each other — either out of the unexpectedness of what happened or confusion and fear. The shock was unimaginably deep. As they left the hall, those present lowered their heads.[13]

Although Khrushchev's speech was described as secret, he fully intended that its contents be known. The speech was read out at party meetings and given to foreign Communists. The KGB made sure the CIA got a copy, and the London *Observer* scooped the world by printing a full version.[14]

In the wake of the speech, the liberation of prisoners was accelerated. Khrushchev formed ninety-seven special traveling commissions. These were troikas, each consisting of a representative of the prosecutor's office, someone from the party Central Committee, and a rank-and-file party member who had been rehabilitated. They were dispatched to the main centers of the Gulag and given the authority to interview prisoners, review their cases, and free them on the spot. In many cases, the time it took to free a prisoner was ten minutes, about as much as it had taken to convict him. By October 1957, the commissions had reviewed the cases of 170,000 prisoners and freed more than 100,000 simply on the basis of the removal of the accusation.[15]

Released prisoners were everywhere. "In railway trains and stations there appeared survivors of the camps with leaden grey hair, sunken eyes and a faded look; they choked and dragged their feet like old men."[16] One former prisoner described the shock of liberation:

> In liberty, we had the good fortune of riding in passenger trains. I went into the bathroom to clean up a bit. I am washing my face and peering at me from the mirror is an unfamiliar old woman with

short hair . . . and a slight face. I was frightened and ran out into the corridor, where an officer asked me: "What's with you?" I pointed to the bathroom. There's some old woman in there. He opened the door—no one was there. And then I understood: that woman was I.[17]

The emotions of a released prisoner returning home were described by Vasily Grossman in his novel *Forever Flowing*. The novel opens with a scene in a compartment of the Khabarovsk-to-Moscow express train, where three of the four passengers are arguing. They all but ignore the fourth passenger, who spends most of the long journey sitting with his elbows on his knees "as if anxious to cover up the patches on his pants." As the train neared Moscow,

> the old man sat at the table, his fists tight against his temples, looking out the window. . . . The train had already entered the green belt around Moscow. The gray tatters of smoke grasped at the fir branches. . . . How very familiar were the silhouettes of those austere northern fires. . . . And the man who for three decades had forgotten that clumps of lilacs still existed in the world — or beds of pansies or garden paths sprinkled with sand, or carts from which vendors sold carbonated soft drinks — this man sighed deeply, seeing once again, this time under a new aspect, that life had gone on without him.[18]

While the commissions had the authority to rehabilitate the prisoners they freed, mass rehabilitation met political resistance. A report by A. B. Artizov on the work of the commissions stated that of a group of 80,000 political prisoners whose cases were reviewed, only 3,271 were completely rehabilitated.[19] Instead, the commissions concentrated on freeing the prisoners and restoring their rights. As Anastas Mikoyan, a Stalin-era politburo member, explained, if all those arrested as "enemies of the people" had been declared innocent at once, it would have been clear that the "the country was not being run by a legal government but by a group of gangsters."[20]

The return of the prisoners created panic in Soviet society. Many of the political prisoners had been the victims of false denunciations, and those who had denounced them were terrified of the returnees' revenge. Polina Furman, a Jewish doctor, was arrested along with her husband and son in

August 1952. During her interrogation in the Lubyanka Prison, she was told that a woman named Khukhrina, a friend of thirty years, had denounced her family. On returning to Moscow, Furman called her old friend, whose panicked response was "You returned!?" They met at a metro station, where Khukhrina said the interrogator had told her that Furman would never come back.[21]

Many of those arrested, of course, never did come back. Officially, those who were executed were sentenced to ten years without the right of correspondence. Wives and children often waited patiently for ten years and then wrote to the authorities requesting information. After Stalin's death, these letters began to be answered, but in keeping with a decision to conceal the scale of the terror and the fact that the victims were shot immediately, the families were given false causes of death — for example, a heart attack — and false dates, usually during wartime, several years after the victims were actually killed.[22] There was no indication of where they were buried.

For most of the freed prisoners, rehabilitation was possible, but it was an exhausting process. The former prisoner or his family had to appeal to the Soviet prosecutor. The prosecutor could then demand the case for review from the KGB, call witnesses, and order material from other archives, particularly the central party archive, where it was indicated whether a party member belonged to an opposition grouping. On the basis of this evidence, the prosecutor could protest a sentence to the USSR Supreme Court. The Court could then issue a decision to rehabilitate. It could also reduce the charges against the accused or reduce the punishment after the fact.[23]

Those who were shot or who died in the camps could be rehabilitated on the basis of an appeal from a family member. If a dead prisoner had no survivors, however, he was not rehabilitated. Well-known persons could only be rehabilitated with the approval of the presidium, which, in this way, put itself higher than the prosecutors or the courts. The ban on the rehabilitation of Trotskyists, Mensheviks, and Socialist Revolutionaries was maintained in force.[24] In April 1956 a commission of the presidium under Molotov was formed to study the 1930s show trials. It met fifteen times without reevaluating the sentences of Bukharin, Radek, Serebryakov, Zinoviev, Kamenev, and others.[25] The authorities' ambivalence was reflected in the fact that in 1957 there was a sharp increase in the number of prosecutions for counterrevolutionary activities, including 2,948 convictions, four times the number for 1956.[26]

The newly freed prisoners frequently showed signs of extreme trauma. Galina Skopyuk, a Gulag prisoner who remained in Norilsk after being released in 1954, did not discuss her camp experience until 1984. "The whole time we were silent," she said, "careful not to say anything, so that we were not sent back to where we had been." In Vorkuta many former prisoners were afraid that if they applied for rehabilitation in 1992, after the Soviet Union had fallen, they would be arrested again. Zoya Marchenko, who spent twelve years in labor camps (nine in Kolyma) and eight years in exile, said, "I always lived with the sense of being a second-class citizen. I understood that my fate did not depend on me but on the forces that governed the country and I had to try somehow to survive."[27]

Some former prisoners had the doorbells removed from their homes. "They were afraid of doorbells because that's how their arrest and misfortune began. . . . You had to knock on the door when you visited," said Roy Medvedev in an interview. "Some even feared telegrams." The wife of Soviet army general Yakov Smushkevich, who was arrested in June 1941, refused to live in her former apartment in the famous House on the Embankment, the building of the Council of Ministers across from the Kremlin that had been the scene of mass arrests during the Great Terror. She described it as that "accursed building where every apartment counted three, four, five arrests in its turnover of tenants." Other prisoners were haunted by recurrent nightmares and feared that their incarceration would never end. One survivor, Berta Babina, at the age of ninety-seven, sat up in her hospital bed and said, "The convoy is waiting." This was her last image before dying.[28]

The returnees nonetheless had to make their peace with Soviet society, and for this reason many sought rehabilitation. Unlike a revoked sentence, rehabilitation indicated the explicit expunging of guilt. Official questionnaires all asked whether the applicant had ever been convicted of a crime, and it was necessary to fill out a questionnaire to get a job, receive an apartment, continue one's studies, or travel abroad. The lack of rehabilitation could make a successful reintegration into society impossible. At the same time, the children of former prisoners who were not rehabilitated also suffered because the same questionnaires required them to answer whether any persons in the family had been condemned.

As the prisoners returned en masse from the camps, the tempo of rehabilitation increased, but there is no certainty about the numbers. According to an estimate published in 1996 in *Moskovskiye Novosti,* about 30,000 victims a year were rehabilitated from 1954 to 1962, for a total of 258,322.[29] Another source, cited by V. Rogovin, places the number of persons rehabilitated between 1954 and 1961 at 737,182. This figure, however, includes persons who were rehabilitated posthumously.[30]

Rehabilitation brought mixed emotions. Many were furious that the state was exercising the right to forgive. The daughter of a victim told an official at the Military Tribunal, after she received her father's posthumous rehabilitation certificate in 1957, "It took you twenty years to clarify that he was innocent, and I always knew it . . . so tell me how this monstrous injustice that destroyed so many honest, devoted people could have occurred!" A former prisoner described what happened after he received his "so-called rehabilitation certificate" in 1957. "After eighteen years of suffering, I was given two months' salary by the Moscow Historical Archive Institute where I worked until my arrest. I was put in line for an apartment, and led a miserable homeless existence for two years inside and outside Moscow."[31]

As strange as it seems, following civil rehabilitation, the next step for many returnees was to seek restored membership in the Communist Party. After the 20th Party Congress, thousands of party rehabilitations were applied for and granted. Between February 1956 and June 1961, according to a report of the party control commission, 30,954 members were reinstated, many posthumously. The same report attempted to explain how it happened that so many loyal Communists were victimized by their own party. The author blamed the arrests on the failures of individuals. "In the past," the report said, "especially from 1936–40, the party control commission did not verify the . . . political accusations made against party members, and . . . indiscriminately excluded them from the party with the formulations: 'enemy of the people,' 'counter-revolutionary,' etc. In many cases . . . exclusion from the party was made on the basis of lists of arrestees sent by the NKVD."[32]

In other words, although mistakes were made by certain individuals, the party itself was blameless. Some returnees were ready to accept such explanations. Many dedicated Communists insisted during the long years of imprisonment that they were the victims of errors that the party would eventually correct. They often felt vindicated in their views by their release and rushed to seek rehabilitation and readmission to the party. One such person was Galina Serebryakova, a writer who spent twenty-one years in Siberia. In her articles, she disregarded her incarceration and praised her release, for which she credited the "Leninist central committee." In an essay in *Molodaya Gvardiya* in 1964, she wrote, "Of course, I am in love with my time, with my generation. Practically every day new cities and waterways emerge, important scientific discoveries are taking place. . . . New relationships between people are developing, [we see] the new man of the communist tomorrow."[33]

Others, however, had more pragmatic reasons for seeking the return of party membership. After she was handed her rehabilitation certificate, Evgeniya Ginzburg was given a phone number to call to seek reinstatement in the party. She asked the official who gave it to her why she would want to rejoin the party. He said it was necessary if she wanted to find a job. "Otherwise," he said, "when they ask, 'Were you ever a member of the party and, if so, when and how did you leave it?' . . . you will have to use the formula recorded in your case file: 'Expelled from the party for counter-revolutionary Trotskyite terrorist activity.' So I suggest you phone this number!"[34]

According to D. Burg, an émigré literary critic, "In accordance with the unwritten law of the last few years [later1950s, early 1960s], the 'rehabilitated person' should express joy and thank the party for its kindness. He should strive to restore his membership in the party and 'look forward to the future.'" The expected gratitude toward the party was well expressed in a 1959 letter to Khrushchev that was published in *Pravda:* "I am not a party member because 20 years ago . . . my father was jailed. Now, he has been posthumously rehabilitated. For this let me voice tremendous thanks to the party and to you personally, the initiator of the review of many old cases. Even though it be posthumously, a man's memory has been cleared."[35]

The question of the state's responsibility was not raised. Instead, Stalin-era crimes were used politically to destroy Khrushchev's opponents, in particular at the June 1957 party plenum, at which Khrushchev defeated an attempt to remove him. In his "secret" speech, Khrushchev had denounced Stalin's crimes, but at the plenum he gave specifics. He said that Molotov, Malenkov, and Kaganovich were the "main culprits" in the "arrests and execution of party and state cadres," and that between February 27 and November 12, 1938, they had personally authorized 38,679 executions. This was the most direct denunciation yet of the Stalin era, but this time Khrushchev's remarks at the plenum were not made public. They were intended only for the party leadership, and they achieved their purpose. Khrushchev eliminated his rivals and secured his power for the next seven years.

The removal of some of the Soviet leaders most implicated in the repressions did not speed rehabilitation. In fact, there was a gradual reduction in the number of cases being examined. For a few years, at least, there was also no return to the question of Stalin's crimes. Khrushchev no longer needed the exposure of Stalin in his struggle for power. The situation changed, however, in 1961. The leaders of China were demanding that the Soviet party restore Stalin's prestige and were contesting Soviet leadership of the world communist movement. At the same time, difficult economic conditions were undermining Khrushchev's popularity at home. Khrushchev decided to make a new denunciation of Stalin at the 22nd Party Congress. He hoped that this would undermine the Chinese and simultaneously renew enthusiasm for his leadership.

In his speech at the congress, Khrushchev spoke not about thousands of victims, as in 1956, but of millions. He implied that Stalin had ordered the 1934 assassination of Sergei Kirov, and he proposed establishing a monument to Stalin's victims in Moscow. On the next-to-last day of the congress, an old woman who had joined the party in 1902, and who had clearly been coached in advance, raised the issue of Stalin's body still being in the mausoleum. She said that in a dream, she had "asked Ilyich [Lenin] for advice," and he had complained about lying next to Stalin. The congress then voted to remove Stalin's body from the mausoleum. It was taken out that night and buried next to the Kremlin wall.[36]

The wave of liberalization continued with the publication of Solzhenitsyn's *One Day in the Life of Ivan Denisovich* and the publication in *Pravda* of Yevtushenko's poem "The Heirs of Stalin," which raised for the broad public the theme of the camps. In 1961 a new commission to review the show trials of the 1930s was formed under N. M. Shvernik, the chairman of the party control commission. Three years later, it concluded that all of the trials had been falsified and the subjects were entitled to rehabilitation. Before this could be done, however, Khrushchev was deposed.

In the new political situation under Leonid Brezhnev, rehabilitation and the exposure of the Stalin-era crimes came to a virtual end. The new regime halted the work of the Shvernik Commission, and its findings were sequestered. The number of persons rehabilitated each year fell to an isolated few. For the next twenty-one years, Solzhenitsyn's works and other accounts of the camps were banned. Information about Stalin-era crimes was circulated by Soviet dissidents in samizdat. History was falsi- fied, and the victims of repression were afraid to speak. The imperturb- ability of the Brezhnev years rested on the successful burial of the past.

In 1985, however, Mikhail Gorbachev became the new general secre- tary. A year earlier he had supported a proposal to restore party member- ship to Malenkov and Kaganovich, but as general secretary he undertook liberalization.[37] The members of the politburo were provided with the long-suppressed findings of the Shvernik Commission. This led in 1988 to the rehabilitation of Bukharin, Zinoviev, Kamenev, Rykov, and other Bol- shevik leaders purged by Stalin.[38] A new commission on rehabilitation was set up under Yakovlev, and persons who had been afraid to apply for rehabilitation started to ask for their cases to be reviewed.

Gorbachev's policy of glasnost quickly divided society into those who welcomed the revelations and those who resisted them as threatening to the country's stability. In fact, the fears of the latter group were fully justified. The truth about Stalin-era atrocities, when it emerged, shook the faith of millions, undercutting the ideological basis of Soviet society.

Events acquired a powerful momentum. The erosion of faith in social- ism led to the awakening of nationalism in the republics. This was fol- lowed by massive strikes in the coal mines; the elimination of article 6 of the Soviet Constitution, which established the Communist Party's "lead- ing role" in the state; and declarations of sovereignty by the republics. Gorbachev, who, at first, enjoyed wide support among the intelligentsia, became increasingly unpopular as he resisted the full dismantling of the Soviet system. In what was seen by many as an effort to restore his reputa- tion, Gorbachev, on August 13, 1990, issued a decree denouncing the Stalinist repressions and calling for the restoration of rights for the vic- tims. But there was no immediate action to translate the decree into law.

On August 19, 1991, pro-Communist elements staged a coup in a last-ditch effort to hold the Soviet Union together. The failure of the coup two days later sealed the country's fate.[39]

In October 1991, with the final collapse of the Soviet state only two months away, an extraordinarily far-reaching law on rehabilitation was adopted by the Supreme Soviet of the Russian Republic. A request to rehabilitate a victim of repression could now come from anyone, not just a family member. It could also be granted by a prosecutor without a judicial decision. The law applied not just to Stalin-era victims but to anyone who suffered political repression after November 7, 1918. In its preamble, the law for the first time explicitly condemned the Soviet regime for terror against its own people and expressed "deep sympathy" for the victims.[40]

The passage of the law on rehabilitation represented a high point in the recognition of the criminal nature of the Soviet regime. The basic idea of rehabilitation as forgiveness by the state, however, remained the same. Even under the new law, it was necessary to compare the acts of a person applying for rehabilitation with the requirements of then-existing laws. This meant that persons who had resisted the Soviet system on moral grounds were not eligible for rehabilitation, whereas the regime's executioners were eligible if it could be shown that the specific charges on which they were convicted were false.

The Soviet Union was abolished on December 31, 1991. Many Memorial activists hoped that the law on rehabilitation would be followed in the new Russia by a legal act specifically acknowledging the responsibility of the Russian state for Communist crimes and defining the responsibility of individuals and organizations. After the Soviet Union collapsed, however, the drive to establish historical justice faltered. In post-Soviet Russia, revelations about Soviet crimes no longer served the political opposition, and attention shifted to the transition to a market economy and the growing impoverishment of the population.

Between 1992 and 1997, four million persons applied for judicial rehabilitation for themselves or others.[41] As of January 1, 2002, 1.8 million certificates of rehabilitation had been issued.[42] For many, the rehabilitation of family members was emotionally liberating, confirmation that they or their relatives were not enemies of the state. Victims of repression were also eligible for various forms of compensation. They received the equivalent of two months' back pay — paltry recompense for those who had spent years as slave laborers, but nonetheless something. In Moscow, they received a 50 percent discount on utility payments, free installation of a telephone, free travel on public transport, free travel by rail once a year and free travel on electric trains, free drugs and medicine, and payment for visits to sanatoria. In a period when people were not being paid their salaries, these benefits could be of significant help.[43]

But the victims of Communism were still having their convictions expunged by a state that did not acknowledge its own guilt. In Germany, anyone who was a prisoner in a Nazi concentration camp was considered automatically a victim of fascism because the regime had had no right to exact extrajudicial punishment. In Russia, there was no comparable move to declare the whole process of repression criminal and, on that basis, to try and punish the organizers.

The notion that it is the role of the state to judge rather than be judged had its effect on the victims, who, in a cruel irony, often identified with the state and found it difficult to condemn the Soviet regime unreservedly for what had been done to them.

"In the ten years that I have worked with the repressed," said Tatyana Nikoltseva, director of social services at Compassion, a center that provides medical and psychological assistance to Gulag survivors, "I have never heard them use the word *government* to describe the party that was guilty in their misfortunes. Only in very confidential conversations, in rare cases where a person lost a lot, for example, a promising career, will someone say, 'the country did this to me.' They can say that Stalin arrested people, but they won't identify him as the leader of the government. They won't acknowledge that it was state policy to develop the economy on the basis of slave labor."[44]

"Those who resisted in the camps were killed," said Elizaveta Zhirikova, the director of Compassion.

The best among the repressed did not survive. Those who survived did so because they stayed in the shadows. In the 1990s, when we began working with them, they were in a bad psychological state. They showed either extreme aggression or they were closed, blocked. They were convinced that no good could come to them. The women were constantly whining and crying.

If there are bureaucratic obstacles to help from the government, the victims of repression usually do not have the strength to over-come them. First come war heroes, then heroes of labor. These are deserving people. By comparison, the victims of repression are peo-ple of the second type. It's impossible to say in a government clinic, "I was repressed and I am entitled to this help" or to say, "I was in the Stalin camps." They will never demand anything because, if they do, people will say that you could not have been arrested for nothing.[45]

Many repressed persons were passive before the government but abu-sive toward the volunteers from Compassion who cared for them. "They could scream at them and even fight," said Zhirikova.

One woman, the daughter of a famous military leader, died in early 2005. She was helped in her last days by a simple woman from Compassion who sat with her and kept her company. Before she died, she was very sick and she began to behave as if she was a prison guard. She tried to beat the woman who was caring for her with a cane.

In another case, an elderly man who had lost his legs from frost-bite and had to move around in a wagon began to terrorize the German volunteer who was helping him.

He had survived a ghetto and then had been in a Stalinist labor camp. After three months, the German boy said he could not con-tinue. The apartment where the old man lived had long corridors, and he had begun to hunt his caregiver, propelling himself in his wagon and chasing him.

The rehabilitation of millions with no acknowledgement of the histori-cal responsibility of the state meant that the sufferers remained within the relationship of the individual to the state that had long been inculcated by the Soviet regime. The government had victimized a person, and yet the individual had to appeal to the same government to clear his name. The recognition of the Soviet regime's responsibility in the preamble to the new law on rehabilitation was important, but it came in October 1991, as the Soviet Union was about to disappear. The process did not and could not make the point that, in the case of mass atrocities, accepting respon-sibility and making restitution is the obligation of the state.

CHAPTER 7

The Trial of the Communist Party

■

On January 2, 1992, the new Russian government headed by Yegor Gaidar freed prices and unleashed hyperinflation. Overnight, the life savings of Russians disappeared. Money that had been put aside to buy a car or apartment or as security for a lonely old age vanished. The desperation such loss inspired was brought home to me in March 1992, when a woman knocked on my door late at night in Moscow and said a neighbor had died and she was collecting money from people in the building to help pay for her funeral.

During the first quarter of 1992, prices rose 800 to 900 percent for most goods, but for basic items the increases were much greater. The price of salt increased a hundredfold, the price of matches 250 times. The factories of Goznak, the state money printing organization, were not prepared for the increased demand for paper money. As a result, as prices exploded, tens of millions stopped getting their salaries.

Yeltsin decreed that anyone was now free to sell anything anywhere, and the streets were soon full of people hawking assorted goods. Moscow began to resemble a giant outdoor bazaar, as impromptu markets appeared on busy corners, along streets, and in courtyards. Members of the World War II generation, some of them wearing battle ribbons on the lapels of frayed jackets, lined the walls of the metro stations selling cigarettes, items from the wholesale warehouses, or their own belongings.

Suddenly it seemed that everyone in Russia was carrying a gun. If during the Soviet period it had been unheard of for guns to exist in private hands, in the new Russia they were everywhere. The local bandits all had guns, and so did the security guards who appeared in every office and store. Soldiers and police charged with guarding the country's weapons preferred to sell them, and army bases and military factories became huge suppliers of illegal and unregistered military hardware.

Russians were accustomed to trusting television and the printed word because in the Soviet Union, behind the media had stood the full authority of the government. Now advertisements appeared for mysterious investment funds that offered to help one overcome the effects of inflation. They featured graphs showing how a person's money would grow, but as soon as thousands of persons invested in them, they disappeared. Advertisements on message boards offered care for old and sick persons who lived alone in return for rights to their apartment once they died. The bodies of those who agreed were later found in forests and garbage dumps, the victims of their caretakers.

The social hierarchy was turned upside down. Those who had been the most despised — criminals, speculators, and black marketeers — were the new elite. Their late-model European cars dominated the roads. An ordinary citizen involved in a traffic accident with a gangster was quickly advised for his own safety not even to think about filing a complaint.

Marx wrote that the period of "primitive capital accumulation" in a capitalist society is always accompanied by crime, and this lesson was fully absorbed by Russia's new entrepreneurs. Everyone borrowed to buy up cheap assets, and many forgot to repay their benefactors, leading to a wave of contract killings. A nation that had given its soul to communism was now confronted with the rule of thieves. Many citizens became convinced that there was nothing to believe in, that the only thing that mattered was the rule of force.

It was in this atmosphere that Russia, in the summer and fall of 1992, set out to hold a trial of the Soviet Communist Party. During six years of perestroika and glasnost, Soviet citizens had learned much about the crimes of the Soviet regime, but what was missing was a final determination on the regime's legitimacy. In the trial before the Constitutional Court, the accusation that the Communist Party was criminal was posed directly, and evidence was presented to support it.

The proceeding was described as a second Nuremberg trial. In fact it was far from this. But the possibility that a judgment might be rendered on more than seven decades of Communist rule led to its being treated initially in both the Russian and the foreign press as an epochal event.

Ironically, the impetus for the trial was a complaint filed by the Communists themselves. In late 1991 Yeltsin issued decrees that banned the party's activity, seized its property, and then banned the party itself.[1] A group of former Communist legislators appealed to the Court, arguing that the 1990 Soviet Law on Public Associations stated that a party could be banned only by the courts. In May 1992 Oleg Rumyantsev, a liberal deputy and the secretary of the drafting commission for a new Russian constitution, citing a recent amendment that gave the Court jurisdiction to rule on the constitutionality of political parties, filed a separate petition asking the Court to determine whether the Communist Party was inherently anticonstitutional.[2] With the exception of the preamble to the law on rehabilitation, there had been no official Russian condemnation of the Communist regime. Rumyantsev's motion created the possibility of such a condemnation based on a judicial determination of guilt.

On May 26 the Constitutional Court ruled that it would consider both petitions. The trial, however, would be held under constrained circumstances. The Constitutional Court had been created by the Russian government in July 1991, while the Soviet Union still existed, and the constitution it was supposed to defend was the Soviet one. Under these circumstances, it had to assess the Soviet era on the basis of Soviet legal precedents rather than in the light of universally recognized moral principles, as had been done at Nuremberg.[3] The results were paradoxical, and in the eyes of many Russians, the trial was doomed in advance.

A few months earlier, Russian society had faced another test of its readiness to reckon with history. The issue arose of what to do about the millions of informers who had worked for the Soviet secret police. As the Soviet Union headed toward collapse, the Soviet Parliament began to discuss the need for "lustration," a term derived from the Latin *lustrum*, "purifying sacrifice." Members proposed banning high-ranking Communists from certain professions and also making public the list of KGB informers. Of these issues, revealing the identities of Soviet informers was by far the more explosive. It meant ruining lives and forcing people to reevaluate countless relationships, but it would have stood as an unambiguous condemnation of the informers' actions and served as a warning to those tempted to denounce others in the future.

During the Great Terror, the fear of informers paralyzed Soviet society. The writer Mikhail Prishvin wrote in his diary on November 29, 1937, that the moment a person shared his feelings, he was overheard and "disappeared." As a result, Russians had almost lost the gift of speech. "My dear friend N . . . was delighted to spot me in a crowded [train] compartment, and when at last a seat was free, he sat down next to me. He wanted to say something but . . . he became so tense that every time he prepared himself to speak, all he could bring himself to say was: 'Yes . . . ' And I said the same . . . and in this way, for two hours . . . from Moscow to Zagorsk: 'Yes, Mikhail Mikhailovich.' 'Yes, Georgy Eduardovich.' "[4]

With the death of Stalin, the results of denunciations became less devastating. But the KGB still wanted to know what people were saying and thinking, which they learned with the help of informers. It was generally assumed in the post-Stalin period that every workplace, social organization, and apartment building had informers who reported what was going on to the KGB.

Under Stalin, an incautious word could bring ten years in a labor camp. Under Khrushchev, one could still be arrested for telling antiregime jokes. Under Brezhnev, people were no longer arrested for jokes (at least, Vladimir Bukovsky did not meet anyone in the labor camps who was there for that reason), and Brezhnev himself was said to enjoy them. But antiregime remarks were risky, and a Soviet citizen knew that anything he said could become known to his boss the next day, with unpredictable consequences. Vyacheslav Luchkov, a Moscow psychologist, told me in the 1970s that any reasonably freethinking person always felt the KGB's boot on his throat. "Without confronting you, without ever saying anything to you, they can silently ruin your life."

Despite the anger they inspired, however, informers were not outcasts. On the contrary, they were often the most sought-after members of society. General Valery Velichko, the former head of the ninth directorate, which guarded the Soviet leaders, said, "We recruited the most active and visible."[5] General Viktor Ivanenko, the first chairman of the Russian KGB, in 1992 cautioned Sergei Grigoriants, a former Soviet dissident, not to overestimate the new Russian "democrats." "Take a look at the Supreme Soviet," he said. "They are all ours."[6]

In the first days after the failure of the August 1991 coup, Vadim Bakatin, the newly appointed head of the KGB, announced that he opposed opening the dossiers on millions of informers. He said that guilt for the fact that many people became informers lay with the system, and that calls to open the archives "can only further divide our already sick society." The democratic forces, he cautioned, "should not lower themselves to a shameful 'witch hunt.'"[7] The question, however, was not settled.

Under the law on rehabilitation, victims and their families could view the investigative files in their cases, including the interrogation records and court transcripts, but they could not see the KGB's operational intelligence. This protected the identities of the persons who had betrayed them. But after the failure of the August 1991 coup, in which KGB director Vladimir Kryuchkov took part, the KGB was in a delicate position. Its headquarters had only narrowly avoided being sacked, and many in the KGB feared revenge at the hands of the democrats. To win goodwill, the KGB granted the requests of journalists and deputies for access to the archives. It did not provide access to operational material, but the ability to peruse the files beyond a relative's case file made it possible to draw conclusions, and some information about informers was revealed.

In November 1991 Gleb Yakunin, an Orthodox priest and Supreme Soviet deputy, joined the commission investigating the coup. In that capacity he was admitted to the KGB archives. He asked for the records of the fourth department of the KGB fifth directorate, which was in charge of the church. As a result, he found the annual reports of the KGB to the party, with the nicknames of church leaders who carried out KGB assignments and a description of their activities. The activities were then matched to the known movements of top church leaders, making it possible to decipher the nicknames. "Adamant" was Metropolitan Yuvenaly of Krutitsy and Kolomna, "Antonov" was Metropolitan Filaret of Kiev. "Abbat" was Metropolitan Pitirim of Volokolamsk, and "Drozdov" ("Blackbird"), was found to be Alexei II, the Russian Orthodox patriarch. The entire top leadership of the Russian Orthodox Church had been KGB agents.[8]

Other information about informers became known. The newspapers *Rossiya* and *Izvestiya* published excerpts from annual reports by the KGB fifth directorate on the surveillance of prominent cultural figures. The information made it possible to identify at least one agent in the Soviet Writer's Union.

In early 1992 the KGB began to refuse to produce documents from the archives, with the explanation that they could not be found. Later the archive was closed for repairs. It never reopened. In February, Ruslan Khasbulatov, the speaker of the Russian parliament, disbanded the parliamentary commission that was investigating the coup. Yakunin was convinced that this was done under pressure from the patriarch. Yakunin had begun to discuss what he was learning in the archives about the connection between the KGB and the Russian Orthodox Church.

The question of publishing the list of informers continued to be raised in the press, but as Russian society plunged into the chaos of the economic transition, it grew increasingly clear that a decision would have to be taken quickly. Galina Starovoitova, a leader of Democratic Russia who was later assassinated, was in favor of publishing the names of informers, as was Gleb Yakunin. The system of mutual spying and personal betrayal, however, was deeply rooted in Russia, and revealing its tentacles was a serious act. In the wake of fast-moving and frequently discouraging events, the will for such an action was evaporating.

The issue of informers put Russian society to an excruciating test. In the first place, the scale of the KGB's penetration of society was extraordinary. Sergei Kovalyev, a former Soviet dissident who became Yeltsin's human rights commissioner, took part in a commission on the opening of the Soviet archives that was chaired by General Dmitri Volkogonov, the former director of the Institute of Military History. In the course of that work, Kovalyev was shocked by the numbers and identities of the informers, which could be gleaned from references to their activities and nicknames. "If two-thirds of the union of writers were informers," he said, "what does this say about society?"[9]

Kovalyev feared that publishing the names of informers would lead to open confrontation. "I was not sure that society could stand the shock," he said later. Others in the democratic movement undoubtedly did not want their own roles exposed, or were afraid of revelations about their relatives and friends. Officials of the security services, playing on these fears, confided that the most active democrats were their agents and warned that, in the event of lustration, those opposed to reforms would win.

There were other problems with revealing the names of informers. Between 1989 and 1991, huge numbers of documents were destroyed. In the event of lustration, some informers would be protected by this destruction. At the same time, the KGB had been forbidden to recruit as agents the directors of factories, chief editors, and high party functionaries. When the KGB asked for their help, they were expected to give it. But their names would not show up in any list of informers. In a conversation with Arseny Roginsky, the head of Memorial, a former party leader said, "Ours are all clean — and as for yours, we'll see."

At the same time, the role of any given informer required clarification. Informers sometimes had protected those that they spied on by filing reports indicating that their activities were innocent. There were also cases where KGB records identified an individual as an informer despite a lack of evidence that the person had ever signed anything. This raised the possibility that he was actually not an agent.[10]

Finally, and perhaps most important, there were signs that Yeltsin was opposed to lustration because he intended to preserve the security agency for his own use. The KGB was broken up to a degree. Separate organizations were created for foreign intelligence, border guards, the protection of leaders, and the monitoring of communications. But there was no fundamental reform such as had occurred in Germany with the Stasi. There were proposals from Russians, including Gavril Popov, the mayor of Moscow, who asked Yeltsin in 1991 to make him chairman of the KGB, that it be reorganized and pared down, with its old personnel replaced, and put under strict civilian control. Had this occurred, the subsequent history of Russia might have been very different. But Yeltsin told his aide Gennady Burbulis that if the Communist Party had been the Soviet Union's brain, the KGB was its spinal cord, and he "clearly did not want to rupture the spinal cord now that the head had been lopped off."[11] Yeltsin retained members of the KGB old guard in top positions, including those who had been involved in the persecution of dissent.

In March 1992 the Supreme Soviet considered a new law on operational investigative activity that declared the names of persons who had cooperated with the special services, on either a closed or an open basis, a state secret.[12] The Supreme Soviet, whose members reportedly included many KGB informers, approved the law overwhelmingly.

With the passing of the law, the question of revealing the names of

KGB informers appeared to be closed. Russian society continued to live with its secrets. A few people publicly confessed to their former ties with the KGB. One of these was the Lithuanian Archepiscop Khristosom, the only hierarch of the church to confirm that he had been an agent (under the nickname "Revstavrator").[13] Another was Anatoly Kim, a deputy in the Russian parliament who, at a decisive moment during the August coup, stood on a tank alongside Yeltsin.[14] For the most part, however, Russians kept silent about their involvement with the security services, and as a result, suspicion fell on everyone. Betrayal came to be treated as mundane, an inevitable part of life in that period.

One of those who came to believe that this was a mistake was Kovalyev. He had opposed lustration as too divisive for society, but he soon saw evidence that Russia's failure to adopt it left the institution of informers free to reestablish itself. At a meeting of a group of deputies in 1992, Khasbulatov read a report in which it was alleged that deputies were being too frank in their conversations with foreign diplomats and journalists. Kovalyev asked whether this information came from informers and demanded an investigation. Khasbulatov appointed a small group, including Kovalyev, to study the matter. But when the group suggested asking the Ministry of Security, the renamed KGB, whether it had informers among the deputies, Khasbulatov took no action, and the matter died.

In late November 1994 the issue of informers in the government arose again. In his capacity as human rights commissioner, Kovalyev tried to organize a group, including members of the State Duma, to go to Chechnya, where tensions had reached the breaking point. He made calls using the internal Kremlin telephone system, the *vertushka,* which is protected against eavesdropping. But his calls, first on the ATS-1 system, which was the most secure, and then on the ATS-2 system, went dead. The phones in the office of Mikhail Poltaranin, the minister of information, did not work, either. Kovalyev assumed that someone with the authority to turn off the phones was eavesdropping and had decided to prevent people from speaking. Kovalyev finally went to Chechnya alone, but the incident with the telephones demonstrated to him that the old system endured.

The opposing sides began presenting evidence in the trial of the Communist Party on July 7. In their petition, the Communists claimed that existing law gave Yeltsin no right to ban the party. Yeltsin's lawyers replied that in light of the Russian Republic's declaration of sovereignty in 1990, no Soviet laws were valid in Russia except those adopted by the Russian legislature. They argued that the relevant legislation was a decree, issued by Stalin in 1932 and ratified by the RSFSR Supreme Soviet, that permitted the "liquidation" of political parties by executive order. They thus justified Yeltsin's acts with the help of Stalin-era legislation intended to strengthen the dictatorship. The second petition was even more problematic. Rumyantsev sought to have declared anticonstitutional a party that until 1990 had enjoyed a legal monopoly of power under that same constitution.[15]

The atmosphere outside the court building on Ilynka Street was tense. An angry crowd of pro-Communist demonstrators with red banners demanded to be let in. Yeltsin warned that any support for the Communists could lead to civil war. That day's issue of *Pravda,* which now identified itself only as the paper founded in 1912 by Lenin, carried statements by three of the Communists' principal accusers, Gennady Burbulis, the state secretary, Rumyantsev, and Sergei Shakhrai, Yeltsin's former legal adviser, as well as by Gorbachev and former politburo member Alexander Yakovlev, in which they expressed orthodox Communist beliefs. The headline above the statements was, "Gentlemen! When did you tell the truth? Yesterday or today?" It referred to Yeltsin's long party career and said, "Weathervanes adapt quickest of all."[16]

In the courtroom, the thirteen Russian judges, all but one of them former Communists, appeared wearing freshly sewn long black robes. F. M. Rudinsky, a lawyer for the Communist side, found the robes farcical. "In Western countries, such costumes are an ancient tradition. But here in Russia at the end of the twentieth century . . . ? At least they weren't wearing wigs."[17] The judges sat in a semicircle under a tricolor Russian flag with Valery Zorkin, the chief justice, at the apex. He had a gold chain around his neck, and in front of him was a bronze gong, which he hit with a small hammer to call the court to order.

The Communists were shell-shocked from their loss of power, but the atmosphere in the hall was on their side. Technically, the case concerned only the legality of Yeltsin's decrees banning the party and the party's conformity with the constitution. The presidential side, however, had announced that the case would be a trial of the Soviet regime, and many of the Communists welcomed the opportunity to seek historical vindication.

Viktor Zorkaltsev, a Supreme Soviet deputy representing the Communist Party, said, "The party that is banned here consolidated society and rallied it against fascism, ensuring the victory in the Great Patriotic War." He acknowledged mistakes, especially during the 1930s, but said that "there were forces in the party that rose up to correct them."[18]

Zorkaltsev was followed by Dmitri Stepanov, another Communist deputy. He rejected the idea that the party was against the people. "The 1930s were not only years of arbitrariness and repression but years of the dramatic improvement of the conditions of . . . the lives of the workers." He said that millions of Soviet soldiers did not turn their weapons against the party. "Such massive military and labor heroism [as during the war] was not seen by any other nation. It could not have been the result of compulsion."[19]

The deputy B. Tarasov said, "I became a candidate member of the party at the age of 18 and all these years acted . . . for the good of the people. Even my first parachute jump . . . I recall that I stood on the ledge and far in the distance saw the earth and a certain timidity stole into my soul, I told myself, 'Tarasov, you're a communist' and jumped. . . . I want to emphasize that millions of people believed in this . . . despite the cynical laughter that resounds here from former, by the way, communists whose morality in this way is well demonstrated."[20]

The presidential side argued that what was banned was not a political party but a criminal organization. Andrei Makarov, a lead lawyer for the presidential side, said, "The CPSU inflicted on its own people a reign of terror unprecedented in history. . . . From the first moments of the assumption of power by Lenin it was clearly established that this was a regime that was not limited by any laws and did not respect rules of any kind."[21]

The presidential side called three former political prisoners, Lev Razgon, Bukovsky, and Yakunin, who described their experiences. Razgon, a prisoner in the Stalin-era camps, recalled that each morning the prisoners had been lined up and told by the guards that they were enemies of the people. The party, he said, divided the country into "hangmen and victims" and "we are the results of this deformation."[22] Bukovsky said that as a prisoner he had been confronted with "monstrous arbitrariness" and punishment "with hunger and cold." He had witnessed the deaths of "many of our friends." Yakunin said that religious believers had been constantly under surveillance, and if they distributed copies of sermons in public places, they were subject to arrest.[23]

The presidential side presented archival documents demonstrating the criminal character of the Communist Party beginning in 1917. Some of the documents were from the 1930s, including telegrams increasing the quotas of persons to be shot in response to requests from local branches of the NKVD. Other documents, however, were more recent. One indicated that the politburo had ordered the creation of special KGB units to fight domestic enemies just two days after the party had supposedly given up its monopoly of power.[24]

On July 10 the justices ruled that insofar as the Communist monopoly of power had been enshrined in the constitution until March 1990, evidence of the party's "unconstitutional" activities should be limited to the period after that date.[25] The ruling was observed mainly in the breach. As Roy Medvedev, a historian who testified as an expert for the Communist side, put it:

> There were a lot of tendentious speeches, with both sides missing the point. The Constitutional Court called upon the communist party lawyers and Boris Yeltsin's representative to present their case from a juridical standpoint, not a political one, but neither side has so far complied. The problem for the court is not just to rule "to be or not to be" for the communist party but also whether or not we are going to have an independent Constitutional Court. This circumstance, no doubt, will influence the court's members . . . when they prepare their final decision.[26]

Nonetheless, after July 10 the opposing sides began to devote less time to history and more time to the legal issues — the lawfulness of Yeltsin's decrees and the behavior of the party after March 1990. This caused the public to lose interest in the trial. Demonstrators stopped gathering outside the court, and the police cordons were removed. Inside the courtroom, the press benches emptied. Of the reporters who remained, some were observed sleeping. On August 3 the hearings were postponed indefinitely to allow the Court to consider the evidence from about forty witnesses, which by then covered a wide range of issues and was in danger of becoming incoherent.

On September 15 the hearings resumed. First the Court heard from experts who testified on the legality of Yeltsin's decision. It then called former members of the politburo, who it hoped could shed light on the party's behavior after March 1990.

The person whose testimony was most wanted by both sides was Gorbachev. But he refused to appear. He could expect little support either from the Communists, who regarded him as a traitor, or the presidential side, which was eager to destroy his authority, and he justified his refusal by saying that the trial was a political show being used for posturing by both sides.[27] On September 29 the Court devoted its afternoon session to a discussion of Gorbachev's refusal to testify. They voted to send another summons to him, warning of possible "legal consequences." The most the Court could do, however, was levy a fine of one hundred rubles. When Gorbachev refused the second summons, the foreign ministry, acting at the Court's request, impounded his passport, preventing him from leaving on a lecture tour.[28]

On October 6 the Court heard Yegor Ligachev, the leader of the conservatives in the politburo. In answer to a question from V. G. Vishnyakov, a lawyer for the presidential side, as to whether the party apparatus could be considered unconstitutional, Ligachev replied that the Central Committee, politburo, and secretariat had "worked in strict conformity with the constitution and the laws." He emphasized, however, that the party had been right to command everything in the Soviet Union as it did under its constitutionally mandated "leading role" until March 1990. "I am confident," he said, "that if the Communist Party had functioned, there would not have been the collapse of the Soviet Union, ethnic wars, and the impoverishment of the people."[29]

Ligachev's testimony was followed by that of Yakovlev, the most liberal member of Gorbachev's politburo. S. A. Bogolyubov, an attorney for the Communists, asked Yakovlev whether, in his opinion, Yeltsin had had a right in August 1991 to ban the activity of the Communist Party. Yakovlev said that he had in light of the extraordinary conditions created by the attempt of hard-liners to seize power in the August coup. "We are now talking about a conspiracy," Yakovlev said, "and tanks on the streets of Moscow. I spent all three days [of the coup attempt] on the streets and did not feel anything but horror for what was taking place. . . . This is not a question of justice or injustice. The leadership of the party, especially the force structures, which were led by Communists, we always forget this, embarked on the path of an anticonstitutional conspiracy."[30]

As the weeks went by, it became obvious that the trial would end in some type of compromise. Outside the courtroom, Yeltsin and the Russian parliament were locked in a steadily escalating power struggle over the course of the economic reforms. The deputies charged that the United States was using "agents of influence" in the executive branch to destroy Russia.[31] Yeltsin answered by warning of the danger of fascism. The importance of making a historical judgment on Communism faded in the face of Yeltsin's practical need to deprive the Communists of the means to reemerge as a serious political force.

Olga Sveridova, an assistant to Burbulis, said that although the presidential side made a great show of its intention to judge Communism, it became obvious that the historical arguments would not lead to a legal condemnation of the Communist Party and a determination that it was anticonstitutional because the only thing the Constitutional Court could do was compare the party's actions with the Constitution of the USSR, which the Communists had written and which they had not violated.

"The representatives of the president really wanted one thing," Sveridova said, "to prevent Yeltsin's decrees from being canceled. If that happened, the Communists would be able immediately to resurrect the whole structure of the Soviet Communist Party. There was a firm desire not to let the Communists restore the structure of the oblast and raion party committees and return to the headquarters on Old Square and create their own organizations and claim their property."[32] The arguments over history began to be seen as a distraction from the real goal of the trial, which was to reinforce the position of the president.

By November there were widespread rumors, based on supposed leaks from the judges, that in the matter of the legality of Yeltsin's decrees there would be some type of split decision. Finally, on November 30 the verdict was announced. The ban on the ruling structures of the party was upheld, but the Court allowed the Communists to have a network of basic party organizations. Party property that had been taken from the government would be subject to confiscation, but the party could keep its own property. On the issue of the constitutionality of the Communist Party, the

Court declined to rule altogether on the grounds that the party "fell apart and ceased to exist as an all Union structure" in August 1991.[33]

Immediately after the verdict was announced, the Communists issued a statement welcoming the decision. They told a press conference that they would quickly revive the party. Most of the attention in the pro-Communist press, however, was given to the court's failure to pass historical judgment by ruling on the party's constitutionality. The newspaper *Sovetskaya Rossiya* greeted the verdict with the headline, "Nuremberg Failed." It said that the party had effectively been declared innocent. "If the court did not rule that the Communist Party was unconstitutional, it means it is constitutional."[34] The irony was that, in the wake of a trial that many had hoped would result in the condemnation of the Communist Party, it became the only party in Russia to be judged constitutional.

Anatoly Kononov, the most liberal member of the Constitutional Court, expressed his dismay over the decision. He said that the party needed to be held to juridical responsibility. But the obstacles in the way of condemning the party in the context of a trial before the Russian Constitutional Court were considerable. The judges were susceptible to political pressure, as their split decision showed, but in the matter of historical responsibility, a decision condemning the party would have been difficult because they were being asked to pass judgment on the party within the framework of the party's own laws.

In the end, the party deserved condemnation not because it violated the Soviet Constitution but because it attempted, at the cost of millions of lives, to organize an entire society on the basis of a totalitarian ideology. Reaching this judgment would have required an altogether different type of tribunal. In the wake of this trial, however, there was no further attempt in Russia to pass judgment on Soviet Communism. But the issue of the Soviet regime's crimes against its own people has not gone away. It remains beneath the surface, deepening Russia's moral confusion and facilitating the rise of a new nationalist and authoritarian regime.

CHAPTER 8

Moral Choice under Totalitarianism

∎

The closest Russia came to a day of judgment for Stalin's henchmen was in June 1957, during the Communist Party plenum, when Khrushchev denounced Molotov, Malenkov, and Kaganovich for their roles in mass crimes. This was not done for the sake of justice. If it had been, Khrushchev would have put himself in the dock. Rather it was done to destroy Khrushchev's political rivals.

For decades, the record of the June 1957 plenum was hidden. A paragraph in the Central Committee's public announcement mentioning "mass repressions" in the thirties later was cut. After the fall of the Soviet Union, however, the transcript of the six-day meeting became available, and it showed a remarkable transformation on the part of those who had once been the most feared men in the country. Confronted with their crimes, the leading Stalinists became inexplicably humble. They depicted themselves as cogs in a machine, helpless functionaries who were incapable of taking responsibility for their actions. The accusations, they argued, constituted a monstrous injustice — not because they were guiltless, but because others were as guilty as they were.

Khrushchev, who orchestrated the proceedings, didn't hesitate to depict himself as an avenging angel. Referring to the crimes of the members of the antiparty group, he said that "the mothers, wives, and children who remained alive shed a sea of tears." He was assisted by Marshal Georgy Zhukov, the hero of World War II, who presented a general indictment.

It is difficult to see how Khrushchev and Zhukov were better than the people they were accusing. Khrushchev had been mindlessly zealous in carrying out Stalin's commands. As the head of the Moscow party organization, he raised the quota for "enemies" to be shot in Moscow from five thousand to eighty-five hundred, thus condemning to death thirty-five hundred innocent persons on his own initiative.[1] He assisted in the arrest and murder of his colleagues and friends. Of thirty-eight top officials in Moscow and the Moscow oblast when Khrushchev was in charge, only three survived. Two of Khrushchev's personal assistants, Rabinovich and Finkel, were arrested, their arrests approved by Khrushchev. The situation did not improve in 1938, when Khrushchev became the party boss in Ukraine. According to Molotov, who was hardly objective, Khrushchev "sent 54,000 persons to the next world as a member of the Ukrainian troika."[2]

Zhukov was not innocent either. While commanding the Leningrad front, he issued an order on September 28, 1941, that "any families surrendering to the enemy will be shot and upon returning from captivity, they will all be shot."[3] The order, which required the murder even of young children, was more draconian than Stalin's order issued a month earlier, which called for the families of soldiers falling into captivity only to be deprived of state subsidies.

Zhukov was more wasteful of his soldiers' lives than any other commander, as was demonstrated in the bloody and unsuccessful attacks on the Rzhevsko-Vyazemsky bridgehead in 1942 and during the Berlin operation. During the battle for the Seelow Heights in the last weeks of the war, Zhukov ordered a frontal attack, but one of the officers objected that German fire had not been suppressed and it was necessary to continue using artillery. The officer was threatened with execution if he did not immediately attack. After several assaults, out of eight hundred soldiers, a hundred were still alive. A second officer who resisted Zhukov's order was executed. The first officer survived but lost his mind after seeing such a hill of corpses.[4]

None of this affected the intensity of Khrushchev and Zhukov's attack on the antiparty group, who were depicted as the "main culprits" in the Stalin-era crimes. Between February 27 and November 12, 1938, Zhukov said, Molotov, Malenkov, and Kaganovich personally had authorized 38,679 executions. On one day alone, November 12, 1938, Stalin and Molotov condemned 3,167 people "like cattle to slaughter." Malenkov, according to Zhukov, bore an even greater guilt because he was supposed to be supervising the NKVD. "If only the people had known that their leaders' hands were dripping with blood, they would have greeted them not with applause but with stones."[5]

Khrushchev also attacked party officials allied with his political enemies. Nikolai Bulganin, the prime minister, had ended up on "a pile of manure." Mikhail Pervukhin, a presidium member, once "wavering personified," now "squirmed like a fish on a hot griddle." As for the "academician" Dmitri Shepilov, "he sure knows how to express himself like an artist." He "looks in a book and sees a shnook. He doesn't understand the simplest things, but he wants to instruct others." "You call yourselves politicians," Khrushchev said, addressing all of them. "No, you're just pathetic schemers."[6]

What followed was a strange spectacle. The arch-Stalinists reacted to this onslaught by partially admitting their guilt even as they tried to defend themselves.

> Kaganovich: I'm being asked about railroad workers. There was an endless flow of papers from the NKVD. Ask the railroad workers how I was constantly accused of holding up the questioning. I defended hundreds of thousands of railroad people, and we arrested some of the people who according to the papers appeared to be enemies.

Khrushchev demanded to know who authorized torture to produce false confessions.

"All politburo members," Molotov replied.

"But you were second in command after Stalin," said Khrushchev, "so you bear the main responsibility, and right after you, Kaganovich."

Molotov: "But I raised more objections to Stalin than any of you did, more than you did, Comrade Khrushchev."

Khrushchev quoted a speech by Molotov praising Stalin on Stalin's sixtieth birthday in 1939.

"Why don't you recount your own speeches?" Molotov answered.

Zhukov said to Kaganovich, "You, brother, answer straight out. You had Central Committee members shot — were they our enemies?"

> KAGANOVICH: There were enemies, there was an intense class struggle. Together with our enemies, did we permit distortions, outrages, crimes? We did. I agree with and approve of Khrushchev's

report at the 20th Congress, although I must say that I was very shaken by it. But I don't think that the members of the [party Central Committee] took this dethroning of Stalin and exposed their sores and wounds with a light heart. I suffered through this report and I support it. I consider that we did right in uncovering and exposing these things. But, of course, that does not relieve me of responsibility. I am responsible politically.

ZHUKOV: And criminally. . . . Abuse of power leads to criminal punishment.

KAGANOVICH: I am talking about political responsibility. The situation was drastic, we all acted very fast, and the fact that Comrade Zhukov pulled out the names of only two or three who signed documents and does not mention the others — that's a factional maneuver. . . . Drown everyone it suits you to and keep your mouth shut about the others. The whole Politburo . . . And you, Comrade Zhukov, as division commander, you never signed?

"I never sent a single person to be shot."

"That's hard to believe."[7]

Molotov, Malenkov, and Kaganovich lost their positions but were never convicted of any crime. Once they no longer posed a political threat to Khrushchev, the purpose of denouncing them had been served. The next attempt to hold Communist leaders individually responsible for their crimes would not come for another thirty-four years. On August 25, 1991, four days after the collapse of the coup that was intended to save the Soviet Union, former Soviet dissident Vladimir Bukovsky returned to Moscow, where he met with Gennady Burbulis, Yeltsin's principal aide, and Mikhail Poltaranin, his minister of information. Bukovsky urged that the fourteen leaders of the coup be put on trial and that the trial be used as an opportunity to pass judgment on Soviet Communism. Less than a year later, Yeltsin would support a trial of the Communist Party, but in the immediate aftermath of the coup's collapse, he declined to try the coup leaders out of fear that it would then be difficult for former Communists like himself to remain in politics.

In the following months, as the Soviet Union was coming apart, there was discussion in the media of the need to punish individuals. There was no shortage of persons who could still be put on trial, including the interrogator of Raoul Wallenberg, participants in the World War II execution of Polish officers, the organizers of psychiatric repression, and those responsible for massacres of civilians in Tbilisi and Vilnius.[8] Bukovsky wanted all of these cases to be opened and to enlist relatives of the victims to testify about the impact of the regime's crimes. But no such steps were taken. Bukovsky attributed the decision not to try the coup leaders or persons guilty of Soviet-era crimes to the Russian leaders' instinct for self preservation. "The Soviet 'democrats,'" he said, "were splinters of the Communist nomenklatura that changed sides. The last thing they wanted was to go into the past and see how horrible they all were."[9]

Even after the Soviet Union collapsed, many difficulties stood in the way of judging the Soviet leaders. The first was that the crimes of the Stalin era had been carried out under conditions of mass terror, and the leadership was as terrorized as anyone else. Khrushchev, for example, lived in daily fear that he would be eliminated. As he wrote in his memoirs: "All of us around Stalin were temporary people. As long as he trusted us to a certain degree, we were allowed to go on living and working. But the moment he stopped trusting you, Stalin would start to scrutinize you until the cup of his distrust overflowed. Then it would be your turn to follow those who were no longer among the living."[10] With Stalin's death, the terror abated but fear remained, and it led a new generation of Soviet officials to take part in Communist crimes.

In addition, Soviet leaders were committed to a totalitarian ideology. The Stalinist leaders looked to a better future to justify the hell they created in the present. Even in the Brezhnev era, when allegiance to the ideology became more ritualized, Communist dogma continued to choke off independent thought. A Communist leader who was guided by the ideology was pushed toward compliance and, inevitably, crime.

Judging the actions of a leadership that worked under the influence of ideology and terror was further complicated in the Soviet Union because ordinary citizens faced the same pressures themselves. If those who exercised power were schooled in unthinking obedience, ordinary citizens were almost always compromised by the daily need to dissimulate in a monolithic society. When the time came for the leaders to be held accountable, ordinary Russians found it hard to apply moral standards that they did not live by themselves.

The legacy of ideology and terror guided the judgments of millions of people. Mass murder was often justified in Russia as a condition of industrial progress. This argument, of course, treats the victims exclusively as means to an end. But in a country where it was taken for granted that nothing was higher than the goals of the state, such arguments made perfect sense. Having lived with these destructive assumptions for decades, Russians were loath to break with them.

With the fall of the Soviet Union, Russians found it hard to navigate in the wreckage of their past. It seemed that everyone was guilty, and where all are guilty, it is easy to assume that guilt does not exist. The fact that almost all Stalinist and post-Stalinist leaders, including many perestroika-era reformers, had routinely participated in evil was a reason not to judge. Criminality was treated as unavoidable and even a mark of government service. The totality of the complicity and the difficulty that even persons with decent instincts had in avoiding it was shown in the stories of Soviet leaders' lives, particularly those who, as events showed, were also capable of doing good.

Two important Stalin-era officials were Alexei Kuznetsov, who organized the defense of Leningrad during the war, and Anastas Mikoyan, a politburo member for three decades. Both men were believed by their families to have been secretly opposed to the repressions in which they took part, and both also performed great services.

On February 20, 2005, the news agency Interfax reported that a group of political and cultural figures had asked Putin to honor Kuznetsov in connection with the one hundredth anniversary of his birth. They wanted a monument to Kuznetsov in the Levashovo Memorial Cemetery, where he is buried along with thousands of victims of the Stalinist terror.[11]

The idea potentially had wide support. During Leningrad's darkest days, Kuznetsov had helped to organize the "Road of Life" across the frozen Lake Ladoga, the city's most important supply line and link to the outside world. With thousands of people starving to death in February 1942, he said, on behalf of the political leadership, "We are the fathers of all children," particularly those whose parents had perished. He directed the rapid construction of Leningrad's defenses. Although he was the party second secretary, he eclipsed Andrei Zhdanov, the first secretary, who was frequently outside Leningrad and who, when he was in the city, spent much of his time in bomb shelters. Zhdanov did not hide the reality of the situation. When Stalin asked who was in charge in Leningrad, Zhdanov answered, "Kuznetsov."[12]

In the autumn of 1941, Stalin, in the presence of the members of the State Defense Committee, took a piece of paper and wrote, "Alexei, all hope is in you. The motherland will not forget you." He then took a cigarette box for his favorite Herzegovina Flor cigarettes and with a red pencil wrote on it, "Stalin." He summoned Vsevolod Merkulov, Beria's deputy, and ordered him to fly into besieged Leningrad and hand the letter and cigarette box personally to Kuznetsov.

Unfortunately, Kuznetsov's activities as a political leader were not limited to the defense of a besieged city. He also signed approximately ten thousand death sentences as a member of the troika in Leningrad from January to June 1938. Many of these victims are believed to be buried in Levashovo.

After the war, on August 13, 1949, Kuznetsov was arrested. He was accused, among other things, of forming a group to take over the leading posts in the party and conspiring to move the capital from Moscow to Leningrad. During the interrogations, he was tortured and his back was broken. At his trial he was unable to stand. After his conviction, executioners placed a white shroud over his head, carried him out of the courtroom feet first, and shot him. Later, after the Leningrad case was reopened, the investigator in the case was tried in the same hall and also shot. He too was buried in the Levashovo cemetery.[13]

The proposal to erect a statue of Kuznetsov inspired a controversy in St. Petersburg. In a letter to Valentina Matvienko, the governor of St. Petersburg, S. D. Khakhaev of St. Petersburg Memorial said that a statue of Kuznetsov in Levashovo would be an insult to the memory of the innocent victims who are buried there. Some people in the city disagreed. Many called into Leningrad Radio during a broadcast on the sixtieth anniversary of the end of the Second World War to say that the authors of the letter wanted "to blacken our history."[14] The letter was finally answered by S. Tarasov, the vice governor of St. Petersburg, who assured

Memorial that its position would be taken into account. In the end, the monument was not built.

Like Kuznetsov, virtually all persons in leadership positions signed death sentences during the Great Terror. The petition on behalf of Kuznetsov and other efforts to honor his memory—a meeting in the Hall of Columns in Moscow and a series of programs on radio and television about his role in organizing the defense of Leningrad—were all based on the notion that his participation in the terror could be overlooked.

Sergo Mikoyan, Anastas Mikoyan's son, who married Kuznetsov's daughter, Alla, said that his father-in-law

> never mentioned anything to me [about the purges]. It was Stalin's time and no one spoke aloud about these things. I can only judge by his nature: he was very kind and friendly. He was cheerful, not fanatical. He was not like Molotov, who was dry, stern, and uncompromising. Molotov was able to sign an execution list by himself. On a list of two hundred "enemies of the people," he wrote, "VMN" ["highest measure of punishment"]. This doomed everyone.
>
> It is necessary to know the historical conditions of 1937–38. The troika was made up of representatives of the party, NKVD, and prosecutor. The main person was the head of the NKVD. The list would not have been changed if one member of the troika refused to sign it. It would not have saved anyone. The person refusing to sign would only have added his own name to the next list.[15]

Representatives of Memorial argued that Kuznetsov had to have known that the accused were innocent because the NKVD handed down quotas for arrests. Mikoyan, however, disagreed. "It was necessary to know the NKVD's methods, and not everyone knew them. Only the NKVD knew about the quotas. There was a kind of madness, it cannot now be understood by normal people. The NKVD at that time was like an insane asylum. People in the party did not know the scale of the repression. They thought that perhaps there were some innocent people, but they could not imagine that no one was guilty."

Despite Mikoyan's view that Kuznetsov was not a zealot, the exposure of "enemies" was the path to advancement in Stalin's Russia, and there is evidence that Kuznetsov actively participated. The newspaper *Leningradskaya Pravda* reported in 1937 that beginning in the 1920s, he "exposed the subversive activities of the kulaks." Later, as a local party official, he "threw himself into the struggle with carefully disguised enemies." As a result, the leadership was "renewed."[16]

In his speech at the 18th Party Congress, in 1939, Kuznetsov, unlike many other speakers, discussed the successes in exposing "enemies of the people." He said that much had been achieved by the Leningrad party organization in uniting its ranks and in "the exposure and rooting out of enemies of the people that especially strongly penetrated the party and state apparatus." He said that there had been the "dulling of class vigilance, criminal carelessness bordering on betrayal" in Leningrad, which had made the subversive activities of enemies easier. F. B. Komal, a Soviet historian, commenting on Kuznetsov's remarks in an article in 1990 in the journal *Leningradskaya Panorama,* wrote:

> In this way, the leaders of Leningrad (because it is necessary to assume that A. A. Kuznetsov expressed not only his own opinion) did not make even an attempt to investigate and correctly evaluate the existing situation. Of course, about carrying out some different line in those conditions there could not be any discussion, but a lot nonetheless depended on them. . . . They could either slow down or speed up the general process. They chose to do the latter.[17]

Some of Kuznetsov's own remarks also indicate that he was a zealous functionary. On the subject of hierarchy, he said that it is necessary for people to be "a little bit afraid of their bosses." On the subject of Stalin, he said, "If Stalin said it, it is the law, this is holy, we believe in this and with this, we will be victorious."[18] Sergo Mikoyan believes that Kuznetsov may have taken part in the purges willingly and either did not doubt the legitimacy of what was happening or did not allow himself to doubt it. "If so," he said, "some type of guilt is, of course, here."

Kuznetsov's son Valery obtained the case file on his father in January 2005. He could not recognize his father from the photo in the file. "Looking out at me was a broken, tormented, exhausted person," he said. "Judging by this photograph, he was tortured cruelly. I made a copy of this photo but could not show it to my older sister." In hundreds of interrogations, one dialogue was repeated endlessly. The investigator asks Kuznetsov, "Are you an enemy of the people? Are you a traitor? Were you waiting for the death of Stalin?" Kuznetsov answers, "Yes, yes, yes."[19]

Sergo's son, Vladimir, the grandson of Kuznetsov, was also allowed to see the file. There were twenty-eight volumes, and Vladimir read seven of them in the KGB reading room on Kuznetsky Most. "From the beginning," Vladimir said, "Kuznetsov is agreeing with everything." Vladimir also saw Kuznetsov's last picture. "He was a completely changed man," he said. "He was like an insane person."[20]

On the subject of Kuznetsov's participation in the purges, Vladimir said,

I'm absolutely convinced that he had some doubts. Kuznetsov was a member of the troika for a half a year when Zhdanov was away. The quotas were NKVD quotas. They wanted the approval of the party people, but approval or no approval, the fate of the victims was already decided.

My opinion is that he deserves a monument. Show me an ideal person. We should not overlook his signature. We should understand why he put his signature there and also look at what he did for the benefit of the city and the people. Let the people judge if he was a hero or a bloodthirsty politician.

If a person peels the skin off of his victim we have absolute guilt. As for the person who signed, believing or not believing, I don't know.

Anastas Mikoyan was another person who participated in the crimes of the regime but also did considerable good. To this day he retains a benign reputation in Russia. One reason was his friendly demeanor. When he was in a good mood, he sometimes gave his subordinates oranges from a bowl on his table. When he was in a bad mood, he could throw files in their faces, but such incidents were unusual. In the 1930s he was in charge of food deliveries and was instrumental in bringing out the first Soviet cookbook, *The Book of Healthy and Tasty Food*. It opened with Stalin's words, "Life is getting better, life is getting gayer."[21] Russia's leading sausage factory was named after Mikoyan.

Mikoyan was a strong advocate of de-Stalinization. It was his idea to form a commission to investigate Stalin's crimes, and he introduced Khrushchev to two recently freed political prisoners, Olga Shatunovskaya and Alexei Snegov, who described conditions in the camps. He also convinced Khrushchev that the condemnation of the Stalin regime had to take place at the 20th Party Congress and could not be postponed.

Mikoyan was also a force for moderation in foreign policy. He opposed the invasion of Hungary and forced Khrushchev to back down from unilaterally ending U.S. occupation rights in West Berlin. During the Cuban missile crisis, he successfully opposed Khrushchev's plan to arm Soviet missiles in Cuba with tactical nuclear weapons. After the U.S. naval blockade was announced, he protested against Khrushchev's plan to run the blockade with submarines. Mikoyan's insistence that the submarines would be detected was backed at the last moment by Adm. Sergei Gorshkov, the commander of the Soviet Navy, and Khrushchev finally gave way and ordered the submarine commanders to stay two days' sail away from Cuba.[22]

Like other politburo members, however, Mikoyan signed execution lists. He authorized the arrest of hundreds of workers in the People's Commissariats of Food Supply and Foreign Trade. He also recommended the arrest of members of the All Union Scientific Research Institute for the fisheries industry and oceanography. In the fall of 1937 he went to Armenia to purge the party and government there. A thousand people were arrested, including seven of the nine Armenian politburo members. He was one of six persons who voted to execute nearly twenty-two thousand Polish officers who were murdered in spring 1940 in the Katyn Forest and other locations. His signature is on Beria's proposal to the politburo that the officers be executed, beneath those of Stalin, Voroshilov, and Molotov. (In the margin it is noted that Kaganovich and Kalinin were also in favor.)[23]

Mikoyan's oldest son, Stepan, who was a military test pilot in the Soviet Union, believes that his father was, in principle, against repression but found that he had no choice but to participate. "He signed lists with the names of many people," Stepan said. "But you either had to sign or kill yourself, in which case you would die an enemy of the people, and all of your family would be shot, and all who worked for you would be arrested. The main lists were signed by Stalin, Kaganovich, Molotov, and Voroshilov. How my father avoided this, I don't know. But he participated in the cases of Armenia and Katyn. He was asked to sign and he did. It was shameful, and it was shameful to him, I think."[24]

In his memoirs, Mikoyan acknowledged that, at first, he was completely in agreement with Stalin and fully trusted him. But as the Great Terror got under way, and persons he regarded as honorable were arrested, he began to have doubts. He said that he managed to save a few people. One of them was Napoleon Andreasian, a Moscow party official, arrested because of his first name and accused of being a French spy. Mikoyan spoke about this to Stalin, who said, "He is as much of a Frenchman as I am." According to Mikoyan, Stalin laughed and assigned him to call the NKVD and say that he should be freed."[25]

At the same time, Mikoyan writes, Stalin was determined to force him to participate in the purges. He ordered Mikoyan to go to Armenia to supervise a purge of "wreckers and Trotskyites." The trip took place after the former head of the Armenian government, Saak Ter-Gabrielian, was thrown out of a window in the office of the local NKVD. Stalin sent a letter to the Armenian Central Committee stating that Ter-Gabrielian was a plotter who was killed by his accomplices "because he knew too much." Mikoyan's role was to read Stalin's letter at the party plenum in Armenia and to sign a list, prepared by the Armenian NKVD in agreement with Moscow, of persons to be arrested. His presence was meant to emphasize how seriously the Central Committee viewed the struggle with wreckers and, according to Mikoyan, it was an assignment he could not refuse.[26]

Mikoyan was accompanied to Yerevan by Malenkov. Beria, who at the time was in charge of the NKVD for the Caucasus region, appeared in the hall as Mikoyan was speaking. Mikoyan managed to finish his speech, but he had to struggle to hide his agitation. "Later," he wrote, "I understood that this too was part of the scenario to drive me into a corner and show that I had no choice except complete submission." He signed a list containing three hundred names, but he crossed out the name of Danush Shaverdian, a party comrade from his youth. Shaverdian was arrested anyway.[27]

On December 21, 1937, there was a grand ceremonial meeting for the NKVD in the Bolshoi Theater. Mikoyan praised the NKVD's head Nikolai Yezhov as "a talented faithful pupil of Stalin . . . beloved by the Soviet people," who had "achieved the greatest victory in the history of the party, a victory we will never forget." He concluded, "Learn the Stalinist style of work from Comrade Yezhov, as he learned it from Comrade Stalin."[28]

Mikoyan's grandson Vladimir said, "There was a decision of the politburo forcing him to make this speech. He read it with a grim face."

Mikoyan knew many of the officers caught up in Stalin's purge of the military, and he defended Gen. I. Uborevich, a close associate of Tukhachevsky's, to Stalin as an honest man. Stalin replied that his guilt was demonstrated by information in the hands of the NKVD. Regarding the charge that leading Soviet military officers were German spies, Stalin said, "It's incredible but it's a fact. They admit it." He circulated copies of confessions to members of the politburo in which the accused signed each page to avoid "falsification."[29] Of course, it was not mentioned that the defendants had been tortured. Stepan said, "We suffered over the arrest of people we knew. No one said at home that these are enemies. His conscience bothered him. But you either had to participate or become an enemy of the people."

Whatever his doubts, Mikoyan followed Stalin loyally, and his readiness to conform extended to relations with members of his own family. Sergo married Kuznetsov's daughter Alla in March 1949. Kuznetsov was arrested in August and beaten into giving a signed confession. Mikoyan received Alla in his Kremlin apartment. "It was very hard for me to speak to Alla," her father-in-law wrote in his memoirs. "Of course, I had to tell her the official version. . . . Alla took in my words bravely. Tears appeared in her eyes, and it was all she could do to keep from crying."

A short time later, Mikoyan called Sergo to his apartment and read him several passages from Kuznetsov's confession. To Mikoyan's amazement, Sergo said, "There are no serious charges . . . here. There are only thoughts and intentions. And the thoughts are not his. Maybe this was written by the investigator?" Mikoyan said that Kuznetsov signed each page. But his son was not impressed. He said that Kuznetsov had great respect for Stalin and kept the letter and cigarette box Stalin had sent to him in Leningrad. "I am sure that the case will be clarified and he will return," Sergo said.

"I couldn't tell him," wrote Mikoyan, "that Kuznetsov's fate was already predetermined by Stalin. He would never return."[30]

After the arrest, Mikoyan invited Kuznetsov's children to his dacha, a move that may have saved them from exile and an orphanage. It was a courageous act. Alexei Kosygin, who was minister of light industry at the time of Kuznetsov's arrest and was related to him through their wives, did not help Kuznetsov's children. When Kuznetsov's wife, Zinaida, who was also arrested, returned from Vladimir Prison in 1954, she met Kosygin's wife, who fell on her knees. "Forgive me," she said, "we were terribly afraid." After this, they did not have much contact.[31]

Stepan always assumed that his father was loyal to Stalin. But after Stalin died, Stepan saw for the first time that his father had actually disliked Stalin. For three consecutive days after Stalin's death, Stepan spent an hour in the Hall of Columns, where Stalin lay in state. To Stepan's surprise, when he told his father how he had paid tribute to the dead leader, Mikoyan replied, "In vain."

After Stalin's death, Mikoyan began to have contact with former prisoners and their families. Through his friend Lev Shaumian, who worked in the publishing house of the *Soviet Encyclopedia,* he was reunited with Shatunovskaya and Snegov. He had met Shatunovskaya in 1917 and Snegov in 1930. They told him about their arrests and the use of torture during interrogations, as well as the fates of dozens of mutual acquaintances, and he introduced them to Khrushchev. Their descriptions of the Terror and of conditions in the camps played an important role in the preparations for Khrushchev's speech at the 20th Party Congress.[32]

One story that Shatunovskaya told Mikoyan made a huge impact on him. She had been a prisoner in a women's camp, and she said that at one point, the guards had brought in a genuine Japanese spy. Everyone ran to look at her and began to ask, "Are you a real spy?" She answered angrily, "Yes! And I, at least, know why I'm here. And you cursed Communists are here for nothing, but I don't feel sorry for you." Mikoyan was astounded that there were ten thousand innocent victims and only one spy.[33]

Mikoyan was also informed about Stalin's crimes by Shaumian, who as a result of his work on the *Soviet Encyclopedia* had unofficial access to information. From Shaumian he learned that the majority of delegates of the 17th Party Congress and members of the Central Committee were repressed. According to his memoirs, these revelations were devastating to Mikoyan. "I considered everything," he wrote, "how this could have happened, why Stalin did this in relation to people who he knew very well. I constructed various guesses, but not a single one of them satisfied me or persuaded me."[34] The truth about the Stalin Terror, however, should not have been that surprising. Mikoyan himself had signed an arrest list containing three hundred names, and afterward virtually the

entire leadership of the Armenian party and government had been arrested. Moreover, he could not have been in doubt about the decision to
execute more than twenty-two thousand Polish prisoners of war, because
he was one of those who approved it.

Mikoyan persuaded Khrushchev that there was no more important task
than the condemnation of the Stalin regime. He did this partly by appealing to their shared desire to avoid blame. In statements later echoed by
Khrushchev in justifying his intention to denounce the Cult of Personality, Mikoyan said that if the present leaders failed to expose Stalin at the
first party congress after his death, someone else would do it, and then
"everyone will have a legal basis to consider us completely responsible for
the former crimes." On the other hand, he reasoned, if the present leaders
exposed Stalin's crimes, "we will defend our honor to some extent."[35]

In the end, Mikoyan regretted the Terror, but he was not able to accept
full responsibility for the crimes in which he participated. "There were
many things that we did not know," he wrote. "We believed in many
things and, in any case, simply could not change anything." He said that
those who criticize the Stalin-era leaders "are partially correct."[36] This
"partial" acknowledgement of guilt, however, was accompanied by critical
silences. Mikoyan did not mention Katyn in conversation with his family
or in his memoirs. He seems simply to have blotted out the memory of his
role. He probably came closest to the truth in 1965 or 1966, in the presence of fifty employees of the *Soviet Encyclopedia,* when he said, "We were
all scoundrels."[37]

The members of Mikoyan's family still struggle to evaluate his role.
"Why wasn't he brave enough to challenge what was going on?" said
Vladimir Mikoyan.

> I remember party times. We were also afraid to stand up and lose our
> careers. In the Leningrad museum of political history, there is the list
> of persons who signed the accusation against Tukhachevsky and the
> other generals. One of them was Krupskaya, Lenin's widow. What
> could they have done to her? She was an old, sick lady. Maybe she
> was frightened. Was she saving her position? She had no position to
> save. Everyone was in favor. I guess some really believed. Definitely,
> none of them had the courage to say I am against.

Stepan said, "We should relate to these people as persons who had no choice. Those who did more than necessary we should condemn. If a person did what he was forced to do, it is necessary to forgive. If he did more than was necessary, he should be condemned."

After the end of the Stalinist terror, obedience in the Soviet Union was guaranteed by bureaucratic compulsion rather than the threat of death. But this was more than enough to assure conformity. The post-Stalin leaders saw little alternative to carrying out the dictates of the regime. As a result, those who were in a position to pass judgment on their predecessors were themselves in need of being judged. This is clearly evident in the lives and careers of the two persons who arguably did the most to bring down the Soviet Union, Boris Yeltsin and Alexander Yakovlev.

On July 18, 1998, Yeltsin took part in the ceremonial reburial of the remains of the last tsar, Nicholas II, and his family in the Cathedral of Saints Peter and Paul in St. Petersburg. In his speech, he said,

> For many years, we remained silent about this monstrous crime but it's necessary to tell the truth. The violence in Yekaterinburg became one of the most shameful pages in our history. Committing to the earth the remains of the guiltless victims, we want to expiate the sins of our ancestors. Those are guilty who committed these crimes and those who for decades justified them. We are all guilty. . . . I bow my head before the victims of this merciless killing. . . . Let them rest in peace.[38]

Yeltsin's attendance at the funeral had immense significance. The Russian Orthodox patriarch, Alexei II, refused to recognize the reburied remains as those of the tsar and his family. Yeltsin's presence testified to the state's faith in their authenticity. With pro-Communist feeling in the country still strong in 1998, his attendance also represented a forceful condemnation on the part of the Russian state of the murder of the tsar and his family.

What Yeltsin did not mention, however, was his own role in eradicating the late tsar's memory. While head of the party organization in Sverdlovsk (now Yekaterinburg), Yeltsin had ordered that the Ipatev mansion, where the imperial family spent their last days and in which they were murdered, be leveled. On July 26, 1975, Yuri Andropov had informed the

Central Committee in a memo that the Ipatev house was being mentioned in anti-Soviet propaganda campaigns in the West. To prevent it from becoming an object of attention, he urged, the house should be razed. Eight days later, the Central Committee approved the destruction of the Ipatev house, and the Sverdlovsk oblast party committee was ordered to carry it out.[39] Nothing was done, however, until more than two years later, in the fall of 1977. Local conservationists reportedly had persuaded Yakov Ryabov, the oblast party first secretary, not to destroy a historical monument, and Ryabov, who did not want to go down in history for having destroyed the house, decided to sabotage the Central Committee decision.[40] He apparently hoped that the Moscow authorities would forget about it. They did not. Brezhnev finally sent a note to Yeltsin, telling him to proceed because the preservation of the house was about to be discussed by a committee of the United Nations. Yeltsin said that he found it "impossible to disobey," and a few days later, he sent bulldozers and steamrollers to destroy the house. By the next morning, the place where it had stood was marked only by a fresh patch of asphalt.[41]

Yeltsin later tried to give the impression that he had been shocked by the order to destroy the Ipatev house. In his memoir, *Against the Grain,* written during the perestroika period, Yeltsin said that he was not bothered by the large number of pilgrims who visited the site. When he received the secret politburo decree ordering its demolition, he wrote, he could not believe his eyes. He said that he met "sharp opposition" from his colleagues in the oblast party committee, who, insofar as the order was secret, would be blamed for the decision. Unlike Ryabov, however, Yeltsin dutifully carried out the order. "I can well imagine that sooner or later, we will be ashamed of this piece of barbarism," he wrote in his memoir, at a time when the situation in the country had completely changed. "Ashamed we may be but we can never rectify it."[42]

The historian Vladimir Pribylovsky, discussing the razing of the Ipatev house in an interview in 2009, said that Yeltsin had no real convictions. "You can say that he betrayed the ideas of Communism, but I think he never held them. When it was advantageous he was a Communist, when it stopped being advantageous, he became an anti-Communist. The idea of power—that was the ideology that he supported."[43] In his book, Yeltsin gave a somewhat different interpretation. He said that everything in the Soviet Union "was steeped in the methods of the command system," and he acted accordingly. Everything he did was "expressed in terms of pressure, threats and coercion." At the time, he wrote, these methods produced some results, but eventually "our stock of ideas and methods [was] exhausted." In the end, he experienced a feeling of wariness, of diminishing satisfaction, "of being up a blind alley."[44]

The case of Yakovlev is equally illustrative. After Gorbachev became the new party leader in April 1985, Yakovlev was put in charge of propaganda in the Central Committee, and in June 1987 he became a full member of the politburo. In that capacity he set out to destroy the Soviet totalitarian system and encouraged Soviet newspapers to expose party corruption. This was followed in April 1988 by a press campaign revealing the crimes of Stalin. Operating with Yakovlev's protection, the press published the facts of mass arrests and executions, the testimony of survivors, and even the recollections of executioners. The psychological crisis caused by exposure to this information helped bring about the collapse of the Soviet Union. His role in destroying the totalitarian regime earned Yakovlev the title "Alexander the Liberator."[45]

Yakovlev was put in charge of rehabilitation, and after the fall of the Soviet Union, he said that the rehabilitation of the victims of Communism became his life's mission. He plunged into the archives and spent hours reading through the documentation. "I could not sleep at night," he said, "and, to this day, when I reread the materials that we gathered for publication, it is guaranteed that I will not sleep."[46] The commission rehabilitated millions of individuals and established the truth about the Soviet regime's principal crimes.

Yakovlev, however, had not always been an opponent of the regime. For many years he had been a Communist ideologue. In 1965, as the deputy head of the propaganda department, he organized the disinformation campaign around the trial of Sinyavsky and Daniel, two writers condemned for publishing "anti-Soviet" works in the West. He determined in detail how the trial would be covered, who would be allowed in, and what they could write. The trial was officially "open," but only persons invited by the local party were admitted into the courtroom. Foreign correspondents were banned. A similar "openness" prevailed in Soviet dissident trials throughout the 1970s and 1980s.[47]

In 1969 Yakovlev wrote speeches and reports for Brezhnev. In his memoirs he described the Brezhnev period as characterized by massive corruption, "thievery, wastefulness, and the plugging of endless holes at the expense of the eating up of national resources." Kremlin propagandists tried to write only about successes, "about the flowering of socialist democracy, about the uninterrupted growth of the well-being of the people, about the unlimited support of the people for the party."[48]

Yakovlev acknowledged that he had written in the same vein.

> Especially funny were the reports about agitation-propaganda work. We reported how many agitators and propagandists worked day and night in this or that region or in general in the country, about their influence on people. And in reality none of the party officials ever laid eyes on a living agitator. Sometimes we, the workers of the central committee, during business trips were shown some head of a library or Komsomol official — these were the agitators. Everyone knew that this was a lie, but we created the impression that it was the truth.[49]

The falseness of Soviet propaganda and the real conditions of Soviet life left Yakovlev seething with indignation. When Gorbachev became the party leader and Yakovlev was named the propaganda chief, he resolved to do something about it. "I was the chief ideological official," he said later, "but the ideology I was defending was not Communist ideology."[50]

Yakovlev's championing of glasnost earned him enemies among Communists, who said he was an agent of the U.S. and of Zionism. At the 28th Party Congress, in July 1990, Gen. Alexander Lebed asked him, "Alexander Nikolaevich . . . how many faces have you got?"[51] Yakovlev was visibly embarrassed and did not respond. At a pro-Communist rally, a demonstrator held a sign depicting a soldier firing at a picture of Yakovlev with the words, "This time, he won't miss." In May 1991 Yakovlev was removed from the politburo, and on August 17 he was expelled from the party. When the pro-Communist coup took place two days later, he joined the democratic opposition.

After Yakovlev broke with Communism, he insisted repeatedly that Russians had to recognize their crimes. "There is no future for Russia," he said, "unless we learn a simple lesson. If you sin, you have to repent."[52] He suggested to Yeltsin and Putin that they make personal statements of repentance, but neither would. At the same time, however, Yakovlev was criticized as unwilling to follow his own advice. Alexander Podrabinek, a journalist and former dissident, wrote that when the Soviet authorities had arrested dissidents for anti-Soviet propaganda, Yakovlev had been in charge of propaganda, and "to this day [December 1994], he has not publicly repented for his antihuman activities."[53]

One could argue that Yakovlev's part in the fall of the Soviet Union and his work in rehabilitating millions of innocent victims was a form of repentance. In any case, he did speak of his role in the Soviet regime, though not always with the specificity his critics would have liked. In his memoirs, he wrote that although after the 20th Party Congress he devoted himself to seeking a way to end "this inhuman system," his efforts were based on "hope, not action." While admitting that he had "lived a double life of agonizing dissimulation," he said that he conformed and pretended but tried all the while "not to lose my bearings and disgrace myself."[54]

Yakovlev told me in 2003 that people often deny having committed crimes or having anything to repent for. "I say to such a person, 'You voted?' He says, 'I voted.' You did not object? 'I did not object.' You attended meetings? 'I attended meetings.' This means you participated and should repent. In the final analysis, this is the only path to a new future for this tortured country."[55]

The failure to hold the leaders responsible for the Soviet regime's crimes was, in some respects, the defensive reaction of a compromised society. Widespread criminality and mass complicity meant that the guilty could be judged only by the relatively less guilty. Given the subtlety of the effort at moral judgment this required, it was easiest not to judge at all. This was all the more true in light of the fact that, in many cases, the worst surviving Stalin-era criminals, once out of power, began to behave with a semblance of normality.

After the June plenum, Kaganovich was sent to Solikamsk in the Perm oblast to work as the manager of the Urals Potash Works. He had once insisted at a Communist Party plenum, "We don't shoot enough people," and in his previous jobs he had been merciless with his subordinates. At Solikamsk, however, he was "the model of a fair-minded boss." In 1961, at the age of sixty-seven, he retired to Moscow on a pension of 120 rubles a month. Every year, he vacationed at an ordinary rest home, where he was popular with other vacationers because of his talent as a raconteur. He never touched on the subject of the Terror, or his role in it.[56]

One day in the early 1970s, the actress Alissa Koonen, then over eighty, was visiting the grave of her husband, A. Y. Tairov, the former director of the Kamerny Theater, in the Novo-Devichy cemetery. Once extremely popular, the theater had been closed down in 1949 for "formalism." As she was standing at her husband's graveside, she was approached by an old man who told her how he had admired her performances. "Excuse me," she said, "but to whom am I speaking?"

"I am Lazar Moiseievich Kaganovich," the old man said. "Tell me, Alissa Georgiyevna, after what happened to Tairov and to you did your friends abandon you?"

"No, why should they?" the actress answered. "They always stuck by us."

"Yes," Kaganovich said, "your world is very different from ours."[57]

In the early 1980s Kaganovich could often be found in the courtyard of a building on the Frunze Embankment, playing dominoes with other old men. He was said to be the dominoes champion of the neighborhood. For a time, play had to be called off at the fall of dusk, but Kaganovich, apparently making use of some of his old contacts, persuaded the local authorities to provide a shelter with electric light for the benefit of his new comrades. As a result, the men were able to continue playing until late at night.[58]

After he was expelled from the presidium and the Central Committee, Georgy Malenkov was given the job of manager of the Ust-Kamenogorsk Hydroelectric Power Station in Western Siberia. Like Kaganovich, he acquired a reputation as a tolerant boss, so much so that the local party criticized him for "familiarity with the workers." After the 22nd Party Congress, he was expelled from the party and forced into retirement. This came after the party heard about his crimes, including his friendships with Yezhov and Beria and his presence during the interrogation and torture of prisoners.[59] Party secretaries who were summoned to meet with him were arrested as they entered his office or immediately after the meetings.

He lived in the same building as Kaganovich but, unlike his neighbor, was rarely seen in public and never spoke to ordinary people. He became so thin that members of the older generation did not always recognize him. He sometimes went to his daughter's dacha near Kratovo, traveling in silence on the suburban electric train, occasionally exchanging a word with his wife. He also had two sons, both scientists, of whom, according to Roy Medvedev, there were only good reports.[60] He vacationed at the Voronovo Sanatorium—reserved for official use by Gosplan, the state planning agency—where he avoided other vacationers and spent his time photographing nature. Once at Voronovo, however, he ran into the old Bolshevik Y. Fridman, who happened to pick up a lens that Malenkov had dropped.

"You know, Georgy Maximilianovich," Fridman said, "I spent fifteen years in the camps thanks to you." Malenkov said that he knew nothing about this. Fridman said, "I saw your signature on my file with my own eyes." Malenkov quickly broke off the conversation and left.[61]

In the 1980s there were rumors in Moscow that Malenkov had been baptized and regularly attended church. Some claimed to have seen him in the church in Mytishi or the one in the village of Ilyinskoye near Kratovo. It was also said that he went to the Yelokhov church near the Baumanskaya metro station in Moscow.[62]

The last member of the antiparty group was Molotov, Stalin's closest associate. After the June plenum, he was named the Soviet ambassador to Mongolia, a relatively important assignment. When the Chinese began showing too much respect for him as Stalin's closest comrade, he was transferred to Vienna to be the Soviet representative at the U.N. atomic energy agency. At the 22nd Party Congress, however, where his crimes were discussed publicly, he was removed from his posts and expelled from the party. He began the life of a pensioner, dividing his time between his family's apartment on Granovsky Street and its dacha at Zhurkovka, outside Moscow.[63]

Molotov never changed his views. The writer Ivan Stadnyuk, who succeeded in interviewing Molotov for a novel he was writing about the Second World War, asked him whether it was true, as Khrushchev claimed, that he had confirmed a list of three hundred persons sentenced to death as enemies of the people.

"It's the truth!"—without hesitation answered Molotov and his eyes gleamed with such inflexibility that I was almost beside myself. And he continued, "I would now have signed that list because I knew what all of these people represented. I don't have any doubts."[64]

In his later years, Molotov was seen frequently at exhibitions, concerts, and, most of all, the theater. These public appearances sometimes ended unpleasantly. A middle-aged woman once went up to him in Pushkin Square and screamed at him that he was a criminal and a murderer. Molotov hunched his shoulders and, without saying a word, hurried away. On another occasion, he joined a queue for tomatoes at a shop in Zhukovka. A woman stepped out of line and announced that she would not stand in line with an executioner. Molotov left in silence. Another time, at the opening of the play *The Steelworkers* at the Moscow Arts Theater, some members of the audience spotted him and asked him to autograph their programs. He seemed to come to life, but a young woman began screaming, "What are you doing? This man's an executioner. He destroyed hundreds of people!" The crowd around Molotov scattered, and he quickly left.[65]

Strangely, Molotov went to a cinema in Zhukovka that frequently showed Western films that were not put out for general release.[66] He also took an interest in the Voice of America. Viktor Erofeev, a Russian writer and the son of a Soviet diplomat, used to listen to Voice of America's Russian-language broadcasts as a teenager while sitting on a bench in the area where Molotov was resting. Late at night as he listened, he recalled, a man would emerge from the shadows and sit down on the bench next to him. When the broadcast was completed, he would get up and silently leave. That man was Molotov.[67]

Unraveling the issue of personal guilt involved moral criteria that post-Soviet Russia did not have. In the Soviet Union, a citizen's world shrank to the confines of a claustrophobic society that was based on an ideology and had abolished any higher spiritual sphere. Russians never fully renounced this world, and in the moral vacuum that followed the collapse of Communism, a view of the Soviet past flourished that was far removed from reality.

In her book *For What and with Whom We Fought*, Natalya Narochnitzkaya, a historian and former Duma deputy, wrote that the "demonization" of the Stalinist Soviet Union does not reflect real crimes committed by the Soviet regime but is "an instrument of international strategy" intended to "confirm everything that has been achieved by the West" since the Soviet Union collapsed. The idea, she argues, is not to bring the Soviet Union before some kind of Nuremberg Tribunal but "to drive Russia from the Baltic, Black Sea and Pacific Ocean."[68] Konstantin Zatulin, the first deputy chairman of the Duma, said that Russia needed to refute charges of Soviet atrocities that were being made, in particular, by the former Soviet republics to "adapt history to their goals."[69]

The Soviet past is often viewed not as a fabric of crimes but as a source of inspiration. This was demonstrated in 2009 by an incident around a shashlik, or kebab, restaurant in Moscow. The place had been called the Anti-Soviet Shashlik Restaurant. But at the behest of local city officials acting at the request of war veterans, the owners changed the name to the Soviet Shashlik Restaurant. This inspired an article by Alexander Podrabinek in the internet newspaper *Ezhednevny Zhurnal,* in which he criticized the veterans who helped bring pressure on the owners. "You were so angered by the name 'Anti-Soviet,'" Podrabinek wrote, "because you were at the top in the prisons and camps, commissars in the blocking detachments and executioners. And you, Soviet veterans, defended Soviet power and then were treated kindly by it and now are afraid of the truth and cling to your Soviet past."[70]

Podrabinek's article evoked an angry response from the Kremlin-sponsored youth group Nashi, which sued Podrabinek for slander and began picketing in front of his apartment, demanding that he leave the country. Podrabinek feared that the actions by Nashi were a prelude to physical attacks. "I received information from reliable sources," he wrote, "that . . . there was a decision to settle with me using any means."[71] He left his home and went into hiding. More than three thousand persons signed a statement in support of Podrabinek on the *Ezhednevny Zhurnal* website.

The defensive reaction of many Russians to criticism of the Soviet past was epitomized by Valentina Matvienko, the governor of St. Petersburg, during a speech she gave on Russia's supposed need for a national idea. "All these years, like masochists," she said, "we excoriated ourselves for the past, present, and future. And this depressed the spirit of the nation — we have to deliver ourselves from this, raise our head, straighten up our shoulders, it is necessary to understand that whatever stage in our history we went through, we are a great nation, a great people. However we evaluated the past, this is part of our history, we lived it and don't have the right to speak about it disrespectfully. Millions of people gave their lives for the USSR, whole generations constructed this state, and we can't cross this out, blacken it and stamp on it."[72]

The lack of self-awareness that makes such statements possible is, in fact, the failure of individuals to face the fact that complicity in a criminal system is criminality. Of those who were prominent during the Stalin period and identified with Stalin's policies, very few had the inner strength to renounce their past behavior. One of those who did was the writer Konstantin Simonov, who rose to prominence during the Great Terror and wrote poems praising Stalin, one of which included the lines:

> The whole people
> Are his friends:
> You cannot count them,
> They are like drops of water in the sea.

Simonov was described as "Stalin's favorite," and for decades he enjoyed a privileged existence, but in the last years of his life he came to judge his collaboration with the regime very harshly. In his memoirs, which were dictated as he lay dying in 1979, he wrote:

> To be honest about those times, it is not only Stalin that you cannot forgive, but you yourself. It is not that you did something bad — maybe you did nothing wrong, at least on the face of it — but that you became accustomed to evil. The events that took place in 1937–38 now appear extraordinary, diabolical, but to you, then a young man of 22 or 24, they became a kind of norm, almost ordinary. You lived in the midst of these events, blind and deaf to everything, you saw and heard nothing when people all around you were shot and killed, when people all around you disappeared.[73]

Throughout the post-Stalinist period, many people were prepared to criticize the criminal past of others, but Simonov is one of the few who was ready directly to criticize himself. In the end, his judgment is severe, but he stands out against the background of thousands more culpable than he who remained silent. It's possible that more persons would have stepped forward if there was social pressure to do so, but there was no will in Russian society to force such an outcome. In its absence, those who contributed to the crimes of Communism were left alone, allowed to die with their rewards and their rationalizations.

CHAPTER 9

The Roots of the Communist Idea

■

In the last years of his life, Alexander Solzhenitsyn, who did more than anyone else to call attention to Communism's crimes, became a strong supporter of Vladimir Putin's rule, even though it was blatantly undemocratic. In an interview with the German magazine *Der Spiegel* in May 2007, Solzhenitsyn depicted Putin as Russia's savior. "Putin inherited a ransacked and bewildered country, with a poor and demoralized people," he said. "And he started to do what was possible — a slow and gradual restoration."[1]

The appearance of the chronicler of the Gulag in the ranks of those praising Putin took many by surprise, but in fact Solzhenitsyn was only being true to his long-held beliefs. In the early 1970s, in his *Letter to the Soviet Leaders,* he proposed retaining moderate authoritarian rule in Russia after the fall of the Soviet Union to "preserve the nation's health." In his literary diary, excerpts of which appeared in *Novy Mir,* he described Sakharov's human rights ideology as a form of anarchism. "One ought to have the whole picture in view," he wrote, "including each person's duties and the rights of the state."[2]

Insofar as rights inhere in the individual, Solzhenitsyn's reference to the "rights of the state" was perplexing. The state has rights in relation to other states, but in relation to its own citizens, it has duties. By "rights of the state," Solzhenitsyn apparently meant the prerogative of the state to ignore the rights of its citizens.

During the Soviet period, Solzhenitsyn refused to take part in campaigns on behalf of victims of political repression. Sakharov recalled in his memoirs: "I asked him if there is anything he could do to help Grigorenko and Marchenko. Solzhenitsyn answered sharply: 'No! These people decided to ram, they chose their fate themselves and it is impossible to save them. Any attempt to do so may damage both them and others.' I froze at the sight of his position, so contrary to normal human reactions."[3]

Solzhenitsyn's emphasis on the state reflected the fact that his first concern was the power and position of the Russian nation. In his 1978 Harvard commencement address, he described Russia as a "deeply rooted, ancient, autonomous culture," full of "riddles and surprises" for the West, as well as its moral superior. Communism, he argued, had given Russians a spiritual training "far in advance of Western experience." In the East, life's "complexity and mortal weight" had produced "stronger, deeper and more interesting characters" than the products of standardized Western well-being. The West was less and less likely under these circumstances to provide the world with a model for emulation.[4]

Solzhenitsyn was widely seen as a fighter against political persecution and defender of millions. It would be more accurate to say that he objected to political persecution when it was done for the wrong reasons. This lack of a commitment to universal values was reflected in all the most important aspects of his political thinking.

First of all, Solzhenitsyn did not believe in the priority of what in the West are accepted as irreducible human rights. In spring 2006 the Tenth World Russian People's Assembly, a forum organized by the Russian Orthodox Church, was held in Moscow with the participation of Metropolitan Kirill, the head of external church relations, who, in January 2009, became the Orthodox patriarch. The forum explicitly rejected the priority of human rights, saying that other values are equally important and that observance of human rights should not, in any case, be allowed to threaten the existence of the nation. In the event of a conflict between human rights and the values of the nation, the statement said, state and society should "harmoniously" combine them.[5]

Solzhenitsyn upheld this position. In an interview with the newspaper *Moscow News* in May 2006, he said,

> Metropolitan Kirill pointed out, quite justly, that "realization of freedoms should not jeopardize the existence of the Motherland or offend against . . . religious feelings or ethnic sentiments," and that

sacred things are values on a par with "human rights." Unlimited "human rights" are what our cave ancestor had when no one forbade him to snatch a piece of meat from his neighbor or hit him over the head with a club.

He said it was necessary to defend not "human rights" but "human obligations."[6]

Solzhenitsyn also displayed an openly imperialistic attitude toward the former Soviet republics. In his book *How to Rebuild Russia*, published in 1990, he proposed that Russia, Belarus, and Ukraine, which he called the "three branches" of "our people," become a "Russian Union" after the anticipated breakup of the Soviet Union. Most important, Solzhenitsyn insisted, was that Ukraine was a key part of the "Russian Union."

> Today, to separate Ukraine means to cut across millions of families and people: such an intermingling of populations, entire oblasts with a Russian majority; so many people struggling to choose for themselves one nationality of two; so many — persons of mixed origins; so many mixed marriages although up until now no one ever considered them mixed. . . . Brothers! There is no need for this cruel division! This is the darkness of the Communist years. We together endured the Soviet period, together fell into this ditch and together we'll get out of it.[7]

Solzhenitsyn said that Russia should give up the Baltic republics, the Caucasian republics, and the Central Asian republics except for northern Kazakhstan, which should become part of the new Slavic state. He justified the partition of Kazakhstan with the argument that northern Kazakhstan was inhabited by Russians and, in any case, Kazakhstan's "current enormous territory was divided by the Communists without thought. . . . Wherever a nomad's herd passed once a year, there was Kazakhstan."[8]

When it came to assessing the crimes of Communism, Solzhenitsyn was primarily concerned not with individual responsibility but with the supposed collective guilt of nationalities. He called for repentance but at the same time tried to absolve ethnic Russians of guilt. While he did not deny that Russians bore some responsibility for Soviet crimes, he argued that they were mainly the victims. Those with the most to repent were the Jews.

This attempt to treat ethnic Russians as less responsible than other nationalities for Soviet crimes has the effect — intended or not — of minimizing the crimes' significance. In the Soviet Union, crimes were committed by members of every nationality and for ideological, not national, reasons. The question of the respective guilt of specific nationalities is therefore deeply irrelevant. More important, it suggests that Soviet atrocities were not overwhelming, and by implication should not much occupy us, because a settling of scores between Soviet national groups is more important than the overall tragedy. The interviewers from *Der Spiegel* reminded Solzhenitsyn that Putin had also tried to downplay Russian responsibility for Soviet crimes and criticized attempts to provoke "unjustified remorse" among Russians. Solzhenitsyn refused to condemn Putin's words, saying, "Unremitting reproaches from outside are counterproductive."[9]

Solzhenitsyn's attitude toward Soviet crimes is perhaps best illustrated in his work *Two Hundred Years Together,* which he said was intended to give an "objective" account of Russian-Jewish relations. In the introduction, he writes, "I appeal to both sides — the Russians and the Jews — for patient mutual understanding and admission of their own share of sin."[10] Inasmuch as it was the Jews who were subject to violence and discrimination on national grounds in Russia, the reference to the sins of both groups is itself a sign of tendentiousness. In fact, the book is intended mainly to weigh the guilt of two groups, Russians and Jews, for the Communist regime, with the emphasis on the guilt of the latter.

Although Solzhenitsyn acknowledges that there were injustices against Jews in tsarist Russia, he argues that the support Jews gave to Bolshevism constitutes a burden of Jewish guilt toward Russians. The Bolsheviks appealed to the Jews in the first days of their rule to work in the Soviet apparatus, "and many, very many went — and went immediately." He quotes the recollections of I. F. Nazhivin, who wrote of the early years of Soviet rule that in the Kremlin and the government, "Everywhere there was incredible slovenliness and disorder. Everywhere there were Latvians, Latvians, Latvians and Jews, Jews, Jews. I was never an anti-Semite, but here the quantity of them struck my eyes and all at a very early age."[11]

Solzhenitsyn writes that the "population of Russia, as a whole, regarded the new [revolutionary] terror as a Jewish terror" and offers tacit support for this perception. He quotes Lev Krichevsky's statement that "in 1918, at the time of the Red Terror, ethnic minorities made up about 50 percent of the central staff of the Cheka." Solzhenitsyn adds that Jews were "quite prominent" among them.[12] Cathy Young, in an article in the May 2004 issue of *Reason,* pointed out that Solzhenitsyn omitted Krichevsky's data, according to which Jews made up less than 4 percent of the Cheka staff and held 8 percent of executive positions. But in other situations, Young writes, Solzhenitsyn used exact numbers. He pointed out, for example, that six of the twelve investigators in the "department for the suppression of counterrevolution" were Jewish.[13]

In the 1930s, Solzhenitsyn writes, the Jews were in many respects a "ruling class" in the Soviet Union, at least until 1937–38, the years of the Great Terror. In 1936, in the government, nine of the people's commissars were Jews, the majority of the presidium of Gosplan, the state planning agency, were Jews, and Jews were prominent in the ministries of construction, heavy industry, and internal trade. As a result, Solzhenitsyn writes, "Soviet Jews received in the Soviet Union a weighty share of the state, industrial, and economic leadership of the country."[14]

In his interview with *Der Spiegel,* Solzhenitsyn said that he was not implying in his book that the Jews carry more responsibility than others for the failed Soviet experiment, only calling for self-reflection. "Every people must answer morally for all of its past—including that past that is shameful," he said. "It is in that spirit, specifically, that it would behoove the Jewish people to answer both for the revolutionary cutthroats and the ranks willing to serve them. Not to answer before other peoples, but to oneself to one's consciousness and before God. Just as we Russians must answer—for the pogroms, for those merciless arsonist peasants, for those crazed revolutionary soldiers, for those savage sailors."[15]

Assessing the guilt of various ethnic groups in the Soviet Union, however, avoids the question of the responsibility of the nation as a whole. Some of the extremes to which it leads are illustrated in the writing of Solzhenitsyn's friend the mathematician Igor Shafarevich, whose essays circulated widely in samizdat during the Soviet period and have since been published in a book entitled *The Russian Question.* Like Solzhenitsyn, Shafarevich describes the participation of Jews in the revolutionary movement and the large number of Jews in the first Soviet government and in the Cheka. Unlike Solzhenitsyn, however, who in *Two Hundred Years Together* frequently cites Jewish and Israeli sources in a studied effort to appear reasonable, Shafarevich often lapses into unmistakable paranoia.

After the Bolshevik seizure of power, he writes, power was in the hands of three persons, Lenin, Sverdlov, and Trotsky, the last two of whom were Jews.

> At the head of the army stood Trotsky. Petrograd was run by Zinoviev, Moscow by Kamenev, foreign policy was ruled by Radek, the Comintern by Zinoviev, the press by Steklov. . . . What is even more striking, all of the non-Jewish leaders had Jewish wives. The wife of Dzerzhinsky was Sonya Mushkat, one wife of Bukharin was Gurvich, the other — Luria; the wife of Rykov was Marshak, Molotov — Zhemchuzhina (Pearl Karpovskaya), Voroshilov — Gorbman, Kirov — Markus, Yezhov — Yevgenya Solomonovna Notkina, Kuibyshev — Kogan, Andreev — Khazan.[16]

Shafarevich quotes Vasily Shulgin, a conservative Duma member and anti-Semite, who spoke of the large number of Jews in the Kiev Cheka. Ironically, he also quotes Shulgin as saying that the number of Jews in the Cheka did not really matter. "Even if in these places there was not a single Jew, nonetheless all these violent acts would still be the work of Jewish hands for the simple reason that the Communist Party, in the name of which all this was done on the all-Russian scale, was run by Jews." Addressing himself to Jews, Shulgin adds: "You complained that during the rule of the 'Russian historic power' there were Jewish pogroms, but these were children's games compared to the all-Russian devastation caused by eleven years of your total power."[17]

Shafarevich adds: "Of course, this 'all-Russian devastation' was accomplished not exclusively by Jewish hands but by Communist power. But this does not remove the question of why Jewish forces took part in the 'devastation' with so much enthusiasm."[18]

Inasmuch as Communism was based on the notion of the conflict between classes, not races, and was explicitly internationalist, one might wonder how the nationality of the Communists was relevant to events in Russia. Shafarevich attempts to answer this question. He writes that nationality (not personality, life experience, profession, or moral values) is the most important aspect of a person's identity. It is the factor that makes a person a participant in history. From his people, Shafarevich writes, the individual receives his language, folklore, art, and awareness of his historical fate. When the two-sided interaction between the individual and his people is interrupted, the result is the same as in nature, the creation of a kind of desert. "More concretely, the interest of a person to work disappears as well as his interest in the fate of his country. Life becomes a senseless burden, youth seeks an outlet in irrational bursts of violence, men turn into alcoholics and drug addicts, and women cease to give birth. The nation dies out."[19]

Why, then, given the supposed importance of national characteristics, did the Russian people choose to commit suicide by adopting Communism? Shafarevich argues that Russians did not really embrace Communism, which was an ideology with no roots in the Russian tradition. In the early years of Soviet power, he writes, it was not Russians but Jews who were responsible for Soviet crimes. "In reality there is hardly another case in history, when in the life of some country, representatives of the Jewish part of the population exercised such enormous influence." Shafarevich writes that the reason Jews played such a crucial role in the crisis of Russian history was their conception of themselves as the "Chosen People," who were destined to rule the world. "Twenty centuries were lived among alien peoples in complete isolation from all the influences of the external world which was understood as 'tref' [unclean], a source of infection and sin." It is possible to imagine, Shafarevich writes, "what kind of ineradicable trace should be left in the soul by such an education beginning in children and a life led according to these principles from generation to generation for twenty centuries."[20]

The notion of a special "saving mission" for the Russian state is not new but is an intellectual tendency shared by many of Russia's greatest thinkers and writers. It is part of what prevents present-day Russia from acknowledging the responsibility of the Soviet Union as a nation for the crimes of the Communist period and, in that way, making a clean break with its past. At a psychological level, this failure is easy to understand. If the Russian state has a special, God-given role, it almost by definition could not have been guilty of mass crimes.

Ultimately, the quasi-deification of the Russian state grew out of the fusion of religion and politics that is a distinctive characteristic of Russian history. Christianity came to Russia from Byzantium, but the Russians, under siege from infidels on the edge of the civilized world, clung to the "tenets and rites of their faith with a stubbornness and fanaticism that far outdid the worldly attitudes of the Mother Church."[21]

In 1439, when Byzantium, under pressure from the Turks, agreed to a reunion with the Catholic Church in a desperate effort to save itself, the treaty was denounced in Moscow as a betrayal of Orthodoxy, and one of its signatories, Metropolitan Isidor, the head of the Russian church, was imprisoned in a monastery. When Byzantium fell to the Turks in 1453, Russia took this as a sign that God was punishing the Greeks for their apostasy.

The fall of Byzantium, however, left Russia as the only nation professing Orthodoxy, and Russians came to see their state as the foremost protector of genuine Christianity in a profane world. The idea began to be expressed that Moscow was the Third Rome, the successor to Rome and Byzantium and a new center of religious and imperial authority. In 1510 the monk Philotheus composed an address to the tsar, describing Moscow's role as follows:

> Know then, O pious Tsar, that all the Orthodox Christian realms have converged in thy single Empire. Thou art the only Tsar of the Christians in all the universe. . . . Observe and hearken, O pious Tsar, that all Christian Empires have converged in thy single one, that two Romes have fallen, but the third stands, and no fourth can ever be. Thy Christian Empire shall fall to no one.[22]

From the fifteenth century onward, the role of the Russian state as the protector of Orthodoxy led to its being treated by Russians as semidivine. The state steadily subordinated the Orthodox Church, its only potential competitor for spiritual authority, reducing it to the status of a department of the state bureaucracy. In the absolutist state that emerged, the tsar was infused with mystical authority and came to be regarded as the country's godlike political and spiritual ruler. The state was seen not only as the guardian of the one true Christian faith but also as the vehicle through which Russia brought to the rest of the world "the revelation that had been granted to her alone."[23]

The way Russians viewed the state had consequences for how they viewed themselves. Tibor Szamuely has written that the Tsar of Muscovy was surrounded by an atmosphere of religious worship that was "truly Oriental" in character, with "Byzantine ceremonial, resounding incantations, hyperbolic praise, and groveling obeisance." Through the tsar, an "aura of sanctity was transmitted to the state . . . and *mutatis mutandis,* to the Russian people as a whole."[24] Russia's greatest writers frequently felt that they could not oppose the state without rejecting Russia itself.

Writers and poets in Russia have long been considered the country's conscience, but few have sought to challenge the root of Russia's problems in the Russian state tradition. Injustice and oppression in Russia, no matter how vividly depicted in their works, frequently exist in a vacuum unconnected to a system that treats the state as sacred and deprives the individual of the most fundamental rights.

The inherent conflict between moral values and support for a repressive regime was most easily resolved for Russia's conservative writers, who were outspoken in their support of the Russian state. Oddly, however, support for Russia's saving mission and the special role of the Russian state was also demonstrated by those writers who were the most critical of the condition of the Russian people and most inclined to condemn the burden of the nation's past.

Perhaps the most outstanding example of a conservative writer is Russia's national poet, Alexander Pushkin, who started his political evolution as a liberal but came to believe that cultural progress in Russia was dependent on the autocracy. "I cannot fail to note," he wrote, "that from the accession to the throne of the Romanov dynasty in Russia it was the government that has always led in education and enlightenment. The nation always follows lazily, and sometimes also unwillingly."[25]

Pushkin was harassed by official censorship. Nicholas I served as his personal censor. He was also tormented by Count Alexander Benckendorff, the chief of police, who reprimanded him for reading his historic drama *Boris Godunov* in the Moscow salons before it was submitted to the tsar, and by S. S. Uvarov, the minister of education. The result was that he never saw a single one of his plays performed on the stage, and many of his poems had to be passed from hand to hand in manuscript. Despite this, Pushkin's support for the monarchy led him to endorse even preventive censorship.

Pushkin believed that books were potentially dangerous. Every government has the right to forbid people to preach on the squares, he wrote, but this actually accounts for little because "the action of man is instantaneous and isolated." The action of a book, on the other hand, is "manifold and ubiquitous." But laws against the abuse of book printing "do not prevent evil and rarely stop it." The answer is censorship, which "can achieve both."[26]

In a memorandum in 1826, Pushkin agreed with the tsar that the Decembrist revolt sprang from "idleness of minds" and "willfulness of thoughts." His solution was to suppress home schooling and impose severe punishments for the circulation of manuscripts, just as he had been forbidden to circulate his own manuscripts.[27]

Pushkin acknowledged that a gulf existed between Russia and Europe. He once called his fellow citizens orangutans and said that living in Russia was like "living in a privy," but he defended Russia's role in history and said that although he was "far from admiring everything I see around me," nothing would lead him to change his fatherland.[28] He argued that Russia had absorbed the Mongol armies and forced them to turn back, its "martyrdom" saving Christian civilization. Commenting on this "strange and ill informed argument," Richard Pipes pointed out that far from being "absorbed," the Mongol armies had ruled Russia for two centuries and turned back from further conquests only because their khan had died and they wanted to take part in the election of his successor.[29]

Another Russian who supported the autocracy was Nikolai Gogol, Russia's first great prose writer. He regarded Russia's autocratic form of government as far superior to democracy and willed by providence, power's "complete and perfect form." According to Gogol, every event in the fatherland's history, beginning with the Mongol yoke, was aimed at concentrating power in the hands of one person in order for him to raise an empire and direct its people "towards that supreme light to which Russia cries out."[30]

Gogol believed that autocracy was endemic to Russia and praised the Romanov dynasty because it came to power not by conquest but by an act of "love," the election of Michael Romanov to the throne. "All unanimously, from the boyars down to the last landless peasant," he wrote, "decreed with a single voice that he should be on the throne."[31] A state without an absolute monarch, according to Gogol, "is an orchestra without a conductor; all the musicians could be excellent, but if there is no one to control them with his baton, the concert will not take place."[32]

Gogol was devoted to Russia because it professed Orthodox Christianity, which he believed was the only true religion. He accepted the Orthodox principles of submissiveness and acceptance of one's station in life and counseled others to do the same. He died virtually penniless after renouncing his possessions. This meek acceptance of fate also led him to defend serfdom and class privilege, as well as the notion of the tsar as the "head of this supreme harmony." Gogol predicted that the second coming of Christ would occur in Russia.[33]

The greatest supporter of the Russian autocracy, however, was Fyodor Dostoevsky. He often commented on politics in the periodicals he edited, particularly *Grazhdanin* (The citizen), and in his *Diary of a Writer,* always insisting on Russia's special mission. Dostoevsky acknowledged the backwardness of Russians, who he said were "crude and ignorant and given to darkness and debauchery." But it was necessary, he insisted, to judge them "not by that vileness that they often do but by those great and saintly things which in his vileness, the Russian continually aspires to." At the same time, he writes, not all Russians are scoundrels. "There are also saints. . . . They glow themselves and light up the path for others."[34]

Dostoevsky was convinced that there was not "a villain or scoundrel among the Russians that did not know that he was disgusting and vile," whereas among other peoples a person who does evil congratulates himself and pretends he is the flower of civilization. "And if there is great filth, the Russian is saddened by it most of all . . . and believes that all of this is transitional and temporary, a delusion of the devil, that the darkness will end and that there will unfailingly appear some type of eternal light."[35]

For Dostoevsky, Russia before Peter the Great was a society characterized by an appreciation of its own uniqueness. It understood that "it carries within itself a treasure which does not exist anywhere else — Orthodox Christianity, that she is the keeper of Christ's truth, the ultimate truth of the genuine image of Christ which has faded in all other faiths and in all other peoples."[36] The Petrine reforms opened Russia and made it possible for it to present this treasure, Russian Orthodoxy, to the world.

"Through the reforms of Peter," Dostoevsky wrote, "the Russian Moscow idea multiplied and spread." Russians acknowledged their "universal mission" and "could not fail to recognize that our personality and our role was unlike that of other peoples." The difference lay in the fact that every other nation "lives exclusively for itself," whereas Russia acts out of the conviction that "we are everyone's servants in the interests of general reconciliation." In this, he argued, is Russia's greatness, because it leads to the "final unification" of humanity. "The one who wants to be higher than all others in God's Kingdom — becomes the servant of all."[37]

Dostoevsky believed that having been "brought up like beasts" and "suffered tortures . . . such as no other people in the world could have endured," the Russians were uniquely suited to lead humanity to its spiritual redemption. Russia never acted in politics from selfish interests. In fact, it mostly served the interests of others (which, he believed, would be obvious to Europe if it were not so blinded by distrust and hatred). Russia supported the unity of the Slavs, he wrote, not for the sake of seizure but "in the service of humanity." This self-sacrificing unselfishness, according to Dostoevsky, was Russia's strength and the future of the Russian mission.[38]

Like Solzhenitsyn a century later, Dostoevsky was concerned with Russia's relations with its neighbors. In particular, he was obsessed with the "Eastern Question," the fate of Constantinople and the Balkans, an area where he believed Russia's mission was particularly manifest. Russia, according to Dostoevsky, had a "moral right" to Constantinople as the leader of Orthodoxy and as the patron and protector of it, a role it acquired under Tsar Ivan III when he accepted the Byzantine two-headed eagle as Russia's emblem, and when under Peter the country gained the strength to realize its mission and became the single patron of Orthodoxy and the peoples professing it. In the end, he insisted, "Constantinople will be ours." This would happen not through violence, he wrote, but on its own, naturally. The only reason it had not already happened was that the time had not been ripe. Constantinople was the key to Russia's future. "In it," Dostoevsky wrote, "is . . . the main way for us to the fullness of history." Taking over the city would make possible a unification with Europe "on a new, powerful fruitful basis."[39]

Pushkin and Dostoevsky were politically engaged. Gogol was not. But all three, in their political writing, treated Russia as too sacred to be viewed objectively. Their attitude was summed up by another militant defender of the autocracy, the nineteenth-century romantic poet Fyodor

Tyutchev, in lines that are known to every Russian. On the subject of Russia, Tyutchev wrote:

> Russia cannot be understood by the mind
> Nor measured by the common mile
> Her status is unique, without kind —
> Russia can only be believed in.

Other Russian writers were willing to acknowledge the nation's historical vices in a manner that was completely unambiguous. But even in these cases, there was a strong tendency to support the supererogatory claims of the Russian state. Nowhere was this tendency more perplexing than in the two writers who, it can be argued, analyzed the Russian character better than anyone else, Pyotr Chaadaev in the nineteenth century and Nikolai Berdyaev in the twentieth.

Probably no writer, Russian or Western, wrote with greater force about Russia's shortcomings than did Pyotr Chaadaev, a religious thinker who became Russia's first victim of psychiatric repression. Chaadaev composed a series of *Philosophical Letters,* which circulated in manuscript in 1828–30. In September 1836 the first *Letter* was published in Moscow in the journal *Telescope.* Its subject was the fate of Russia. N. N. Nadezhdin, the editor of *Telescope,* obtained a copy and asked Chaadaev for permission to publish it after it had been miraculously passed by the censor and set in type. Chaadaev agreed, seeing in this situation the hand of providence. The article, in which Chaadaev argued that Russia had contributed nothing to civilization, caused a huge scandal in Russian society.

"What is for other peoples simply a habit, instinct," Chaadaev wrote, "for us it is necessary to drive into our heads with the blows of a hammer. . . . We grow but don't mature, we move forward but in an oblique direction, in effect, along lines that don't lead to a goal." He argued that of Russians it is possible to say, "We comprise an exception among peoples. We belong to those of which do not constitute a constituent part of humanity."[40]

Chaadaev said that all the peoples of the West have a family resemblance, but each also has special characteristics rooted in history and tradition. Each individual in these countries possesses a share of this general inheritance. "These are the ideas of duty, justice, rights, order." These qualities are constituent elements of the social life of these countries. This, he said, is "the atmosphere of the West . . . the physiology of the European." Chaadaev contrasted this to the psychology of the Russian, who, he wrote, "is not in a condition to concentrate his thinking on any line of ideas," and whose participation in the progress of human reason "amounts to blind, superficial, very often muddle-headed imitation of other peoples." The result, he wrote, is that there is in Russians "a lack of stability, a lack of a certain consistency in mind, a certain logic. The Western syllogism is to us alien. In our best minds there is something worse than superficiality. The best ideas, in the absence of connections and consistency, like sterile outbreaks, paralyze in our brains. A person loses himself when he is not in a condition to connect with what was before him and what will be after him; he loses any firmness, any confidence."[41]

Chaadaev said that foreigners praise Russians for selfless courage but do not notice the lack of depth and indifference to good and evil from which that quality derives. Russia does not have a group of thinkers capable of inspiring and guiding the nation, he wrote. "The experience of time for us does not exist. Centuries and generations pass for us without result. . . . The general laws of humanity are reduced to nothing. Alone in the world we gave the world nothing and took nothing from the world. We did nothing to assist the movement forward of human reason, and everything we received from this movement we distorted."[42]

The reaction on publication was immediate: Chaadaev's *Letter* was described as "horrible confusion," "noise," and "frenzy." E. M. Khitrovo, an acquaintance of Pushkin's, wrote that Chaadaev "should be unhappy over the fact that he accumulated in himself so much hatred to his country and to his countrymen."[43] The Austrian ambassador, Count Finkelman, in his report to Chancellor Metternich on November 7, 1836, wrote that the letter fell "like a bomb amidst Russian vanity and all attempts at political and religious superiority to which they are very much inclined in the capital."[44]

Perhaps more important, the article outraged Russian officials. Tsar Nicholas I read the *First Philosophical Letter* and wrote, "Having read the article, I find it a blend of insolent senselessness worthy of a lunatic."[45] There was hesitation in official circles over how to deal with the author — whether to charge him with a crime or declare him insane. The minister of education, Uvarov, insisted on Chaadaev's criminality. He said that the article revealed "not the delirium of a madman but instead the systematic hatred of a person cold bloodedly insulting the holy of holy and most precious thing, his country." Nicholas, however, decided in favor of pronouncing him mad. He believed that in this way it would be possible not only to discredit Chaadaev's ideas but place them outside the limits of debate. Many persons wanted to answer Chaadaev, but the delirium of a madman was not a subject for discussion.[46]

Count Alexander von Benckendorff, the head of the gendarmerie, was called to the tsar and told to prepare an order for Chaadaev to be declared mentally ill and subjected to forced treatment. The order was presented to Nicholas, who wrote on it, "very good." In the words of Chaadaev's biographer, M. O. Gershenson, "a more cynical mocking by physical force of thought, the word, and human dignity had not been seen, even in Russia."[47]

The order said that the *Philosophical Letter* by a certain "Mr. Cheodaev" living in Moscow had given rise to general amazement. "In it, the author speaks about Russia, about the Russian people, its understanding, faith and history with such contempt that it is unintelligible even in what way a Russian could lower himself to such an extent to write something similar." Nonetheless, the residents of Moscow, "always distinguishing themselves with common sense and being full of a feeling of the dignity of the Russian people, came to the conclusion that such an article could not be written by a fellow countryman who retained all his faculties." They "not only did not turn their anger against Mr. Cheodaev but, on the contrary, expressed genuine sadness about the extent of the destruction of his mental faculties, which could be the only explanation for the authorship of such an absurdity." Thus "a feeling of compassion about "the unhappy situation of Mr. Cheodaev was shared by the entire Moscow public." The order called for providing him with the necessary care and medical relief and measures to prevent him from being exposed to "the harmful influence of the raw and cold air." In a word, "everything was to be done to restore his health."[48]

In addition to this order against Chaadaev, *Telescope* was banned and its editor Nadezhdin was exiled. The censor, A. B. Boldirev, the rector of Moscow University, was removed from his post. On November 1 Chaadaev was invited to the chief of police, where he was read the order pronouncing him mentally ill. He was ordered not to leave the area and was subjected to daily visits by a physician as well as general police super-vision. According to his contemporaries, Chaadaev was deeply shaken by the punishment. A. I. Turgenev wrote: "He freed his horses, sits at home, has lost weight terribly and has spots on his face." Later, he wrote: "He doesn't leave his home. I fear that he may really go mad." The daily visits by a doctor, however, soon came to an end, and after a year, police super-vision was lifted on condition that Chaadaev not write anything further.[49]

Despite this, he began to work on a new text, *Apology of a Madman*. He did this not to appease the authorities but to develop his own ideas, which now, despite what he wrote in the *First Philosophical Letter*, included a belief in Russia's mission to create God's Kingdom on earth. He came to this belief paradoxically, on the basis of his negative assessment of Russia's past.

Russia's path to the future had been opened, in Chaadaev's estimation, by Peter the Great. Peter found at home "only a sheet of white paper and with his strong hand wrote on it the words, 'Europe' and 'West.'" This "was only possible with a nation . . . whose traditions were powerless to create her future." If Russians were so obedient to the call for a new life, "this was obviously because there was nothing in our past that could justify resistance."[50]

Chaadaev reasoned that culture grows from the work of many genera-tions and, as a result, the happiest nation is the one that came to maturity later because it can inherit the moral and material legacy of past genera-tions. Russia was not only in a position to acquire the results of others' labor. It could also make better choices unhindered by the weight of the past. "I believe," Chaadaev wrote, "that we came after others in order to do things better than they did, in order not to fall into their mistakes, their delusions and superstitions." He said that the position of Russia allowed it "the possibility to contemplate and judge the world" free from "unbridled passions and petty cupidity." Russia was, in fact, summoned to decide many problems of the social order and "answer the most fundamental questions that concern humanity."[51]

Chaadaev believed that Russia was free of prejudice because, having no real past, it possessed no living legends, and dead legends have no force. According to Gershenzon, the more Chaadaev considered this, "the more he saw in it something providential."[52] Under these circumstances, any attempt to assimilate with Europe was contrary to Russia's mission and was therefore absurd and harmful. "We meet every new idea with a virgin mind," he wrote.[53] At the same time, the Orthodox faith, by virtue of its estrangement from the world, preserved the spirit of Christianity in a purer form than Catholicism.[54]

Russia's mission was therefore clear. It was to proclaim, earlier than others, those great truths that should be accepted everywhere. The only thing that was required was "one authoritative act of that higher will [the tsar's] which includes in itself the whole will of the nation" and which "opened to her a new path." The result would be to elevate Russia to heights not yet achieved by the other European peoples. "And this great future, which, without a doubt, will be realized . . . will be only the result of those special characteristics of the Russian people which first were pointed out in the ill-fated article."[55]

Berdyaev wrote more than a century after Chaadaev. Like Chaadaev, he was concerned with the nature of the Russian character and the differences between Russia and the West. But he had to deal not with the issue of tsarism but with Communist totalitarianism, which at first he fiercely opposed. In time, however, his faith in Russia's special mission led him to support the Stalinist Soviet Union.

Berdyaev's evolution was all the more striking because, perhaps better than anyone else, he described Russian Communism in his writings as a metaphysical evil. He argued that this evil lay in its atheism and in the Soviet regime's consequent negation of morality. From atheism, he wrote, came all of Communism's lies: the lie of bloody violence to establish social truth, the lie of tyranny that cannot abide human dignity, and the lie of the right to use vicious means to achieve supposedly noble ends. Communism, according to Berdyaev, was in fact a pseudo-religion, a social theory that owed its strength less to its persuasiveness than to its ability to draw on "man's former religious psychology."[56] In economically backward, agricultural Russia, what was established was not the dictatorship of the proletariat but rather "the dictatorship of the idea of the proletariat." In the name of the idea of the proletariat "it was possible even to shoot real empirical workers."[57]

It is Communism's nonrational appeal, he wrote, that allows it to command sacrifice. If Communism had succeeded in tearing religious feelings from the souls of people, "it would have made it impossible to have faith in communism." The Communists would have destroyed their own existence, and "no one would have wanted to sacrifice themselves in the name of the communist idea."[58]

For Berdyaev, Communism was a pseudo-spiritual (and therefore anti-spiritual) phenomenon. Marxist economic theories provided no scientific explanation of the universe, only an excuse for destroying the restraints imposed by religion and morality. In a letter to "Miss X," apparently a convinced Communist, with whom he corresponded between 1930 and 1939, Berdyaev wrote that what is presented "as an economic or political question" at a deeper level is "a question of God and immortality."[59]

In his article "The Truth and Lie of Communism," Berdyaev wrote: "The organs of the Soviet Communist press are loaded . . . with economic news. . . . But this is a special type of economics, this is spiritual and metaphysical economics replacing God and spiritual life. . . . The five-year plans that set for themselves the prosaic goal of the industrialization of Russia . . . are followed with religious pathos."[60]

Despite his criticisms of Communism, however, Berdyaev did not object to Russian messianism. On the contrary, he continued to believe in a special Russian "mission." He never accepted Marxism but argued that spiritual culture was more fundamental than politics and the economy, the opposite of Marxism. Yet against all logic he agreed with the notion, implicit in the ambitions of the Soviet Union, that Russia was suited to bring "enlightenment" to the rest of humanity.

On December 2, 1944, in newly liberated Paris, a strange spectacle took place. Berdyaev, standing between portraits of Lenin and Stalin, told the members of a new organization, White Russians: The Friends of the Soviet Union, that it was necessary for Christian Russians to rally to the Soviet Union. There were two nations in Europe, Berdyaev said, with a messianism that enabled them to have an impact on their neighbors — Russia and Germany. But it was unfair to compare the two. German messianism was pagan, marked by a glorification of race, the state of nature, and the fighting spirit, and it completely contradicted the spiritual message of Judaism and Christianity. Russian messianism, on the other hand, was deeply rooted in religious ways of thought. It "exalted Russia as a country that would help . . . solve the problems of humanity and . . . accept a place in the service of humanity." Berdyaev concluded that "recent changes in the Soviet Union [a supposed softening in the attitude toward religion and toward Russian traditions] made it not only possible but right for Christian Russians to rally to the Soviet government."[61]

This new attitude shocked Berdyaev's longtime friends and admirers, but it was quickly recognized by the Soviet government. In 1946 he was invited to a reception at the Soviet embassy in Paris, although the official Soviet attitude at the time was that all émigrés were enemies of the Soviet Union.

In an article written in 1948 but published after his death in the Paris-based periodical *Novy Zhurnal,* Berdyaev tried to explain his position. He cited a "Russian idea" that reflects the fact that "the fate of Russia is unique and the Russian people are unique." The idea was based on free communalism. "This idea entered communism but it was deformed by being connected with forced collectivism." Despite this, the experience of Communism was a demonstration of the Russian people's greatness. The Russians were "the first to make a social experiment, extraordinary in its bravery, and raise a new theme for the whole world. Let [the Russian people] once in a while make a mistake but that is better than doing nothing and remaining self satisfied."[62]

In an article published in 1946 in the Paris émigré newspaper *Russkiye Novosti,* Berdyaev wrote that it was necessary to recognize that Bolshevism was not violence against the Russian people on the part of small group, but rather the creation of the Russian people." It was legitimate to support the Soviet regime because the issue was not one's attitude toward that regime and its actions but "one's relation to the Russian people, to the Russian earth, and to the Russian revolution as an important moment in the fate of the Russian people."[63]

Berdyaev was not blind to the mass repression in the Soviet Union. Nonetheless, influenced by the euphoria among Russian émigrés in France with the Soviet victory over Nazi Germany, he came to treat that repression as secondary to Russia's messianic mission. His faith in that mission led him to reject the "bourgeois democracy" of the West. The problem with bourgeois democracy, he wrote, was that it offered only formal freedom. "The enormous working masses are deprived of the opportunity to realize their freedom." In this regard, nothing was more pathetic than attempts to shore up the "dying bourgeois, capitalist world" with the help of Christianity.[64]

In a 1947 article in *Russkiye Novosti,* Berdyaev wrote that freedom was understood in complex and contradictory ways. Some saw in movement the violation of freedom, and in the absence of movement, freedom. "The great slogan of freedom can become in the capitalist world, a cover for capitalist interests."[65]

Berdyaev said that the world could not be divided into the "empire of light and empire of darkness, the empire of Good and the empire of Evil." In an echo of the Marxism he had once been at pains to reject, Berdyaev wrote that capitalism was rotting and should disappear. His answer was to seek an alternative to both Communism and capitalism in what he called "religious socialism," or "socialism with a spiritual base." The radical change necessary in order to overcome the division of the world into two parts, he wrote, should least of all be anti-Soviet. "On the contrary, it should recognize the truth of communism, should recognize that Soviet Russia poses a great question before the world."[66]

One would normally look to a country's writers for a critical attitude to what amounts to a national mythology. But faith in Russia's supposed saving mission affected great artists no less than ordinary citizens. It is one of the reasons Russia finds it so difficult to commemorate the crimes of the Communist era and acknowledge their implications.

Besides being a matter of vanity, the notion of Russia's "special way" and saving mission is a fundamental element of psychological integration. A Russian lives without freedom, but in his own mind he is not a slave. He is a participant in a grand enterprise with which he and his fellow citizens have been entrusted and which requires sacrifice and a readiness to accept total subordination. Calling attention to society's moral responsibility to the victims of Communism, which cannot be done without acknowledging the responsibility of the Russian state, suggests that such subordination is not justified. It would require calling Russians' entire self-identification into question. This is why an admission of guilt by the state is so difficult.

After he was declared a lunatic, Chaadaev was able to avoid additional trouble with the authorities by publishing nothing further. But there are indications that toward the end of his life, the faith in Russia's special role that he expressed in *Apology of a Madman* was waning. In 1854, two years before his death, he wrote an essay which, for security reasons, he pretended was copied from the French periodical *L'Universe*. In it, he suggested that Russia's future was not so glorious after all.

On the subject of the Russian character, he wrote that there was no noticeable difference between a free person in Russia and a slave. "I would say that in the bowing before fate of the latter there is something more dignified and resilient than in the hesitant, wary glances of the former." Regarding Russia's future, he added: "Speaking of Russia, people always imagine that they are speaking of a country that is like the others. In fact, it is not so at all. Russia is a whole separate world, submissive to the will, caprice, fantasy of one man—no matter whether he be called Peter or Ivan." In contrast to all the laws of the human community, he continued, "Russia advances only the direction of her own enslavement and the enslavement of all neighboring nations." For this reason, "it would be in the interest not only of other nations but also in her own that she be compelled to take a different path."[67]

CHAPTER 10

Symbols of the Past

∎

On December 4, 2000, to the dismay of liberals and the West, Vladimir Putin proposed to reintroduce the melody of the Soviet national anthem as the anthem of the Russian Federation. "If we accept the idea that we cannot use the symbols of the previous epochs including the Soviet one," he said, "then we must admit that our mothers and fathers lived useless and senseless lives, that they lived their lives in vain. I can't accept it either with my mind or my heart."[1]

Boris Yeltsin opposed retaining the Communist melody. In an interview with *Komsomolskaya Pravda,* he said that he associated it only with Communist Party congresses, not Soviet sports victories or achievements in space.[2] A group of thirty-five cultural figures, in a letter to Putin, stated that the idea inspired "nothing but protest and disgust."[3] Putin, however, said that this was the wish of the majority of the population.[4]

The issue of a new national anthem had been debated in Russia for almost a decade. After the Soviet Union collapsed, the "Patriotic Song" by the nineteenth-century composer Mikhail Glinka was adopted by Yeltsin's decree as the nation's anthem, but it was never ratified by the parliament. Communists began almost immediately to call for the return of the Soviet anthem, which, although it referred to "the triumph of Communism," was inspiring and easy to sing. Glinka's music was never put to words, but it is complicated and difficult to hum.[5]

In September 2000 Moscow's Spartak soccer team sent a letter to Putin, asking him to propose words for the Patriotic Song and hinting that the absence of a real national anthem was affecting the team's play. "We don't want to hang our heads any longer when our country's anthem is played in domestic and international arenas," the players wrote.[6] The pro-Putin Unity Party then announced that it preferred the tune of the Soviet anthem, which was composed in 1943 by Alexander Alexandrov.

Four days after Putin made his proposal, the Duma overwhelmingly approved it, by a vote of 381 to 51. Gennady Zyuganov, the Communist leader, said in an interview with Ekho Moskvy that the music enabled Russians to be proud of Soviet-era achievements. "We have restored the anthem of the Soviet Union," he said, "the great music of victory [in the Second World War] . . . the anthem that helped us move into space and create a complete system of health care and education."[7]

Alexander Yakovlev, then in charge of the rehabilitation of repressed persons, said, "I am not going to either rise or sing to this music."[8] The new anthem, however, was quickly accepted by the population, which found it comfortingly familiar. In 2001 the hymn received new lyrics that spoke of Russia "our beloved country" instead of invoking the victory of Communism. The melody, however, had the eerie effect of defining Russia not as a new country but as the Soviet Union in a new form.[9]

One of the most difficult questions for post-Soviet Russia is what to do with Communist symbols. At first, it was generally accepted that they should be done away with. Cities were renamed: Leningrad became St. Petersburg, Sverdlovsk became Yekaterinburg, and Gorky became Nizhni Novgorod. Russian leaders changed the names of streets, including Gorky Street, the main avenue in Moscow, which became Tverskaya Street. The statue of Lenin was removed from the Kremlin.

During seventy-three years of Soviet rule, however, the Communist leaders had placed statues and emblems everywhere, and removing them was costly and time consuming. Perhaps more important, Russians often failed to recognize the political cost of preserving—or at least failing to destroy—what was old and familiar. The result was that most of the Soviet-era names and monuments were left in place.

In Moscow, Lenin's body was left in Red Square, and the statue of Lenin in October Square was preserved intact. Familiar street names were retained, including Bolshaya Kommunisticheskaya Street (Great Communist Street), Leninsky Prospect, the Street of the Young Leninists, and Prospect Andropova. Almost every Russian city of more than twenty thousand had a statue of Lenin in its central square. None of these was touched. Communist street names in provincial cities were not changed. In Perm, for example, the main streets remained Kommunisticheskaya, Bolshevitskaya, and Sovetskaya. All this created the impression that, in some ghostly sense, the former regime continued to exist.

After the Bolsheviks seized power, Russia witnessed the nationwide destruction of tsarist symbols. The post-Soviet Russian government had nothing like that degree of commitment. The impulse to rename streets and remove monuments quickly faded, and by 2000, after Putin became president, almost all discussion of eliminating Communist symbols came to an end. On the contrary, beginning with the hymn, Communist symbols began to be seen as useful in emphasizing the importance of the Russian state. There was no surge in the creation of new Communist monuments, but with a taboo broken, there were sporadic attempts to restore the honor of Communist-era saints.

On July 8, 2004, a week before the ninetieth anniversary of Yuri Andropov's birth, a monument to Andropov was dedicated in Petrozavodsk, the capital of the Karelian Republic. It was the first monument to a former leader of the KGB erected in post-Soviet Russia. On June 15, 2004, Nikolai Patrushev, the head of the FSB, published a full-page tribute to Andropov in *Rossiskaya Gazeta*.[10] That article and one in *Izvestiya* by Fyodor Burlatsky, who had worked with Andropov in the early 1960s, stressed the "secret" of Andropov, which supposedly consisted of a desire to improve Soviet society.[11] The articles argued that he had had great plans that he would have realized had his period as general secretary, when he ran the country while attached to a dialysis machine, not been cut short.

Patrushev wrote that Andropov tried to restore legality in the country by declaring war against corruption. All his activity, said Patrushev, was subordinated to "strengthening the state, stabilizing its position in the world." In this respect, Andropov was a model for contemporary Russia.[12]

Burlatsky wrote that the enigma of Andropov was that he "never left Khrushchevism and socialist rootedness but he was drawn to democracy and the West." As general secretary, he had discussed plans for the modernization of the country, the establishment of order, and the liquidation of corruption. But, Burlatsky added, "this could not replace a program of reform. . . . History leaves open the question: how far would Andropov, the great power ideologist and defender of socialism, have gone in the direction of market reform?"[13]

In fact, Andropov's career gives little reason to suspect either a genuine desire to change the Soviet system or any particular nobility of character. In 1950 the bloody trail of the Leningrad case, the postwar purge of the Leningrad party organization, reached Karelia, on the Finnish border. A plenary meeting of the local party was held under the chairmanship of Andropov, at the time the party second secretary. The issue was the proposed removal of the first secretary, Gennady Kuprianov, who had promoted Andropov and whom Andropov had often referred to as his "teacher." The charge against Kuprianov, who directed the partisan war in Karelia, was that agents he planted behind enemy lines were really "enemies of the people," who had collaborated with the fascists. At the plenum, he turned for support to Andropov, who at the time was his right hand. Kuprianov described what happened in his book *Guerilla War in the North:*

> I said, seeking support from my comrades, that here Yuri Vladimirovich Andropov, my first deputy, knows all of these people very well insofar as he took part in the selection, training, and dispatch of these persons to the enemy's rear . . . and can confirm my words. But then to my great amazement, Yuri Vladimirovich rose and said, "I didn't take any part in the organization of underground work. And I can't vouch for any of those who worked in the underground." I couldn't believe my ears and only said, "Yuri Vladimirovich, I don't recognize you." This was the product . . . of the enormous chronic cowardice and unbelievable gift for adaptation that this person [Andropov] possessed.[14]

Kuprianov was excluded from the party and arrested. He was not freed until after Stalin's death in 1955, at which time he was rehabilitated. But in Karelia, the destruction of "Kuprianovism" continued and, according to Kuprianov, helped Andropov earn the trust of Malenkov and Beria and ascend to the highest levels of power.[15]

Andropov's cold-bloodedness was also demonstrated during the 1956 Hungarian Revolution. As the Soviet ambassador to Hungary, he suggested to the Hungarians talks on the possible withdrawal of Soviet forces. The negotiations were to take place at the Tokol Soviet military base, but as soon as the Hungarian delegation, led by Defense Minister Pal Maleter, entered the room, KGB agents burst in and arrested them.[16] Maleter was executed, along with Imre Nagy and others, in a Budapest prison on June 16, 1958.

Another incident involved Colonel Sandor Kopacsi, the chief of the Budapest police.

> I will never forget the last meeting with that terrible man. It occurred on the last day of our revolution. My wife and I were hurrying to the Yugoslav embassy to ask for political refuge. In the street we were stopped by KGB agents, who delivered us to the Soviet embassy. We were met by Andropov. He was cordial and hospitable, as if we were invited guests and he was very glad to see us. He invited us to table for a cup of tea and said with a smile that Janos Kadar was forming a government and he would like to see in it Colonel Kopacsi. I believed the Soviet ambassador. "It is safe now," he said. "If you don't mind, we will give you a car to get you to the head of the new government." I agreed. An armed vehicle drove up to the porch. I will never forget Andropov in that last minute of our meeting. He was standing at the head of the stairs smiling and waving his hand to us in farewell. . . . The Soviet armed vehicle took us straight to prison, from which I was released seven years later in 1963.[17]

Gyorgy Heltai, the deputy foreign minister in the government of Imre Nagy, said that the terror in Hungary was Andropov's responsibility. Maj. Gen. Bela Kiraly, the former chairman of the National Defense Council (and a member of the Hungarian delegation at the Tokol base), said that Andropov "reduced Hungary to the silence of a cemetery. He deported thousands of Hungarians into Russia and executed hundreds of defenseless young people."[18]

When, as head of the KGB, Andropov began his campaign to become general secretary of the party during the dying Leonid Brezhnev's last days, the KGB arrested Yuri Sokolov, the director of Yeliseevsky's, Moscow's most famous grocery store. The arrest marked the beginning of Andropov's "war on corruption," which was unique in that it represented the first time that the government had acknowledged that corruption existed. The campaign focused on persons close to Brezhnev and his children (Sokolov was a friend of Galina Brezhnev) and so was critical to Andropov's drive for power. Sokolov's trial took place after Andropov's death. He was accused of taking bribes, a common practice in the Soviet retail network. In his defense, Sokolov said that to fulfill the economic plan, he had to bribe those who were in authority and also subordinates, including even the drivers who delivered food products. Sokolov's motion for clemency was rejected, and he was shot.[19]

As general secretary, Andropov ordered daytime raids on stores, cinemas, barber shops, and bathhouses, where patrons were checked to see why they were not at work. In many cases, the "loafers" had gotten time off to make up for the extra hours they were forced to work to help their enterprises meet Soviet production quotas. They were arrested anyway. At the same time, Komsomol patrols terrorized suburban trains, picking up "petty speculators." These were usually collective farmers, housewives, or pensioners on their way to Moscow to buy food products unavailable in their home cities for themselves, their friends, and relatives.[20] Andropov was praised in party circles for trying to reform the economy and fight corruption, even though he made no effort to identify the sources of corruption in the economic system itself.

The streets of Petrozavodsk, the capital of Karelia, are lined with tall, snow-covered fir trees. There are five-story buildings with stately balconies. Many are freshly painted and, in their modern, attractive appearance, seem to reflect the influence of nearby Finland. The main street, Lenin Prospect, descends to the steel gray waters of Lake Onega, which is framed by forested hills and has a promenade along the shore.

I arrived in Petrozavodsk on a cold, clear morning in January 2005, checked into the Severny Hotel and walked down Lenin Prospect to Andropov Street. The statue of Andropov stands in a lot across the street from the FSB building. It consists of a bust of the young Andropov atop a pillar engraved with the words, "Yuri Vladimirovich Andropov." The monument is ten feet tall and wreathed in snow. People shoveling snow nearby seem to pay little attention to it.

The monument was first suggested in 2002 by the Karelia Council of Veterans, and money was immediately found — 1.2 million rubles for improvement of the territory and 1.1 million rubles for the monument. A competition was held for the best design, and the winner was Mikhail Koppolev. Yuri Dmitriev, the president of the academy of social legal defense, a human rights group, wrote a letter to Sergei Katanandov, the governor of Karelia, arguing that it was unthinkable to put up a memorial to Andropov because "he was up to his elbows in blood." Katanandov never answered.[21]

I met Dmitriev at the Petrozavodsk Museum of Victims of Political Repression, which he ran in the basement of a building in the city center. The museum consisted of two rooms with photographs and documents, including biographies of victims and execution orders. In a third room, a florist prepared wreaths for funerals.

"The monument reflects the attitude of the nation toward its past," Dmitriev said. "We don't know the past and we don't want to know." He said that long-standing efforts to put up a monument to Stalin-era victims at an execution ground near Petrozavodsk, where twelve hundred people had been killed, had been fruitless, although the amount of money required was only 10 percent of what was spent on the Andropov memorial.

From the museum I went to the office of the Russian Fund for Peace, the successor to the Soviet Peace Fund, where I met with Yuri Vlasov, the director, Sergei Tataurshchikov, who had worked with Andropov in the Komsomol during the war, and several other persons who had known Andropov in Karelia. Since the fall of the Soviet Union, the Peace Fund in Karelia has principally been involved in searching for the bodies of Soviet soldiers who died in the Finnish war and World War II. Vlasov said that they have found thirty-five hundred sets of remains, but that these are often difficult to identify. "Many soldiers threw away their medallions [capsules with personal information, the equivalent of dogtags] because they thought that keeping them meant they were going to die," Vlasov said. "Instead, they kept the keys to their apartments, which meant they were going home. They died anyway but were impossible to identify."

Tataurshchikov said of Andropov:

> He had great intellectual ability. He was very erudite. For him, the scale of Karelia was too small. Stalin, Yezhov, and Beria destroyed their enemies. Andropov did not do this. For example, Andropov fought desperately for Sakharov. The majority of the politburo wanted to send him out of the country. But Andropov persuaded Brezhnev to keep Sakharov in the Soviet Union but make sure he was out of sight. This was his wisdom. Andropov's methods were far from repressive.

Today, there is democracy. This is the word that is used. But for whom is there democracy? In the Soviet time, the ordinary people chose the government at all levels of power. Today, 10 percent have huge wealth that was stolen from the government and all the rest live in wild poverty.

Andropov is our worker, our hero. This was an unusual person. Why can't we make a monument to a person who devoted such efforts to Karelia? We were obliged to do this. This is why he is depicted as a young man.[22]

Another effort to resurrect Communist-era symbols was ultimately unsuccessful but, if anything, reflected an even deeper moral blindness than a statue to Andropov. It took place in Orel, 240 miles south of Moscow, and concerned Stalin.

In a meeting on March 31, 2005, the city council of Orel overwhelmingly approved a motion to rehabilitate Stalin and put up a bust of him in the center of the city. The council called for returning Stalin's name to streets and squares and restoring monuments to him "as a symbol of the indestructibility of the Russian state."[23] The decision provoked a strong reaction in the Russian and foreign press. This led the city council to issue a statement in which it conceded that some viewed Stalin with horror, but asserted that "there is a great deal to be grateful to Stalin for, including the Victory."[24]

During the Stalin period, the population of the present-day Orel oblast was about 800,000. Of these, 40,000 to 50,000 were arrested. A third were shot.[25] The best-known crime was the murder of 157 prominent political prisoners who were being held in the Orel prison. They were shot on Stalin's orders on September 11, 1941, just before the area was occupied by the Nazis. Among them were Maria Spiridonova, the leader of the Left Social Revolutionaries, an uncompromising opponent of Lenin; Olga Kameneva, the sister of Leon Trotsky and ex-wife of Lev Kamenev; and Professor Dmitri Pletnev, a Kremlin doctor who had treated Stalin.

The atmosphere in Orel as the Germans were about to enter the city was powerfully described by Vasily Grossman in his war notebooks:

I thought I'd seen retreat, but I've never anything like what I am seeing now and could never even imagine anything of the kind.

Exodus! Biblical exodus! Vehicles are moving in eight lanes, there's the violent roaring of dozens of trucks trying simultaneously to tear their wheels out of the mud. Huge herds of sheep and cows are driven through the fields. They are followed by trains of horse-driven carts. . . . This isn't a flood, this isn't a river, it's the slow movement of a flowing ocean, this flow is hundreds of meters wide. . . . Everyone keeps looking up into the sky but not because they are waiting for the Messiah. They are watching out for German bombers. Suddenly, there are shouts: "Here they are! They're coming, they are coming straight for us!"[26]

In 1989 a case was started against Vasily Ulrich, the chairman of the Military Collegium of the Supreme Court, who had passed sentence against the 157 victims of the prison massacre. The case was closed in April 1990 after the Court found that Ulrich was only carrying out the orders of the State Defense Committee, at the time the highest organ of authority in the country. The investigation, however, uncovered many details of how the victims met their deaths. K. F. Firsanov, the head of the NKVD for the Orel oblast, testified that the order from Ulrich to carry out the death sentences arrived as Orel came under heavy bombardment from German forces. Nonetheless, the NKVD had time to prepare the prisoners for death.

They were taken to a special room where . . . [a member] of the prison staff shoved a cloth gag into the prisoner's mouth and secured it with a rag so that he could not spit it out and then announced that he was sentenced to the highest measure of punishment — execution by shooting. After this, the victim was taken by the arms and led into the yard of the prison and put into a covered car with bullet-proof sides.[27]

The prisoners were then driven, according to Firsanov (who testified that he learned about it from subordinates), to a place in the Medvedevsky Forest about six miles from Orel, where they were shot. The trees that had existed on that spot had been pulled up by the roots, and after the victims were buried, the trees were replanted over them. Although the German advance was causing total chaos, until October 3, 1941, when Orel was finally captured, NKVD officers regularly returned to the burial ground posing as mushroom pickers to make sure it had not been discovered.[28]

In 1989, almost fifty years after the massacre, the KGB tried without success to locate the site of the executions and burial. Human remains were found in several places in the approximate area of the executions, but it was impossible to be sure to whom they belonged. The Germans also executed people in the area. After the war, a large part of the former forest was cleared and the area was built over. The bones of the Orel prison victims could lie under an apartment building, garage, or factory.[29]

Despite these uncertainties, in 1990 the local authorities erected a monument, a jagged piece of red granite, at the largest site where remains were found. The monument contains the words, "to the memory of the victims of repression in the thirties, forties, and beginning of the fifties." When it was dedicated, at the height of the anti-Stalinist wave in the Soviet Union, about two hundred persons attended the ceremony, including local officials, survivors, and members of democratic organizations.

A month after the vote in the city council, I went to Orel to ask residents about their attitude toward Stalin. The city is dominated by a central square and Lenin Prospect, whose nineteenth-century façades have changed little since the days when Ivan Turgenev was growing up there. The Oka and Orlik Rivers flow past Soviet-era housing blocks and restored churches. Dmitri Krayukhin, a local human rights activist, met with me in the office of United Europe, an organization he heads that is dedicated to combating racism. As well as being appalled by the vote of the city council, Krayukhin was in danger from local ultranationalists. In June 2003 he protested acts of vandalism and distribution of anti-Semitic literature by the nationalist group Russian National Unity (RNE). A criminal case was opened and charges were filed against two members of the group. In February 2004 the prosecutor gave RNE the case materials. Leaflets then appeared in Orel with Krayukhin's photograph, home address, and telephone number, calling for him to be killed. His requests for police protection were denied.[30]

Krayukhin said that corruption of local officials had led to a wave of nostalgia for the Soviet era. "People see that it is hard to find work, that the authorities can do what they want. They see corruption and banditry, and they don't see any other way to deal with it but repression. . . . They say that under Stalin, corrupt people were shot."

We went to see Gennady Godlevsky, the editor of the local newspaper,

Orelsky Meridian. "All that is left of the former superpower," he said, "is the victory in the Second World War. In the mass consciousness, the symbol of that victory is Stalin. Until 1993 the immunity to Stalin was very strong, but now I think that we will resurrect Stalin. There is a strong demand for a firm hand. This comes from the chaos and disorder in the country."

Later in the day, I spoke to members of the staff of *Gorod Orel,* the newspaper of the city council. Sergei Zarudnev, one of the reporters, said, "Stalin was the embodiment of a powerful Russia. Under Stalin, there was no feeling of inferiority, and the Soviet Union was victorious. He did what he did so that Russia could be a great power. Most people want to live in a powerful country that is respected. I think the vote in the city council reflects a strong mood in the area."

In the early 1990s, ceremonies continued to be held at the monument on the anniversary of the massacre of the political prisoners. But soon the only officials who attended were members of the Commission on Rehabilitation. After a few years, they too stopped coming. In 1998 Krayukhin suggested that members of the city council take part in the ceremonies. Sergei Markov, the deputy chairman, answered: "Why should we leave flowers on the graves of Trotskyites and various anti-Soviets?" By 2000 no more than five or ten persons were attending the commemorations. "The question of the victims left social consciousness," Krayukhin said, "and there was no one who could raise it."

Krayukhin and I visited the monument on a Saturday afternoon. The weather was warm and the air was thick with mosquitoes from the nearby woods. There were red tulips in front of the monument, identical to the ones in front of the statue of Dzerzhinsky at FSB headquarters in the city.[31] Cars on the Moscow-Simferopol Road sped by, their occupants possibly not noticing the slab of red granite on a mound at the edge of the forest. A short distance away, a group of picnickers sat around a tablecloth that was spread on the ground and laden with prepared dishes. In addition to the 157 political prisoners, the Medvedevsky Forest is believed to contain the remains of thousands of other purge victims.

People often have picnics on the edge of the woods. These picnickers were celebrating the thirty-seventh birthday of Andrei, a member of their group. We asked their opinion about the vote in the city council. One of the picnickers, a female history teacher, called the idea of a monument to

Stalin absurd. "What should we do, have a monument to Stalin in one place and a monument to his victims in another?"

They invited Dmitri and me to join them. They said that they knew there were mass burial grounds in the woods. Nonetheless, they were ambivalent about Stalin. One of Andrei's male friends said, "It's necessary to respect history. We have monuments to Peter the Great, and he killed many people. St. Petersburg was also built on the bones of serfs." A middle-aged woman said that Stalin deserved a monument. "He was an outstanding personality who did a lot for the country, although I'm neither an opponent of his nor a supporter."

Andrei's wife objected. "What did he do for this country? The war was won by the people, by the military leaders, not Stalin." "Stalin freed the whole world," said one of the men. "He also raised the economy. If it hadn't been for the war, we would have caught up with and surpassed America in standard of living. The Americans destroyed the Indians. But they don't cry and cover themselves with ashes. Why should we?"

Anna, a fifteen-year-old girl who was with her mother, said, "When Stalin was alive, everyone loved him. Now they all hate him. When he died, entire apartment buildings cried. People were crushed trying to go to the funeral."

Another of the women, Lena, said, "I'm not totally against the monument. It's all right if it is in a square. If it is ideological on a big pedestal, then I'm against it."

In subsequent months, veterans groups and local Communists collected money for a statue of Stalin and circulated petitions in support of the idea. Nonetheless, as the weeks passed, interest in a statue of Stalin in Orel gradually declined. Attention turned again to economic issues, the cost of housing and food, and the crumbling city services. At many factories, there were still delays in paying salaries. Finally, discussion of a statue of Stalin was dropped altogether, but by that time sympathy for Stalin in official circles and in Russian textbooks was already a national reality.

In Volgograd, a drive to put up a monument to Stalin culminated in the creation of a private museum dedicated to the Soviet dictator. It was opened on May 15, 2006, on Mamayev Kurgan, the 330-foot hill where Soviet defenders engaged and stopped the Nazi invaders in the battle of

Stalingrad. No place is more symbolic of Russia's World War II history than Mamayev Kurgan. Its summit was critical to the defense of Stalingrad, and it changed hands repeatedly in ferocious hand-to-hand combat. Today the entire hill is a memorial, visited each year by thousands of people. It is treated, however, as a monument to the Soviet victory, not, except in relatively minor respects, as a memorial to the soldiers who died there. It was this emphasis that made it possible to make Mamayev Kurgan the site of a Stalin museum.

The victory at Stalingrad was long described by Soviet historians as Generalissimo Stalin's outstanding accomplishment. In fact, as personal accounts show, the victory was possible only because of a surge of patriotism from below that Stalin did not appreciate and even tried in some ways to stifle. After the massive German bombardment of Stalingrad on August 23, 1942, G. Skiruta, the commander of the 81st Krasnoznamenny regiment, recalled, "Everything that could burn burned. . . . There was nothing to breathe, no water. . . . But . . . both soldiers and ordinary citizens fought. . . . Many [civilians] worked in factories and plants under bombs and shells. Stalingrad was the first frontline city from which they did not evacuate the industry. The products of Stalingrad's factories were sent straight from the factory gates to the most dangerous parts of the front."[32]

Lydia Plastikova, an employee in the Stalingrad Tractor Factory, said that the outpouring of popular support for the resistance in the face of the German invasion was overwhelming. "The patriotic fervor at the tractor factory was so massive that not only individuals but entire shops signed up for the home guard. The boss of the shop became the commander of the detachment, the secretary of the party organization, the commissar, the secretary of the Komsomol organization, the deputy political officer." A young Komsomol who became a soldier explained his motivation in a letter to his mother:

Mama, don't leaf through the wax-covered pages of ancient books. Don't go to grandfather Arkhip Naidenov. Don't seek, together with him, some type of sacred miracle in our unbelievable deeds. Listen to me: we triumph over death not because we are invulnerable but because we fight not only for our life; we think in the battle about the life of the Uzbek boy, the Georgian woman, the elderly

Russian. We go onto the field of battle in order to defend the holy of holies — our Motherland.[33]

Despite this outpouring of patriotism, however, Stalin had no faith in the Soviet people's readiness to defend their country. Stalin's order no. 227 — "Not One Step Back" — required each army command to organize three to five blocking detachments of up to 200 men each, to be stationed in the rear to shoot any soldier who tried to flee. In all, 13,500 soldiers were executed during the five-month battle of Stalingrad.[34] Anyone caught with a German leaflet was turned over to the NKVD. Anyone who criticized the regime or argued with a commanding officer could face charges of "counter-revolutionary propaganda" or "non-belief in our victory."[35]

When the massive air bombardment of Stalingrad began, the available boats were monopolized by the NKVD. As a result, thousands of civilians were trapped in the city. Stalin refused to evacuate the civilian population. The purpose was to induce the troops and, especially, the home guard, to defend the city more fanatically. "No one bothered about human beings," said a boy trapped in the city with his mother. "We too were just meat for the guns." Soviet civilians who sought shelter from the fighting on the German side were shot by Soviet soldiers. The same fate awaited Russian children who, in exchange for a crust of bread, filled German water bottles in the Volga or civilians who, forced at gunpoint by the Germans, ventured into the no-man's land to bring bodies of German soldiers back to the German lines.[36]

The alacrity with which Soviet commanders exploited their own people was rationalized by General Vasily Chuikov, the army commander in Stalingrad, in his memoirs. "Bourgeois writers," he wrote, "have said that the Russians, defying death as no nation has ever done, seemed not to care about life. They cannot understand that a Soviet citizen, loving life, cannot conceive of it apart from his Soviet country."[37]

Under Yeltsin, the official attitude toward Stalin was still sharply negative. After all, the revelations about Stalin under glasnost had helped bring Yeltsin to power. But after Putin was elected president, in April 2000, official attitudes underwent a change. On the 125th anniversary of Stalin's birth, December 21, 2004, Boris Gryzlov, the speaker of the Duma, said in response to journalists' questions that Stalin was an "outstanding person" who did a "great deal during the Great Patriotic War," and that the negative attitude toward him would not last. Regarding the mass terror, he said only, "Of course, the excesses that took place in internal policy do not flatter Stalin."[38]

The changed attitude at the national level quickly found an echo in Volgograd. On January 21, 2003, the Volgograd oblast Duma asked the State Duma to discuss changing the city's name back to Stalingrad. The central court of Volgograd invalidated the request because the city had not been informed of the cost of renaming the city as required by law. In 2004, however, the name Volgograd in the list of "hero cities" on the Tomb of the Unknown Soldier in Moscow was changed by Putin to Stalingrad.

In February 2005 Alevtina Aparina, the leader of the Volgograd Communists, announced that the sculptor Zurab Tsereteli would donate to the city his statue of the seated figures of Churchill, Roosevelt, and Stalin at the Yalta conference. Tsereteli had wanted to put the sculpture in the Crimea, but Crimean political organizations objected. Aparina and Evgeny Ishchenko, the mayor of Volgograd, then suggested their city. The plans were subsequently shelved because of the high cost of moving the ten-ton monument, but in the wake of the failure, a private Stalin museum created by Vasily Bukhtienko, a wealthy Volgograd businessman, was opened on Mamayev Kurgan with the permission of the Volgograd city government.

When the Stalin museum was opened, the only public objection came from Eduard Polyakov, the head of the Volgograd branch of the All Russian Association of Victims of Political Persecution. He said that creating a museum to Stalin was a mockery of the more than 100,000 families in the Volgograd region who had suffered from the repression. This idea was not widely shared. In an informal survey on the streets of Volgograd after the museum opened, a reporter for the newspaper *Russky Kurier* found that nine out of ten of the persons questioned supported the idea of the museum, including some persons who had lost relatives in the Stalinist terror.[39]

The museum contains nearly four hundred unique photographs and archival documents and many of Stalin's personal belongings. It includes a replica of his office and a life-size wax figure of Stalin standing over a large map, plotting strategy.[40] Bukhtienko said that he began to read about

Stalin and came to the conclusion that although one could not ignore the repressions, Stalin's political achievements compensated for his crimes.

Volgograd today is a verdant city of hills and tree-lined boulevards. The central square, where Paulus, the commander of the German sixth army, had his headquarters in the basement of the main department store, is filled with shoppers and trolleybuses. The riverfront is lined with cafés. Bathers swim in the Volga, and passenger boats and cargo ships ply its waters.

Nonetheless, there are reminders of the war. In July 2005 a worker found a bomb in his yard while digging a basement, a fairly common experience in a city of which 95 percent was destroyed during the war. The worker called the Ministry of Extraordinary Situations (MChS), which informed him that the device was an aviation bomb and therefore the responsibility of the local military headquarters (voenkomat). The voen-komat said that the bomb was the responsibility of the MChS. Finally, the worker called the police. They said that since the house was private, the bomb belonged to him. The worker sent his family away and called the local newspapers, which published photos showing him posing next to "his" bomb. Finally, the MChS came and removed it.[41]

Besides unexploded bombs, Volgograd is the site of vast quantities of human remains. It is generally accepted that much of the city rests on bones, but the government takes no responsibility for digging them up. Various youth clubs seek to locate the remains of soldiers. The effort, however, is haphazard, and the young volunteers are sometimes hindered by "black archeologists," who illegally search for arms, medallions, and medals to sell to collectors. Confrontations between volunteers and these grave robbers are frequent and have led to pitched battles.

The soldiers' remains, when found, often cannot be identified. Soviet soldiers in Stalingrad, as elsewhere, frequently threw away their medallions. If they kept them, they often put letters to their girlfriends instead of their names and addresses in the identity capsules. As a result, even when a medallion is found with a soldier's remains, it is often impossible to know who he was.

Shortly after I arrived in Volgograd, I met Yelena Silantieva, the editor of the local weekly newspaper *Den za Dyem,* who said that the controversy over Stalin was less about the war and Stalin's role than about the state of contemporary Russia. "Stalin wanted to be equal among equals," she said. "He sacrificed his own son. Today, not a single oligarch has a son in the army. He had no palaces. He did not take more than he was entitled to. When people see how officials take bribes and build palaces, they say if only Stalin were alive, this wouldn't be happening."

I went with Yelena to Mamayev Kurgan. By official count, the bodies of 34,505 Soviet soldiers are buried in common graves there.[42] At the height of the struggle for the hill, Soviet battalions fed into the inferno were being annihilated every six minutes. After the battle, Galina Kotelnik, a young girl from Stalingrad who survived the war on the east bank of the Volga, returned with her brother and some soldiers to Mamayev Kurgan, which before the war had been a favorite spot for lovers and strollers. What she saw there haunted her for the rest of her life.

> When we came to Mamayev Kurgan and the truck stopped, we turned to stone from what we saw. We could not bring ourselves to get out of the trailer. Mamayev Kurgan is large, but the entire hill was covered with layers of corpses. To walk on the hill without stepping on a dead soldier was impossible. This picture so stunned me that for ten years it gave me no peace. At night, I leaped up, cried and screamed. But that day my brother and I were struck dumb. We sat on the floor of the trailer and cried.[43]

Despite this legacy, the design of Mamayev Kurgan is concerned with the victory, not with fallen soldiers. As we ascended a series of granite staircases, at each level the monument at the summit, a 270-foot-high statue of a woman with a raised sword and a flowing gown entitled *Motherland Calls,* came closer into view. At the top of the first staircase, where two rows of tall poplar trees frame the statue in the distance, we reached the Stand Until Death square. In the center of the square is a pool, and on an island in the pool, the figure of a muscular, bare-chested soldier, an automatic rifle over his shoulder. On the base of the statue are the slogans "Stand Until Death," "Not a Step Back," and "There Is No Land for Us beyond the Volga."

The next staircase led up to the Square of Heroes. On one side of a wall were six statues depicting soldiers in heroic poses, including a marine advancing with grenades on a tank. An inscription described the awe that the bravery of Soviet soldiers supposedly inspired in the enemy: "A feeling of superstitious dread seized the enemy: people attack, are they mortal?"

At the next level was the Hall of Military Glory, a cylindrical building 130 feet in diameter. In the center of the hall is a metal hand holding a torch with an eternal flame. The melody of Schumann's "Reverie" is carried over speakers, and on the walls are thirty-four banners, carved out of red smalt, engraved with the names of seventy-two hundred defenders of the city. Above them is a ribbon with the words "Yes, we are simple mortals and few of us survived, but we fulfilled our patriotic duty before the sacred motherland."

Next on the ascent was the only place on Mamayev Kurgan that acknowledges the tragedy of those who lost loved ones in the epic battle. A statue of a mother holding her dead son in her arms is mirrored in a small pool. This is the Place of Sorrow. From here, we reached the first of two hundred steps leading to the statue at the top of the hill. The eight thousand–ton statue is surrounded by mass graves, as well as the gravestones of thirty-five Heroes of the Soviet Union. In the gathering dusk, the epic scale of the monument seemed almost inhuman, too great a celebration of victory in a place that contains so many dead.

We left Mamayev Kurgan and went by trolleybus to another spot with relevance for recent Russian history. This was a gray granite stone on the river bank marking the place where a monument to the victims of the Stalinist terror was to have been erected. The stone was laid in 1994, but the monument was never built.

During the rest of my time in Volgograd, I visited other signs of the city's unreconstructed past. Near the city center, the Square of the Chekists contains a monument to the 10th NKVD division, which, in addition to distinguishing itself in combat, controlled the river crossings and was responsible for the terror against Soviet soldiers and civilians during the battle.

Finally, I met Konstantin Kalachev, the deputy mayor of Volgograd, who opposed the monuments to Stalin in the city. He said that support for such monuments is typical only of a zealous few, but the fact that the issue exists at all reflects the moral confusion of the population.

"In this situation," he said, "Stalin is a symbol of principle. There is an absence of moral leaders. People hate the hypocrisy that they see every day. People go to work honestly and see that for this they get nothing. Stalin lived modestly. He did not accumulate property. He did not use his authority to enrich himself. He was bloodthirsty but honest. He murdered honestly. He was a symbol of asceticism. He did not go to ski resorts in Switzerland."

At the same time, however, Kalachev said it would be a mistake to overestimate the support for Stalin in Volgograd. "Many people just want to get on with their lives. They are tired of the history of the city. They don't want to live in a city of museums, cemeteries, and monuments.

"There was a competition for suggestions to humanize the city. There is a big movement to put up a monument to lovers. The war ended long ago. People want music, balloons. There are three hundred monuments in the city, and all of them are military monuments. Volgograd was once a big trading city."

I went to see Irina Litvinova, the director of the museum of the Volgograd State University, who supported Kalachev's views. "The fate of the city," she said, "was tied up with the personality of Stalin. The reason why Stalingrad was defended was because it was named after Stalin. But most people don't want to live in a place called Stalingrad. The image of Stalin as a dictator has stayed. People remember the famine in the 1930s, dekulakization, the repression of the Cossacks. The Communists back the idea of changing the name back to what it was, but for normal people, the thought of living in a city that is named after Stalin is depressing."

From the windows of the Moscow-Volgograd train, *Motherland Calls* stands out against the horizon, freezing in time the moment when the residents of an otherwise unremarkable city were called on to decide the fate of the entire world. What they did was heroic, but the victory at Stalingrad came as a result of the Soviet Army's complete disregard for its soldiers' lives. Unfortunately, there is no judgment of that fact in Volgograd, just as there is no judgment of the Stalin-era purges. This is why the issue of honoring Stalin still arises periodically in the city. The lives of the soldiers and civilians who died paled next to the goals of the regime. Their inherent value has not been recognized in Volgograd to this day.

CHAPTER 11

History

■

On November 7, 1941, with German units fifty miles away and the fate of the city hanging in the balance, preparations were completed in almost total secrecy for the annual Revolution Day parade in Moscow's Red Square. Most of the participating commanders received their instructions at 2 A.M., only a few hours before they had to muster their troops. At 8 A.M., the parade began. Stalin and the other Soviet leaders stood atop the Lenin mausoleum; General Budenny rode out on a white stallion from the Spassky Gate and saluted. He was followed by T-34 tanks and columns of troops. In driving snow and wind, the troops marched through Red Square and then out of the city directly to the front.

The effect of the parade on Soviet morale was dramatic. Word spread quickly that, despite rumors, Stalin had not left Moscow. Soldiers at the front, told about the parade by soldiers who had just participated in it, were awed by what they heard.

The parade became a legend in Russia, a symbol of patriotic defiance in the face of mortal danger. On November 7, 2007, Moscow marked the ninetieth anniversary of the Bolshevik Revolution by honoring not the revolution but the parade. Several thousand military cadets dressed in World War II uniforms marched through Red Square, as did the cavalry group of the presidential regiment and more than three thousand Moscow schoolchildren and pupils of the Moscow military-musical academy. From the tribune, a large group of elderly war veterans looked on, sixty-five of whom had taken part in the parade of 1941.

Mayor Yuri Luzhkov said that the parade inspired the battle for Moscow, the most important battle of the war. "The leadership of the country in that tragic period," he said, "made the decision to hold the parade on Red Square, and from there, military units left for the front. We gained the first, the most significant, and the most important victory in the battle for Moscow. This is the universal significance of the parade on Red Square on November 7, 1941."[1]

The decision to celebrate the anniversary of the parade was Russia's answer to a delicate problem. Sixteen years earlier, the Soviet regime had ceased to exist. It therefore made no sense to celebrate the anniversary of the revolution. Russians, however, had grown up with the November 7 holiday. In the 1990s the day was renamed the Day of Accord and Reconciliation. But no one could say with what they were in accord and with whom they needed to be reconciled. In 2005 Putin eliminated November 7 as a holiday, but in deference to the custom of having a day off in early November, he created a new holiday on November 4, People's Unity Day, to celebrate the expulsion of the Polish invaders from Moscow in 1612. There remained, however, an unspoken wish to mark November 7 as people always had. This led to the decision to celebrate the parade. In effect, Moscow celebrated the sixty-sixth anniversary of the twenty-fourth anniversary of the revolution.

During the Yeltsin era, the official view of the Soviet regime was negative. Yeltsin came to power as a result of a peaceful anti-Communist revolution, and as president he encouraged a rejection of the Soviet past. Immediately after the accession of Putin, however, there were signs of change.

In February 2000 Putin, then the acting president following Yeltsin's resignation on December 31, 1999, was asked during a call-in with readers of the newspaper *Komsomolskaya Pravda* about his attitude to the Soviet system. To the surprise of many, he said, "Anyone who does not regret the passing of the Soviet Union has no heart." He then added that anyone who wanted it restored "has no brains."[2] The official attitude had been that there was no reason for Russians to be attached to the Soviet system in their "heart."

After he was elected president in April 2000, Putin promoted the idea that the purpose of Russian history was the creation of a strong state regardless of ideology. In 1998, under Yeltsin, the remains of Tsar Nicholas II and his family had been ceremonially reburied in the Peter and Paul Cathedral in St. Petersburg. Under Putin, the honoring of tsarist-era figures continued. Maria Fyodorovna, the mother of Nicholas II, was reburied, as were Gen. Anton Denikin, a leader of the White Army, and Gen. Nikolai Batyushin, the head of Russian counterintelligence during the First World War.[3] At the same time, Putin praised Stalin and Andropov and expressed the view that the Soviet Union, whatever its faults, was a fundamental part of the Russian state tradition.

During the Soviet period, Russian nationalists insisted that Russia and the Soviet Union were fundamentally different and that Russia was as much a captive nation as any of the other Soviet republics. Under Putin, the fact that Russia and the Soviet Union shared the same political tradition was not only acknowledged but treated as something positive.

On December 28, 2004, Viktor Cherkesov, the director of the Federal Narcotics Control Service (FKSN) and a former interrogator of dissidents, sought to explain the new "statist" philosophy. Because of its geopolitical position and national composition, he wrote, a strong state was necessary to Russia's survival. Without it, Russia would share the fate of many African countries, including "chaos and intertribal genocide." He acknowledged that Communism was, "in many respects, defective," but he said that most of those who opposed the Soviet system really had been "aiming at the heart of the state."[4] This was why KGB agents (including himself) had felt justified in prosecuting them.

On April 25, 2005, in his address to the Federal Assembly, Putin described the fall of the Soviet Union as "the greatest geopolitical catastrophe of the twentieth century."[5] By formulating the issue in this way, he avoided saying whether the collapse of the Soviet Union was a good thing in moral terms. But with this remark, the era of anti-Communist revulsion in Russia came to an end.

The Putin-era notion that the purpose of Russian history is a powerful state without any idea that might justify it, other than to keep the country from falling apart, makes so little sense that it is scarcely credible. Yet in a relatively short period, the notion that Russia's goal is the creation of a strong state has become the official view, inspiring the way students are taught and influencing Russia's relations with other nations.

In June 2004, traveling with a reporter for the education newspaper *Pervoye Sentyabrya,* I made a trip to schools in the Vologda and Novgorod oblasts, between Moscow and St. Petersburg. We visited teachers and students in schools in three towns and two villages. I decided to make the trip after a widely used textbook, *A History of the Homeland in the Twentieth Century,* by Igor Dolutsky, lost the endorsement of the Ministry of Education.[6]

Dolutsky, a historian and teacher, was determined to write frankly about Soviet and post-Soviet crimes. His book described the Baltics under the Soviet regime as "occupied" and included estimates that in 1941–42 at the beginning of the war, 150,000 persons were shot in the Soviet Union for "cowardice and spreading panic." Dolutsky pointed out that in 1939, Britain fought Hitler alone while Germany and the Soviet Union divided up Eastern Europe between them.[7] In the early 2000s his textbook had sold 600,000 copies in two years. The withdrawal of the endorsement appeared to be a sign that the Russian regime was preparing to take a different attitude toward teaching about the Soviet Union.

In a high school in Ustyuzhna, an idyllic 750-year-old town that was the setting for Gogol's play *The Inspector General,* the students at school no. 2 did not regret the coming of a new age. Maxim Mikhailov, eighteen, said, "In the Soviet Union, people were all the same. They wore identical clothes and lived in identical apartments. I prefer to live in this time. I support the collapse of the Soviet Union." Dmitri Yukhta, sixteen, said, "It's better now. Each can show his ability. Before everything was decided for you." Alexei Kazachaev, sixteen, said, "The Communists destroyed many innocent people. They should have asked forgiveness. But there was no remorse."

Students' sentiments were similar in Borovichi, an industrial town of seventy thousand on green hills along the bank of a slowly flowing river. At school no. 2 Marian Tera, sixteen, said, "In Soviet times, there was stability but there was no freedom of speech and no freedom of thought and there was censorship." Irina Sheretskaya, eighteen, said, "It's not realistic to build Communism." Alyona Boldina, sixteen, said, "In the Soviet Union there was one center and everything was commanded from that center. That's why we won the war. Now, if there is a war, no one will go." Nastya Potatuyeva, seventeen, corrected her, "They'll go — but only for money."

In a high school in Konchansko Suvorovskoe, a rural village outside Borovichi, Masha Osipova said, "Now, it's a lot better. Before, even books could not be published. This was unjust." Dmitri Ryabinin, fifteen, said,

"My grandmother says that in the Soviet times, it was better. Prices were lower and it was easier to live. But in those days, if a person went against the government, they eliminated him."

The teachers had a more positive attitude toward the Soviet past. In the village of Zhelezkovo, on the territory of a collective farm, Lyudmilla Zelenikina, a history teacher, said, "In Soviet times, people were kinder, souls were more open. There was pride in the country. The world took note of our opinion, and people felt that they were part of this great country. Now, people feel more pain. Mutual help, which was always typical of Russians, disappears, even in the countryside."

Galina Stepanova, a history teacher in Borovichi, said, "Collectivism is the national idea. World War II was won on the basis of volunteers who were ready to give their lives." She recalled a film about the Western Front that was shown on Russian television. The Americans, she said, found it difficult to recruit volunteers who would be placed in the enemy's rear. The word *volunteer* itself was often treated as an insult. In Russia, however, soldiers were ready to take risks. "This was the result of the spirit of collectivism."

In a high school in Valdai, a city of seventeen thousand in a scenic region of forests and lakes, Nadezhda Gerasimova, a history teacher, said, "The drive to be together is typical of the Russian people." She recalled that in 1984 the students had spent thirty-five days together harvesting potatoes. "As a result, they formed strong ties," she said. "They are friendly to this day because they were always together. The students in 2004 are atoms. They will not meet after they graduate."

"The students are less patriotic," her colleague Marina Vasilieva said. "Pride in their motherland is not there. When I lived in the USSR, I felt pride. Now, the students don't know who Lenin was. Old people lived their whole lives and ended up poor and they see that there is no place for them and that everything that they believed in was wrong."

Three years after I made that trip, on June 20, 2007, Russians were exposed to the new official view of history. A teacher's manual covering the period 1945 to 2006, released by Prosveshcheniye, the country's leading textbook publisher, offered a dramatically more favorable assessment of the Soviet Union than had been current in Russia until then. "The Soviet Union," the manual said, "was not a democracy, but it was an example of the best and most just society for millions of people all over the world." Stalin was "the most successful leader of the USSR," a man who built industry and led the country to victory in the Second World War. Repression was used to "mobilize not only rank-and-file citizens but also the ruling elite." The concentration of power in Stalin's hands suited the country; indeed, the conditions of the time "demanded" it.[8]

As for Gorbachev, the manual said that his policies led to a decline in economic growth, the first in the postwar period. As a result of his cession of Central and Eastern Europe, "the Soviet Union lost its security belt, which a few years later would become a zone of foreign influence with NATO bases an hour away from St. Petersburg."[9] The manual insisted that Russia did not lose the Cold War but rather ended it, and in return, the United States pursued an anti-Russian policy and fomented revolutions in Georgia and Ukraine, turning them into springboards for future attacks. In the final chapter, on "sovereign democracy," the manual praised Putin and said that "practically every significant deed" of the most recent period is connected with his name. Regarding the Yukos case, the author wrote: "A government that had become stronger sent business an unambiguous message: Obey the law, pay your taxes, and don't try to put yourselves above the government. They took the hint."[10]

The manual was written by Alexander Filippov, a political operative with close ties to the Kremlin, and was a preliminary version of the recommended history textbook for the eleventh grade. Also released was a social studies manual, *The Global World in the Twenty-first Century*. It stated that since the early 1990s, the United States had tried to create a global empire using tactics of divide and rule, and had sought to isolate Russia from the former Soviet republics. America itself, however, faced a grim future because it can "no longer integrate into a single unit . . . 'whites' and 'blacks,' 'Latinos' and others."[11]

The change in the country's textbooks was not an isolated event. The authorities started to justify decisions that earlier had been seen as criminal, such as the Molotov-Ribbentrop Pact.[12] At the same time, the Russian media, which had become largely state controlled, became anti-Western. It promoted the view that the West is deceitful, has double standards, and never wanted good for Russia. There were repeated references to a statement by Alexander III that Russia had no friends except its army and its fleet. Documentary films depicted Russia as a besieged fortress.[13]

The new manuals were presented at the All Russian Conference of Social Science Teachers in Moscow. On the following day, twenty-six delegates met with Putin in Novo-Ogareva, where he discussed the proper teaching of history. There was a "mishmash" in people's minds, Putin said, that had to be corrected. While there were "problematic pages" in the country's history, he argued that this was true of any country, and Russia had fewer of them than did others. He said the events of 1937 should not be forgotten. But other countries had "even more horrible things." "At least, we didn't use nuclear arms against a civilian population and we have never dumped chemicals on thousands of kilometers," as had U.S. forces in Vietnam. "We should not allow anyone to force a feeling of guilt upon us," he concluded. "Let them think about themselves."[14]

Leonid Polyakov, the chairman of political science at the Higher School of Economics, responded to Putin's remarks. "You are right," he said, "there is mush in everyone's heads! We have ideologically disarmed ourselves. In 1990–91, we rejected Marxism and Communism. . . . What did we get instead? We got some shaky, abstract ideology of universal values! We adopted the words 'freedom,' 'democracy,' 'market,' 'human rights' and 'civil society.' It's like giving children blocks but not teaching them how to spell words . . . and so far we've been stacking them and . . . someone is looking at us from a distance, like we're in school or not even in school but in kindergarten!" Putin replied, "You are right. These people are appropriating the right to teach and want to continue that. No one can take away from us our distinctive national character, our traditions!"[15]

Teachers reacted enthusiastically to the new manual. At government-organized conferences to discuss the book in provincial cities, a representative comment was, "At last there is an objective textbook that is patriotic." Filippov, in an interview in *Rossiiskaya Gazeta,* said that until recently, Russian history had been the object of a propaganda offensive from both inside the country and abroad, whose purpose was to prove that Russia "deserved a place only on the periphery of world politics" and was "doomed forever to repent for . . . real or invented crimes." The idea was "to inject Russian society with an inferiority complex and a feeling of historic guilt" and then use these feelings to detach the former Soviet republics from the Russian sphere of influence.[16]

In October, the new textbook based on the teachers' manual was published. A chapter on Stalin's role in history, with its claim that Stalin was the Soviet Union's most successful leader, had been dropped. But the textbook defended his policies, and the chapter on "sovereign democracy," although renamed and slightly revised, interpreted every major event of the Putin period from the point of view of official propaganda. It said that the motto of the Yeltsin period was "reform at any price," whereas Putin operated according to a different principle: "Improvement of the living conditions of the population."[17]

The appearance of the textbook for 1945–2007 was followed by the publication on the website of Prosveshchenie of a summary of the proposed new volume covering 1900–1945. The history of this period was, if anything, even more sensitive than that of the later period because it included the years of the Great Terror. The summary announced that the purpose of the textbook would be to see history from the point of view of the state. This, in fact, already had been accomplished in the first textbook. "Particular attention" would be devoted to the "motives and logic" of the authorities. The book would begin not with 1917 but with 1900, because another of its tasks would be erasing "the artificial border between pre- and postrevolutionary Russian history."[18]

The summary then gave an interpretation of Soviet history that justified the regime's worst crimes. Stalin, it said, was a "rational manager." Terror in the 1930s "made it possible to achieve an industrial breakthrough." At the same time, there was no way other than collectivization to obtain the means necessary for industrialization. The 1932–33 famine was not deliberate but a result of weather conditions and the poor functioning of the newly created collective farms. The death toll was not ten million in Ukraine, as claimed by Ukrainian historians, but only one to two million persons in Ukraine and two to three million in the entire Soviet Union. Stalin acted as he had to create a centralized system capable of achieving rapid industrialization against the prospect of imminent war. Other countries had industrialized with fewer losses but over a much longer period. For the Soviet Union in the 1930s, the summary said, this had not been an option.[19]

The Great Terror, according to the summary, was Stalin's reaction to opposition tendencies that threatened him with the loss of his position and even physical destruction, creating a danger of general political destabilization. "Stalin did not know who would deal the next blow and, for that reason, he attacked every known group and movement, as well as those who were not his allies or of his mindset." The summary described the Second World War as "one of the most heroic chapters" in Russia's history. The difference in the casualty rates on the Eastern and Western Fronts showed the decisive influence of the Soviet contribution. The summary mentioned the killing of the Polish officers in Katyn and said that it could not be justified but also said that, from Stalin's point of view, this was not just a question of "political expediency" but an answer for the deaths of tens of thousands of Red Army soldiers in Polish captivity after the war of 1920, which was initiated not by the Soviet Union but by Poland.[20]

The interpretation of recent Soviet history in the summary loosed a flood of criticism. Sergei Lebedev wrote in *Pervoye Sentyabrya* that the authors had acted not as historians but as lawyers for the authorities.[21] Anatoly Bershtein, a columnist for the newspaper *Vremya Novostei,* wrote that the summary made no moral or ethical evaluation of the authorities' actions. "The greatest gap in the 'know how' of the authors of the future textbook," he wrote, "is that explaining the logic of the authorities, they ignore the logic of their victims."[22]

Alexander Tsipko, a philosopher and critic of Marxism, wrote that during the Brezhnev period, not even the most diehard Stalinist would have risked suggesting that terror was a necessary tool in the service of industrial development. He said that the summary showed that Russians have not rejected a "Red" view of their history, the conviction that without Lenin it would not have been possible to carry out an industrial and cultural revolution. "However, from the conviction that the Bolsheviks thanks to Lenin saved Russia from . . . backwardness it is only one step to the philosophy of mass executions."[23]

The objections fell on deaf ears. In the fall of 2008, the first textbook was introduced into the schools. Isaak Kalin, the deputy minister of education, said that its basic ideas would be used in the state exam. Yuri Afanasyev, the founder of the Russian State University for the Humanities, said, "The textbooks . . . soon will consist of nothing but lies," and the "pragmatic, value-free approach" to Russia's history would set the stage for future horrors.[24]

On December 28, 2008, Stalin barely missed being voted the greatest Russian of all time in a contest sponsored by the state-controlled RTR television station. The competition was modeled on the BBC's 2002 *Great Britons* series, which was won by Winston Churchill, with viewers casting their votes online or by text message. In the Russian contest, Stalin finished third, about 5,500 votes behind the "winner," Prince Alexander Nevsky, who received 524,575 votes, and 4,500 votes behind Pyotr Stolypin.[25]

Public opinion polls, meanwhile, showed increasingly that Russians preferred cruel rulers to those who introduced reforms. Peter I, for example, was more popular than Alexander II, and Lenin and Stalin more popular than Khrushchev or Gorbachev. The reason for the popularity of despotic leaders was that they supposedly had forced the world to respect Russia and fear it. That they had done so at a huge cost in human life apparently was given little weight. Not only did Stalin receive favorable ratings, Russians even gave a favorable assessment to Ivan the Terrible, who used to boil his victims alive. In a 2008 survey by the Fund of Public Opinion (FOM) and RTR, Ivan finished tenth in list of great Russians, ahead of Catherine the Great and Alexander II, who liberated the serfs.[26]

After Stalin's third-place finish in the RTR contest was announced, some Russians speculated that only cheating had prevented him from finishing first. He had led in the early voting. This may have caused consternation among Russian leaders, who although they have partially rehabilitated Stalin, did not want him declared the country's leading hero. In August, Alexander Lyubimov, the head of the project, announced that Stalin's lead was the work of hackers. The voting was nullified and restarted. This time, Tsar Nicholas II pulled ahead, but his lead soon disappeared and Stalin again proved to have huge support. He was beaten only by Stolypin, who was known to be Putin's choice, and the winner, Alexander Nevsky, who in addition to being a symbol of defiance of the West for Russian nationalists is the patron saint of the FSB.

Besides shaping the teaching of history, Russia's emphasis on the power of the state as the purpose of its history affected its relations with other nations. The rehabilitation of the Soviet Union extended to a Russian claim that the Soviet Union's role as a liberator entitled Russia to a "zone of privileged interests" that included the former Soviet republics. Many of these republics, however, made it clear that they had no interest in being part of Russia's zone of privileged interests. The result was a steady worsening of relations, leading to boycotts, diplomatic confrontations, energy cutoffs, and even wars.

Two of the most serious conflicts involved Estonia and Ukraine. Confrontations stemmed from Estonia's insistence that it was occupied and Ukraine's conviction that it had been a victim of genocide.

The dispute with Estonia, which led to a minor Cold War between Russia and the former Soviet republic, was, on the surface, deeply senseless. It came as a result of the decision in April 2007 by the Estonian authorities to move a Soviet war memorial, a six-foot bronze of a Red Army soldier, from its place in the center of Tallinn to a military cemetery. The almost hysterical Russian response that this action provoked was fully consistent with a view of history that emphasizes the supreme importance of the Russian state, irrespective of values. The Russian reaction was so extreme that it raised fears that Russia might have resorted to overt aggression had Estonia not been a member of NATO.

The background to the dispute was the annexation of the Baltic republics during the Second World War. The Russians insist that Soviet troops entered the Baltics in 1940 "on the basis of an agreement."[27] The "agreement," however, was in response to an ultimatum after the Soviet Union had massed 500,000 troops on the borders of the three Baltic republics. Hopelessly outnumbered, Estonia and the other Baltic republics agreed to the entry of Soviet troops in order to avoid the needless loss of life. Sham elections led to pseudoparliaments that "requested" that the republics be incorporated into the Soviet Union.

On September 22, 1947, the third anniversary of the reentry of Soviet forces into Tallinn after the defeat of the Germans in 1944, the so-called Bronze Soldier was unveiled in Tonismagi Square in the center of the city and dedicated to the "liberators of Tallinn." In fact, the German Army had withdrawn ahead of advancing Soviet troops. To support the myth of a battle, however, in 1964 an eternal flame was added to the site.

In 1991, after Estonia regained its independence, the eternal flame was put out. But the monument remained and became a source of tension. Ethnic Russian war veterans living in Estonia gathered at the statue every year on May 9 to dance, sing, and drink in honor of the Soviet victory. They began to have frequent clashes with Estonian nationalists. In 2004 the confrontations escalated. On May 9, 2006, a group of nationalists arrived at the square with an Estonian flag and a placard denouncing the Soviet occupation. Fights broke out, and the police ordered the Estonians to leave. On the night of May 21, Estonian extremists doused the statue with paint. Russians then formed a group called Night Watch to protect the monument. At that point, the government decided to relocate the statue.

As preparations were made for relocating the monument, Russia warned Estonia that moving the statue was "blasphemous," and the chairman of the Duma's foreign affairs committee, Konstantin Kosachyov, said that a recently passed law that authorized the relocation was part of the "glorification of Nazism."[28] The Estonians offered to discuss the removal of the statue, but the Russians refused. In the meantime, representatives of the Russian embassy met frequently with groups of ethnic Russians who were determined to prevent the removal of the monument.

On April 26, 2007, the Estonians decided to act. The monument area was covered with a tent. As word spread that the statue was going to be removed, a crowd formed across the street from the monument and grew steadily larger. Toward dusk, members of the crowd attacked police lines, setting off a full-scale riot. Demonstrators hurled rocks and Molotov cocktails at police, smashed shop windows, and looted liquor stores. An ethnic Russian, Dmitri Ganin, was stabbed to death by unknown persons, and 153 others were injured. At 4 A.M. on April 27, the government, meeting in crisis mode, decided to move the monument. It was taken to the Fitri Street military cemetery. This touched off another night of rioting. By the time the disturbances were over, the police had detained more than 1,000 persons, most of them ethnic Russian teenagers who had come to Tallinn from all over Estonia.[29]

Russian officials were quick to react. The Federation Council unanimously passed a resolution calling on Putin to consider breaking diplomatic relations with Estonia. Konstantin Kosachev, the head of the foreign relations committee of the State Duma, alluded to possible economic sanctions. The state-controlled Russian press described the rioters in Tallinn as peaceful demonstrators who had suffered from police brutality.

At the same time, a large group of members of the Kremlin-sponsored youth organizations Nashi and Molodaya Gvardiya laid siege to the Estonian embassy. They were given flags, loudspeakers, and tents, and their numbers increased steadily as reinforcements arrived by bus from surrounding cities. They sang Soviet war songs and shouted, "Estonian fascists, go home!" The demonstrators distributed printed material showing the Estonian ambassador, Marina Kaljurand, with a Hitler mustache, and pictures of the statue surrounded by candles.

While this was going on, there was a massive cyberattack from Russia on government computers in Estonia. The main targets were the websites of the Estonian presidency, parliament, ministries, and political parties. Also attacked were the websites of three of the country's biggest news organizations and two of its biggest banks. The attackers infiltrated computers all over the world with "bots" — software that automatically performs some function on an infected computer — and used them to swamp Estonian websites with tens of thousands of visits, jamming and disabling them.[30]

The first attacks came at 10 P.M. on April 26. The Estonians, anticipating trouble, had erected firewalls around the government websites, set up extra computer servers, and put staff on call. But the attack was so intense that Estonia was forced to shut down key computer systems for its own protection.[31] The government urged banks to keep their services running and protected an important government briefing site, but other sites, including that of the Estonian presidency, were sacrificed as being of lesser importance.

In all, 128 separate strikes were launched against Estonia's cyber infrastructure.[32] The attacks tailed off after May 3 but resumed on May 8 and May 9, the anniversary of the Soviet victory. Estonian officials said that some of the attacking computers belonged to Russian state institutions, including the Russian presidential administration.[33] On May 10 the Estonian state prosecutor asked the Russian prosecutor for help under the countries' mutual legal assistance treaty, but the Russian prosecutor refused. This made it impossible to identify specific Russian suspects in the attacks.

The demonstrators besieging the Estonian embassy, meanwhile, showed no sign of relenting. Each time the ambassador left the embassy, demonstrators blocked her car. When she finally succeeded in leaving to go to the office of the newspaper *Arguments and Facts* to hold a press conference, several Nashi activists gained access to the room and shouted slogans at her before they were subdued with pepper spray and removed. As he left the embassy, the Swedish ambassador was attacked by demonstrators who vandalized his car, tearing off the Swedish flag. Signs appeared in stores in Moscow and St. Petersburg and elsewhere saying, "We don't sell Estonian goods."[34]

The siege was lifted only on May 3, when the Estonian ambassador left Moscow for consultations. Other forms of harassment continued. In late June a group of deputies in the State Duma called for putting up a replica of the Bronze Soldier in Moscow next to the Estonian embassy and asked Luzhkov to set aside a site for that purpose.[35] On September 19 Konstantin Goloskokov, a Nashi activist, began to picket the Estonian embassy, demanding a visa so that he could "stand guard [in Tonismagi] in memory of the fallen Soviet soldiers who liberated Estonia from fascism."[36] On September 25 Goloskokov was formally refused a visa. On October 1 he began a hunger strike, drinking only mineral water. He put up a tent in front of the embassy and promised to remain at his post day and night. On the street in front of the embassy, Nashi organized an exhibit on the subject of "Estonian state fascism."

In the immediate aftermath of the confrontation over the Bronze Soldier, a public opinion poll conducted by the Levada Center showed that 60 percent of Russia's citizens considered Estonia to be an enemy of Russia, a higher percentage than for any other country.[37] Luzhkov called for a boycott of all things Estonian. "We must say to Russian companies, halt your contacts with Estonia," he said. "It has shown to us its most negative and — if I may say so — a Nazi face."[38]

The idea that the meaning of Russian history comes from the creation of a strong state also brought Russia into conflict with Ukraine. If the issue with Estonia was the supposed sanctity of Soviet war symbols, in the case of Ukraine it was the Soviet state's responsibility for the 1932–33 famine or *Golodomor* (literally, murder by starvation), which caused five million to seven million deaths, most of them in Ukraine.

Of all the crimes committed by the Soviet Union, none was more terrible than the famine. The grain crop in 1932 was sufficient to avoid widespread starvation, but large amounts of grain were lost during the harvest because dekulakization had deprived the countryside of its best workers, and the peasants had destroyed their draft animals rather than turn them over to the collective farms. When the state imposed draconian quotas for grain, the peasants were seized by a fear of famine and began to resist the removal of grain from their villages by any means, including theft. The government reacted by requisitioning virtually the entire harvest. Local Communist activists, with the help of volunteers from the cities, scoured cellars, attics, barns, and holes in the ground and confiscated not only hidden grain but all reserves. At the same time, military units prevented the peasants from leaving their villages, which in many cases was their only hope of survival. The result was the greatest catastrophe the Ukrainian countryside has ever seen.

In the past, Russian leaders, including the Soviet leaders in 1921–22, had reacted to famines by trying to save lives. This time, Stalin and the Soviet leadership refused even to acknowledge that a famine was taking place. Instead they tried to create the impression that the country was successfully completing the first Five Year Plan. The Soviet leadership declined foreign assistance and not only did not purchase grain abroad to relieve the famine but continued to export grain, using the hard currency that was earned to develop heavy industry, dooming millions to death from starvation.

In the end, the famine devastated all of the principal grain-growing regions of the Soviet Union, including Ukraine, the North Caucasus, the lower and middle Volga region, the central black earth zone, Kazakhstan, western Siberia, and the southern Urals. But its impact was greatest in Ukraine, where resistance to collectivization had been particularly strong. It left a wound in Ukraine that is felt to this day.

The idea that the famine was an act of genocide directed against Ukrainians had long been held by survivors, who whispered it behind closed doors. During the Soviet period, it was forbidden to mention the famine publicly. In his speech in November 1987 marking the seventieth anniversary of the Bolshevik seizure of power, Gorbachev referred to collectivization as one of the great achievements of the party. As the policy of glasnost gathered momentum, however, details of the famine appeared in the Ukrainian press. Rukh, the Ukrainian movement for national identity, used the memory of the famine to rally support for an independent Ukraine, and memorial services were held in Ukrainian villages.

In 1993 Leonid Kravchuk, the president of Ukraine, referred to the famine as an act of "genocide against one's own people" but "directed from a different center."[39] It was only in 1998, however, under pressure from nationalist deputies and the Ukrainian diaspora, that Leonid Kuchma, Kravchuk's successor, established the fourth Saturday in November as a day of commemoration for the victims of the famine. On the day of remembrance in 2002, Kuchma called the famine the planned genocide of the Ukrainian people and urged efforts to gain international recognition of this fact. In 2003, at the request of Ukraine, the U.N. General Assembly approved a declaration marking the seventieth anniversary of the famine, recognizing it as the national tragedy of the Ukrainian people, but not as genocide. Efforts to have the famine classified as genocide received a new impetus with the election of Viktor Yushchenko as president of Ukraine in 2004.

Yushchenko was determined to move Ukraine toward the West and to strengthen its separate national identity. He did this in part by focusing on Ukraine's bitter historical experience as a part of the Russian Empire. He commemorated the memory of the famine, honored the anti-Soviet Ukrainian partisans who continued fighting until 1952, and commemorated the followers of the Hetman, Ivan Mazepa, who had taken the side of Charles XII in the Northern War of the eighteenth century. Of these national symbols, the famine was the most important. In November 2006, at Yushchenko's urging, the Ukrainian parliament adopted a law declaring the famine a genocide of the Ukrainian people.[40]

The Ukrainian effort to have the famine recognized as genocide drew attention to the famine in Russia. During perestroika, it had been discussed in Russia, along with the famines of 1921–22 and 1946–47, as an indictment of the Soviet system, but there had been no attempt to memorialize the event or commemorate the victims. But as the issue of the Golodomor (*Holomodor* in Ukrainian) became increasingly important in Ukraine after the breakup of the Soviet Union, Russians tried to prove that the famine was not genocide and that all nationalities in the vast famine area had suffered equally. The resulting debate became increasingly heated, provoking extreme positions on both sides.

Ukrainian political leaders and scholars have advanced a number of arguments to support the view that the 1932–33 famine was a case of genocide directed against Ukrainians. A leading Ukrainian historian, Stanislav Kulchytsky, said that it was necessary to draw a distinction between the famine that affected large parts of the Soviet Union in 1932–33 and was the result of the attempts to force the pace of economic transformation, and the terror famine in Ukraine and the Kuban region (which was 75 percent ethnic Ukrainian). The latter, he argued, was a carefully organized mass crime intended to destroy Ukrainian national aspirations.[41]

Kulchytsky said that beginning in the final quarter of 1932, the Kremlin imposed fines in kind on farmers who were not meeting their quotas for grain. But if the authorities in other areas confiscated the grain necessary to fulfill the state procurement quotas, local authorities in Ukraine also confiscated all of the reserves. Deprived first of bread and then of all other food products, Kulchytsky wrote, the farmers lacked the physical strength to resist. They died meekly in villages isolated from the outside world. As a direct result of the confiscation of all foodstuffs in Ukraine, the death rate from the specifically Ukrainian terror famine, according to Kulchytsky, was ten times higher than that of the general famine.[42]

Kulchytsky's argument was supported by Vladimir Vasilenko, another Ukrainian historian. Vasilenko said that the greatest resistance to the Soviet collectivization of agriculture was in Ukraine. Though spontaneous and disorganized, this resistance had the potential to turn into a national uprising. The terror famine was a "preventive, punitive operation" intended to prevent such an uprising. "With the help of an artificially organized famine," he wrote, "a crushing blow was delivered to the Ukrainian peasantry with the goal of physically destroying the heart of the nation, and cutting off any potential resistance."[43]

In response to the Ukrainian arguments, Russian historians have insisted that the famine was not directed against Ukrainians. Viktor Kondrashin, in *The Famine of 1932–33: The Tragedy of the Russian Village*, writes that, in contrast with the genocide of the Armenians in 1915 and of the Jews during the Second World War, as well as the ethnic slaughter in Rwanda, there are no documents testifying to an intention to destroy Ukrainians by famine. On the contrary, between February 7 and July 20, 1933, there were thirty-five government decisions mandating the delivery of food aid amounting to 320,000 tons of grain to the stricken areas. Of this total, 264,700 tons was delivered to Ukraine and the Kuban region and 55,300 tons to all other regions. "These figures," writes Kondrashin, "refute the theory of the famine as genocide directed against Ukraine."[44]

With the passage by the Ukrainian parliament of the law on the Holo-domor, Ukrainian diplomats intensified their efforts to gain international recognition for the famine as genocide. Russian diplomats worked to defeat these efforts, which, on the whole, were not a success.

In June 2008 Gorbachev said that the effort to describe the famine as genocide of the Ukrainians was political. "In my native village of Privolny [Stavropol region], 40 percent of the population died. Of six children of my grandfather on my father's side, three died of hunger," he said.[45]

The diplomatic battle, however, called attention to the difference be-tween the way the famine was commemorated in Ukraine and how it was marked in Russia. In 2008 a national memorial was dedicated in Kiev to the victims, a high column in the form of a candle, which became the center of a memorial complex. But in Russia there is no monument to famine victims on either the federal or the regional level. Memorial also has no record of a commemoration of the famine victims being established in any Russian village.

The difference in the attitudes in Russia and Ukraine toward the 1932–33 famine is explained by a number of factors. In the first place, of the estimated five million to seven million deaths, the overwhelming majority were in Ukraine and Kuban, with the rest spread among the other Soviet republics. Only the Ukrainians saw the famine as a specifically national tragedy. At the same time, Russians, more than Ukrainians, identified with the process through which the modern Soviet Union was created. Russian historians argue that without the collectivization of agriculture, which led to the famine, the Soviet Union could not have won the Second World War.

On April 2, 2008, the seventy-fifth anniversary of the famine, the Rus-sian State Duma for the first time adopted a special resolution on the tragedy. It acknowledged that the famine claimed the lives of seven million persons, but it attributed the disaster to a combination of economic mis-management and repression. "Striving to resolve at any cost the prob-lem of food supply for rapidly growing industrial centers," the resolution said, "the leadership of the USSR and union republics used repressive measures in grain procurement which aggravated considerably the dire consequences of the crop failure of 1932." At the same time, "there is absolutely no historic proof that the famine was organized under ethnic principles. . . . The tragedy does not have and cannot have internationally established signs of genocide and must not be the subject of present day political speculations."[46]

The resolution was framed in reasonable language, but it also contained a chilling hint that, in the final analysis, Russia considered the famine to have been part of a process that was, on the whole, positive. It said that while the peoples of the USSR paid an enormous price for industrialization, the industrial giants of the Soviet Union, the Novokuznetsk Metallurgical Combine, the Magnitogorsk Metallurgical Combine, and the Dniepr Hydroelectic Plant, will be "eternal monuments" to the victims.[47]

On November 22, 2008, Ukraine commemorated the seventy-fifth anniversary of the famine and dedicated the memorial. In his speech at the ceremony in Kiev, Yushchenko called the famine "a well planned act of genocide." At the peak of the Holodomor, he said, twenty-five thousand people died every day. "Stalin wanted to break the spine of the Ukrainians who were the second largest ethnic group in the empire and potentially the biggest threat to it."[48]

Russian President Dimitri Medvedev was invited to attend the ceremonies but declined. In a letter to Yushchenko explaining his reasons, he wrote that the theme of the famine was being used for political ends. The famine was not, he insisted, directed toward the destruction of any particular nationality, and to speak otherwise is "cynical and amoral." Konstantin Grishchenko, the ambassador of Ukraine in Russia, said that Medvedev's letter caused disappointment in Ukraine. In an interview with Ekho Moskvy, he said: "We would have wanted that on this day [the seventy-fifth anniversary of the famine] we could have been together to give their due to the memory of the millions of Ukrainians and persons of other nationalities who were victims of the Stalinist terror."[49]

The famine, by some estimates, destroyed about a sixth of the population of Ukraine. It killed indiscriminately. No category of the population was spared, and survival in the affected areas depended not on personal traits but on skill in hiding food, twists of fate, and cannibalism. Death was so pervasive, gruesome, and indiscriminate, and it affected Ukrainians so disproportionately, that that what took place can justly be described as genocide whether the wiping out of an entire people was the Soviet leaders' underlying intention or not. Miroslav Popovich, a Ukrainian historian and philosopher, said that the problem is with the legal definition of genocide. "The United Nations' definition of genocide is exclusively the mass killing of people on the basis of their nationality or ethnicity," he said. "So formally, one can regard [Holodomor] as a massive tragedy rather than genocide. But in actual fact, one can regard it as genocide."[50]

In the years since Yushchenko sought to make the famine a pillar of Ukraine's national identity, Russia, which was exalting the history of the Russian state, has reacted to the Ukrainian accusation of genocide legalistically and with little attention to the essential truth in the accusation. It did this although leaders in Ukraine stated repeatedly that this was a question of the responsibility not of contemporary Russia but of the Stalinist regime.

In a front-page comment in the daily *Izvestiya*, Solzhenitsyn attacked the argument that the Ukrainians were victims of genocide. "This provocateur's cry of 'genocide,'" he wrote, "began to germinate decades later — first secretly, in the moldy minds of chauvinists maliciously set against [Russia], and now elevated to government circles of today's Ukraine." He implied that the Ukrainian appeal might be supported by Western governments for geopolitical purposes. "They have never understood our history. All they need is a ready fable, even if it is an insane one."[51]

The notion that there is something sacred about the Russian state creates a psychological gap between Russia and the rest of Europe. This immediately becomes clear whenever Europeans make any attempt to condemn the crimes of Stalinism. On July 3, 2009, the parliamentary assembly of the Organization for Security and Cooperation in Europe (OSCE) voted to support making August 23, the anniversary of the Molotov-Ribbentrop Pact, a day of memory for the victims of Stalinism and Nazism. The OSCE resolution urged its members to take a united stand against totalitarian rule "from whatever ideological background."[52]

The Russian reaction was sharply hostile. The Russian delegation boycotted the voting, and Alexander Kozlovsky, its head, said that any attempt to equate Nazism and the Soviet regime was an "outrage against history."[53] The leaders of the Russian parliament called the OSCE declaration "an attempt to destroy the . . . dialogue between Russia and the West" and "a direct insult" to the memory of millions of Soviet citizens who died "for the liberation of Europe."[54] Oleg Morozov, the first vice speaker of the State Duma, said the attempt to equate Nazism and Stalinism was "simply infuriating."[55]

The idea of a strong state as the goal of Russian history is now well established, but its implications for those subject to Russian power are a serious matter. The statist-FSB philosophy means that the Russian regime will not be morally restrained when it believes its political interests are at stake, or worry excessively about the value of its citizens' lives.

One of the most dramatic illustrations of the results of the exaltation of the Russian state was Russian behavior during the battle of Grozny in the First Chechen War, December 1994 to March 1995. At that time, Yeltsin was in charge, but he shared the statist psychology that became explicit with the elevation of Putin.

When initial hopes of suppressing the Chechen separatist movement "in two hours" disappeared in the face of fierce Chechen resistance, the Russian Army began the block-by-block leveling of an inhabited city with the help of intense artillery fire and carpet bombing. By the time Russian forces occupied the last parts of Grozny on March 7, it was estimated that twenty-seven thousand civilians had been killed, most of them ethnic Russians.

The dismay of elderly Russian pensioners trapped in Grozny because they were penniless and had no family in Russia was expressed to Anatol Lieven, who covered the war for the London *Times*, by Lydia Mukashenko, an elderly Russian widow:

> The Russian Federation is killing us Russians. Two of my neighbors are dead. Why? For what? Russian television said that Grozny is empty of people, that it's a military target. Are they lying, or do they really not know that there are still women and children here? Tell them, you must tell them that we are still here, that they are killing us, that the Russian army is killing its own people.[56]

Lieven was so shocked by the Russian Army's disregard for the lives of civilians in Grozny that he assumed Yeltsin's political career would be finished when Russians learned what had occurred. He even predicted Yeltsin's fall in an editorial.[57] Nothing of the kind happened. There was no reaction to the massacre from the political leadership, and it had almost no impact on the national consciousness.

Ultimately, the statist interpretation of Russian history is a justification for unaccountability and an absolution of past crimes. It frankly acknowledges that the issue for the Russian state is not an idea but power. But the fact that it is put, however clumsily, in the form of a political doctrine further complicates the task of Russian society in searching for a new direction.

Russia has long been burdened with a false state tradition that elevates gangsters to positions of power and devalues the lives of its citizens. To free itself, it needs to view the past objectively, without spurious justifications. Tolstoy wrote, "In order to cure a disease, you must first of all recognize it, and this is what we do not do." As a result,

> the disease does not pass but only changes its appearance, penetrating deeper in the flesh, in the blood, in the bones and in bone marrow. . . . We say, why should we remember? In fact, if I had a terrible and dangerous disease and I was cured, I would always with pleasure remember this. . . . We don't understand only because we know that we are sick nonetheless and we want to fool ourselves.[58]

CHAPTER 12

The Shadow of Katyn

■

On a night in December 2009 in Smolensk, at the Church of the Immaculate Conception of the Virgin Mary, Father Ptolomeusz Kuczmik, the Catholic priest in the city, recalled an incident from his boyhood in Poland. "When I was growing up in the 1950s," he said, "my grandmother pointed out a woman to me and said that her husband was killed at Katyn. I asked her, 'What is Katyn?' She refused to answer. She just said, 'When the time comes, you'll find out.'"

Today, Father Ptolomeusz meets relatives of the victims of the Katyn Forest massacre and accompanies them to the memorial in the Koziye Gori (Goat's Hills) section of the forest, where more than four thousand Polish officers are buried. He listens to their stories and tries to comfort them.

The family members come from Poland but also from the United States, Britain, and other countries. "Overwhelmingly," Father Ptolomeusz said, "they want to forgive. There is not a person who wants to live in hate. There are persons who came specifically to say the prayer 'Ochi Nashi,' in which they ask forgiveness for those who transgress against them. In some cases, they say that only here could they find the strength to forgive those who deprived their father of life."

The Poles who visit the memorial, however, are often troubled by two facts that have implications for the issue of forgiveness. The Russian government has never officially apologized for the Katyn massacre or described it as a crime against humanity, and most of the record of the Russian investigation, which began in 1990 and lasted for more than fourteen years, is classified. Even the reasoning behind the decision to classify 116 volumes of evidence is secret, although Russian law forbids classifying information relating to abuses of human rights.[1]

The events that led to the Katyn Forest massacre and the long cover-up that ensued began on September 17, 1939, when the Soviet Union invaded Poland, which was already at war with the invading Nazis. Polish commanders ordered their troops not to fire on the Red Army in order to concentrate their efforts against the Germans, and as the Soviets overran the eastern part of the country, 250,000 Polish servicemen were taken prisoner. The Soviets allowed ordinary soldiers and low-ranking officers to return to their homes. But high-ranking officers, agents of the Polish intelligence service, military police, and prison wardens were placed in three prisoner of war camps: the Kozelsk camp, 150 miles southeast of Smolensk; the Starobelsk camp, 125 miles southeast of Kharkov; and the Ostashkov camp, 100 miles west of Kalinin (now Tver). In all, 14,856 Polish prisoners were placed in the three camps.[2]

The Kozelsk camp, three miles from the city of Kozelsk, was guarded by high walls topped with barbed wire and lit at night by searchlights. The prisoners slept on boards and were tormented by bedbugs and lice. "There is nowhere a free place," a prisoner noted in his diary. "There is nowhere to sit, nothing to read. The days pass in a senseless manner. There are long lines for food, water, to go to the toilet, to the grave."[3]

The prisoners at Kozelsk included four generals, one rear admiral, twenty-one university professors and lecturers, some of Poland's most outstanding surgeons and journalists, writers, lawyers, judges, and prosecutors. Father Zdzislaw Peszkowski, one of the prisoners, recalled that in the early evening, officers went through the crowded quarters announcing the time, location, and subject matter of classes and lectures given by fellow prisoners. Each night at 9 P.M., the prisoners began three minutes of spiritual devotion despite the camp ban on religious activity. Members of all religions — Protestants, Orthodox, Catholics, and Jews — observed these periods of silence. Father Peszkowski, one of the few survivors from the camp, was later to recall, "At Kozelsk, I discovered Poland."[4]

The prisoners were subjected to constant interrogations, mostly at night. The Red Army entered Poland on the pretext of establishing public order after the "collapse" of the Polish government, whose disappearance, in the Soviet interpretation, left the Polish prisoners stateless. The Soviets extended de facto Soviet citizenship to the prisoners from eastern Poland. This, however, denied them the protection of the Geneva Convention on the treatment of prisoners of war, and since they had served in a capitalist army, it left them vulnerable under Soviet law to charges of counterrevolutionary activities.

A prisoner who was transferred to the Smolensk prison in early March and later escaped to the West described his interrogation by a political officer named Samarin.

SAMARIN: Let us imagine that the public prosecutor annuls your case. Let us suppose that your request to return to German-occupied Poland is complied with, that the Germans allow you to live at liberty in Warsaw at your apartment. What would you do?

PRISONER: I would rest after my exhausting experiences.

SAMARIN: Supposing I turned up at your apartment for one day, would you give me a cup of tea?

PRISONER: I don't know if there would be any tea there.

SAMARIN: And would you put me up for the night?

PRISONER: You have the large Soviet legation in Warsaw. You would be better off and more comfortable there.

SAMARIN: But if I did not want the Soviet Legation to know of my arrival; if I came incognito as a spy, would you take me in and report to the Gestapo that a Soviet agent had arrived?

PRISONER: I do not know the regulations in Warsaw about reporting. I do not know what has happened to my apartment. In these circumstances, I cannot give you an answer.[5]

On April 22, 1940, an NKVD commissar at Kozelsk named Niechorochev wrote in a report to Beria's aide, Gen. Vsevolod Merkulov, in Moscow:

The majority of the officers coming from the German territories . . . want to go to neutral countries such as France where they would volunteer for the French army and fight against Germany, then turn against the Soviet Union and restore Poland from the Oder to the Dnieper. . . . Some officers dream of . . . joining the Weygand army [in Romania] and forming an armed detachment against the Soviet Union. . . . Some offer the following opinions: "The Soviet Union is worried because there is danger from their [German] allies." "The Soviet Union is very large but it has feet made of clay. It's enough to touch it and it will fall." . . . During the political indoctrination talks, the audience is very passive. . . . Some others challenged us. For example . . . "You gave us a knife in the back. Poland is going to exist anyway and it will pay you back. You are going to be our prisoners."[6]

Although the Polish Army had just been defeated, the prisoners were optimistic. They believed that Hitler would be crushed and Poland would outlast its oppressors. Many believed that a British and French attack on Germany was imminent, and in March 1940 there were rumors that the Soviets had reached a firm decision to close the camps. NKVD officers encouraged these rumors to create a false sense of security.

In fact, the prisoners could not have imagined how dire their situation was. In a memorandum to Stalin dated March 5, Beria stated that in the camps for war prisoners of the NKVD and in the prisons of the western oblasts of Ukraine and Belorussia, there were "a large number of former officers of the Polish army, former employees of the Polish police and intelligence organs, members of Polish nationalistic counter-revolutionary parties, participants in secret counter-revolutionary insurgent organizations, traitors and others."[7]

Inasmuch as all of them were "committed and incorrigible enemies of Soviet power," the NKVD considered it necessary to examine the cases of the 14,700 persons in the prisoner of war camps and the 11,000 persons in the prisons of the western parts of Ukraine and Belorussia — "members of various counterrevolutionary and espionage and terrorist organizations" — in a "special regime" in which the prisoners would be subject to "the highest measure of punishment — shooting." The review of cases would proceed without the arrested persons being called and without the presentation of any accusation. It would be carried out by a troika consisting of Merkulov, Bakhcho Kobulov, a deputy head of the NKVD, and Leonid Bashtakov, the head of the first special department of the NKVD. The memorandum was signed by J. Stalin, K. Voroshilov, V. Molotov, and A. Mikoyan, and in the margin was written, "Kalinin — yes, Kaganovich — yes." It sealed the fate of more than 22,000 persons.[8]

The transport of prisoners to their deaths began on April 3, 1940. It continued for seven weeks, after which it was reported that 14,587 officers had been evacuated from the three camps.

As the Polish officers left the camps, every effort was made to convince them that they were about to be liberated. At Kozelsk, the camp authorities arranged a farewell reception for an early departing group that included three generals. The prisoners formed an honor guard and cheered as the generals passed. At the Ostashkov and Starobelsk camps, the prisoners were given a sendoff by military bands.

According to the few who escaped death, and descriptions contained in diaries found on the bodies of Polish officers exhumed at Katyn, once the prisoners had cleared the camp gates at Kozelsk, the friendly atmosphere disappeared. Waiting for them were NKVD guards with truncheons, machine guns, and dogs. The prisoners were ordered into cars or trucks and driven through the woods to the railroad station, five miles away. The station was heavily guarded, and the men were pushed into windowless prison cars called Stolypin wagons, where as many as sixteen were forced into compartments intended for six to eight persons.[9]

The train from Kozelsk came to a halt at Gnezdovo, eight miles west of Smolensk. There the men were taken out of the train in groups of thirty and put into the rear of cramped prison vans. Those who hesitated were shoved in. Only one prisoner, Stanislaw Swianiewicz, witnessed what happened next and survived. His group arrived on the morning of April 30. The prisoners heard the sounds of running motors and shouted commands. Men from other cars were being offloaded when an NKVD colonel came to the door and ordered Swianiewicz, an expert on the Nazi and Soviet economies, outside. He was taken to an empty carriage and locked in one of the compartments, where he discovered a small hole near the roof. Climbing onto the upper luggage rack, he watched through the hole as the NKVD removed his fellow prisoners from the train. He saw that the area was guarded by NKVD soldiers with fixed bayonets, and he wondered why unarmed prisoners from whom even penknives had been taken were thought to pose such a risk.[10]

From the road, a bus whose windows were whitewashed with lime entered the ground. Swianiewicz tried to understand why the bus had whitewashed windows. The bus drove off and returned after half an hour to take the next contingent. He concluded that the place to which the prisoners were taken was nearby, but again he was puzzled. "What was the purpose of such a . . . procedure instead of ordering the prisoners to march, as on previous occasions?" The NKVD colonel who had picked him out from his group "was directing the whole operation. I wondered what kind of operation it was. . . . At that moment, in the rays of this wonderful spring day, the thought of execution had not entered my mind."[11]

The prison wagons traveled for about three miles into the woods, to an area halfway between the main road and the Dnieper River, where open pits had been readied. One prisoner, Major Adam Solski, described his final moments in such a wagon in his diary, which was recovered in 1943 from one of the mass graves.

> April 9. A few minutes before five in the morning — wake up call in the prison railway cars and preparations to leave. We are to go somewhere by car. And what then? . . . 5 AM . . . departure in a prison car in cells (awful!). We were driven to some place in a wood; something like a summer resort. Here, a detailed search took place. They took my watch, showing 6:30. They asked about my wedding ring. . . . They took rubles, main belt, penknife.[12]

There are no known eyewitnesses to the killing of the Polish officers. The place where the prisoners were buried, Koziye Gori, was an NKVD dacha settlement that had served as an execution site and burial ground for victims of the Great Terror. It was first thought that all of the Polish officers had been shot at the edge of the burial pits. But few shell casings were found in the pits or nearby. And the hands of the vast majority of the victims were unbound, which means that they were taken by surprise — an indication that they were shot elsewhere. Local Russians testified that prisoners were taken to or near the main building of the NKVD summer resort. It is now thought likely that many were shot in an execution room in one of the NKVD dachas and in the NKVD headquarters in Smolensk. The hands of 20 percent of the victims, however, were tied behind their backs. Some had sawdust in their mouths, and the rope binding their hands was looped around their necks, so that if they moved they would suffocate. Probably the prisoners with tied hands were shot at the burial site. Those with rope around their necks were almost certainly the ones who had tried to resist.

The prisoners from the Ostashkov camp met their deaths in the internal prison of the Kalinin NKVD. Dmitri Tokarev, who was the head of the Kalinin NKVD, described the execution of the prisoners during his interrogation by Russian prosecutors in 1991. He said one of the cells had been covered in advance with felt so that the shots would not be audible. The Poles were taken one by one to the "Red Corner" (the Lenin room), where officials collated information — last name, first name, patronymic, year of birth. Each prisoner was handcuffed and taken to the execution room, where he was shot in the back of the head. The body was then brought to the yard and loaded into a closed truck.[13]

The shooting of the Starobelsk prisoners took place in the Kharkov prison and followed the same procedure as in Kalinin. The only surviving eyewitness was Mitrofan Syromiatnikov, an NKVD militia lieutenant who was interrogated by Soviet and Polish prosecutors between June 1990 and March 1992. According to Syromiatnikov, the guards escorted the unsuspecting prisoners to a special room, where a prosecutor and NKVD official asked the prisoner his family name, patronymic, and date of birth. "The prisoner was then told, 'You may go.' There was a clack and that was the end." Syromiatnikov said that he did not see the shooting, only heard it.[14]

In addition to the inmates in the three special prisoner of war camps, the NKVD executed 7,305 Polish prisoners held in the NKVD prisons in western Ukraine and Belorussia. The fate of these prisoners is not fully known. The names of 3,435 Polish prisoners in Ukraine who were transferred to NKVD prisons in Kiev, Kharkov, and Kherson and shot were found by Ukrainian authorities, but their burial place is unknown. There is no trace of the presumed 3,870 prisoners taken from the NKVD prisons in Belorussia and sent to the NKVD prison in Minsk. The government of Belarus has declined to release documents or to permit archeological investigation of presumed burial sites.

For reasons that are not clear, 395 of the prisoners in the three camps were spared. They were sent first to the Yukhnov camp, near Smolensk, and then to the Griazovets camp near Vologda. Some of them were sympathetic to the Soviet Union. Natalya Lebedeva, a Russian historian at the Institute of Universal History, said that about 100 were probably agents. In most cases, however, those who were not executed disappointed their

Soviet captors. They proved to be no less patriotic and hostile to the Soviet Union than their murdered comrades.

The Polish officers were murdered at a time when the Soviet leadership did not fear an imminent war with Germany. But after France fell, in June 1940, the situation changed, and an attack on the Soviet Union became a real possibility. In October, Beria and Merkulov selected a group of pro-Soviet Polish officers led by Col. (later Gen.) Zygmunt Berling, who had been held at Starobelsk but was sent to Griazovets, to draw up plans for a Polish division in the Red Army. According to Berling's account, he and Col. Eustachy Gorczynski, another prisoner who had come to Griazovets from Starobelsk, drew up a list of five hundred officers for this division. Beria asked whether it included those held in the Kozelsk and Starobelsk camps. They said that it did. Beria replied that those men had left the country.[15]

After war broke out and Soviet-Polish relations were restored, it was agreed to raise a separate Polish army. General Władysław Anders, who was being held in the Lubyanka prison, was accepted as the commander and set free. Polish military authorities noticed, however, that almost all the officers from the Kozelsk and Starobelsk camps were missing, as were the policemen and gendarmes from Ostashkov. In late November 1941, General Władysław Sikorski, the head of the Polish government in exile, flew to Moscow and met Stalin. During their meeting, Sikorski said that many Poles were still in prisons and camps. They were losing their strength and health instead of serving the common cause. Stalin replied that all the Poles who were imprisoned had been released under an amnesty. The rest of the conversation was recorded by Anders, who was also present.

> SIKORSKI: I have with me a list of nearly 4,000 officers removed by force and now located in prisons and camps, and even this list is not complete because it contained only the last names that have been listed by memory. I gave the order to verify if they were in Poland with which we have constant ties. It turns out that there is not a single one of them there. Nor are they in the prisoner of war camps in Germany. These people are located here. Not a single one of them has returned.

STALIN: That's not possible. They fled.
ANDERS: Where could they have fled?
STALIN: Well, to Manchuria, for example.[16]

The Germans attacked the Soviet Union on June 21, 1941, and the Smolensk region was quickly overrun. In July the German 537th Signals Regiment established itself in the Katyn Forest at Koziye Gori. In early 1943, four Russian prisoners of war working for the Germans discovered a hole dug by a wolf. When Col. Friedrich Ahrens, the commander of the regiment, examined the area about four weeks later, he saw that "there were graves and the wolf had been digging for bones."[17] The Germans began digging and uncovered a mass grave.

For Germany, the discovery was a godsend. German propaganda chief Joseph Goebbels believed he had found a way to divide the Allies. The Germans began exhumations at the site. On April 10, 1943, a delegation of Poles from German-occupied Poland was taken by the Germans to Katyn to view the burial site. Except for one pro-German journalist, they refused to make statements useful to the Germans, but they secretly reported what they had seen to the Home Army in Warsaw. On April 11, 1943, German radio announced the discovery of the corpses of some three thousand Polish officers killed by the NKVD. After the return of the Polish delegation, a technical commission of the Polish Red Cross visited and concluded on the basis of identification of the victims, as well as newspapers and diaries found on the corpses, that the killings had taken place in the spring of 1940. At a difficult moment for the Allies, proof had emerged that the missing Polish officers had been murdered by the NKVD.

In June 1943, nine or ten plywood chests containing items found on the Polish corpses were sent to the former Polish State Institute of Forensic Medicine in Kraków, then under German control. A team of forensic experts under Dr. Jan Zygmunt Robel began examining the items. As the Russians closed in on Kraków, Werner Beck, the German director of the Institute, arranged for the evacuation of the items, repacked in fourteen chests, to Breslau (Wrocław), where they were stored in the anatomical institute of the university. But as the line of the front advanced, Beck decided to evacuate the chests again, this time to Dresden. When the Russians entered Dresden, he gave the order to burn the chests.

The chests were destroyed, but over the years, some Katyn documents

have surfaced. In March 1991, workers renovating the Institute of Forensic Medicine in Kraków found in the attic a well-preserved sealed packet
with typed copies of the diaries. It had been put there by a worker at the
institute, who had not mentioned it to anyone. Additional Katyn documents, apparently salvaged from the fire at the Polish Red Cross office
in Warsaw during the 1944 uprising, were hidden in Kraków. Finally,
some of the Katyn items, still in the original envelopes, were hidden by a
staff member of the Kraków city archives. After the war they were found
by Professor Marian Friedberg, the director, who continued to conceal
them. The Polish Security Police eventually seized the items in November
1953 and took them to Warsaw. But they did not destroy them — or report
them to the Soviets. They were turned over to the Metropolitan Curia in
Kraków on April 3, 1990, ten days before the Soviet Union admitted guilt
for Katyn.

The Smolensk area was liberated by the Red Army on September 25,
1943. Shortly afterward, a report was prepared on the "so-called Katyn
question." It was signed by Merkulov, who blamed the Germans. When
Soviet investigators reopened the case in 1990, they learned that the NKVD
operatives had put forged documents with dates later than May 1940 in the
clothes of selected victims. They also detained persons who worked for the
Germans in the area and, under threat of death for cooperating with the
enemy, turned them into "witnesses."[18]

On January 13, 1944, an official commission on Katyn was established
under Nikolai Burdenko, the chief surgeon of the Red Army. Burdenko's
commission supported the conclusion of the NKVD operatives. In the
summer of 1945, when the victorious powers agreed to try German war
criminals in Nuremberg, the Soviet charges against the Nazi leaders included the massacre at Katyn. In order to compel the tribunal to accept the
findings of the Burdenko commission, the Soviets relied on article 21 of
the tribunal's charter: "The Tribunal shall not require proof of facts of
common knowledge but shall take judicial notice thereof. It shall also take
judicial notice of . . . the acts . . . of the committees set up by the various
countries for the investigation of war crimes."[19]

The Allies showed no desire to raise the subject of Katyn, but Dr. Otto
Stahmer, the lawyer for Hermann Göring, who was charged with complicity for Katyn, asked to call as defense witnesses the commanding of-

ficers of the 537th Signals Regiment, who were listed in the Soviet accusation as directly responsible for the massacre. The Soviet prosecutor, Roman Rudenko, objected, but the tribunal agreed and Stahmer's examination of the German officers cleared them completely. As a result, the Katyn case was not listed in the tribunal's verdicts. But to avoid a conflict between the Allies, Göring and the other top Nazi leaders were nonetheless found guilty of all the crimes with which they were charged, and until April 1990, the Soviets insisted that they had won their case on Katyn at Nuremberg.

After the Nuremberg trials, silence descended over the issue of Katyn in the Soviet Union. Dachas were built on the execution site at Koziye Gori, which was surrounded by a six-foot-high wooden fence topped with barbed wire. In front of the fence was a small plaque on which it was written in Russian that on that site Polish officers had been shot by the Hitlerites.

Khrushchev did not mention Katyn in his secret speech in 1956 denouncing the crimes of Stalin, although there are reports that he discussed admitting the crime and blaming it on Stalin with the Polish party leader Władisław Gomulka, who rejected the suggestion for fear of the Polish reaction.

On March 3, 1959, in the absence of any further action, Alexander Shelepin, the head of the KGB, suggested destroying the personal files of the victims on the grounds that they had neither "operational interest" nor "historical value." He wrote that, on the contrary, an unexpected turn of events could lead to the Katyn operation being revealed. This, he said, would be highly undesirable in light of the well-publicized official version putting the blame on the Germans. Shelepin proposed saving only the protocols of the NKVD troika that had condemned the prisoners and the documents that confirmed the carrying out of the sentences. The protocols, however, were destroyed along with the personal files.[20]

It was not until the beginning of glasnost that attention in the Soviet Union returned to the question of Katyn. In spring 1987, during a visit to Moscow by Wojciech Jaruzelski, the Polish Communist leader, Gorbachev agreed to set up a Soviet-Polish joint commission to study "historical blank spots" in relations. Alexander Yakovlev was assigned to supervise the commission's work, on behalf of the politburo. But Yakovlev quickly discovered that Gorbachev was not as cooperative as he pretended. Each time Yakovlev asked for help in finding documents, Gorbachev told him, "Keep looking!" Yakovlev turned for help to Valery Boldin, who was in charge of the archives. Boldin insisted that he did not have the documents, but he did so, Yakovlev later wrote, "with a slight smile." Yakovlev began to have doubts about Gorbachev's and Boldin's sincerity. "But I began to chase away these doubts, because I did not see any understandable reason why it was necessary to conceal the truth."[21]

In the meantime, Katyn was drawing the attention of the Soviet intelligentsia. Natan Eidelman, a historian, investigated the issue and presented his conclusion that Katyn was a crime of the NKVD at a meeting in Moscow of the Union of Cinematographers that included Polish historians and was attended by Vladimir Abarinov, a correspondent for *Literaturnaya Gazeta*.

On May 11, 1988, Abarinov published an article entitled "Blank Spots: From Emotions to Fact," in which he gave the reasons for believing Katyn was the work of the NKVD. In response, *Literaturnaya Gazeta* received hundreds of letters from readers. Most insisted that the Soviet forces could not have shot unarmed prisoners for no reason. A few letters, however, conceded it was possible and hinted that it was justified. D. I. Ovchinnikov, from Yuzho-Sakhalinsk, wrote, "Is it really possible that our Polish friends cannot assess what happened from a clear cut class standpoint? After all, these people were the top echelons of the old Polish army that was in the service of the bourgeoisie."[22]

One of the letters was particularly important. It came from Alexei Lukin, who said that he had served in the convoy troops that guarded the Kozelsk POW camp from 1939 to 1941. While denying that any crimes had been committed, he identified his battalion — the 136th. Abarinov went to the central archive of the convoy troops and looked up the records of the 136th battalion. They showed that the POWs in the Kozelsk camps had been transported by the convoy unit to Smolensk but never came back.[23]

For forty-five years, no one in Poland at the official level had had the courage to tell the truth about Katyn. But in February 1989, as glasnost spread in the Soviet Union and round table talks progressed between the government and the banned Solidarity trade union movement, the Katyn report of the Polish Red Cross was published in Poland. On March 7 Jerzy Urban, the Polish government spokesman, told a press conference that

Polish historians on the joint commission believed that the massacre had been carried out by the NKVD. It was the first time the Polish authorities had publicly placed the blame on the Soviets.

The changed atmosphere led to new thinking among high-ranking Soviet officials. On March 22 Foreign Minister Eduard Shevarnadze; Valentin Falin, the director of the Communist Party International Department; and Vladimir Kryuchkov, the chairman of the KGB, wrote in a note to the party Central Committee that it was now advisable to admit what really had happened, "thus effecting closure to the problem." They called Katyn the subject of a campaign whose subtext gives Poles the idea "that the Soviet Union is in no way better, and perhaps even worse," than Nazi Germany and that the Soviet Union is no less responsible for the outbreak of war and even for the military rout of the government of Poland.[24]

The politburo decided on March 31, 1989, to instruct the prosecutor, the KGB, the foreign ministry, and other branches of government to produce an explanation of what happened to the Polish officers. Natalya Lebedeva and two other Russian historians, Yuri Zoria and Valentina Parsadanova, found documents in the archives with the names of the Polish officers sent out of the camps. Yakovlev reviewed the documents and told Gorbachev that there was finally something to show the joint commission. Gorbachev reacted without emotion and, in Yakovlev's view, without particular interest.[25]

In the meantime, Falin suggested that Gorbachev admit the massacre to Jaruzelski and attribute it to Beria. His proposal was rejected, but on March 25, 1990, *Moskovskiye Novosti* published documents on the convoy units that it had received from Abarinov, as well as an interview with Lebedeva, under the title "The Katyn Tragedy." This forced Gorbachev's hand. On April 13, 1990, the fiftieth anniversary of the official German radio communiqué on the Katyn graves, Jaruzelski was in Moscow and Gorbachev gave him the NKVD dispatch lists with the names of the 14,589 murdered prisoners. On the same day, the Soviet news agency Tass reported that archival materials allow the conclusion that "Beria and Merkulov and their subordinates bear direct responsibility for the evil deeds in the Katyn Forest." It expressed "deep regret" and declared that the crime represented "one of the heinous crimes of Stalinism."[26]

The acknowledgment of responsibility for the murders was a momentous step. It marked the end of a cover-up that had gone on for fifty years. In its wake, however, Gorbachev came under pressure from the Poles to provide more information, and on November 3, 1990, he instructed the state military prosecutor to begin an investigation of the Katyn crimes. There is evidence that Gorbachev did not want to delve further into Soviet responsibility for Katyn. In his memoirs, Boldin wrote that Gorbachev asked him to find documents on Katyn in March 1989, twelve months before the Soviet Union admitted its responsibility. When Gorbachev opened the two sealed envelopes that Boldin brought him, he quickly resealed them and told Boldin not to show them to anyone. "This is a hanging matter," he said.[27]

Meanwhile, the investigators located the two most important living witnesses to the crime, Tokarev and Pyotr Soprunenko, who was in charge of all prisoner of war matters for the NKVD and supervised the evacuation of the three special camps. They also located Syomiatnikov and, after the fall of the Soviet Union, Shelepin. During the years of Stalinist terror, these men had held the power of life and death. But as subjects of a criminal investigation, they were obsessed with only one thing, to avoid responsibility and depict themselves as civil servants who were merely doing their job.

Tokarev was discovered living in Vladimir, in a single room in a wooden building near the headquarters of the oblast KGB. He was questioned by Lt. Col. Anatoly Yablokov, the military prosecutor. Yablokov's first impression of Tokarev was of a sick old man. His figure was bent, and he walked with a shuffling gait and had a weak voice and dull eyes. His room was clean but bare. The only item of luxury was a mechanical wall clock, which kept the exact time. Yablokov knew that Tokarev could refuse to answer questions at any time, so he adopted a friendly, respectful tone. It was soon clear to Yablokov, however, that despite appearances, Tokarev was far from helpless. "His physical weakness had not led to the degradation of his personality," Yablokov wrote. "He immediately demonstrated internal organization, rapid and logical thought, a sharp memory, erudition and a deep intellect and—what was particularly striking—unquenched authoritarianism."[28]

Tokarev insisted that because he had been newly appointed as head of the Kalinin oblast NKVD, he had not participated directly in the murders. He said that he was summoned to a meeting in Moscow with Kobulov, who informed those attending that a decision had been taken at the highest level to shoot the fourteen thousand Polish prisoners of war. Tokarev said he understood that the order came from the politburo. Nonetheless, he said, he refused to participate in the shootings but agreed to provide all organizational assistance.[29]

On Tokarev's orders, cells were vacated so that they were available for the Polish officers, a room was prepared for the final identity checks, and an execution room was readied. Also, five dump trucks for removing bodies were provided, as was an excavator for digging pits on the territory of an NKVD dacha colony near Mednoe, twenty miles from Kalinin. Most important, executioners were selected from among the guards and drivers at the prison. Tokarev admitted that he had threatened a driver who did not want to be an executioner, but he said he did this to save the man's life. Kobulov had told him not to leave alive a single witness not implicated in the crime. Tokarev said he told the driver, "Lad, if you refuse, they will shoot you."[30]

Tokarev said that the operation was directed by Vasili Blokhin, the NKVD's main executioner, with the assistance of M. S. Krivenko, the head of the staff of the convoy troops. Blokhin brought with him an entire suitcase of German Walther pistols because the Soviet Nagans overheated. Each day at dawn, five or six cars took the bodies to Mednoe, where an excavator had already dug holes into which the bodies were afterward thrown and covered up.

During the Khrushchev thaw, Tokarev told his oldest son what had happened to the Poles and about their burial near Mednoe. But he tried to persuade his son that although he had known about this operation, he had not personally participated in it and so was not rewarded by the NKVD leadership. Tokarev's attempts to evade responsibility were transparently flimsy, but the information he provided to the investigation was critical. He tied the shootings to the politburo and explained the mechanism of the executions. He also revealed where the prisoners' bodies were buried. This made it possible to carry out an exhumation, which in turn helped to force the testimony of Soprunenko.

Yablokov's first impression of Soprunenko was similar to his impression of Tokarev. Both were badly dressed, emaciated, and ill. But unlike Tokarev, Soprunenko did not seem intelligent and articulate. After being repeatedly shown a videotape of Tokarev's testimony, Soprunenko expressed amazement at Tokarev's memory and ability to speak effectively without apparent preparation.

Soprunenko's apartment was in the center of Moscow, in a building on Sadovo-Samotechnaya Street. It had expensive furniture, antiques, and paintings, but Yablokov was struck by the atmosphere of moldiness, disorder, and neglect. Tokarev lived alone but managed to maintain himself decently, whereas Soprunenko, with two daughters living in Moscow, could not keep up elementary cleanliness and order. "In fact, it became clear to me that Soprunenko was the same type of lonely old man as Tokarev," Yablokov wrote. "His daughters came to him rarely and only when it was necessary to them." Their primary concern was that the attention to their father's crimes not affect their own position in society.[31]

Soprunenko was interrogated for the first time on October 25, 1990. At that time, the investigation had comparatively little evidence about his role, and the questioning produced little result. But after Tokarev was interrogated, Yablokov asked to question Soprunenko a second time. Soprunenko refused. His daughters characterized talk of their father's participation in the Katyn massacre as slander. Finally he agreed to be questioned in the presence of his daughters. The interrogation took place on April 29, 1991.[32]

Initially, Soprunenko insisted that he did not know anything. He avoided serious questions and tried to lead the interrogation into secondary matters. He said that in April and May of 1940, he had worked in Vyborg as part of a Soviet-Finnish commission on the exchange of prisoners. When documents were presented to him showing that that commission had been in force during a different time, he tried to place responsibility for Katyn on his deputy, I. I. Khokhlov (who was already dead). Only after being presented with archival documents and being shown a videotape of the interrogation of Tokarev did he confirm his participation. He admitted that he had held in his hands the politburo decision bearing Stalin's signature ordering the execution of the Polish officers, and that he directed the "unloading" of the three camps, compiling the lists of prisoners for execution.

The prosecutors also interviewed Syromiatnikov, who denied having taken part in the shootings and refused to sign a protocol of the interrogation on grounds of blindness. He said that his only role had been to lead the officers to the place of execution. Syromiatnikov was later interviewed by a Polish journalist, Jerzy Moravsky, who found him in a small village near Kharkov, the only survivor of 143 persons who had received awards for their "work" in the murder of the Polish officers. The interview was published in the Polish journal *Slad kuli* in 1991. Moravsky wrote that Syromiatnikov, who was eighty-three years old at the time, sat in a miserable room on an iron bed. "He had gray hair and his face was lined with wrinkles. He had been blind for several years. His eyes were dead and without expression."[33]

Syromiatnikov said that the prisoners had been shot by the commandant, Timofei Kupry.

"And he alone destroyed four thousand persons?" Moravsky asked.

"What else could he do? Hire someone and pay him for this work? Where would you find someone?"

Syromiatnikov said that there were instructions on how to kill people. "A good shooter doesn't spend a bullet in vain. On the front, you shoot and go further without knowing if you've hit anything or not. But in peacetime, you received an order and had to fulfill it in the best way possible. If you performed badly, they would put you on trial. It was better to carry out your instructions blindly."

Moravsky asked whether the executions took place during the day or at night.

"What are you saying?!" Syromiatnikov said. "Who is going to shoot people during the day?! Someone might see how these officers were being led to their deaths. How would that look from a moral point of view? No, this task was secret. So work began with the fall of darkness."

Syromiatnikov said that they had thrown the bodies into the back of a truck and taken them into the woods. "They didn't wait for the bodies to decompose. This is clear to a drunken hedgehog." During the war, he said, Kupry was convicted of speculation and sentenced to death, but the sentence was reduced to twenty-five years, and he was freed and sent to the front. After the war he went to Poltava, where he became the head of a milk factory.[34]

Moravsky asked Syromiatnikov about his own fate.

"In 1955, I was removed from the KGB," he said.

You can say that they threw me out, giving me on departure fifty rubles. They squeezed me like a lemon and then discarded me. In fact, I honestly served Soviet power. I asked them to at least help me with an apartment so that I would not live in poverty. Bandits murdered my only son. In one night, I turned completely gray. And my wife simply lost her mind. She sat for days in the cemetery at the grave of our son. And that would have continued had we not followed the advice of a doctor and left Kharkov. Now we live here.[35]

Yablokov interrogated Shelepin after the fall of the Soviet Union. On December 9, 1992, he went to the apartment where Shelepin lived with his daughter's family, in an elite building on Alexei Tolstoy Street. After Yablokov explained that he wanted to question him about his letter to Khrushchev, Shelepin said that he was not feeling well and did not remember anything. Finally he agreed to be interrogated if his successor as head of the KGB, V. E. Semichastny, who lived in the same building, also participated. Fearing that Shelepin might otherwise refuse, Yablokov agreed.[36]

The interview took place on December 11. Semichastny repeated the questions to Shelepin and helped him formulate his answers. Yablokov said that by comparison with Semichastny, who was tall, strong, and self-confident, Shelepin, who had small features and was of below-average height, appeared to be a typical elderly Russian man. His only purpose seemed to be to avoid responsibility for his acts as head of the KGB. He said that he agreed to head the KGB only because he had been ordered to do so, and while new to the job, he approved everything that was presented to him by his subordinates. He said that he gave permission for the destruction of the personal files of the Katyn victims without knowing what was in them.[37]

The fall of the Soviet Union interrupted the investigation of Katyn only temporarily. If anything, it ultimately gave the investigation new momentum, because it made possible the release of the most secret document in Soviet possession, the politburo order to execute the Polish officers.

In December 1991, in their last meeting before the dissolution of the Soviet Union, Gorbachev gave Yeltsin an envelope with documents about Katyn, including the execution order—the same documents that Gorbachev had repeatedly said he could not find. Yakovlev also attended the meeting. "In dismay, I looked at Gorbachev but did not see any sign of embarrassment," he recalled. In his memoirs, Gorbachev said that he was calm because he had received the file with Beria's memorandum earlier. "It took my breath away to read this hellish paper," he wrote.[38]

Gorbachev was not the only one to hesitate. Yeltsin waited almost a full year before making the contents public. The memorandum was finally released because Yeltsin want to use it for the trial of the Communist Party. On October 14, 1992, the text of the politburo decision was published in the Russian press, and it and other previously secret documents concerning Katyn were presented to Polish president Lech Wałęsa in Warsaw. In a letter of appreciation, Wałęsa thanked Yeltsin for his courage and called the decision to release the documents "heroic."[39]

The release of the documents ushered in a period of Russian-Polish cooperation. In August 1993 Yeltsin made his first visit to Poland and laid flowers at the Katyn cross in Warsaw's Powaski cemetery. He knelt before a Polish priest, kissed the ribbon of a wreath he had placed at the foot of the Katyn cross, and quietly said, "Forgive us, if you can."[40] He and Wałęsa promised to punish the guilty and to make reparations.[41]

In February 1994, in Kraków, an agreement was signed on the creation of Polish military cemeteries in Katyn and Mednoe. It was clear, however, that besides the Polish victims, both Katyn and Mednoe also contained Soviet victims. In 1994 Smolensk Memorial, with the help of a team of volunteers, found 277 common graves in the area. To create a Polish memorial, when next to it were the unmarked graves of Soviet victims, would have been too blatant a demonstration of Russia's disregard for its own citizens, so plans were developed for a memorial complex honoring all of the victims of totalitarianism.

In the meantime, the Russian investigators continued to collect evidence and interrogate witnesses. On June 13, 1994, after three years of work, Yablokov proposed that Stalin and his politburo collaborators be found guilty of crimes against peace and humanity, war crimes, and genocide, on the basis of articles 6a and 6b of the charter of the International Military Tribunal at Nuremberg. The motion was rejected by the main military prosecutor's office.

The Polish government viewed the crime as genocide under article II of the Genocide Convention of 1948, "actions directed toward the full or partial destruction of a national, ethnic, racial or religious group."[42] Russians, however, argued that the Poles had been killed as "implacable opponents of Soviet power," which would make the crime political rather than national.

In 1995 the cornerstones were laid for Polish military cemeteries alongside Russian and Ukrainian cemeteries in Katyn, Mednoe, and Kharkov. Public opinion in Russia, however, was undergoing a change. Economic reforms had impoverished millions, and it appeared that the Communist candidate, Gennady Zyuganov, would win the next presidential election.

Yeltsin appeared at the ceremony to lay the cornerstone for the cemetery at Katyn, but there was no repetition of the gesture he had made in Warsaw. This time, he emphasized that totalitarian terror did not only affect Poles. "In the first place," he said, the victims were "citizens of the former Soviet Union." Ten thousand bodies of the "most varied nationalities" had been found in the Katyn Forest. He said the tragedy should not "divide our nations" and "be the subject of political games." Less than two weeks later, a Russian foreign ministry spokesman warned Poles insisting on an apology not to sow "distrust between Russia and Poland." He said that totalitarian rule had "killed, among others, millions of Russians."[43]

On June 20, on the eve of elections to the State Duma, claims circulated that what had happened at Katyn was no worse than the treatment of Russian prisoners of war in Poland in 1920. Some Russian nationalists called for a Polish apology. "After fifty years of lying about Katyn," said Vyacheslav Bragin, the head of the Russian half of a Russian-Polish commission created to memorialize the victims of repression in Katyn and Mednoe, "it was difficult to find the moral force to be honest about the question."[44]

The commission had been set up to carry out exhumations and set aside pieces of land for the two Russian memorial complexes. An unstated objective was to normalize Russian-Polish relations. But both Russian and Polish members of the commission were sometimes shocked by what they found. Bragin was stunned that the NKVD chose to bury bodies in the area where they vacationed with their families. "Their children played on graves and collected berries on the bones. There is no way to explain this, except as a result of the lack of anything sacred in a person." In Mednoe, several dachas — including Tokarev's — were built directly on the ravines where the bodies were buried. His toilet emptied into one of these ravines, a fact that evoked revulsion on the part of the Polish members of the commission. "This," said Bragin, "is the essence of Bolshevism."

Ironically, the Germans' attitude was very different. In his testimony at the Nuremberg trials, Lt. Gen. Eugen Oberhauser, the liaison chief of Army Group Center, testified that the 537th signals regiment could not have carried out the massacre of the Polish officers at Katyn, if only because "the commander . . . would certainly never have chosen as a place for his headquarters this spot next to 11,000 dead."[45]

In September 1998 the Russian prosecutor general, Yuri Chaika, sent a letter to the Polish minister of justice, demanding an official inquiry into the deaths of Soviet soldiers during the Polish-Soviet war of 1919–21. Chaika said that 83,500 prisoners died in Polish concentration camps, and that it was possible to conclude that they were victims of genocide. There was no documentary support for this figure.[46]

Jaruzelski, in an interview, objected. "The Red Army prisoners died first of all because of the difficult conditions in the camps," he said. "However, this was not a case of planned murder, directed from above and covered up in the course of decades."[47] According to an article by Tomasz Nalecz in the Polish newspaper *Wprost,* 100,000 Red Army soldiers had been taken prisoner in 1919–21, of whom 16,000 to 18,000 died, victims not of murder but of Spanish flu, typhus, and dysentery.[48]

In July 2000 the memorial complex at Katyn was formally opened. The Russian representative was Viktor Khristenko, the deputy prime minister. In his speech, Khristenko tried to deflect attention from the Polish nature of the tragedy, saying that "it was the peoples of the former Soviet Union who became the first and principal victims of the inhuman Stalinist machine which broke and mangled millions of human lives."[49] Aside from such speeches, however, the Russians showed little interest in commemorating their compatriots. When the Mednoe memorial complex opened, on September 2, 2000, the Polish part contrasted sharply with the section for Soviet victims, where little had been done besides surrounding some of the largest mass graves with metal borders.

As the years passed, the Poles waited anxiously for the results of the Russian Katyn investigation. One issue was the identification of the nearly four thousand prisoners who had been shot in Belorussia. Many of the children and grandchildren of the victims wanted to know where and how their relatives had died. To the dismay of many Poles, however, the Russian investigation seemed to be making little progress. Finally, on

March 11, 2005, Alexander Savenkov, the head of the office of the chief military prosecutor, announced that the investigation was being closed due to the deaths of the guilty parties. He concluded that there was no evidence of genocide and said the statute of limitations had expired for a criminal case. Stalin and the members of the wartime politburo were neither charged nor officially condemned. Of the 183 volumes of collected material, Savenkov said, 116 were secret and 67 would be open to the public. The open volumes, however, contained documents the Poles had already seen. The basis of the decision was also a state secret.

That the Russian investigation ended without a condemnation of Stalin inflamed public opinion in Poland. In response, the Polish prosecutor's office began its own investigation of Katyn as an act of genocide and a crime against humanity. A resolution of the Polish Senate, adopted on April 1, 2005, said that what was at stake was the liquidation of Poland by means of the "liquidation of the most valuable of its citizens."[50]

On the basis of their own investigative efforts, the Poles determined that nearly two thousand persons had participated in the Katyn massacre.[51] The Polish position was supported by Memorial, which argued that even if the murder of the Polish officers did not constitute genocide, it should be treated as a war crime or crime against humanity. Memorial also supported publication of the names of all participants in the crime and objected to the decision to treat most of the materials in the case as state secrets. It said that, according to the law on state secrets, "information about . . . the violation of rights" cannot be treated as secret.[52]

Families of some of the murdered officers have tried to prevent the closing of the case. In 2008 the relatives of ten of the murdered Polish officers appealed to the Moscow regional military court against the military prosecutor's decision, but without success.

Russia's unwillingness to give satisfaction to the Poles over Katyn reflects the Russians' inability to commemorate their own dead. It could even be argued that the Russian government's response to the Poles is generous compared with the way it treats its own people.

The Russian and Polish parts of the memorial complex at Katyn are different. In the Polish part, there is a wall of memory behind the altar with the names of the 4,410 victims. Metal plates around the perimeter of the memorial area show the name, rank, and dates of birth and death of each officer. The altar, the altar wall, and the looming cross behind them are of iron meant to corrode to an orange hue symbolizing the color of blood. A bell set in a depression behind the altar sounds a hollow knell that evokes the fate of the men who are buried there.

On the Russian side, black metal borders have been put around the sites of the largest mass burial sites, but little else has been done. According to witness testimony, the Soviet victims were buried in many locations. The first Soviet mass graves were discovered by Poles probing for Polish graves, who uncovered male and female corpses in civilian clothing and even children's shoes. Russian efforts to establish the locations of the burial pits were cursory. Elevated walkways have been constructed throughout the Russian part of the memorial so that visitors will not walk on bones.

According to various estimates, between twenty-five hundred and sixty-five hundred Soviet citizens are buried in various locations in the Katyn Forest. Beyond the officially designated Russian and Polish zones and extending to the Dnieper River is a forested area called the Valley of Death. At the entrance to this area is a plaque that states that it "became a place for the secret burial of many thousands of Soviet citizens," victims of the Stalinist regime. On the day I visited, local people had left two wreaths of artificial flowers near the plaque. Deep in the woods, a granite stone dedicated in 1995 indicates the future site of a memorial to the Soviet victims of political repression. The memorial itself, however, has never been built. The reason most often cited has been lack of money, to which Lilya Turchenkova, the head of the Smolensk association of victims of political persecution, responded, "For bullets, to shoot, they had money."[53]

According to an official statement of the FSB, almost ten thousand Soviet citizens were executed in the Smolensk region between 1928 and 1938.[54] But with the exception of Katyn, there is no significant memorial to the Soviet dead. There is a plaque in Roslavl, at a place of mass shootings, and in Vyazma at a burial site. The inscription on the plaque in Vyazma, however, says, "Apparently, here there are remains . . . "[55] In the cemetery in Smolensk a common grave for the repressed is unmarked.

The former Metropolitan Kirill, now the Russian patriarch, once said that Katyn is first of all the Golgotha of the Russian people and the Russian church, but no one visiting the memorial could imagine that Russians consider it particularly important.

In an interview, A. F. Volosenkov, the director of the memorial complex, said that one of the greatest problems is "the sharp contrast in impressions for the visitor between the Polish military cemetery and the Russian burial grounds, which is not in favor of the latter. There is a contrast between the consideration to the smallest details in the formation of the graves of the Polish officers and the external facelessness of the common burial grounds of our citizens which is the vulnerable place of the memorial."[56]

Residents of the area wrote to *Moskovskiye Novosti* in 1989, after the newspaper published the first materials about Soviet responsibility for the shooting of the Poles, with stories about the fate of Soviet citizens in the Katyn Forest.

"Beginning in the 1930s, NKVD camps dotted the length of the road between Minsk and Moscow," wrote Leon Kotov, a lecturer at a Smolensk institute. "Tens of thousands of prisoners worked from dawn to dusk. The offenders and the sick were carried away to the Katyn Forest. It was rumored at first to be a health resort for the Cheka. But the trucks rumbling there and back suggested otherwise. Still, no one dared to go there and find out. I heard that mass shootings occurred in the Katyn Forest right up until the war."

Zinaida Merkulenko, a former resident of the Koziye Gori district, wrote: "Sometimes the kids found pits with bodies still stirring in them because the killers had left in a hurry to collect the next contingent of victims. The pits were deep but the bodies were barely covered with soil. . . . I don't know how often trucks came there. No one counted."

Ivan Kiselyev, a resident of Gnezdovo, wrote, "Trucks with bodies started arriving in Katyn Forest from the direction of Smolensk as early as 1935. I don't know where they were shot. There wasn't barbed wire at that time. Berry pickers could see the prepared pits and the ones already filled in. They made no secret of it then. The fence appeared later, but you can't conceal everything. They started to cover up the pits with turf and to plant trees. But tell me, why plant grass and young pines in a forest?"[57]

Mednoe presents a similar contrast. The area where the Poles are buried is circled by a path bordered with rows of iron plaques that identify each of the more than six thousand Polish victims. Nearby is a field of birch crosses with photos and plates attached. They date from the early

1990s, when it first became known that Mednoe was also a place of burial, but before the Poles were able to construct the official memorial.

The area of Soviet graves takes up thirty acres. Borders have been placed around two burial sites with dense concentrations of bones. How many other mass graves exist and where they are located is not known.

S. A. Seredina recalled an incident involving her father, Andrei Seredin, that took place about 1940. Seredin lived in a veterinary clinic near Mednoe. One night, returning from a call to attend a sick animal, he took a shortcut through the woods. When he emerged on a road, he saw cars heading in the direction of the dachas. A man got out of the last car and asked what he was doing on that road so late at night. He said he was a veterinarian and had been on call. The man asked if he had been standing for a long time on the road, and Seredin replied that he had just come out of the woods and was eager to get home. The man advised him to hurry home and never tell anyone about this meeting. When he told his wife what had happened, she became terrified and told him never to travel on that road again.

After the Mednoe burial ground was discovered as a result of the investigation into the murder of the Polish officers, relatives of Soviet victims put pictures of the repressed on the trees at Mednoe with black ribbons attached as a sign of mourning. Many of the victims had died during the Great Terror: Vasily Fyodorovich Shuvalov, 1907–38; Pyotr Akimovich Maximov, 1902–37; Vasily Sergeievich Nechaev, whose photograph shows him sitting at his writing desk surrounded by newspapers and lamps, 1900–1937.

Now Mednoe has few visitors. As the children of the Polish victims age, fewer and fewer make the trip to the remote site. On the December day in 2009 when I visited the memorial complex, there was not a single visitor, and the parking lot was empty except for the staff's cars. In Tver (formerly Kalinin), the onetime NKVD headquarters in the old city center is now a medical institute. A plaque commemorating the Polish officers who were executed there is affixed next to the old entrance to the building, which is separated from the street by a fence. To gain access to it requires the permission of a guard.

The Soviet regime carried out mass crimes mainly against its own population. Katyn was the most dramatic exception: the Polish prisoners of war were there subjected to the kind of treatment that was the fate more routinely of Soviet citizens. This is one of the reasons Russians have a difficult time treating the Polish victims differently from their own dead.

The reluctance of the Russians to fully commemorate the murdered Polish officers may also reflect an unconscious awareness of the circumstances surrounding the Katyn atrocity. Documentary evidence uncovered recently by Natalya Lebedeva shows that, but for an accident of timing, the Polish officers could very easily have been spared.

On December 4, 1939, agents from the NKVD were sent to the Ostashkov camp with orders to investigate the six thousand prisoners and present their findings to a special commission by the end of January. The Finnish war was in progress, and there apparently were plans to evacuate the Poles so that the camp could receive a large number of Finns. By the end of February, the commission had reviewed the cases of six hundred Polish prisoners and sentenced them to three to eight years' hard labor in the Soviet Far East. This is a clear sign that there had been no decision to execute the Polish prisoners.

On February 20 Soprunenko proposed to Beria that three hundred ill or elderly prisoners be released to their homes from the Starobelsk and Kozelsk camps, as well as four hundred to five hundred reserve officers and residents of the conquered territories on whom there was no compromising information. He also asked for permission to prepare cases on another four hundred prisoners for a commission that imposed labor camp sentences. In this case too, there was obviously no plan to execute the prisoners.[58]

Beria, however, apparently decided to ask Stalin. That meeting took place on February 25 or 26. The Chief Allied Council was making plans to send an expeditionary force to Finland to support the Finnish armed forces, and the Polish government in exile in London was insisting that Polish units be included in the force. Polish Prime Minister Sikorski said on January 24, 1940, that the dispatch of an expeditionary force to Finland would involve Britain and France in a war with Russia, "which, for us, is very desirable." This information reached Stalin, who already knew of the Polish prisoners' anti-Soviet sentiments from the network of NKVD interrogators and informants in the camps. In the meantime, the Red Army's poor performance in the Finnish war was followed by increased activity by the Polish underground in the Soviet-occupied areas of Poland under instructions from the Polish government in London.

Beria's meeting with Stalin appears to have been decisive. On February 26 orders went out to collect detailed information about the social position and rank of the officers in the Kozelsk and Starobelsk camps. This information, combined with data about the Ostashkov prisoners and delivered to the NKVD department responsible for prisoners of war, provided the basis for Beria's proposal to the politburo that the Polish officers be executed without investigation or trial, which was approved on March 5, 1940.[59]

The murder of the officers continued until late May. A month later, the fall of France forced the Soviet leaders to face their vulnerability before the German war machine. On June 15 the Red Army entered Lithuania and Latvia. Polish officers in those countries were arrested and interned in the same camps from which the Katyn Poles had been taken to be executed. But the Polish officers from Lithuania and Latvia were not shot, because the threat of Allied intervention in Finland had been replaced by the threat of an invasion of the Soviet Union by Germany. NKVD brigades were sent to the prisoner of war camps not to prepare for executions but to decide which units would fight on the side of the Soviet Union.[60]

In early January 1941, when Berling presented Beria and Merkulov with a list of officers and NCOs for the projected Polish division that included the names of officers from the Kozelsk and Starobelsk camps, Merkulov added to Beria's statement that they were "no longer in the country," a haunting remark. He said: "We made a big mistake with them."[61] It was a testimony to how little independent value human lives held for the Soviet leadership that if the Katyn Poles had not been shot before the fall of France, there is every likelihood that they would have survived.

CHAPTER 13

Vorkuta

■

In July the sun in Vorkuta never sets. It traces an arc over the tundra and for a few hours approaches the horizon, during which time the city is cloaked in gray. Scattered lights appear in the city's silent apartment blocks. This eerie twilight, however, does not last. The sun is already shining brightly by 2:30 A.M.

Lenin Street, Vorkuta's main artery, recalls the Soviet Union. It is six lanes wide but carries little traffic. Pedestrians cross wherever they like, and drivers slow down for them. The surrounding buildings are painted in bright colors—yellows, reds, oranges, blues—and streaked with dirt. They are still adorned with Soviet slogans: "Peace to the World!" "Coal is the bread of industry!" "Glory to the Conquerors of the North." But there are also more recent posters, put up by Vorkutaugol, the coal trust. One shows a miner proudly holding a piece of coal and says "Vorkuta and Coal: Formula for the Future." Another shows a smiling young boy in a school uniform next to a miner in soot-covered clothes. The boy is saying, "I'll be a miner."

The city is shadowed by things left unsaid. On Lenin Street, a tall pillar holds a medal given to the miners of Vorkuta, a star backed by two pick-axes surrounded by a wreath. The monument is dedicated to "Fifty years of exploitation of the coal basin." There is no hint that this was done by slave labor. A parkway lined with trees was built in 1945 to mark the victory over Nazi Germany. A plaque states that it was created through the "selfless labor of the residents of Polar Vorkuta." It doesn't say that it was built by prisoners.

There is also no sign that the city is built on bones. When the modern city of Vorkuta began to be constructed in the 1940s and 1950s, cemeteries and burial grounds were built over, eliminating any chance that most of the victims could ever be properly remembered. Mikhail Baitalsky, a former prisoner in Vorkuta, described in his memoirs a scene that he witnessed in the 1950s.

When they began to dig the foundation ditch for a new school, they found human skeletons. They were in a heap, barely covered with dirt. Prisoners were digging the ditch. Some of their shovels flung aside the intermingled skulls, ribs, and hands: others scooped everything into a new pile. Passersby tried to peer through the cracks of the fence surrounding the site, but the convoy official dispersed them. "Move along, citizens. There's nothing here that concerns you." . . . Soon a school went up over the secret grave.[1]

On a day in July 2008, the people of Vorkuta were enjoying the brief Arctic summer. Temporary cafés were set up in tents on Lenin Street, and shashlik cooking on open grills sent flames and clouds of smoke into the sky. Russian rock music played over portable CD players. Old women sat on stools selling bags of seeds and cloudberries, and salesgirls stood smoking insouciantly in the entry to a nearby shopping arcade.

For a moment, Vorkuta could have been any Russian city. But even as people enjoyed a break from the cold, there were reminders that Vorkuta is an island in the far north, separated from the rest of Russia by hundreds of miles of uninhabited waste. The brutal winters have stripped the buildings of paint. Wooden balconies are weathered, the metal entryways rusted and bent. Old women sweep up with metal dust pans and twig brooms. The sun shares the sky with a pale moon and rows of concrete panel apartment blocks line streets that lead to an empty horizon.

In the warmth of the sun, pensioners sitting on benches feed bread to the pigeons. The birds, infrequent visitors to Vorkuta, arrive on the roofs of the trains. But even the cooing of the pigeons can lead to dark memories. The railroad from Kotlas to Vorkuta was begun in 1937 and finished in 1941. An army of slave laborers put down an average of 1.2 miles of track per day in Arctic conditions to finish the last 287 miles, an effort unprecedented in world practice. Of 20,000 prisoners who worked on the railroad in 1938, only 3,851 were still alive in 1940. Eighty percent of the 50,000 prisoners who worked on the railroad in the winter of 1940–41 died. The bodies of those who died while working were left out in the tundra or dumped into pits. To this day, the crowded trains to Vorkuta run past their bones.[2]

In the mild weather, some of the city's young people relax on the banks of the placid river. They go swimming or cook over campfires. The trees are fully in leaf, and smoke rises from the fires. Many of the young people are without shirts, enjoying the warm weather.

On a ridge overlooking the river is Vorkuta's monument to the repressed, a boulder ringed with a strand of barbed wire on a metal base. Across the river is the site of Vorkuta's first labor camp and coal mine — Rudnik no. 1. The mining settlement that grew up there is now abandoned, a ghost town of buildings with blackened walls awash in piles of garbage. In the distance, the tall chimney of a heating station pours a stream of brown smoke into the blue and white sky.

The monument was meant to be temporary. In 1990 Memorial and the Vorkuta city council signed an agreement with the sculptor Ernst Neizvestny to construct a more elaborate one, sixty-five feet high, that was to consist of "myriad human heads sprouting from rocky crags, caves, and cliffs," as well as flames and pools of water. Neizvestny produced a model in bronze. But after the fall of the Soviet Union, economic hardship led to widespread opposition to spending any more on the memorial, and it was never built.

Despite the lack of an imposing monument, however, the presence of the dead prisoners in Vorkuta is hard to avoid. The very existence of the city in a region where the sun doesn't set from May to July, and doesn't rise in December and January, poses the question of how it came to be. "When I go through Vorkuta," Neizvestny said, "I have the impression that the shadows of the dead accompany me everywhere."[3]

Even by the standards of the Gulag, Vorkuta was exceptional for its cold and cruelty. In the endless darkness of the Arctic winter, the temperature hovers for weeks near minus 60 degrees Fahrenheit, and there are frequent blizzards. The presence of coal in the region was known in the nineteenth century. But when advisers to Tsar Nicholas I suggested that the area be made into a colony for exiles, the idea was rejected because "it was too much to demand of any man that he should live there."[4] In 1930, however, after Soviet geologists identified a high-quality coal seam in the Pechora Basin, a decision was made to exploit the deposits. A year later, a group of prisoners arrived by boat along the waterways from Ukhta to the place that is today Vorkuta. The party consisted of twenty-three persons — geologists, prisoners, and a small contingent of OGPU guards. They began building Vorkutlag, the camp for those who would exploit this new source of coal. The prisoners survived the winter in tents and in the spring opened Rudnik no. 1. By 1938 Vorkutlag had grown to fifteen thousand prisoners; that year it produced 188,206 tons of coal.[5]

Slave labor made it possible to exploit Vorkuta coal at little cost. The coal was mined with picks and shovels, and until 1940, when horses arrived, it was brought to the surface by hand in wooden carts. Prisoners mostly slept in freezing tents or dugouts. Barracks were a rarity. The summers could be warm, but without fresh food the prisoners developed scurvy, and they were tormented by mosquitoes and gnats. Of three million prisoners who passed through Vorkuta from 1931 to 1956, between 500,000 and a million are believed to have perished, most of them in the late 1930s and 1940s.[6] As the machine of repression was perfected, it assured that there were always new prisoners to replace those who died.

Among the prisoners in Vorkuta in 1936 and 1937 were thousands of persons convicted of "counterrevolutionary Trotskyite activity." Some were barely literate peasants who had no idea what Trotskyism was. But others were dedicated revolutionaries who believed that political struggle was still possible. The political prisoners were placed under the authority of criminals, who terrorized them. In October 1936 they began hunger strikes, demanding better conditions and separation from the criminals. The strikes lasted 132 days and ended when the camp administration agreed to the strikers' demands. Instead of fulfilling the agreement, however, the authorities made plans for the mass execution of the Trotskyites, beginning with the participants in the hunger strike. In August 1937 V. Baranov, the head of Vorkutlag, and A. Grigorovich, a leading NKVD official in the region, began to look for a place that could serve as a holding area and execution site. They finally chose a remote brick factory, which became a prison. In September they started bringing prisoners to the new location. At one point it housed 1,053 of them. The first to be condemned were 400 participants in the hunger strike. They were followed by an equal number of persons guilty of other "offenses," such as resistance to the criminals.

Yefim Kashketin, an NKVD officer, was sent from Moscow to interrogate the most prominent prisoners. The interrogations took place around the clock in January and February 1938 at a prison in Vorkuta. The victims were brought from the brick factory to the prison, where, to extract confessions, they were put in the punishment cell, an empty room without plank beds or a stove, where the temperature was between zero and 60 below, the same as outdoors. To survive, a person had to run back and forth continually without sleep. If he fell down, the guards tied him up and left him on the floor until his hands and feet were frostbitten. Rations were seven ounces of bread and a mug of cold water each day.[7]

One night in February, Kashketin arrived at the brick factory and summoned to a guard post three men who had known him years earlier in Kharkov. He told them that the prisoners would be shot and "cracked open like nuts." It was obviously intended that this information be shared, and it sent a tremor of fear through the inmates. Nonetheless, they were not sure what it meant. On March 1, 1938, three groups of prisoners, 173 men in all, were taken from the tents at the brick factory. They were told that they were being transferred to new assignments. They were escorted under guard out into the tundra, forced to take off their outer clothes and shoes in the bitter cold, and executed with machine guns. They were probably not buried — there were no machines to dig in the frozen earth — but simply covered with snow. In a report to his superiors, Kashketin called the operation, which began at 9:30 A.M. and was completed at 7:30 P.M., a success. "There were no excesses or problems in carrying out the operation," he wrote.[8]

After that, groups of prisoners were led away every few days. Each time, the other prisoners were told that they were being taken to new assignments. Finally the prisoners realized that the inmates were being led away to be killed. Baitalsky, a metal worker imprisoned at the brick factory, wrote:

Kashketin's assistant began to come into the tents with surprising frequency, lending credibility to the talk of more convoys. Only a month ago, Kashketin had threatened to crack us all open, and now suddenly they were promising us more convoys to the pit, to Usa. But suddenly new people were brought in: from the pit from Usa. We began asking them what they knew about those who had been sent there, from the brickworks, in three convoys. They answered: "We know nothing; no convoys came to us from here, either March 1 or later." What happened to a hundred and fifty persons?[9]

By March 27 the executions at the brick factory were apparently finished. But a new round of killings began at the prison in Vorkutlag. Two of the most prominent prisoners, V. Krainov, a veteran of the Odessa Komsomol, and Viktor Kosior, the brother of Stanislaw Kosior, the secretary of the Central Committee of the Communist Party of Ukraine, were among the victims. They had been tortured repeatedly in the punishment cell before being shot. By May 8 the cells of the Vorkutlag prison were empty except for a few women. On that day, they too were shot, including Rosa Smirnov, the wife of Ivan Smirnov, a prominent oppositionist, and their daughter, Olga.[10] The workers left in the brick factory were transferred back to the mine with orders to remain silent. But this did not mark the end of executions. Although the prison had been emptied, convoys of prisoners from camps downriver were brought to Vorkutlag to be shot. In all, during that period, in the Ukhto-Pechorsky region camps that included the Vorkutlag camps, 2,755 persons were executed.[11]

During the war years, Vorkutlag expanded rapidly. In 1940 and 1941, tens of thousands of Soviet Germans were exiled there, as well as large numbers of Latvians, Lithuanians, Estonians, and western Ukrainians. They formed the bulk of the "free" population who labored in the mines alongside the prisoners. Work began on creating the infrastructure of a modern city, and by 1943, an unlikely metropolis rose on the tundra, with modern buildings, schools, theaters, and parks. Most of the population, however, lived behind barbed wire in labor camps next to the mines. There were eleven mines and, in every camp, fifteen to twenty barracks with from one hundred to two hundred persons in each. In 1943 the mines produced 1.6 million tons of coal; in 1944 more than 2 million tons. In 1945–47, there was a new influx of prisoners. This group differed from its predecessors in that it included many anti-Communists: Baltic and

Ukrainian nationalists, officers of the Polish Home Army, and Vlasovites, as well as Soviet citizens who had spent time in Germany as slave laborers. The number of prisoners in Vorkutlag reached 60,000.[12]

Prisoners were roused at 5 A.M. and usually walked one or two miles from their huts to the mines. The shift was from 8 A.M. to 8 P.M. Despite electrification, the technological level was primitive. Baitalsky estimated that for every worker with a drill, there were seven with spades.[13] The prisoners were fed twice a day. In the morning, they received a bowl of oat broth, and in the evening watery soup and a pound and a half of black bread. Anyone who didn't fulfill his norm received a punishment ration of seven ounces of bread. Refusal to work was treated as sabotage and punished with death. The bodies of miners who died in the frequent accidents were taken to the tundra and left in the snow.[14]

> Winter dragged on slowly, and, after it, the summer flew by. And then winter was upon us again. Each day was like the one before, and you ceased being able to distinguish yesterday from a day last year. You came home from work, ate quickly, and jumped onto your plank bed. This was the only place where you could read, daydream, and mainly get lost in another world. And to get lost in another world is the strongest desire prisoners have.[15]

Consigned to a slow death, many prisoners dreamed of escape, but escape was impossible. Vorkuta was surrounded by miles of impassable tundra, and the territory was monitored by helicopter. Hunters of the local Komi people, many of whose family members worked as guards, were paid bonuses for any escaped prisoner they captured. Nonetheless, attempts did occur. In the 1940s escapees were shot and left lying at the camp gate as a warning to others. Later, according to Joseph Scholmer, a German doctor who was a prisoner in Vorkuta, they were simply brought back to the camp and beaten "within an inch of their lives."[16]

In 1948 Rechlag was established for political prisoners, while Vorkutlag continued to receive thieves, embezzlers, and murderers. The number of prisoners in Rechlag came to 14,880.[17] Of these, many were western Ukrainians, including many supporters of the faction of the Organization of Ukrainian Nationalists led by Stepan Bandera. There were also Nazi collaborators and Baltic nationalists, as well as Germans. In addition, there were persons convicted of telling political jokes or committing acts of "terrorism," such as using a newspaper with Stalin's portrait as toilet paper, as well as Jews who, in a triumph of Stalinist logic, were accused of being both "cosmopolitans" and "bourgeois nationalists" at the same time.

The Baltic prisoners and the Ukrainians created effective underground anti-Soviet organizations. The Balts showed almost complete unity, and the Ukrainians killed suspected informers. As a result, these organizations were difficult to infiltrate and suppress. They were destined to play an important role in what later became known as the Great Vorkuta Slave Revolt.

In March 1953 Stalin died. Beria was arrested three months later. Suddenly, the prisoners dared to hope that they might some day be freed, and for the first time, fear spread among the guards, a few of whom nervously asked the prisoners, "What do you think will happen now?" On June 18 the prisoners learned from *Pravda* and radio broadcasts the electrifying news that a workers' revolt had broken out in East Berlin. They had put all their hopes into the idea that the West would declare war and liberate them. But now an uprising had broken out in the Soviet bloc. The lesson was clear: they did not have to wait for the West. They could act on their own.

In the wake of Stalin's death, thousands of political prisoners petitioned for review of their cases. An amnesty was announced, but it applied only to the criminals, who had the lightest sentences. The political prisoners, who had fifteen- to twenty-five-year sentences, remained behind barbed wire. In June several thousand political prisoners from the Karaganda camps, many of them Ukrainians and Lithuanians, were shipped to Vorkuta. When they left Karaganda, they were promised that their cases would be reviewed and they would be given improved conditions. Instead, their cases were not reviewed, and they were subjected to some of the worst conditions in the Gulag. This intensified the atmosphere of incipient revolt.

Many of the former Karaganda prisoners were concentrated in mine no. 7. On July 19 they and other prisoners in the mine went on strike. The wheels in the no. 7 mine elevator stopped turning, and this alerted other prisoners that something was happening. Coal cars from the mine began arriving three-quarters empty at points along the internal Vorkuta railroad. A message was written in chalk on the cars: "TO HELL WITH YOUR COAL. WE WANT FREEDOM." The strike spread. In one mine after another, the miners refused to go into the pits, expelled the guards, and took over the camps. By July 29, tens of thousands of prisoners were on strike. They demanded improved conditions and a review of their sentences.

At first, the camp authorities tried to negotiate. This in itself was a sign of a new era. They negotiated regulations governing letters and visits and even talked about the removal of numbers from uniforms and bars from windows. But officials refused to discuss the prisoners' main demand, a review of their cases. On July 29 Gen. Ivan Maslennikov, the deputy head of the Ministry of Internal Affairs (MVD), arrived in Vorkuta and went from camp to camp trying to persuade the prisoners to return to work. In the camp for mine no. 3, the prisoners presented their demands and, with Maslennikov listening uncomfortably, delivered lectures to him on the immorality of the Soviet system.

Finally, on August 1, the authorities started to act. Armed guards took a small group of inmates from the labor camp for mine no. 7 into the tundra. The prisoners were told to return to work or be shot. They reluctantly agreed to go back to work. A new group of prisoners was then led into the tundra. As they were given the same ultimatum, they could see the first group returning to work. In this way, all of the miners in mine no. 7 were eventually forced back to work. Soon the other striking miners saw that the mine's elevator wheels were again turning. Maslennikov went to other camps and issued the same ultimatum: work or die. He also promised the prisoners that their cases would be reviewed. This false promise helped to break the prisoners' morale.

One camp, however, continued to hold out. This was the labor camp attached to mine no. 29, whose inmates, including many Baltic prisoners, showed "an utter fearlessness and an uncompromising attitude." Late in the afternoon on August 1, Maslennikov entered the camp with his retinue. Patriotic songs blared over the loudspeakers, and a thousand troops, as well as tanks, fire trucks, and ambulances surrounded the perimeter. Machine guns were set up in the watchtowers. Nearly twenty-five hundred prisoners stood with their arms locked in front of the camp gates, confronting the troops. Maslennikov ordered the prisoners to return to work. They refused. A fire hose was brought forward to turn on the prisoners, but a young Polish prisoner grabbed the hose and turned it on the NKVD. He was immediately shot, and guards in the watchtowers opened fire with machine guns. The gunfire lasted one or two minutes, and when it ended, the ground was littered with the dead and wounded. The stunned survivors were then set upon by guards, who beat them with clubs and iron bars. "After the firing," said Miron Zakharia, an inmate in the camp, "we heard the cries of the prisoners. . . . It is very difficult to describe those cries. Everything came together in one blood-chilling sound, the wails of the injured, the screams and moaning of the dying. . . . 'What for?!' The prisoners' cries were audible in the tundra for miles."[18]

According to Zakharia, 62 prisoners were killed. Their bodies were left to rot in the 85-degree F. Arctic heat. Some of the prisoners brought in to identify their comrades said that more than 70 prisoners were killed. Many died in the camp hospital in the following weeks. Nonetheless, the official figure reported from Vorkuta to the Ministry of Internal Affairs was 53 dead and 123 wounded. The strike leaders were put on trial, and ten to twelve persons were given additional sentences.[19] Nonetheless, the slave revolt of 1953 did produce some results. The bars were removed from the prisoners' barracks windows, and numbers were taken off their clothing. In 1955 and 1956, more amnesties were granted. This time, political prisoners were released.

In the late 1950s, thousands of prisoners in Vorkuta were freed. Each one had to sign an agreement not to discuss what he had seen or even to acknowledge that he had been in a labor camp. This imposed a curtain of silence in Vorkuta, where many of the liberated prisoners remained because they had not completed the majority of their sentences or because they had nowhere to go. Former prisoners developed the habit of speaking about a sensitive subject only to one other person, the better to deny that a conversation ever took place. Even free workers refused to talk. Many had been forced to sign pledges of secrecy in order to get work.

With the biggest wave of liberations, in 1956, Vorkuta began to change. The barbed wire was removed, and villages developed on the sites of the former labor camps. Sometimes the newly freed prisoners were given materials and paid to build the houses they later lived in. The workers often built on the sites of cemeteries and places of burial.

Larissa Akhtirko, a sound director at Vorkuta television, was born in Vorkuta in 1957. Her father, Georgy Akhtirko, was a German prisoner of war who was rearrested by the Soviets. Her mother, Zinaida, was arrested for having been a teacher under the occupation. They met in a labor camp of mine no. 40 and married in 1954, after they were liberated. Georgy, at the time of his liberation, was forbidden to leave Vorkuta for life. At first they lived with friends. In 1956 they helped build a barracks and received a room. It was their first home as free workers. They did not receive their own apartment until 1981.

Gradually, the old Vorkuta of grim huts and twisted alleyways gave way to a modern city that was forbidding, monotonous, and gray. A polar coefficient was established for work in the Far North, and thousands of new workers attracted by high pay arrived to work in the mines. Many stayed for decades.

At first there was a tolerant attitude toward the former prisoners, with whom the new arrivals worked side by side. Nonetheless, the former prisoners avoided talking about the past. They recalled interesting people or amusing incidents, but the conversations were deliberately superficial. When Larissa asked what had happened in the camps, her parents told her it was not necessary for her to know. It was too terrible.

As the face of Vorkuta changed, however, there was less tolerance. The Soviet media depicted the young workers arriving in the late 1950s and 1960s as "heroes of the North," and the heroes cared little about how Vorkuta had been established. To the extent that they were aware of it, they were often irritated by the presence of the former prisoners. If they had been arrested, there must have been a reason. Former prisoners of war who had been rearrested after liberation and put in the camps were asked why they didn't commit suicide instead of allowing themselves to be captured. The usual reply was that there was nothing to do it with. During the 1960s the war veterans in Vorkuta were invited to the Palace of Miners every year on the anniversary of the victory. On one occasion, after the ceremonies, Georgy Akhtirko went with a group to a restaurant. He was asked where he met the victory. When he replied, "In a labor camp," the atmosphere changed immediately. There was suddenly nothing to talk about. Akhtirko did not attend the ceremonies again.

Official histories did not mention that Vorkuta had been built by prisoners. Yet reminders of the camps were everywhere. There were burial grounds in and around the rebuilt settlements, and children regularly found skulls and bones. Boys tried to frighten each other with the skulls. The first prisoners were buried on top of each other and without coffins. In the summer, the snow melted and the ground thawed to a depth of five feet. Under these conditions, the bodies, which had sunk into a pile of bones, were moved by ground water, often far from the original site of interment. At the same time, the ground opened, revealing remains and even causing them to rise out of the earth.

In 1964 the restrictions on Georgy Akhtirko were lifted, and he was finally free to leave Vorkuta. But he no longer had the strength to move away from the place where he had spent twenty years of his life. In Vorkuta, there were many people who had been in the camps and shared his experiences. He did not want to go to a new place where everything would have to be explained.

At first, he also refused to ask for rehabilitation. He said, "They arrested me, they should rehabilitate me." He took pride in the fact that he never asked for anything, "not from the Chekists, not from the Fascists." He finally relented when Larissa was denied permission to travel to East Germany and to become a journalist because of his status. To spare her further problems, he applied for rehabilitation and received it. At that point, he thought again about returning to his native Ukraine. He found it more and more difficult to tolerate the temperatures in Vorkuta, but it was already late to make such a change. It also required money, and he had saved very little.

In 1981 the family was given a separate apartment overlooking the site of the labor camp attached to mine no. 40. The site of the former camp now held a factory that processed timber, but several structures were left over from the camp. Akhtirko sometimes looked at the factory with a sad expression, recalling those who had died. He said that prisoners dying of starvation sometimes had been thrown into common graves while they were still alive. Larissa's mother recalled that during the periods of deep frost, bodies were stacked in the women's camp in rows, one on top of the other, alternating heads and feet. There was a central square on the territory of the camp, and everyone could see the bodies.

One year a group of former prisoners went with the Akhtirkos to a burial ground near their residence on May 9, Victory Day, drank a glass of vodka, and observed a minute of silence for those who died. Larissa read *One Day in the Life of Ivan Denisovich* in 1972, when she was seventeen. She saw the friends of her father in the book's characters, and when she realized what had been done to them, she started to cry.

Yet despite the weight of the past, Larissa's childhood was a happy one.

The harsh environment instilled a spirit of collectivism, and she grew up in a place where people were friendly to each other and took care of each other. During the long, dark winters, people visited one another's homes. If guests arrived unexpectedly, they were immediately invited in, even if it was 2 or 3 in the morning or they were with strangers they had picked up on the street. If there was no food to feed the newly arrived guests, a person could always wake up a neighbor and get what he needed. The partying could go on for two or three days, and no one was ever asked to leave. Hospitality was the rule because a person who did not entertain would end up alone.

People borrowed money from one another. Once when Larissa was vacationing in the south, she ran out of money and sent a telegram to her place of work asking for 160 rubles. They immediately sent it to her. She then went to Odessa and ran out of money again. This time she asked for 200 rubles. It too was immediately sent. She traveled in the Caucasus, and when she returned to Vorkuta, she paid back the loan. If a miner from Vorkuta ran out of money while on vacation on the Black Sea, his first move was to find someone from Vorkuta from whom he could get a loan. He then took down the lender's address and paid the money back when he returned. The lender could be confident that the money would be returned.

During the Brezhnev era, Vorkuta residents became wealthy by Soviet standards. The miners earned from five hundred to six hundred rubles a month, four times the average salary of a worker in the south. A Vorkuta miner could fly with his family to Sochi in the summer and be sure that, for a month, he would live "like a baron." The miners' work was heavy and dangerous, and they spent all but a few months of the year in polar darkness and bitter cold, but in a country where very few people had money, they were rich. In Soviet resorts, they spent ostentatiously.

The fate of the prisoners who built Vorkuta was far from the minds of most people in the city in those years. But during perestroika, the situation changed. The impact of glasnost was especially powerful in Vorkuta because so much had been concealed. Partly in response to the revelations about Stalinism and the camps, the miners of Vorkuta went on strike, demanding the elimination of article 6 of the Soviet Constitution, which guaranteed the "leading" role in society of the Communist Party. The miners declared that the Communists had victimized "our fathers and grandfathers." There was also strong support for a memorial to the repressed, which was widely seen as payment of an overdue debt.

This concern for historical justice did not last. After the fall of the Soviet Union, hyperinflation wiped out the savings of almost the entire population. Soon thousands of persons who counted on one day being able to return to the south found that they were trapped in Vorkuta. At the same time, subsidies, including the northern coefficient on salaries, were eliminated. Vorkutaugol then stopped paying miners their salaries. This situation prevailed in all the mines of Vorkutaugol from 1994 to 2003, and it led to an epidemic of heart attacks and premature deaths among miners who could not adapt to the radical change in their lifestyles.

These conditions brought a wave of nostalgia for Communism. Sergei Medvedev, an officer in the union of power workers, said, "There was no competition in Communist society. In our building, all birthdays were celebrated in the yard. All the neighbors were invited. There was music, food. Suddenly, no one celebrated that way. Instead, the entire city was divided up by criminal structures." Concern for the memory of the victims of the Gulag was overwhelmed by the daily struggle to survive.

The economic situation improved in 2005 and 2006, but better conditions were accompanied by an upsurge in Russian nationalism that worked against historical introspection. "People began to be proud," Larissa Akhtirko said, "There was a time when we had to ask for tolerance from other countries. Now we don't have to ask. We can even wag our finger."

I arrived in Vorkuta on an overcast evening in mid-July, after a two-hour flight from Syktyvkar. Parts of the city are abandoned, islands of derelict buildings with blackened interiors. But the inhabited areas of Vorkuta, in the town center, were enjoying the fruits of the new prosperity. Satellite dishes had blossomed on the balconies of apartment buildings, cafés serving reindeer meat and moose were full of patrons, and the stores on Lenin Street were crowded with shoppers buying designer clothes, computer equipment, and mobile phones.

It was obvious even from the street scenes that many people in Vorkuta had little desire to think about the past. On the evening I arrived, a banquet was in progress in the Hotel Vorkuta restaurant to celebrate the local police chief's birthday. A noisy band performed in the cavernous hall under strobe lights, and the partying continued late into the night.

During the day, when the sun is shining, and particularly on weekends, friends meet each other in the central square. They sit at red and blue plastic tables enjoying the warm weather. Everywhere there is the smell of shashlik cooking on open grills. The miners are in shirtsleeves, smoking and drinking beer from bottles. All the benches are crowded, and empty bottles pile up in the trash receptacles. Crowds form around amateur acrobats, and children line up for the slide and swings or drive battery-powered cars. In the new, patriotic atmosphere, the city is riveted by the fate of Russia in international sports. For the first time, it is possible to hear women discussing soccer in buses on the way to work.

The failure of memory in Vorkuta is not complete. The victims of repression receive government benefits equivalent to those of war veterans and are no longer objects of resentment. Many schoolteachers include lessons about the Gulag in their classes, and the regional museum has an exhibit devoted to the history of the labor camps. It includes copies of prisoners' memoirs and their personal items; a *telogreika,* the prisoners' jacket; a wooden suitcase, a pick, and a lantern; and a chess set made out of bread that was chewed, baked in an oven, and then painted. There are advertisements from 1945 for the Vorkuta musical drama theater. The actors were prisoners who were escorted under guard to the theater and then back to the camps. But the chance to participate in theatrical productions for the camp bosses saved their lives.

These efforts, however, do not adequately memorialize the hundreds of thousands of persons who died building Vorkuta and whose bones are everywhere under the city. Vorkuta consists of a city center and a collection of far-flung mines and mining villages, many of them abandoned. They are linked by a ring road that traverses a bleak empty landscape. While in Vorkuta, I revisited the largely neglected sites of past tragedies along that road.

The mining village of Zagorodny was once known as Berlin-2 because of the many Soviet German exiles who lived there. Now most of them have emigrated to Germany, and only the shells of buildings remain. A road runs through the middle of the cemetery, but although many people are buried on the left side of the road, no crosses or gravestones are visible, only a wilderness of tall, thick bushes. The part of the cemetery that is still active, on the right side of the road, is a field of wooden and metal crosses in the middle of a mosquito-ridden swamp. Boards have been put down on a bed of twigs to make it possible to reach the graves, but the water of the bog is everywhere. In a few cases, fresh stones have been placed around the graves to protect them from the water. On a metal cross above one grave, a poem was left in a large cellophane envelope. Unfortunately, the water had reached it anyway. The poem, written in Russian, read:

> Years go by that's a tragedy
> Health always passes away
> Let happiness to you on wings fly
> Let not your heart be troubled
> By hurts and worries.

The members of Memorial try to preserve the cemetery, but they can do only so much. Valentina Dolgopolova, a retired railway worker, cut back the vegetation, which otherwise would have run riot, and restored ten of the graves. Members of the small surviving German community also helped. One of those with an emotional attachment to the site is Maria Shalma, a Soviet German whose infant son is buried there. Maria met her husband, Vladimir, another Soviet German, in 1947. Their son was born in 1953 and died eight months later. After 1953, burials were forbidden because a road was going to be laid through the cemetery. "And who thought about us?" said Maria. "They didn't care about the living, let alone the dead. . . . The bulldozers did their work and they took no pity on the grave of our son."[20]

Another stop on the ring road is the abandoned settlement of Yur-Shor, near the labor camp that was the site of the 1953 massacre and the cemetery where the victims are buried. Exceptionally, the cemetery has not been forgotten. Orthodox and Catholic crosses stand in even rows, a reminder of how the men once stood at the gate of the labor camp defying their enslavers. There are wreaths of artificial flowers on the graves, and the scene is dominated by a Lithuanian monument, an iron canopy over the figure of a Lithuanian saint. There is also a German monument, a black metal cross on a marble base.

On August 5, 1953, five days after the killings, fourteen of the victims were buried in a common grave. The prisoners protested that their comrades were being buried like dogs, and the authorities relented. After that, the victims were interred individually, in coffins, and the burial brigades succeeded in putting up a pole with the prison number of the victim over each grave.

As prisoners began to be freed, those who remained in Vorkuta tried to look after the graves. But their number dwindled, and the tundra encroached on the remote burial ground. In the 1950s and 1960s, very few persons knew that a burial place of the revolt's participants existed there. If they saw the crosses and poles, they thought it was just another abandoned cemetery. In those years, many residents departed for the south, leaving the remains of relatives behind. In the 1960s laborers working on the ring road that was to connect Vorkuta's mining settlements began to strike skulls and bones with their excavators as they approached the cemetery. They were ordered to continue working, but on their own initiative they altered the route, digging a path that avoided the cemetery and thus saved it.

The burial ground became more accessible with the completion of the ring road, but it was still threatened by nature. Stanislavas Grintsyavicius, a Lithuanian who had come to Vorkuta in 1956, worked with other local Lithuanians to drain the bog that had formed and put crosses on some of the graves. They knew that many of the victims had been Lithuanians.

As new arrivals poured into Vorkuta, attracted by the high pay, the memory of the revolt receded further in the city's collective consciousness. Evgeniya Khaidarova, the chairwoman of Memorial in Vorkuta, arrived from Donetsk in 1969 but heard about the revolt only in 1987, the third year of perestroika, from a Polish survivor in Warsaw. Once she was aware of what happened, she sought out survivors in Vorkuta and other parts of the Soviet Union, and Memorial began to care for the cemetery and collect money for its restoration. The vegetation was cut, and at the insistence of Grintsyavicius, Memorial replaced the rotting wooden poles with new wooden crosses. With the numbers on the poles, the names of the victims were located in the Russian state archive in Moscow, and memorial plates were put on the crosses over thirty-nine of the graves. The remaining fourteen names were listed on the cross above the common grave. On August 1, 1989, people gathered at the cemetery for the first time to honor the memory of the victims. This became an annual event, attended by survivors from the Baltic republics, Ukraine, Poland, and Germany. In 2003, the fiftieth anniversary of the massacre, a commemoration was organized with the help of Memorial, the city of Vorkuta, and Vorkutaugol. More than three hundred persons attended the ceremony.

The site of the former labor camp met a different fate. At what was once the entrance, bricks, rags, broken glass, metal, and other construction waste is scattered over the ground. Wooden poles trailing rusted barbed wire stand in the bushes, and on the ground amid the wildflowers, moss-covered window frames still hold iron bars. A separation in the bushes marks the spot where a road led into the tundra. Prisoners who died were often loaded in the middle of the night onto a wagon that was pulled by a bull and taken to the tundra, where they were dumped in a gulley and covered with snow.

When the cemetery was being restored, Grintsyavicius insisted that a monument be put up at the massacre site. There was not enough money from private donations, however, for an additional monument. Yuri Voroshilov, the mayor, said that the city had no money, so the idea was abandoned, leaving the site gradually to disappear. Now, amid the wreckage of the camp, it is impossible to say exactly where the shooting took place.

Another point on the ring road is the Vorkutinsky mine, which is still in operation. There was once a cemetery next to the mine, containing the remains of many Polish prisoners, but with the improvement in the economic situation in Vorkuta, many miners bought cars, and the cemetery was turned into a parking lot.

In the late 1940s two Polish teenagers, Jeremi Odynski and Janek Prewzner, were arrested and sent to Vorkuta for having helped the Polish Home Army. They escaped from the labor camp by digging a trench under the snow. Lost and freezing, they returned to the camp with their arms raised. They were met by guards who shot them in the chest and throat. The bodies were left for ten days in the mine entrance. But after they were buried, a commission was convened to determine whether they had been killed while trying to escape or simply shot. The bodies were exhumed. When they were reburied, other prisoners knew where they were interred.

Stepan Kostewicz, a prisoner in the camp who remained in Vorkuta, made crosses and metal borders for the two teenagers' graves. Over time, other small Catholic crosses were placed in the cemetery in memory of persons who had died in the camp. In the meantime, the barbed wire was removed from the labor camp and the mine expanded to include the cemetery. In 1990 as agitation against the Communist regime in Vorkuta reached its height, the mine director, Yuri Lobis, agreed to memorialize the camp victims. An Orthodox cross with the words "Here are buried the prisoners who built the Vorkutinsky mine" was erected on a mound at the entrance to the cemetery. At the time, the gesture had wide support.

With the fall of the Soviet Union, however, sentiment changed. Miners in the Vorkutinsky mine, like those elsewhere in Vorkuta, did not receive their salaries for months, and an accident in the mine claimed four victims. The crosses began to seem like a bad omen. Miners complained that the first thing they saw when they left the mine was a cemetery. In 1997 a Polish prisoners' organization asked to put a Catholic cross on the burial ground. The administration refused. The cross was allowed only on a spot next to the highway, one thousand feet away.

The following spring, when Khaidarova returned to the mine, all of the crosses were gone. At the mine headquarters, she was told that they had been removed by a vote of the miners, who said it was necessary to think about the living, not the dead. A short time later, the parking lot was built, and today all that is left to indicate that people are buried near the mine entrance is a metal post that once helped to cordon off the cemetery.

On my last day in Vorkuta, I traveled deep into the tundra with Khaidarova and Nikolai Zinoviev, another member of Memorial, to the site of the old brick factory, the scene of the mass execution of Trotskyites. It was the wish of many former prisoners that this factory be found. In 1991 Tamara Romankova, a member of the Belarusan branch of the International Helsinki Committee, met Mikhail Melnikov, a writer and former prisoner in Vorkuta, in the Belarusan city of Krichev. She had investigated massacre sites in Belarus, and he urged her to go to Vorkuta and find the old brick factory. "Tell everyone," he said. "Write about how in the deep tundra, they shot an enormous number of people." Romankova went to Vorkuta in 1994 but could not find anything.[21] The brick factory was not found until 2005, after more than thirty expeditions organized by Memorial.

The road leading out of Vorkuta passed by a reindeer farm before entering the tundra, which stretched in rolling green waves to the horizon. After turning onto a gravel lane and driving past a lake filled with reeds and white flowers and surrounded by the parked cars of berry pickers, we arrived at the Yun-yaga station ("bright river" in the Komi language), an outpost for servicing engines. We parked and began to walk south along railroad tracks lined with violet willow herbs. After an hour, we left the tracks and, putting on mosquito netting, entered the tundra, where the spongy ground sank with each step. After another half-hour, we arrived at the site of the brick factory.

The first sign of the former location of the camp was a stand of tall bushes that towered over the surrounding vegetation, an indication that the permafrost had once been penetrated by the heat of human activity. We descended to the river bank and found stones and logs that had reinforced dugouts carved into the side of the hill. It was here that the interrogations took place. We also saw the rusted remains of rails and wagons. The prisoners dug clay for bricks, and the bricks were transported in wagons to a barracks, where they were baked.

We tried to guess where the prisoners were taken for execution, but there were few clues. On the opposite side of the river, the straight line of a road was barely discernible in the green of a distant hill. The story of the brick factory shootings is well known in Vorkuta, but few persons have visited the site. As a result, there is nothing to indicate that anything out of the ordinary occurred in this remote place, with its swarms of mosquitoes and limitless tundra, where so many of those who tried to struggle with the Stalinist regime for minimal rights lived their last days.

The city that rose on the tundra one hundred miles north of the Arctic Circle was left by history with a dilemma it has been unable to resolve. To commemorate those who died to build Vorkuta means living with the memory of the horror they endured. Ignoring the city's past, however, creates an atmosphere of moral indifference that encourages people to turn their backs on other, more recent crimes.

The authoritarian regime that was introduced by Putin all over Russia is reproduced to an even greater degree in Vorkuta. Officials used any excuse to reduce pensions in order to divert money to themselves. At the same time, on the basis of a decree by Vorkuta's mayor, Igor Shpector, utility charges were raised first by 200 percent and then by another 50 percent, but the extra income disappeared.

Lyudmilla Zhorovlya, a local human rights defender, won a judgment invalidating the decree and then began to work actively for the return of the overpayments, amounting to hundreds of millions of rubles, to the city's residents. On July 21, 2005, Zhorovlya and her twenty-one-year-old son, Konstantin, were murdered in their apartment by intruders. Two days earlier, she had been visited by persons who asked her to withdraw her motion.

For eight months, the connection between the killings and Zhorovlya's human rights activities was not investigated. Instead, the prosecutor tried to build a case against Zhorovlya's husband, although he had an alibi confirmed by numerous witnesses. Shpector was eventually questioned — as a witness. But three years after the murders, the prosecutor of the Komi Republic admitted the case was not likely ever to be solved. A demonstration held in Vorkuta in 2008 on the anniversary of the murders was attended by only fifty persons, most of them representatives of human rights organizations.

There is also a lack of free expression in Vorkuta. The television center is city property, and the city decides what to charge for rent. This gives the city considerable power to impose political conformity. Shpector regularly called the director of Vorkuta Teleradio or Radio Vorkuta to denounce specific journalists or to give orders on when and how to film him. Olga Shutova, the chief editor of Radio Vorkuta, did a story about how the police gathered up stray dogs, drove them in trucks out of town, and then shot them, leaving the bodies in the tundra. She compared this with the way stray dogs were sterilized or humanely euthanized in other countries. The report was about to be aired when the director of the station banned it, with the explanation that the dogs had been rounded up and shot on Shpector's direct orders. In another incident, Shutova was assigned to prepare a broadcast on Shpector in honor of his birthday. But the report was not acceptable to station management. According to Shutova, "it did not show in full measure the love of Vorkuta residents for their mayor." She refused to redo the program and, aware that she was going to be fired, she resigned.

Rima Yakovenko, a correspondent for the newspaper *Zapolarye,* said,

We cannot write all we know because there is an unspoken instruction not to worsen the atmosphere and create the feeling that everything is bad. There was a report on the loss of people's savings that showed a man setting fire to his money. This was not allowed. The unspoken rule comes from the mayor's office. There is a feeling that if we write about all the bad things that people simply won't want to live. People come to me with complaints. But if I write about each case, it would create such a negative impression that it would be unbearable.[22]

A mural on the wall of the Palace of Pioneers on Lenin Street shows children in red scarves holding aloft a glider and petting a reindeer. In the background is a rocket heading for the cosmos. In many ways, the mural captures how Vorkuta would like to be envisaged even today. Its citizens know that they live in a vast graveyard, but there is a citywide consensus that it is better to avoid anything that would remind them of this. "There are many things that we have to live through," said Larissa Akhtirko as we sat together on a bench in the central square, surrounded by others who were out enjoying the warm summer evening. "What happened here is part of life experience, like unsuccessful love. There is no point in dwelling on it. There is nothing you can change. It's desirable that it not happen again. We paid too high a price."

But not everyone is happy with this type of forgetting. Shortly before leaving Vorkuta, I spoke to Ursula Negretova, the daughter of German political refugees who were executed by Stalin and the widow of Pavel Negretov, a former political prisoner and historian of Vorkuta.

"I never noticed that anyone was concerned about those who died building Vorkuta," she said. "They promised us a radiant future. It was absurd, and what we have now is absurd. The majority still does not want to remember these crimes. In my husband's class in Kirovograd, of those born in 1923, only three out of a hundred remained alive. Unfortunately, our people forgive everything."

There are periodic attempts to press the case for a monument to the victims of political persecution, but they never get very far and are frequently misunderstood. Instead of a monument, Shpector suggested creating a "gulag park" as a tourist attraction. In an interview in the newspaper *Tribuna,* he explained that the park would offer "extreme tourism." He said that in Sweden there was a hotel in a prison, and the idea was so popular that visitors had to book a place a year in advance. "We can gather old materials in order to re-create completely all the horrors of the Stalin regime. We'll have dogs, sentries in watchtowers, and we'll feed the tourists the food that the prisoners ate."[23] Memorial denounced Shpector's idea as blasphemous. But Galina Dahl, a Soviet German who was a prisoner in Rechlag, said that she supported it if Shpector would be the first prisoner. Shpector replied this did not interest him, because "I'm not a tourist."

Valentin Dorogovtsev, an engineer whose father was repressed, believes the indifference can be traced to the damage done by Communism. "There is a biological kindness," he said. "But in our souls, we are invalids. In the best case, there is nothing, in the worst case, rot. We are kind inside the herd but there is no social conscience. We lost memory. People don't know and don't want to know what happened here. The idea of commemorating a place of burial is foreign to us. For that, there is only Memorial."

CHAPTER 14

The Odyssey of Andrei Poleshchuk

■

On a warm night in July 1985, Leonid Poleshchuk, a KGB agent normally resident in Lagos, was drinking with his son, Andrei, in a beer hall near their apartment in Moscow. It was a time of transition. Poleshchuk was home on leave and had been trying to exchange his small apartment, where the family had lived for years, for something better. Andrei had just been hired by the Novosti Press Agency and was starting a career as a journalist. In the crowded, smoke-filled hall, Andrei and Poleshchuk stood at a circular metallic counter. Poleshchuk told his son about Nigeria, where he served as the KGB's head of counterintelligence. He described the foreign community, his travels in the country, the beaches and the gigantic waves. For the first time, Poleshchuk allowed Andrei to smoke in his presence.

Andrei had always been fascinated by his father's work in the KGB, but he tried not to ask questions that he knew his father probably could not answer. But this time, for some reason, he asked his father whether anyone had ever tried to recruit him. The question was unexpected, but Poleshchuk showed no reaction. Andrei recalled later that he did not even blink. He said there had been attempts, but he always refused them. Andrei was not surprised. He regarded his father as a Soviet patriot. But after Poleshchuk gave this answer, a strange thing happened that Andrei would never forget. His father looked at him for a long time. It seemed to Andrei that he wanted to tell him something.

It was the last time Andrei and his father went out together. Years later, when he recalled that meeting, Andrei wondered what it was that his father wanted to say.

While Poleshchuk was organizing his affairs in Moscow, a discussion was taking place in CIA headquarters in Langley, Virginia, about the best way to deliver twenty thousand rubles ($28,000) to him. Sandy Grimes, an officer in the Soviet–East European division, suggested leaving the money at a dead drop in Moscow. "Eventually he is going to be recalled [to Moscow]," she told Burton Gerber, the division head, "and he could really help us there." She believed the successful use of a dead drop would show Poleshchuk that the CIA could communicate with him safely in Moscow.[1]

Aldrich Ames, another CIA agent, objected, saying that communicating with Poleshchuk with a dead drop was too risky. Grimes did not say anything, but she suspected Ames of petty jealousy. She had just been promoted to the GS-15 pay level, whereas Ames remained stuck at GS-14. Ames did not even make a pretence of congratulating her. But Gerber and his deputy, Milton Bearden, agreed with Grimes on a dead drop, and she ordered an officer in Moscow to set it up. A fake rock filled with Soviet rubles was left at a site in Izmailovsky Park. No message was put in the rock, and it was agreed that no one would check on it. If Poleshchuk did not pick up the rock, it would stay where it was.[2]

What Grimes, Gerber, and Bearden could not know was that on June 13, Ames had met Sergei Chuvakhin, a Soviet diplomat, for lunch at Chadwick's, a restaurant facing the Potomac River in Georgetown under the Whitehurst Expressway. During the meal, Ames gave Chuvakhin a bag filled with classified documents that contained the names of nearly every Soviet citizen working for the CIA and the FBI. In return, Chuvakhin handed Ames a shopping bag filled with cash.

The consequences of Ames's actions were felt in Moscow almost immediately. On the morning of August 2, 1985, Poleshchuk and his wife left their apartment to go shopping. They returned at about noon, and Poleshchuk left again to park his car in a garage just fifteen minutes away. By evening, he had not returned. Andrei was working late, reporting for *Novosti* on the 12th Moscow World Youth Festival, and was anxious to get some sleep before another long day. But when he returned home at 2 A.M., the lights were on in the family's ground-floor apartment, the curtains were drawn, and he could see the shadows of people moving around. He immediately sensed danger. He rang the bell and the door was opened by a huge man in a dark suit. Andrei's mother, Lyudmilla, and his grandmother were behind him looking pale and devastated. Several persons were searching the apartment. The colossus showed Andrei a search warrant and said, "Your father has been arrested."

The search lasted until 8 A.M. The KGB agents took Poleshchuk's personal belongings, letters, photo albums, cigarette boxes, liquor bottles, medications, and electronic devices. At 11 A.M., more KGB officials arrived at the apartment. They took Andrei, his grandmother, and his mother to the Lefortovo prison. Lyudmilla was taken to see Viktor Chebrikov, the head of the KGB. He tried to interrogate her, but she could tell him nothing. She had had no idea that her husband was involved with the CIA. In response to Chebrikov's questions, she only burst into tears.

Andrei was also interrogated. He was asked about his father's personal life, his habits, his hobbies, what books he read, how he spent his time, whether he had a mistress, whether he was abusive, and whether he was often drunk. Andrei realized that he was expected to say negative things so that Poleshchuk would be shown his answers and would thus be convinced that he had no support from his family. Andrei asked who his father was supposed to have worked for, but the interrogator refused to give him any details. He said only that Poleshchuk had collaborated with "enemy intelligence."

Leonid Poleshchuk was born in 1938 in Shadrinsk, in central Russia, and grew up in Dushanbe, the capital of the Tadjik Republic. He was recruited by the KGB in 1967 while teaching English in a local college. Two years later, he was transferred to Moscow for special training at the KGB academy, and upon graduation he was assigned to the KGB's 17th directorate, which dealt with South Asia. In 1970, at the age of thirty-two, he was sent to Kathmandu, Nepal.

Andrei remembers Kathmandu as picturesque, charming, and dirty. People relieved themselves in public in the shadow of beautiful Buddhist temples. Cows were sacred animals. They walked untouched down streets filled with lepers and beggars. The family lived in a three-bedroom house near the Royal Palace, with banana trees in the courtyard. Andrei quickly made Nepalese friends and played soccer with them. But there was no Russian school in Kathmandu and, after only a few months, he was sent to live with his grandparents in Anapa, a city on the Black Sea, to attend school in the Soviet Union.

Life in Kathmandu started out successfully for Poleshchuk. He was very sociable, particularly in comparison with other Soviets officials, and he and Lyudmilla had a lot of guests, both Nepalese and foreigners. Besides entertaining at home, however, Poleshchuk frequented the Kathmandu casinos, a fact duly noted by the CIA. On one occasion, he lost five thousand Nepalese rupees (about $300) of the KGB's money at the roulette table, with no way to pay it back. A CIA officer who had befriended him gave him the money as a "personal loan." Some time later, Poleshchuk began working for the CIA.

During his last two years in Kathmandu, Poleshchuk provided information to the CIA in return for spending money. When his tour ended, the CIA provided him with spy gear. He promised to get in touch once he returned to Moscow. Instead, he burned the spy gear in Moscow, and for ten years the CIA did not hear from him. The FSB later depicted Poleshchuk as a gambler, womanizer, and drunk who agreed to cooperate with the CIA for money. The amount of money he received, however, hardly justified the risk. When he returned to Moscow from Kathmandu in August 1975, Poleshchuk bought a Volga automobile. He paid for it with hard-currency coupons that Soviet diplomats received for working abroad. But he did not have enough money to buy an apartment and instead was given a modest two-room flat by the KGB, in a building built in the 1940s by German prisoners of war. It was full of cockroaches and mice, and Andrei's mother struggled for years to get rid of them. If Poleshchuk had been well paid by the CIA, he could have joined a cooperative and made a down payment on a much better apartment without raising suspicion.

Probably more significant than money was Poleshchuk's conflict with his superiors. Even as a boy, Andrei noticed his father's frustration with his bosses. "My father was restless, energetic, focused, and highly motivated to do his job right. He was ready to think outside the box in order to get results. He was creative and adventurous. Unfortunately, the KGB station chief, Seliverstov, was an old fashioned Soviet apparatchik. He drove my Dad crazy by ignoring his ideas and putting on hold or terminating his projects." In 1973, when Poleshchuk's father died, he was denied permission to attend the funeral. Andrei's mother told him that after this happened, Poleshchuk was "like a raging bull. He would smash things," While living in Anapa, Andrei became ill on one occasion and had to be hospitalized. But Poleshchuk was not allowed to leave Kathmandu to visit him.

After Poleshchuk returned to Moscow in 1975, he went to work in the 19th department, where he dealt with Soviet Armenians who were working as illegals in countries with large Armenian communities. In November 1984 he was named deputy chief of the KGB station for counterintelligence in Lagos. There he resumed his contacts with the CIA. If American intelligence had gotten very little of use from Poleshchuk previously, in Lagos he became extremely productive. He passed on 120 to 130 reports that he had collected during the course of ten years working at the headquarters of KGB foreign intelligence in Yasenovo. It is possible that after Ames gave Poleshchuk's name to Chuvakhin, Poleshchuk was told that an apartment was available for him in Moscow in order to lure him home. In any case, he asked for permission to return. He also asked the CIA for the twenty thousand rubles, presumably to buy the long-awaited apartment. There is no sign that Poleshchuk had any notion he was returning to his death.

In August and September, Andrei and Lyudmilla were each interrogated four or five more times. On one occasion, Andrei asked Colonel Gusev, one of the interrogators, who his father had worked for. Gusev did not answer directly. Instead, he showed Andrei a document with a single line written in his father's hand: the phrase "I met Joe." From this, Andrei assumed that his father had contact with either the British or the Americans, most likely the latter.

Andrei and his mother asked to see Poleshchuk but were told that there would be no visits until the investigation was complete. There were several more searches of the apartment. During one of them, Andrei asked Capt. Sergei Kruglov, one of the investigators, how the case was progressing. He said, "It's going to be a long investigation. He has a lot of information and a computer of the third generation in his head."

In the meantime, Lyudmilla started to deteriorate mentally. She neglected her appearance and started to walk around singing nonsensical songs. When she looked at Andrei, her eyes were expressionless. Finally, he called the KGB and told them that if they wanted to talk to her, they would have to provide her with some therapy. They sent a group of doctors, and she was put in a KGB hospital, where, with the help of drugs, she was restored to a seemingly normal state. During her treatment, however, they continued to question her.

After her release, Lyudmilla returned to work as a part-time bookkeeper in a local café, but Andrei never saw her smile again. With his mother ill and the family's books and personal items all removed in repeated searches, the apartment began to feel haunted. Andrei stayed away as much as possible. His mother retreated to her own inner world and remained there until she died. The only time that Andrei could remember when she betrayed her feelings was when she prepared a parcel for her husband. Holding it in her hands, she burst into tears.

The trial began on June 10, 1986, before the Military Collegium of the Supreme Court. Poleshchuk was assigned a public defender, but this person was given only limited access to the case. Lyudmilla was allowed to attend the opening session, but she began to feel faint and was led out. She did not attend the subsequent sessions. On June 12 Poleshchuk was found guilty and sentenced to "death by means of shooting, with confiscation of property."

Andrei and his mother were informed of the sentence by mail. It was not unexpected, but Andrei was deeply shaken. Each member of the immediate family wrote to Gorbachev, asking for a pardon. They asked for forgiveness for Poleshchuk and said that his death would be devastating for the family. They got no response. While they waited, however, they were told that they would be allowed to visit the prisoner.

The first person to see Poleshchuk was his brother Alexander, who had come to Moscow from Leningrad. After the meeting, he told Andrei that he would not recognize his father. "He's changed dramatically," he said. "Be prepared for a tough meeting." Poleshchuk's mother was second; she came back engulfed in tears. Lyudmilla was unable to go, she was too sick and feeble. Andrei went last. The meeting took place in mid-July.

Andrei was told the meeting would be at 10 A.M., but it did not take place until 4 P.M. For six hours Andrei waited in a reception area, with no explanation for the delay. Finally he was escorted to a room where two men in suits occupied two of five chairs arranged around a long table. On the wall was a portrait of Gorbachev. One of the men introduced himself as Gen. Alexander Petrenko, the head of investigations. He was in his seventies, friendly and polite. He said, "You are about to meet your father.

You have twenty to thirty minutes. You are not allowed to talk about the case, and he's not allowed to discuss it with you. You can only speak about everyday life, your family, and your work."

A short time later, a door opened and Poleshchuk was ushered in, escorted by two men in uniform. Andrei got up and went to his father and they embraced. Poleshchuk was taking heavy breaths, trying to control his emotions. Andrei could feel his father's heart pounding. "Dad, calm down," he said. Poleshchuk was pale and very thin, at least thirty pounds thinner than when Andrei last had seen him. His eyes were constantly moving, and Andrei felt he was having a hard time just focusing. He was wearing glasses that he had just started using to read. They sat down on opposite sides of the table, with two KGB men nearby. The first thing that Poleshchuk said was, "Andrei, trust me, I did what I did not because I hated my country but for personal reasons."

He then took out a piece of paper and held it in front of him. He began reading haltingly from a list of questions. The first question was "How is your work going?" This was followed by "What are you doing?" "What is your current position?" "Do you like your job?" "How's Mom?" "How is your personal life?" "What do you think about the World Cup soccer match?" (The tournament was being held in Mexico, and the Soviet team was doing very well.) At last, Poleshchuk put down the piece of paper. He managed to look at his son. They talked further about the Soviet soccer victory over Hungary. Andrei said that the score had been 6–0. Poleshchuk asked, "Was it really 6–0?" He then asked, "Do you have enough money to live on?" Andrei lied and said that they did. Finally, after thirty minutes, Petrenko said their time was up. Poleshchuk got up and he and Andrei hugged again. Two men in uniform led Poleshchuk to the door. Poleshchuk turned, and Andrei and his father looked at each other for the last time.

After his father had left the room, Andrei asked Petrenko if he could see his father again. Petrenko said, "Don't worry, Andrei Leonidovich, this is not your last meeting. We don't destroy people like your father. We need him. We'll work with him. He will still be useful to us. You will meet with him again." Andrei asked whether it would be possible to take a vacation before the next meeting. Petrenko said, "Go ahead and give me a call when you get back. We will arrange another meeting."

Andrei returned from Anapa in late August. The following day, a letter arrived advising the family to pick up Poleshchuk's death certificate. The date of death was given as July 31, 1986. In the space for the cause of death was written, "On the basis of the decision made by the Russian Federation Supreme Court." A short time later, an official called and asked the family to bring the certificate back so that an error could be corrected. They were asked to surrender it and were given a new one. In the second death certificate, the space for the cause of death was left blank.

Andrei called Petrenko. He said that he had just received his father's death certificate. Petrenko's tone was now cold and official. Nonetheless, he agreed to meet Andrei at the Lefortovo prison. At the meeting, Andrei asked Petrenko about his promise of another meeting. Petrenko said that Poleshchuk was taken into custody by a special team, and he had been unable to interfere.

"Can you confirm that my father is dead?" Andrei asked. "Can you show us his grave?"

"I am not authorized to answer these questions. No one will ever do this."

After Poleshchuk's death, a KGB team arrived to pick up his property. After spending hours cleaning out the apartment, they claimed that there were some missing items, mainly books, and demanded that Andrei reimburse them by paying a total of 317.17 rubles.

Lyudmilla never recovered her health. She had suffered for years from inflammation of the pancreas, and after her husband's execution, she stopped taking care of herself and died of pancreatic shock in 1988. Andrei kept his job at *Novosti* due to the intervention of Sergei Ivanko, the deputy chairman, who insisted that Andrei was not guilty of anything. But in December 1988 he was refused permission to travel to London to work as a trainee in the editorial office of the newspaper *Soviet Weekly.* Viktor Bukharov, the KGB representative at *Novosti,* told him that he was refused because "there will be an immediate provocation against you."

Andrei became depressed and began to smoke and drink heavily. Only concern for his mother had made him hold on to his job, but after her death, his life seemed to have lost all purpose. The one thing that kept him interested in his career was the unexpected change taking place in the Soviet Union. Under Gorbachev's policy of glasnost, Soviet citizens watched with amazement as people published information that, months earlier, would have led to their arrest. At the same time, supposedly loyal Communists at all levels of the hierarchy began to attack the system, revealing themselves to have long been bitter enemies of the regime.

In May 1989 Andrei left *Novosti* and joined the staff of *Moskovskiye Novosti,* one of the flagships of glasnost. In May 1990 he was allowed to travel to Sweden. A KGB agent told him, "We decided to let you go. But behave appropriately in case of an emergency." Finally, in November 1990, Andrei left *Moskovskiye Novosti* to join the newly established newspaper *Nezavisimaya Gazeta.*

The shock of his father's execution weighed on Andrei. He wondered what could have motivated Leonid. He did not believe it was sex or money. It was more likely frustrated ambition and political principle. He wanted the answer to this question. He also wanted to know where his father was buried, and to see his father's final resting place. It was the last thing he could do for his father.

At one time it seemed to Andrei that he would never find the answers to these questions. But as glasnost expanded and society was swept by anti-Communist sentiment, he became more optimistic. It began to be reasonable to ask whether Poleshchuk was really a traitor or whether he acted, at least in part, to help rid the Soviet people of a totalitarian regime. At the same time, Andrei was establishing himself at *Nezavisimaya Gazeta,* where, to his surprise, as the Soviet Union veered toward collapse, he was assigned to report on the KGB.

The years of glasnost and perestroika had completely upended the KGB's position in Soviet society. Where once the KGB had not only dominated society but been idealized by it, the revelations about past atrocities carried out by the secret police had made it an object of wide-spread revulsion. In response, the organization tried to improve its image with the public. On July 27, 1991, the KGB called a press conference at which Gen. Alexander Karbainov, the head of the KGB's newly created Center for Ties with Society, expressed support for democratization. *Nezavisimaya Gazeta* sent two reporters: Vladimir Abarinov and Andrei. To Andrei's surprise, the KGB gave him permission to attend.

The press conference included a moment Andrei had not expected. After the current situation was discussed, one of the journalists asked Karbainov about the activities of foreign intelligence services. "In the last ten years," Karbainov said, "counterintelligence exposed more than thirty Soviet citizens who were recruited by foreign intelligence. To my shame, among these people were officers of the KGB." He then gave the names of the KGB "super agents" who, in his opinion, had done the most serious damage to state security: Oleg Gordievsky, Sergei Vorontsov, and Leonid Poleshchuk. At that point, the whole room turned and looked at Andrei. Poleshchuk was not widely known at that time. The only "super agent" well known to the public was Gordievsky.

That press conference was the first example of the ambiguous situation in which Andrei now found himself. As the son of an executed CIA agent whose motivations and fate he could not establish, he was a reporter for a leading organ of the newly liberated press. Ironically, the KGB now needed his goodwill. Despite Karbainov's assurances that the agency supported democratization, Vladimir Kryuchkov, the head of the KGB, played a key role in the attempted coup of August 19–21. When the coup collapsed, many agents feared for their futures and, in some cases, their lives. More than ever, the KGB sought to find common ground with society.

On August 27, 1991, Andrei again entered KGB headquarters, this time to interview Vadim Bakatin, the first "democratic leader" of the KGB. After the interview was over, Andrei received a call from Capt. Sergei Trubin, an officer in the 5th directorate, which had been responsible for persecuting dissidents, and the son of Soviet prosecutor general Nikolai Trubin. He suggested that they meet; Andrei agreed. This was the beginning of a collaborative relationship in which Trubin and others provided Andrei with detailed information about the internal workings of the KGB. Andrei began to receive extraordinary access to high KGB officials. After the KGB was split up in the wake of the break-up of the Soviet Union, Andrei established good relations with the SVR, the Russian foreign intelligence service created on the base of the former First Chief Directorate, where his father had worked.

It began to seem to Andrei that, with time, he would learn the full story of what happened to his father, including where he was buried. Russia had renounced Communism, and he hoped there would not be a continuing vendetta against those KGB agents who had fought against Communism from within. Once, Nikolai Rafaenko, an officer of FSB press service, said, "I know who your father was. I know the whole story. It won't affect our cooperation in any way." Andrei became friendly with Yuri Kobaladze, the head of the press office, and two of his associates, Tatiana Samolis and Boris Labusov. On Andrei's birthday, they sent him a fax that said, "We love you very much!"

In 1992 Andrei was awarded a place in a U.S. journalism exchange program. He spent a month that summer working in Denver for the *Rocky Mountain News*. While there, he called the CIA after finding a contact number in the yellow pages. He said he was the son of Lt. Col. Poleshchuk and that he could be reached in Denver or, on his way back to Moscow, in New York. A second person got on the line and promised that someone would contact him in New York. Shortly after he arrived there, Andrei got a call at his hotel, and a meeting was arranged at the Plaza Hotel. He was met by a Russian-speaking woman from the CIA and two men from the FBI. The woman confirmed that Poleshchuk had worked for the U.S. government. She said he had made an outstanding contribution to the democratization of Soviet society and that he was a much loved and highly respected person.

Andrei met with the CIA several more times during trips abroad. Each time, he told everything he knew about his father's case, even handing over copies of the protocol of arrest and the death certificate. Although he did not realize it at the time, he was aiding an intensive mole hunt that was going on in the CIA.

On February 22, 1994, Aldrich Ames was arrested and charged with having been a KGB mole. Andrei sensed immediately that Ames had a connection to his father's case. Ironically, he was now in the position of writing about the arrest for *Nezavisimaya Gazeta*. His first step was to call Col. Gen. Vyacheslav Trubnikov, the deputy director of Russian foreign intelligence, with whom he was already acquainted, and ask for comment. Trubnikov demanded anonymity but confirmed Russian involvement in the case. Asked whether he considered the arrest a failure for foreign intelligence, Trubnikov answered, "I would look at this incident from the other side and say the fact that our intelligence for such a long period of time had such an agent is without a doubt a big success. There is no question but that he was worth the large sum of money that he was paid."

Andrei began to follow the Ames case closely, collecting everything written about him and eventually writing fourteen stories, all under various pseudonyms. In September 1994, during a weeklong vacation in Cyprus, he met a CIA officer who confirmed that his father had been betrayed by Ames.

Although the Ames case was covered in the Russian press, for months there was almost no mention of the Soviet citizens he betrayed. This may have reflected uncertainty as to how to relate to them. Finally an article appeared in *Izvestiya* by Vladimir Nadein, the paper's Washington correspondent, under the headline "These People Were Shot by the KGB: They Are Known in America But Not in Russia." The list of persons executed after being exposed by Ames included KGB Lt. Col. Gennady Smetanin, who provided information from Lisbon; KGB Lt. Col. Gennady Varennik, who revealed a plan to murder American soldiers in Germany; Lt. Col. Vladimir Piguzov, who provided information from Indonesia; Maj. Sergei Motorin and Lt. Col. Valery Martynov, both of whom worked in the Soviet embassy in Washington; Adolf Tolkachev, a scientist who gave information to the CIA about Soviet MiG fighters; Dmitri Polyakov, a general in military intelligence who provided highly classified military information; KGB Maj. Sergei Vorontsev, who revealed KGB operations against the U.S. embassy in Moscow; and Vladimir Vasiliyev, a colonel in Soviet military intelligence, who helped trap an American who had sold NATO defense plans to the KGB. Also on the list was Poleshchuk.

"One of the striking moments, characterizing post-Soviet society," wrote Nadein, "is the complete indifference to the fate of these people, to the motives which inspired them and to the atmosphere in the KGB that led to such widespread betrayal. . . . American intelligence has released the names of those who died after a closed trial in the KGB. Our Chekists consider themselves justified not to tell us anything and not to explain anything."[3]

In the wake of Ames's arrest, Andrei made a more active effort to learn his father's fate. His first step was to ask some of his contacts for help. He had good relations with Rafaenko, and he asked him whether he might get access to his father's file. Rafaenko said, "Forget it, don't even try." He then approached his former classmate Yuri Ursov, who worked for *Trud* and *Sovetskaya Rossiya* and had excellent sources in the intelligence services. Ursov promised to inquire but finally told Andrei that the FSB did not know where Ames's victims were buried. The executions had been carried out by the MVD.

Andrei finally decided to speak directly to Trubnikov, who by that time was the director of the SVR. He had met Trubnikov a number of times since calling him about the Ames arrest, and relations between them were friendly. On October 25, 1997, Andrei wrote to Trubnikov requesting his assistance. In his letter he wrote:

> I am the son of Leonid Poleshchuk, a former KGB officer. You must be aware of my father's case. His death and the death of my mother who could not bear the sufferings came as a severe shock to me. This is the pain that never goes away especially when one does not know all the truth. Despite everything that happened, my father will remain the person I loved most. It is a son's duty to find and visit his father's burial place. Please, help me do it.

Having sent the letter, Andrei carried on with his normal duties. Among other things, he scheduled an interview with Trubnikov for December 17, the official Day of the Chekists. He did not intend to raise the subject of his father but meant only to interview Trubnikov in connection with the holiday.

On December 17 Andrei met Trubnikov at SVR headquarters in Yasenovo as planned. Trubnikov, however, was upset and tired. He had just come from the funeral of a close friend. Andrei asked a question about the holiday, but Trubnikov apparently misheard him. He began pouring some cognac. "Andrei," he said, "trust me on this. We've done our best. We wanted to help you, but we're not in a position to provide you with information about your father's grave. We failed."

Andrei was momentarily confused. But when he realized what Trubnikov was saying, he thanked him and went on with the interview. A few weeks later, he received a certified letter from Trubnikov repeating that he had failed to find Andrei's father's burial place and adding, "Please, do not consider this reply to be a mere formality."

Though grateful to Trubnikov for his response, Andrei was not ready to give up. He sent an almost identical letter to Nikolai Kovalyev, the director of the FSB. Kovalyev did not answer. On May 12, 1997, Andrei had a meeting with Rafaenko, who told him that he would never be trusted by some important people at the FSB. "Like father, like son, you know . . ."

By this time, Andrei had decided to leave Russia. His patron, Vitaly Tretyakov, had been forced to step down as editor of *Nezavisimaya Gazeta*, and the quality of the paper had declined. At the same time, Andrei felt he could not stay in the country that had killed his parents and refused to help him find his father's grave.

On May 20, 1997, Andrei and his wife, Svetlana, left Russia for America and settled in Reston, Virginia. A month later, a memorial service for Andrei's parents was held in the Russian Orthodox Cathedral of St. John the Baptist in Washington, D.C. Following the service, a traditional Russian reception was held at the home of a CIA agent who had worked with Poleshchuk, and Andrei had an opportunity to meet some of those who knew his parents, as well as people involved in investigating the Ames case. At the memorial service, "Joe," who came from his retirement home, made a speech in which he called Poleshchuk "my brother" and burst into tears. He said that Poleshchuk was "an amazingly modest man, a principled man, a thinker with the ability to see both sides of an issue, hence his code name, 'WEIGH.' He loved his country but was angry with the system, the KGB. He could see how harsh the system was to an individual."

Joe later told Andrei that he and Poleshchuk had become genuine friends. They did not discuss politics, he said, but talked about their countries. They spoke about someday opening a motel in some remote place, with both wives working as greeters. Joe said that Poleshchuk told him that he was grateful that Joe never tried to compromise him but only tried to persuade him to work for the good of the Russian people against Communism. The offer was made in February 1974. It took Leonid half a year to make a final decision. Joe said that Poleshchuk's decision was not abrupt, and that he had fully recognized the danger.

Andrei set about organizing a new life in America. In Russia, however, discussion of the fate of the Russians betrayed by Ames continued, largely in reaction to the publication of books about the Ames affair in the United States.

Of these books, the best known was *Confessions of a Spy: The Real Story of*

Aldrich Ames, by Pete Earley. What made Earley's book unique was that it was based on fifty hours of face-to-face interviews with Ames in federal prison, without third parties present. Earley later said that he was able to get so much time with Ames because the prison administration had not been told that Ames was forbidden to meet alone with journalists. In any case, after interviewing Ames, Earley left for Moscow to meet Russian intelligence officials. It was suggested in the Russian press that Earley's access to Ames might have been arranged by the FBI and CIA to give the Russians an incentive to talk to him and so possibly shed light on unknown aspects of the case.

On April 11, 1998, *Izvestiya* ran a long article about Earley's book that focused on the fate of Varenik, another of Ames's victims. Earley had succeeded to talking to Varenik's relatives. (Andrei was contacted by Earley in December 1994, but declined to talk with him out of fear of jeopardizing his attempts to learn about his father's fate.) The newspaper ran a large photo of Varenik with his daughter, next to a smaller photo of Ames with his son. It also included excerpts from Earley's book.

According to Earley, Varenik told Charles Leven, a CIA agent working in Germany, that there was a plan to murder American soldiers and their families. Varenik was supposed to locate restaurants near American military bases where small bombs could be placed. The KGB intended to detonate the bombs when the restaurants were packed with people and then implicate German terrorists. The object was to disrupt relations between the United States and Germany and create the impression that American forces were not wanted on German soil. Leven said that "Varenik was nauseated at the thought of the murder of the innocent Americans."[4]

Izvestiya also quoted from Earley's interviews with Varenik's wife and a KGB investigator who worked on the case. Varenik's wife said,

> My husband was a good man — honest, kind and strong. We met in the theater and it was love at first sight. . . . Unlike the majority of his colleagues, he did not drink, smoke, or have affairs with other women. . . . Our life was a fairy tale. We had much love. . . . The packages that I brought for him at Lefortovo prison were not given to him. When they allowed me to see him, he resembled a corpse. . . . I tried to restrain myself but burst into tears. . . . We were not allowed at the trial. We received a notice that he was executed on

February 25, 1987. I will never marry again. We Russian women, once we fall in love, it cannot happen again.[5]

The KGB investigator who worked on the case, however, had a different view. "This man was a traitor," he said.

Why romanticize him? He was a nobody. We did not find any real basis to suppose that he committed this treason for ideological reasons. Of course, at the trial, he spoke about this alleged plot to kill U.S. servicemen and about corruption in the KGB. What would you expect him to say? The law was very clear about his fate. I am proud of the job that I did and shed no tears for this traitor.[6]

It is not surprising that those who took part in the arrest and sentencing of the CIA's Soviet agents would defend their actions. But in post-Communist Russia, their attitude is widely shared. Boris Yeltsin freed those CIA agents who avoided execution and were still in labor camps in 1992, but none of them was rehabilitated — despite their significant contribution to the fall of the Soviet Union and the rise of the new Russia.

Valery Savitsky, a Russian legal expert, argued in an article in *Izvestiya* that Russians who cooperated with the CIA deserved their fates and were not candidates for rehabilitation. He said that it was his "deep conviction that treason remains treason even if it is committed in relation to a bad, antidemocratic, totalitarian state. . . . If today we were to rehabilitate these people . . . we would lose that moral standard which defines eternal values and the categories of good and evil."[7]

In a few sentences, Savitsky illustrated the core of the problem in Russia's notion of its history, the failure to recognize that "eternal values" do not come from the structure of the state but require a transcendent source. As a matter of practice, treason is understood as the betrayal of a particular government. But it can also be understood in light of a higher appreciation of right and wrong. It is for this reason that the members of the Stauffenberg Conspiracy of July 20, 1944, are remembered as heroes in Germany, not as traitors, for their attempt to kill Hitler.

Savitsky argued that treason is a violation of an individual's obligation to the state, regardless of the nature of that state. This understanding of treason is consistent with the Soviet ideology, which excluded the possibility of a standard of right and wrong above the goals of the Communist regime.

In "Crito," the dialogue in which Plato offers an uncompromising view of the citizen's obligation of obedience to the state, Socrates argues that he cannot flee to avoid the death sentence that has been passed on him by Athens because he agreed during the entire course of his life to be governed by the state; he had had the opportunity to convince the state that the laws were wrong and had not done so. Moreover, he argued, he always had the option of leaving Athens if he was dissatisfied, an option he did not exercise. The import of these facts was that Socrates entered into an "implied contract" that he would do as the state commanded him.

The Soviet citizen, however, did not enter into any implied contract with the Soviet government. He had no opportunity to convince the state that the laws were wrong or even to express himself on the subject, and he was denied the opportunity to leave. Under these circumstances, he did not have an ultimate, as opposed to relative and conditional, obligation to demonstrate loyalty to the Soviet state. In fact, he had a higher, human obligation to oppose the Soviet state to the extent he could — an obligation that was recognized by those Soviet citizens who worked in what they believed to be their country's interest, by cooperating with the CIA.

On July 28, 1998, after thirteen years during which Poleshchuk had barely been mentioned in Russia, ORT, the principal state television station, broadcast a thirty-nine-minute documentary film about him entitled *Blackout in Kathmandu*. It was a joint production of the FSB press service and the RTS television company. There were also long articles about the affair in the press. The only other of Ames's victims to be the subject of a similar documentary was Tolkachev.

According to the film, in July 1985, at a time when the confrontation between the Soviet and American secret services was at its most extreme, KGB counterintelligence carried out a special operation aimed at identifying the CIA agents in Moscow. As a result of this operation, the KGB managed to locate the site of a dead drop used by the CIA station officer for an agent. On August 2, 1985, the KGB caught the agent, who turned out to be Poleshchuk. For at least a month, according to the film, Poleshchuk denied everything. But in the end, investigators were able to force him to confess. How this was done was not explained. The documentary gave the KGB credit for exposing and arresting Poleshchuk. Ames's role in the case was not mentioned.

Watching the film, Andrei reflected on the fact that the FSB was not ready to help him learn about his father or tell him where his father was buried but was ready to make a tendentious film that damaged his reputation. Andrei wrote an article criticizing the film and gave it to Tretyakov, who was visiting him in the United States. It was published in the military affairs supplement of *Nezavisimaya Gazeta* in March 1999.[8]

In the article, Andrei pointed out that the documentary made no mention of Aldrich Ames. The person filmed picking up the material from the dead drop was not Poleshchuk but an actor, and the film's depiction of how the KGB found the dead drop contradicted other published accounts. On the basis of what he recalled of his father's movements that day, Andrei suggested that he was arrested not at the dead drop but in another part of Moscow.

According to the filmmaker, Poleshchuk's "blackout" was the result of his weakness for alcohol and the roulette table. But Andrei pointed out that it was typical of the Soviets to depict those who turned against the system as motivated by money and those who helped the Soviet Union as idealists. This was even true of Ames, who stated very clearly that he betrayed his country for money.

A little more than a month after Andrei's article appeared, there were signs that it had had an effect. *Nezavisimaya Gazeta* published a round-table discussion on a newly released history of the Russian counterintelligence services, in which an answer of sorts was finally given to the question of where Poleshchuk was buried. Vadim Soloviev, a correspondent for *Nezavisimaya Gazeta,* said, "Let us clarify one topic which was broadly discussed in our newspaper. How accurate is the documentary about the arrest of Leonid Poleshchuk? And where is his burial place?"[9]

Maj. Gen. Alexander Zdanovich, head of the FSB Public Relations Center, said,

Recently, we've had some discussions on the article about the Poleshchuk case that was published in *Nezavisimaya Gazeta*. The documentary does, in fact, contain a number of staged scenes; therefore, there could've been some inaccuracies. . . . For instance, due to some reasons, our team was unable to videotape the capture of the real Poleshchuk. So we used the related scene from the KGB training movie for our documentary. However, it's possible to do this in a documentary. Naturally, we had to omit some other important details.

As for Andrei's request . . . here's my short answer: there is no-place where he can go to pay tribute to his father. No one bothered to bury him. They didn't even have a cremation urn. And we were about to tell Andrei about this, but he'd already left Russia. The Ministry of Interior was in charge of conducting executions at that time, not the Ministry of Justice.[10]

In short, Poleshchuk's remains were cremated with no attempt to save the ashes or mark the spot where they were deposited. Even such a pre-dictable disposition of the remains, however, left a number of questions. In the first place, where exactly did the cremation take place? This is a question of no small importance to a dead person's family. It is also rea-sonable to ask: why was it not possible to give this answer in 1997, when Andrei first officially asked for it? And why was Andrei denied access to the file in his father's case once still classified material was removed from it?

According to Orthodox tradition, if a body is not buried, the soul will never rest in peace. Until the relatives and close friends pay a last tribute, the soul of the dead person is somewhere in limbo, and the suffering affects the children and the spouse. "To me it's not execution, it's more like murder," said Andrei. "Murderers also do not reveal the place of burial."

The attitude of the Russian intelligence services toward Poleshchuk, almost a decade after the Soviet Union ceased to exist, reflects the FSB's vision of itself as the rightful heir to the KGB. This attitude was shown not only in the treatment of the CIA agents like Poleshchuk but also, paradox-ically, in the attitude toward Ames.

During Earley's interview in Moscow with Boris Solomatin, a retired KGB general, Solomatin introduced him to an intelligence officer who gave his name only as "Yuri." Earley then met with Yuri separately. Yuri asked whether Ames thought that someone in Moscow had betrayed him. Understandably uncomfortable with the question, Earley said that Ames had not mentioned anything. Yuri told Earley that those arrested in 1985 and executed were caught not because of Ames but because of their own mistakes and the KGB's efforts. This inspired Earley to ask why, if Ames did not provide any useful information, he was paid $2 million.[11]

A year later, Earley traveled again to Moscow, where he asked Yuri some final questions about the Ames case, very few of which he answered. Before they parted, however, Yuri asked for a favor. He wanted Earley to give Ames a personal message. "Tell Rick that we have not forgotten him," he said. "If we can find an appropriate way to help him, we will. Good friends do not forget each other."[12]

Earley had previously written a book about John Walker Jr., the retired American navy warrant officer who had betrayed military secrets to the Soviet Union, and he asked Yuri why the Russian government, which had never done anything to help Walker, now claimed to be ready to help Ames. According to Early, "Yuri was quiet for several moments and then he said: 'There is a real difference between these two men, my friend. Walker was a good source for us, that's true. He produced a lot and we appreciate that. I am sorry that he is in prison. But Rick, you see, with him it is different. We must keep our commitments to him.'"

"Why?" Earley asked. "Why is he different?"

"Because Rick Ames is a professional intelligence officer," Yuri said. "He is one of us. That is the difference."[13]

As of 2011 the victims of Aldrich Ames, including Leonid Poleshchuk, were still treated as traitors in Russia, demonstrating the extent to which Russia identifies with the Soviet regime. *Blackout in Kathmandu* was updated in the late 2000s with new material and renamed *The Hiding Place on Serebryakov Passage*. It continues to be shown on Russian television as part of a series on Russian "turncoats" that includes the documentary on Tolkachev and also a new documentary on Polyakov. If the men betrayed by Ames were traitors, however, it means that the Soviet Union was a country that it was possible to betray, and that a country can legitimately impose obligations even when it denies its citizens any rights.

The Hiding Place on Serebryakov Passage includes an interview with Igor Kozhinov, a colleague of Poleshchuk's in Nigeria, who states that Poleshchuk, while being interrogated by the KGB, had accused him of being an agent of the CIA. Kozhinov died of a heart attack in 2006, twenty years after Poleshchuk's execution, and the film implies that the supposed accusation by Poleshchuk was responsible for Kozhinov's premature death. The film concludes with a passage about Burton Gerber, who had directed the Soviet intelligence operation for the CIA and, at one time, was the CIA station chief in Moscow. As the film shows pictures of snarling wolves ripping apart prey and skies full of lightning, the narrator says that Gerber loved wolves, but the only person he associated with wolves was himself. The agents who worked for him he considered "jackals." The film then refers to a book published on the fortieth anniversary of the establishment of the CIA (there is no indication of whether the book was published *by* the CIA) in which the opinion is supposedly stated that those who work for American intelligence as agents are "traitors" who, in most cases, offer their services for money.

This was a different message from the one that Andrei received in August 2000 at CIA headquarters in Langley, when he was there to attend a memorial meeting for his mother and father. Before the meeting, CIA director George Tenet met with Andrei and Svetlana in his office. Tenet said that Andrei's parents were real heroes and that his father made a great contribution to the cause of the democratization of the former Soviet Union. At the meeting, Andrei made a short speech about his father and was presented with a framed photograph and a medal. On the photo was written, "To the Poleshchuk family: On behalf of many I wish to again express our deepest respect and sincerest regards, George Tenet." The medal was inscribed: "In memory of Leonid Georgiyevich Poleshchuk, for his courageous service in the pursuit of democracy and world freedom."

Conclusion

∎

Russia today is haunted by words that have been left unsaid, sites that have not been acknowledged, and mass graves that have been commemorated partially or not at all. In the years since the fall of the Soviet Union, there has been little attempt to understand the Soviet period or to draw inspiration from those, like Andrei Sakharov, who stressed that what Russian society needed was a new morality. The failure to face the moral implications of the Communist experience, however, has meant that real change in Russia was not possible. The psychology of state domination was left intact to influence the new post-Communist Russia.

Russia today is relatively prosperous by historical standards, and compared with the Soviet Union it is quite free. But the failure to acknowledge and atone for the mass crimes of Communism has contributed to a situation in which the average Russian is as powerless before the apparatus of the state as was a citizen of the Soviet Union. He can be used for any purpose, and there is nothing to prevent him from becoming a victim if this is judged to be in the interest of the state.

On September 9, 1999, an explosion ripped through the nine-story building at 19 Guryanov Street in the Pechatniki section of Moscow, a working-class neighborhood. By the end of the first day, the death toll had risen to 98. On September 13 another explosion reduced a nine-story brick building at 6 Kashirskoye Highway in Moscow to a pile of rubble. The death toll soon reached 118. These explosions were part of a series of four bombings of apartment buildings that were used to justify a new invasion of Chechnya and created the conditions for Putin's rise to power.

From the beginning, however, there were signs that not Chechens but the FSB was behind the bombings. Suspicion increased when a fifth bomb was discovered in the basement of a building in Ryazan on September 22 and the persons who planted the bombs were captured. They proved to be not Chechen separatists but agents of the FSB.

The question of who was responsible for the terror bombings was far from settled in the spring of 2000 as Russians prepared to vote in the presidential elections. Putin, posing as the savior of the nation, promised to avenge bombings in which he may have been complicit. But what was truly surreal was that many Russians, fully convinced that the FSB had carried out the bombings, were ready to vote for Putin regardless.

In late March, Patrick Cockburn, the Moscow correspondent of the *Independent,* went to the site of the bombing on Kashirskoye Highway and spoke to residents. Only one of the ten persons he interviewed said that Chechens were behind the bombing. Cockburn found that Putin nonetheless had strong support. Svetlana Nikolaevna, a woman who lived in a building next to the one that had been destroyed, said, "At the beginning, we thought that it was the Chechens. Now we think it was people in the Kremlin administration who wanted to stay in power." Despite this, people supported Putin because "he can really get things done."[1]

This passivity on the part of ordinary Russians, combined with a seeming inability to make moral judgments, gives Russia's rulers the conviction that they never will be held to account.

Perhaps the most hated symbol of their impunity is the flashing blue light, or "migalka," affixed to the tops of officials' cars, which confers on the owner the right to drive on the wrong side of the road at high speed, ignore traffic lights, and careen onto sidewalks. In August 2005 Mikhail Evdokimov, the governor of the Altai region, was killed along with his driver and bodyguard when their car, which was going 120 miles per hour on the wrong side of the road, hit a car in front of him that had slowed down to make a left turn at the bottom of a small hill. Evdokimov's car flew into the air and crashed into a tree. The driver of the other car, a Siberian railroad worker named Oleg Shcherbinsky, who was en route to a nearby lake for a picnic with his wife and daughter, was arrested and sentenced to four years' imprisonment for violating traffic rules.

Tensions over the driving habits of officials had already been high because in May a car driven by Alexander Ivanov, the oldest son of Deputy

Prime Minister Sergei Ivanov, had struck and killed Svetlana Beridze, a sixty-eight-year-old Moscow resident in a pedestrian crosswalk. The younger Ivanov was not charged.

Atypically, Shcherbinsky's sentencing led to mass protests in Russia, with thousands of drivers in cities all over the country driving in long processions with flashing accident lights and black and orange ribbons to represent the death of justice and to hint at Ukraine's Orange Revolution, which was both hated and feared by the Russian authorities. There were also slogans calling for the release of Shcherbinsky and the arrest of Ivanov. In the end, Shcherbinsky was freed by an appeals court, which vacated his conviction. But officials continued to use migalkas on Russia's clogged roads to evade safety regulations, with fatal results.

One such fatality was Olga Aleksandrina, a thirty-five-year-old doctor who was killed along with her seventy-two-year-old mother-in-law, Vera Sidelnikova, in Moscow in February 2010 in a head-on crash with a Mercedes belonging to Anatoly Barkov, the vice president of the LUKoil oil company, which according to witnesses was driving in the wrong lane, apparently to avoid a traffic jam. After the crash, the driver of the Mercedes removed the license plates from the car. The police claimed that surveillance cameras did not capture the accident, which took place on Moscow's busy Leninsky Prospect. Nonetheless, it was ruled that Olga had caused the accident, and Barkov was not charged.

The passivity of the population and the impunity of officials creates a situation in which an exceptionally low value is attached to human life. In the wake of the terrorist attack on Domodedovo Airport on January 24, 2011, that claimed thirty-five lives, it was revealed that police assigned to guard the arrivals area had been spending most of their time not protecting the public but shaking down passengers from Central Asia and elsewhere who arrived without valid work permits.[2]

It is an eerie reminder of the lack of concern for human life in Russia that three hundred persons disappear in Moscow every year. In many instances, due to indifference and bureaucratic inefficiency, they are never sought. Information is received daily about the disappearance of pensioners or alcoholics, but no one makes a formal statement and there is no search. Soon, unknown persons appear in the apartments of the "disappeared." As of October 2008, twenty-four hundred persons were listed as missing in Moscow and suspected of having been victims of foul play.[3]

Perhaps the most graphic example of the low value attached to human life is the reaction of the Russian authorities in hostage situations. There have been two grave hostage crises in Russia in the 2000s: the mass hostage taking at the Theater on Dubrovka in Moscow in October 2002, and the Beslan school siege in September 2004. Both times the regime recklessly sacrificed its own citizens.

On October 23, 2002, a total of 979 persons were taken captive when forty Chechen terrorists stormed the Theater on Dubrovka during a performance of the popular musical *Nord-Ost*. Early in the morning of October 26, the theater was filled with toxic gas and stormed by FSB and special forces. As the gas flooded the theater, the terrorists had time to fire on the hostages with automatic weapons but did not do so. The effect of the gas, however, was devastating. The official estimate of the number of dead was 129, but 75 persons believed to have been in the theater were unaccounted for.[4] As a result, unofficial estimates put the number of dead at more than 200. In the months after their "rescue," hostages continued to die from the effects of the gas. In October 2003 it was estimated that 300 of the former hostages were dead.[5]

The Russian prosecutor cleared the authorities of any responsibility for the deaths, ruling that the gas was harmless without determining what gas had been used.[6] Three years later, the content of the gas was still a state secret, although 80 percent of the survivors were still suffering from the consequences of the poisoning. In a statement at a press conference on the third anniversary of the hostage taking, Svetlana Gubareva, who lost her thirteen-year-old daughter Sasha and her American fiancé, Sandy Booker, in the siege, said, "The impression is created that all us — former hostages living and dead and relatives of hostages — for the prosecutor are absolutely nobody."[7]

Arguably an even more chilling example is the authorities' reaction to the seizure by terrorists of a thousand hostages during the takeover of a school in the Russian city of Beslan in September 2004. Russian forces stormed the school, causing the death of 332 persons, including 186 children.

In the succeeding years, a great deal of information about Beslan has emerged. It has come from many sources: Yuri Saveliev, a parliamentarian and member of the federal commission investigating the terrorist act; a commission of the North Ossetian parliament; the trial of Nurpashi Kula-

yev, a surviving terrorist; and the work of two journalists, Marina Lit-
vinovich, the editor of the website pravdabeslana.ru, and Elena Milashina
of *Novaya Gazeta*.

This information showed that although the Russian authorities blamed
the deaths on the Chechen terrorists, the authorities themselves shared
responsibility for the tragedy. The Putin regime refused negotiations that
could have ended the crisis and, in the absence of hostile action, ordered
Russian special forces to open fire with heavy weapons on a gymnasium
packed with hostages.[8]

On September 2 Akhmed Zakayev, the representative of the Chechen
resistance in London, announced through the foreign press that Aslan
Maskhadov, the Chechen separatist leader and deposed president, had
agreed to come to Beslan to mediate the crisis. There were no preliminary
conditions. At noon on September 3 the news that Maskhadov was ready
to come to the school was reported to Vladimir Pronichev, the head of
the FSB operation on the ground. The attack on the school began one
hour later.[9]

Survivors at Kulaev's trial said that Russian forces attacked the school
with flamethrowers and grenade launchers. Officials at first denied that
flamethrowers had been used, but survivors recovered used tubes that they
found near the school and presented them in court. The flamethrower in
question fires a capsule that on detonation creates a fireball and a shock
wave that destroys everything in its path.

In a report on the tragedy, Saveliev, an expert on the physics of com-
bustion, said that the explosions caused an inferno and the collapse of
the roof of the gymnasium. For more than two hours, Gen. Alexander
Tikhonov, the head of the special forces, *forbade* anyone to extinguish the
fire. This led to the deaths of the majority of the hostages. By the time the
fire began to be suppressed at 3:28 P.M., more than a hundred hostages
had been burned alive. Another 106 to 110 hostages died after terrorists moved them from the burning gym to the cafeteria, which came
under heavy fire from security forces using rocket launchers, flamethrowers, and tanks.[10]

Russia differs from the West in its attitude toward the individual. In the
West, the individual is treated as an end in himself. His life cannot be
disposed of recklessly in the pursuance of political schemes, and recogni-

tion of its value imposes limits on the behavior of the authorities. In Russia, the individual is seen by the state as a means to an end, and a genuine moral framework for political life does not exist. The result is that the weight of a lawless state apparatus is slowly destroying Russia's immense human potential, rendering the country's authoritarian stability precarious. Russia has little protection from a recurrence of murderous political fanaticism that, under normal circumstances, would be rejected immediately in the West.

Russia needs to end the imbalance between the status of the individual and the prerogatives of the state. This is not possible, however, without breaking with the Russian state tradition, acknowledging the reality of the state's crimes and the human worth of its victims.

Unfortunately, many Russians prefer nationalist delusions to serious thought about their country's future. There is a tendency to protest against "the demonization of the Communist 'Stalinist' USSR," which obviously takes little account of Stalin's victims. At the same time, there is a penchant for making a scapegoat of the West. Russia is often described as under attack by the West, and official statements depict the West as seeking to encircle Russia, just as Soviet officials accused the United States of seeking to encircle the Soviet Union in the 1970s and 1980s.

It could be argued that renouncing the Russian state tradition means rejecting Russia's past, because the state tradition is what tsarism, the Soviet regime, and contemporary Russia have in common. To a degree this is true. But breaking with the past, if it is done consciously and in light of ultimate values, does not imply a loss of identity. At the same time, the dominant tendency in Russia is not the only one. There are figures in Russian history who fought for democracy, from the Decembrists to members of the Provisional Government to the Soviet dissidents, and each of them played a role in bringing about the degree of freedom that exists in Russia today.

Sharp breaks with tradition are also not unheard of in the history of modern nations, and they are often accomplished with reference to alternative tendencies in a country's own history. In the final analysis, a nation cannot look with confidence to the future if the proclivity of its institutions is to crush the individual. Ultimately, it is on the talents of each person in his capacity as an individual that the nation depends. The Soviet regime treated individuals as inputs in production, and its ideology explicitly deprived them of spiritual value. It was therefore entirely logical for the regime to destroy millions in its effort to create a "new man" capable of living in a "classless society" that would change the course of history.

The Russian earth, however, is no longer giving forth an unlimited number of individuals to be exploited by the apparatus of the state. It is now necessary for Russia to value the people that it has. But this means restoring the dignity of those who were so recklessly sacrificed under Communism, and condemning unreservedly the regime which so devalued the individual as well as the state tradition out of which it arose. This is a difficult prospect. But it is certainly well within the capacity of a nation that tried to create heaven on earth. And it is the only hope for a better future.

NOTES

■

A few of the websites cited in these notes are accessible only by subscription. Those interested in accessing articles published on these sites may, of course, subscribe but otherwise are advised to search key words or phrases in order to find other versions of the materials online.

Introduction

1. Vladimir Ryzhkov, "Privivka ot Terrora," *Novaya Gazeta,* February 21–27, 2008, 9. All translations not otherwise specified are my own.

2. Ibid., 8. The scale of murder in the Soviet Union was so immense that estimating the number of victims with any degree of accuracy is difficult if not impossible. Figures cited in recently available archival materials are often in conflict with demographic data which places death tolls considerably higher. In this book, I accept 20 million as the number of direct victims of the Soviet regime. This figure includes only those put to death by the regime or who died as a direct result of its repressive policies. It does not include the millions who died in wars, epidemics, and famines that were predictable consequences of Bolshevik policies but not entirely the result of them. The figure of 20 million includes a minimum of 200,000 victims of the Red Terror (1918–22); 11 million victims of famine and dekulakization in the 1930s; 700,000 persons who were executed during the Great Terror (1937–38); 400,000 additional execution victims between 1929 and 1953; 1.6 million persons who died in forced population transfers; and a minimum of 2.7 million persons who died in Gulag camps, labor colonies, and special settlements. To the resulting figure of 16.6 million should be added persons who died in prisons, 975,000 Gulag prisoners released during the war to punitive battalions, where they faced almost certain death, the victims of partisan warfare in Ukraine and the Baltic republics after the war, and Gulag prisoners freed so that their deaths would not count in the mortality totals for the labor camps, as well as other categories of victims across the length and breadth of a vast country.

3. Vyacheslav Nikonov, interview with the author, November 10, 2003.

4. In other former Soviet republics, the situation is different. In Kazakhstan,

which had an enormous labor camp population and to which more than a million and a half persons were deported, the effort to commemorate is led by the president, Nursultan Nazarbayev. After Astana was chosen as the new capital, a memorial was constructed on Nazarbayev's initiative. There are already more than a hundred museums and memorials dedicated to the victims of repression, and their number is growing. Nazarbayev travels to the sites of the main Kazakhstan camps — Steplag, Karlag, Dalnego, Peschanogo, the special camp Kengir — and opens new memorials and museums. In the Baltic republics, the restoration of memory is regarded as the key to the new posttotalitarian national identity and as a guarantee of democratic development. Memorials and museums are located in central locations. The Lithuanians put their museum in the former headquarters of the KGB in the center of Vilnius, the Latvians put theirs in the former building of the Museum of the Latvian Red Rifles. Ryzhkov, "Privivka ot Terrora," 8.

5. Karl Jaspers, *The Question of German Guilt* (New York: Capricorn, 1961), 21, 22.

6. Ryzhkov, "Privivka ot Terrora," 8.

7. Ibid.

8. Ibid.

9. Valerii Shiryaev, "283 Shaga," *Novaya Gazeta,* February 21–27, 2008, 6.

10. *Razrushennye i Oskvernennye Khram* (Frankfurt: Posev-Verlag, 1980), 146.

11. Shiryaev, "283 Shaga," 6.

12. Ibid.

13. Survey conducted by Analiticheskii Tsentr Yuriya Levady, February 22–25, 2008, http://www.levada.ru/press/2008030506.html. Accessed October 19, 2010.

14. Aleksei Levchenko, "Stalin Vstaet iz-pod Zemli," Gazeta.ru, August 26, 2009, http://www.gazeta.ru/politics/2009/08/26 a 3240785.shtml.

15. Vladimir Kremlev, "ROAR: Stalin's Portraits Appear and Disappear in Russian Cities," *Russia Today,* May 6, 2010, http://rt.com/politics/roar-stalin-portraits-russia/.

16. This is described in my previous book, *Darkness at Dawn: The Rise of the Russian Criminal State* (New Haven: Yale University Press, 2003).

17. Jaspers, *The Question of German Guilt,* 32.

18. Ibid., 32, 71.

19. Although Jaspers rejects the notion of collective guilt, insisting that guilt adheres only to an individual, he does identify some aspects of co-responsibility of the citizens of a nation that has committed atrocious crimes. They consist, he writes, "first, in the unconditional political surrender to a leader as such, and second, in the kind of leader surrendered to. The atmosphere of submission is a sort of collective guilt." Referring to the German situation, Jaspers said that the German-speaking individual feels concerned by everything growing from German roots. "That the spiritual conditions of German life provided an opportunity for such a [Nazi] regime, is a fact for which all of us are co-responsible." Ibid., 78–79.

20. The current attitude recalls the sadly famous words of Count Benkendorff, the chief of the political police under Tsar Nicholas I, who wrote, "Russia's past was admirable, her present is more than magnificent, and, as for her future, it exceeds all that the boldest imagination can envision; this . . . is the point of view from which the history of Russia ought to be viewed and written." Richard Pipes, *Russian Conservatism and Its Critics: A Study in Political Culture* (New Haven: Yale University Press, 2005), 107.

21. Quoted in Andrei Piontkovsky, "The Hubris of Russia's Governing Elite," *Insight on the News,* April 8–21, 2008, www.insight mag.com.

22. Ibid.

23. Petr Potapkin, "Glukhie Telefony," *Novaya Gazeta,* January 24, 2002.

24. Ibid.

1. The Statue of Dzerzhinsky

1. Andrei Antonov, " 'Kholodnye Golovy' Dzerzhinskogo i Luzhkova," Prima-News, September 16, 2002, http://prima-news/news/articles/2202/9/16/16826 .html. Accessed September 27, 2005.

2. Boris Sokolov, "Nerzhaveyushchiy Feliks," Grani.ru September 11, 2002, http://pub.tagora.grani.ru/Politics/Russia/FSB/m.9142.html. Accessed April 18. 2011.

3. S. P. Melgunov, *Krasny Terror v Rossii* (Moscow: PUICO, 1990), 27.

4. L. A. Golovkova et al., *Butovskii Poligon* (Moscow: Al'zo, 1997), 59.

5. Vladimir Varfolomeev, interview with Nikolai Kharitonov, Ekho Moskvy, July 6, 2000.

6. Alexander Podrabinek, a former Soviet dissident, recalled: "In 1986–87, when perestroika began and they started to allow cooperatives, I wrote to Mossovet [the Moscow city council] asking to register a cooperative and publish a newspaper. I received a letter saying that my idea of freedom of speech did not conform to Marxist-Leninist teachings and so the application could not be approved. The letter was signed by Luzhkov. When perestroika got under way, he became different. When they began renaming streets, he was in favor; he rejected Communist names, but this is a Soviet person. He has no principles. He had none and never will have them." Interview with the author, September 27, 2005.

7. "Keep Iron Felix on Scrapheap of History," editorial, *Moscow Times,* September 18, 2002.

8. "Zheleznomu Feliksu Ne Mesto na Ploshchadi," PrimaNews, September 16, 2002, http://prima-news.ru/news/2002/9/16/16837.html. Accessed September 27, 2005.

9. "Miting Protiv Vosstanovleniya Pamyatnika Dzerzhinskomu," PrimaNews, prima-news.ru, September 27, 2002, http://prima-news.ru/news/news/2002/ 9/27/17070.html?print.

10. "Soyuz Pravoslavnykh Grazhdan Vystupaet protiv Pamyatnika Dzerzhins-komu," Pravoslavie.ru, September 18, 2002, http://www.pravo slavie.ru/news/020916/07.html. Accessed August 20, 2005.

11. "56% Rossiyan Podderzhivayut Ideyu Vozvrashcheniya Feliksa," Grani.ru, September 28, 2002, http://www.grani.ru/Society/m.10471.html. Accessed October 31, 2005.

12. Ibid.

13. Quoted in Ivan Atlantov, "Gosduma Reshit Sud'bu Pamyatnika Dzerzhin-skomu," *Izvestiya,* September 27, 2002.

14. Alexei Pankin, "A Debt of Gratitude to Dzerzhinsky," *Moscow Times,* October 1, 2002.

15. Boris Kagarlitsky, "'Iron Felix' and Fetishism," *Moscow Times,* October 1, 2002.

16. Gavriil Popov, "Vokrug Pamyatnika Dzerzhinskomu," *Moskovsky Komsomolets,* October 11, 2002.

17. "SPS protiv Dzerzhinskogo," Dni.ru, September 16, 2002, http://www.dni .ru/news/russia/2002/9/16/14168.html. Accessed October 29, 2005.

18. "Luzhkov Predlagaet Vosstanovit' Pamyatnik Dzerzhinskomu kak Pam-yatnik Vuchetichu," Polit.ru, September 13, 2002, http://old.polit.ru/printable/503713.html. Accessed October 29, 2005.

19. Georgii Poltavchenko, "Pamyatnik Dzerzhinskomu Vosstanovlen Ne Bu-det," *Leningradskaya Pravda,* September 23, 2002.

20. Simon Saradzhyan, "Iron Felix Panned by Kremlin, Patriach," *Moscow Times,* September 23, 2002.

21. Andrei Sinyavsky, *Soviet Civilization* (New York: Arcade, 1990), 126.

22. Christopher Andrew and Oleg Gordievsky, *KGB: The Inside Story* (New York: HarperCollins, 1990), 42, 40.

23. Sinyavsky, *Soviet Civilization,* 128.

24. Orlando Figes, *A People's Tragedy: A History of the Russian Revolution* (New York: Viking, 1997), 536. One of the Cheka's first Moscow victims was the well-known circus clown Bim-Bom, whose repertoire included anti-Soviet jokes. Chekists burst in on the clown during one of his performances, and the audience at first thought it was part of the act. But Bim-Bom, understanding the real situation, fled, and the Chekists shot him in the back. Panic broke out. Because the population had not yet become accustomed to living according to the new rules, hundreds of people turned out for the clown's funeral, which became a demonstration against terror.

25. Nikolai Svanidze, interview with Boris Nemtsov, Ekho Moskvy, www.echo .msk.ru, October 6, 2002, http://www.echo.msk.ru/programs/beseda/19862/. In the program *Mirror,* which was hosted by Nikolai Svanidze on NTV, Nemtsov and Vladimir Zhirinovsky, the leader of the Liberal Democratic Party, discussed whether to return the statue of Dzerzhinski to the square. Nemtsov said that the "crazy idea [of restoring the statue] was put forward simply to agitate society." He

went on to describe what he learned as a result of his research in the state archives.

"The terror began officially on September 5, 1918, after Fanny Kaplan tried to kill Lenin," he said. "On the following day, the Bolsheviks indiscriminately killed five hundred persons and then began to mow down everyone. They let themselves go to such an extent that [Patriarch] Tikhon called them a satanic herd. They began to issue a weekly bulletin. . . . In it, they published the names of those murdered and shot."

Zhirinovsky said, "The Bolsheviks came to power. Dzerzhinsky was placed in the most difficult sector, the battle with counterrevolution. To fight with counter-revolution without blood, without terror, was impossible. This was an honest person who carried out the will of the party. This was not bin Laden, who hides in alien mountains in a foreign country. Dzerzhinsky was assigned to this work. And you accuse him for this. . . .

"And you speak of the Tambov farmers," Zhirinovsky continued. "Should the country have died of starvation? This was a forced measure: either take bread from the farmers and save millions of city dwellers from starvation, or leave the bread with the farmers and there will be freedom but they will not bring the bread to market. They will wait higher prices. And during this time, millions will die in the cities. This was a choice between the lesser and the greater evil. Now you emphasize only this lesser evil but the greater evil was avoided because of this lesser evil. . . .

"And what about the new [post-Soviet] democratic authorities who did not use such terror but nonetheless, five million people died from hunger, unemployment, suicide, desperation. At least the Bolsheviks wrote down who they killed. The first husband of my mother was a Chekist. After executions, he came home and puked. Chekists were honest people. There was an order from above, shoot every day. Otherwise, the hold on the country would be lost."

There were calls from listeners. A retired teacher of history said that she favored the return of the monument. "My family and those close to me are for this. There is such disgrace and absence of limits in the country."

"I want to add a small commentary," said Zhirinovsky. "At least someone in the country one hundred years ago imposed some kind of order."

Nemtsov said that in the notes that he saw, Dzerzhinsky wrote, cynically, " 'Kill without investigation, so that they will be afraid.' The monument is not important artistically. It is a symbol of lawlessness, terror and arbitrary rule."

Zhirinovsky said, "Regarding symbols. You say that there is too much blood connected with the name of Dzerzhinsky. But there are other considerations. Today we have the FSB. The FSB needs something to be proud of. They celebrate their holiday every year and their founder is somewhere in an empty lot. Without the FSB, the country cannot develop further. What should thousands of officers of the FSB do if their founder is considered a criminal? That means their organization is criminal. It's impossible to say that Dzerzhinsky committed a crime. This was a crime of the existing regime. . . . The government would have dissolved. . . . The only way to preserve the country was to create the Cheka. If they had not suppressed others, they would not have remained in power."

26. Nikolai Berdyaev, *Samopoznanie* (Moscow: Mysl', 1991), 215.

27. Vitalii Shentalinsky, "Filosofskiy Parokhod," from "Oskolki Serebryanogo Veka," *Novyi Mir,* nos. 5–6 (1998).

28. Berdyaev, *Samopoznanie,* 216. Berdyaev may have underestimated Dzerzhinski's depravity. An indication of this was the use of sadistic torture by the Cheka of which Dzerzhinski could not have been unaware. Each local branch of the Cheka developed its own methods. In Kharkov a victim's hands were submerged in boiling water until his skin peeled off. In Tsaritsyn a victim's bones were sawed in half. In Voronezh the victims were rolled naked in nail-studded barrels. In Kiev the Chekist torturers attached a cage with rats to the victim's torso and heated the cage so that the rats would devour him alive. Other local Chekas used fake executions or buried the victim alive, put him in a coffin with a corpse, or forced him to watch loved ones being tortured or killed. Figes, *A People's Tragedy,* 646.

29. Leon Turrou, "An Unwritten Chapter," manuscript, 1926, Hoover Institution Archives.

30. Ibid.

31. Andrew and Gordievsky, *KGB,* 42. The OGPU, the Joint State Political Directorate, was the successor organization to the Cheka. It was established in 1922.

32. Vladimir Mayakovsky, "Khorosho!" (1927), translated in Sinyavsky, *Soviet Civilization,* 130.

33. Eduard Bagritsky, "TVS" (1929), translated ibid., 131.

34. Aleksandr Dobrovolsky, "Slezy Edmundovicha," *Moskovsky Komsomolets,* October 21, 2002.

35. Yuri German, *Rasskazy o Felikse Dzerzhinskom* (Leningrad: Lenizdat, 1974).

36. Andrew and Gordievsky, *KGB,* 43.

37. In December 1918 a special commission was formed under the government of Gen. Anton Denikin to investigate the actions of the Bolsheviks on the territory of southern Russia that was under its control. It succeeded in gathering and then bringing to the West a huge amount of documentary material about the actions of the Cheka.

38. Melgunov, *Krasny Terror v Rossii,* 30, 22–23.

39. Ibid., 23.

40. Dobrovolsky, "Slezy Edmundovicha."

41. Nabi Abdullaev, "Luzhkov Wants to Restore Iron Felix," *Moscow Times,* September 16, 2002.

42. Varfolomeev interview with Kharitonov.

43. Popov, "Vokrug Pamyatnika Dzerzhinskomu."

44. Nabi Abdullaev, "The Bronze Chekist," Transitions Online, October 4, 2002, www.tol.cz. Subscription required to access the full article.

45. Kevin O'Flynn, "City Rejects Return of Dzerzhinsky," *Moscow Times*, January 22, 2003.

46. Golovkova et al., *Butovskii Poligon*, 60.

47. Zoya Svetova, "Muzey ili 'Diskoteka na Kladbishche'?" *Novye Izvestiya*, April 26, 2006. Marshal Mikhail Tukhachevksy was a commander of the Red Army during the Russian Civil War and the head of the Red Army from 1925 to 1928. He was known for his ability as well as his ruthlessness. He suppressed the Kronstadt sailors' revolt in 1921 and used poison gas against the peasant rebels in the Tambov oblast who revolted against Bolshevik rule in 1921 and 1922. He was arrested in 1937 on charges of spying for Nazi Germany and executed. Marshal Alexander Yegorov was a commander of the Red Army's southern front during the Russian Civil War, during which time he was a close colleague of Stalin. He was officially listed as one of the judges at the trial of Tukhachevsky but was arrested in February 1938 and died in prison.

48. Rustam Rakhmatullin, " 'Rasstrel'nyi Dom' pod Pritselom," *Izvestiya*, January 20, 2006.

49. Irina Vlasova, "Feniks v Kozhanom Pal'to," *Novye Izvestiya*, November 9, 2005.

50. Kim Murphy, "Soviet Spy Chief Is Back — on a Pedestal," *Los Angeles Times*, November 10, 2005.

2. Efforts to Remember

1. D. Gai, "Pomni o GULAGe," *Vechernyaya Moskva*, October 31, 1990, 2.

2. Zoya Marchenko, "Kak Byl Ustanovlen Solovetskii Kamen' v Moskve," *30 Oktyabrya*, no. 1 (1999): 4.

3. G. Zaichenko, "Chernoe na Krasnom," *Moskovskaya Pravda*, October 31, 1990.

4. Vadim Dormidontov, "Istoriya Solovetskogo Kamnya," *30 Oktyabrya*, no. 10 (2000): 10.

5. Hannah Arendt, *The Origins of Totalitarianism* (New York: Schocken, 1948), 461.

6. Quoted in Stephane Courtois et al., *The Black Book of Communism*, trans. Jonathan Murphy and Mark Kramer (Cambridge: Harvard University Press, 1999), 75–76, 59.

7. Ibid., 78.

8. Ibid., 82, 107. The Bolsheviks also glorified terror while the White leaders depicted the atrocities of their side as eruptions of savagery that they were powerless to prevent. In the words of Melgunov, the Bolshevik terror "was a system of the methodical application of violence in life, the open apotheosis of murder as an instrument of power. . . . These were not excesses which you can find in the psychology of civil war or for which there is some other type of explanation. The

white terror was a phenomenon of a different order–first of all it consisted of excesses on the basis of unbridled power and revenge. Where and when [among the white leaders] did you hear voices with calls for systematic, official murders?" S. P. Melgunov, *Krasny Terror v Rossii* (Moscow: PUICO, 1990), 6.

9. Courtois et al., *Black Book*, 109, 123.

10. Ibid., 112–14.

11. Ibid., 137, 138.

12. Ibid., 155.

13. Ibid., 161, 159.

14. Ibid., 202, 205.

15. Ibid., 205, 219, 231.

16. Ibid., 4.

17. Mikhail Heller, *Cogs in the Wheel* (New York: Knopf, 1988), 1.

18. V. Gordin and N. Goryacheva, "A KGB Molchit . . . " (interview with Alexander Milchakov), *Vechernyaya Moskva,* October 20, 1990.

19. In an interview, January 16, 1991, in *Vechernyaya Moskva* ("Po sledam ras-strelnikhk spiskov"), Milchakov said that the commission that had been established in the Moscow City Council to search for the burial grounds of victims of political repression had voted in favor of creating an eternal flame in the Alexandrovsky Garden between the Borovitsky and Troitsky Gates, and there was already a good place to put the flame. In 1978, three Soviet dissidents, Pyotr Starchik, Mikhail Makarenko, and Alexander Podrabinek, traveled to the site of the Belomor-Baltisky canal and gathered and put in a special bag the remains of prisoners who were buried near one of the sluices where the work conditions had been the most terrible. They then brought the remains to Moscow, where they were taken to the apartment of the priest N. Pedoshenko, who performed a funeral service. The dissidents then went to the area between the Borovitsky and Troitsky Gates and, taking advantage of the fact that construction was going on, buried the remains near the Kremlin wall. They photographed the site and made a video, which was twice shown in the U.S. Congress. Milchakov said that there was no need to argue, there was already a place for the eternal flame. Alexander Milchakov, "Poisk novikh adresov zakhoronenii prodolzhaetskya," *Vechernyaya Moskva,* July 12, 1990.

20. Viktor Svinin, "Ten' Vyshinskogo v Nekhoroshem Dome," *Nezavisimaya Gazeta,* April 3, 2006.

21. Ibid.

22. "UFSIN po Magadanskoi Oblasti," Magadan Oblast Directorate of the Federal Service for Corrections website, www.ufsin-magadan.ru/index.php?news id=44.

23. Aleksandr Glushchenko, "Pis'mo iz Magadana: Maska," *Sovetskaya Rossiya,* June 27, 1996.

24. David Raizman, *Maska Skorbi* (Magadan: Russian State University for the Humanities Press, 2003), 4.

25. Zh. Vasilieva, "Iskusstvo i Vlast' — Nesovmestny?" interview with E. Neizvestniy, *Literaturnaya Gazeta,* August 24, 1994.

26. *Maska Skorbi,* documentary film, Magadanskaya Studiya, Televidenie, 1996.

27. Penny Morvant, "Memorial to Stalin's Victims Unveiled in Far East," Radio Free Europe/Radio Liberty, no. 115, part 1, June 13, 1996.

28. Ellen Mickiewicz, *Changing Channels* (Durham, N.C.: Duke University Press, 1999), 182.

29. John Round, "The Legacies of the Gulag System in Post-Soviet Magadan," paper presented at Conference on the Soviet Gulag: Its History and Legacy, Harvard University, November 2, 2006.

30. Ibid.

31. In the late 1960s, after the invasion of Czechoslovakia, the democratic movement in the Soviet Union gained strength and the authorities began making plans to crush it. Political prisoners were already being held in labor camps in Mordovia, about three hundred miles east of Moscow. But the authorities decided to organize new camps and to cut off the channels of communication that were allowing information from prisoners to reach the West.

The Perm camps were well suited for this role. They were farther from Moscow, in an isolated location, and, in the case of Perm 36, already equipped with reinforced security. The first train with prisoners from Mordovia arrived in the Perm oblast on July 13, 1972, with prisoners for Perm 36 and Perm 35. From that time on, prisoners were steadily transferred from Mordovia to the more secure camps of the Perm triangle. Perm 36 became the main political prison camp in the Soviet Union. In fact, the political labor camps were only the tip of the iceberg of repression in the Soviet Union. In addition there were political prisoners in ordinary labor camps and psychiatric hospitals. But the political camps contained the most uncompromising and politically conscious of those who fought the totalitarian regime, and among those who served their sentences in Perm 36 were Sergei Kovalyev, Natan Sharansky, the writer Leonid Borodin, the psychiatrist Semyon Gluzman, and many of the leaders of the nationalist movements in Ukraine and the Baltics. The prisoners were convicted of "anti-Soviet propaganda" and "anti-Soviet agitation." These were the political articles of the criminal code. As a rule, their only offense was circulating information.

32. Yevhen Sverstiuk, "Return to the 'Zone of Death': Perm Camp 36," *Ukrainian Weekly,* October 11, 1998. The political labor camps were cut off from the world, but what took place there often became a major issue in international relations. This was because the prisoners regularly succeeded in smuggling out word of their condition. They wrote surreptitiously on thin cigarette paper in tiny handwriting with pencils that were constantly sharpened. The writing was so small that the messages, which contained details of hunger strikes and abuse, later had to be read with a magnifying glass.

The guards tried to prevent information from leaving the camp. Wives, who were allowed annual visits, were often subjected to gynecological examinations before and after meetings. The prisoners, however, wrapped their messages tightly in packaging from food products purchased in the camp canteen and swallowed them. A prisoner would then excrete the capsule, wash it, and have his wife swallow it before leaving the camp. In this way, information about the camps reached the West.

An example of the prisoners' communications was a letter to President Reagan signed by ten men in Perm 36 that reached the West in March 1983, urging an international inspection of the camps.

The letter read, "It is often difficult for a resident of the West to imagine the atmosphere of lawlessness in which the inmates of Soviet political prison camps exist today." The prisoners went on to describe how three of their number were dragged away from a "a humble, prison table" at which fourteen prisoners "had gathered to celebrate Easter with prayer and an Easter meal." They told how prisoners were deprived of long-awaited visits with family members for failing to fulfill their work quotas and described ideological censorship of their letters and the confiscation of poems, prayers, and even the text of the Universal Declaration of Human Rights because of its "suspicious content."

The prisoners wrote that "an impartial commission of politically unaffiliated Western humanitarians" would, after visiting the camps, be able to "draw up an authoritative conclusion about the prisoners here and, consequently, about the moral right of the government of this country to condemn others [the British in Ulster, South Africa] for using imprisonment to suppress dissent."

33. Marchenko, a philologist from Kiev and member of the Ukrainian Helsinki group, one of the unofficial groups formed by Soviet citizens to monitor Soviet observance of the 1975 Helsinki Accords, died on October 7, 1984, after labor camp authorities waited three months to hospitalize him for an infected kidney despite a call for his immediate hospitalization from the U.S. State Department. Stus, another member of the Ukrainian Helsinki group and a celebrated poet, died in the camp after declaring a hunger strike on September 4, 1985. Tikhy, a founding member of the Ukrainian Helsinki group, died on May 5, 1984, after being subjected to harrowing treatment. Although he suffered from tuberculosis and a severe duodenal ulcer, he was not excused from hard labor and was put in a punishment cell despite the agonizing pain that near-starvation causes an ulcer victim. He died on emerging from the cell. Litvin, also a member of the Ukrainian Helsinki group, committed suicide in the Perm 36 camp in August 1984.

34. Marina Nikitina, "Zona Svobodnykh Lyudei," *Novaya Gazeta,* January 30, 2009.

35. "Muzei 'Perm-36' Budet Vosstanavlivat'sya na Den'gi Kongressa SShA," *RIA "Novyi Region,"* http://pda.nr2.ru/perm/41506.html. December 26, 2006.

36. As the project got under way, volunteers began to collect documents about the camp and to tape oral histories. Some of the former guards participated. They said that they were told that the political prisoners were dangerous criminals and that any escape attempt would be made with the help of the CIA and the use of

helicopters. Despite this, the guards were warned that if a prisoner escaped, they would pay for it "with their heads." To some extent, this indoctrination had its effect on the guards. A former guard named Chugainov, in an interview with Cherepanov, recalled Sergei Kovalyev, who had been a prisoner in the camp and, at the time of the interview, was in charge of human rights under Yeltsin. "Sergei Adamovich," Chugainov recalled, "this is very nasty person. He stuck his nose into everything. I understand that this was his work. Just as now, he is in charge of human rights, he fulfilled that function then." Chugainov said, "Once one of the political prisoners came up to me, I don't remember his name. He said, 'I identified you among the other guards as literate and thoughtful. Well, I tell you that sooner or later, we will be over you.'" Chugainov said, "It turns out that even then they had everything planned." Mikhail Cherepanov, interview with the author, April 9, 2006.

3. Butovo and Kommunarka

1. "O Sobornom Proslavlenii Novomuchenikov i Ispovednikov Rossiiskikh XX Veka," *Russkoe Voskresenie,* http://voskres.ru/golgofa/svyat.htm.

2. G. Polonskaya, *Tak My Zhili* (Haifa, 2005), Memorial Society collection, 182, 186.

3. Nikolai Lyubimov, *Neuvyadaemyi Tsvet: Kniga Vospominanii* (Moscow: Ya-zyki Slavyanskoi Kultury, 2004), 200, 201.

4. Avis Bohlen, conversation with the author, 1975.

5. Mark Rafalov, *Raspyatye Sud'by* (Moscow, 2002), unpublished memoir, Memorial Society collection, 21.

6. Nelli Tachko, *Zhizn' Kazalas' Takoi Bezoblachnoi* (Moscow: Moskovsky Memorial, 2005), 30.

7. Valery Bronshtein, *Preodolenie* (Moscow: Adamant, 2004).

8. Golovkova et al., *Butovsky Poligon,* 64.

9. Aino Kuusinen, *Gospod' Nizvergaet Svoikh Angelov* (Helsinki: Muistelmat vuo-silia, 1972), 138. Aino Kuusinen was the wife of Otto Kuusinen, a Finnish communist and member of the Presidium of the Supreme Soviet.

10. Golovkova et al., *Butovsky Poligon,* 67.

11. Ibid., 64–65.

12. V. Gordin and N. Goryacheva, "Khozyain Rasstrel'nogo Doma" (interview with Alexander Milchakov), *Vechernyaya Moskva,* July 27, 1990.

13. Ibid.

14. Ibid.

15. Ibid. Milchakov said he could not walk past the building of the Military Collegium without experiencing the most painful recollections from his childhood. His father was tried in that building. As a child, his mother took him to the court building with her. She went nearly every day, and while she waited in line for news of his father, he played with other children near the statue of Ivan Fyodorov,

the pioneer of printing, which was located nearby. "Mother came to me, always sadly, having received the standard answer, 'The sentence for your husband has not been handed down. Come next time.' This was the same answer that thousands of other people received."

In fact, "The arrested persons were taken to the third floor . . . and led into the hearing room one by one." On the table in front of the judge, V. Ulrich, was a pile of already prepared sentences. "What happened next was a horrible parody of a trial. In his last words, the accused tried to explain logically that he wasn't an enemy of his people . . . but his fate was already decided. . . . Ulrich, usually after a few minutes and as was required by the law, left for consultations, and then after two or three minutes returned and announced his verdict. The defendant was taken out to a neighboring room. The condemned were shot here in the dark basements of the building of the Military Collegium on 25th of October Street. . . . And all this time, relatives in the reception area waited for news."

The executions were described by Aleksei Snegov, an old Bolshevik and party member since 1917, in a conversation with Vladimir Pyatnitsky, the son of I. A. Pyatnitsky, a leader of the Comintern who was shot in 1938. According to Pyatnitsky, Snegov said, "The condemned person was taken down the same stairway [he had ascended to the courtroom] under guard to a deep basement and shot in the back of the head. The executioner was the commandant of the Military Collegium. The executed person was pulled into the corner of the basement, his shoe was removed from his right foot, and on his large toe was fastened a plywood name tag in which was written in pencil the number of his case. From that moment, the last name of the of the former person was nowhere mentioned."

Pyatnitsky recounted that Snegov told him that "after he was taken to the basement by mistake after the pronouncement of his sentence, although he received only ten years in prison, in the corner, in the pile of corpses, he recognized his friend — a Leningrader and member of the party Central Committee, V. Pozern. He was lying with his beard pointing up." Vladimir Pyatnitsky, "Khronika posledgnego puti," *Novaya Gazeta*, "Pravda GULAGa," April 3, 2008, http://www.novayagazeta.ru/data/2008/gulago3/05.html?print=201114021122.

16. Golovkova et al., *Butovsky Poligon*, 160.

17. Valentin Gordin, "Kak Sobrat' Ubityi Narod" (interview with Alexander Milchakov), *Vechernyaya Moskva*, February 18, 1992. Milchakov notes that Sadovsky was forced to change his name.

18. Golovkova et al., *Butovsky Poligon*, 61.

19. Ibid., appendix.

20. Ibid., 71–72.

21. Gordin, "Kak Sobrat' Ubityi Narod."

22. Golovkova et al., *Butovsky Poligon*, 85–86.

23. Ibid., 86.

24. Ibid., 84.

25. V. Gordin and N. Goryacheva, "Dvorik v Varsonofievskom, ili Kto Strelyal v

Zatylok?" (interview with Alexander Milchakov), *Vechernyaya Moskva*, September 28, 1990.

26. Golovkova et al., *Butovsky Poligon*, 92.

27. Ibid., 87.

28. Ibid., 90.

29. Ibid., 71.

30. Leonid Novak, "Loza: Fragmenti budushchei knigi," *30 Oktyabrya*, no. 2 (1999).

31. *Rasstrelniye Spiski, Moskva 1935–53, Donskoye Kladbishche (Donskoi Krematorii)*, (Moscow: Obshchestvo "Memorial" — Izdatel'stvo "Zven'ya," 2005), 565.

32. Ibid.

33. Leonid Novak, "Loza: Fragmenty budushchei knigi," *30 Oktyabrya*, no. 3 (2000): 7.

34. V. Gordin and N. Goryacheva, "Duel': Aleksandr Milchakov protiv KGB" (interview with Alexander Milchakov), *Vechernyaya Moskva*, April 14, 1990.

35. V. Gordin and N. Goryacheva, "KGB: Rasstrel'nye Spiski Naideny" (interview with Alexander Milchakov), *Vechernyaya Moskva*, November 27, 1990.

36. V. Gordin and N. Goryacheva, "Vstrecha Sostoyalas', Duel' Prodolzhaetsya" (interview with Alexander Milchakov), *Vechernyaya Moskva*, August 10, 1990.

37. Golovkova et al., *Butovsky Poligon*, 157.

38. V. Gordin and N. Goryacheva, "A KGB Molchit . . . " (interview with Alexander Milchakov), *Vechernyaya Moskva*, October 20, 1990.

39. Ibid.

40. Gordin and Goryacheva, "KGB."

41. V. Gordin and N. Goryacheva, "Po Sledam Rasstrel'nykh Spiskov" (interview with Alexander Milchakov), *Vechernyaya Moskva*, January 16, 1991.

42. Ibid.

43. Golovkova et al., *Butovsky Poligon*, 170.

44. Ibid., 170–71.

45. A. B. Roginsky, "Posleslovie k Spiskam Zakhoronennykh v 'Kommunarke,'" www.memo.ru/memory/communarka/komm.html. Accessed February 21, 2005.

46. Gordin and Goryacheva, "KGB."

47. Ibid.

48. Golovkova et al., *Butovsky Poligon*, 160.

49. Ibid.

50. "Ob Obshchestvennoi Gruppy po Uvekovecheniyu Pamyati Zhertv Politicheskikh Repressii," www.netda.ru/martirolog/t1/butovo_02.htm.

51. Golovkova et al., *Butovsky Poligon*, 161.

52. Ibid., 163.

53. Gordin, "Kak sobrat."

54. Golovkova et al., *Butovsky Poligon*, 165.

55. Ibid., 167.

56. "Svyatiye Butovskiye mucheniki, molite Boga o nas (kommentarii v svete

very)," Sedmitza.ru, "Pravoslavnaya Entsiklopediya," http://www.sedmitza.ru/text/409916.html.

57. Andrei Sakharov, "Memorialu v "Kommunarke" — Byt'!" *30 Oktyabrya*, no. 1 (1999): 10.

58. Pamphlet, " 'Spetsob" ekt 'Kommunarka' — Khram Svv. Novomuchenikov i Ispovednikov Rossiiskikh."

59. Ibid.

60. Golovkova et al., *Butovsky Poligon,* 172–73.

61. Ibid., 96.

62. Stalin deliberately played to Russian nationalism in order to win support for the war effort. He spoke of Russia's heroic past and called on Russian soldiers to follow the example of the great Russian military leaders Alexander Nevsky, Dmitri Donskoi, Alexander Suvorov, and Mikhail Kutuzov. Neither he nor the soldiers to whom he appealed saw a conflict between Russian nationalism and Soviet patriotism. More Russians served in the Soviet Army than any other group, and they graciously suggested that members of other national groups were all "Russians" in their hearts. The Russian parts of the country were swept by a wave of patriotic fervor. In Moscow recruitment centers were jammed around the clock. In the Kursk province, seventy-two hundred people applied for front-line military service in the first month of hostilities. See Catherine Merridale, *Ivan's War: Life and Death in the Red Army, 1939–1945* (New York: Picador, 2006), 92, 132, 290.

63. "President Rossii pervim iz rukovodstva strain posetil mesto massogo rasstrela repressirovannikh," news.ru.com, October 30, 2007, http://www.newsru .com/russia/30oct2007/butovo.html. Accessed November 11, 2010.

64. Ibid.

65. Ibid.

4. St. Petersburg

1. Veronique Garros, Natalia Korenevskaya, and Thomas Lahusen, eds., *Intimacy and Terror: Soviet Diaries of the 1930s* (New York: New Press, 1995), 356.

2. *Leningradskii Martirolog,* vol. 2 (St. Petersburg: Izdatel'stvo Rossiiskoi Natsional'noi Biblioteki, 1996), 430–31.

3. Garros, Korenevskaya, and Lahusen, *Intimacy and Terror,* 357.

4. *Leningradskii Martirolog,* 2: 435.

5. *Leningradskii Martirolog,* vol. 4 (St. Petersburg: Izdatel'stvo Rossiiskoi Natsional'noi Biblioteki, 1999), 668–69.

6. Liana Ilyina, interview with the author, January 25, 2004.

7. R. Efrussi, "Zapiski Inzhenera," in "Memorial Sovesti," *Zvezda,* no. 6 (1991), 147.

8. *Leningradskii Martirolog,* 2: 448.

9. Efrussi, "Zapiski Inzhenera," 147.

10. *"Nam Ostaetsya Tol'ko Imya . . . "—Pamyatniki Zhertvam Politicheskikh Repressii Petrograda-Leningrada* (St. Petersburg: Izdatel'stvo DEAN, 1999), 7.

11. Pavel Gutiontov and Andrei Chernov, "Ikh Prodolzhayut Rasstrelovat' do Sikh Por," *Novaya Gazeta,* September 9, 2002.

12. *Leningradskii Martirolog,* vol. 1 (St. Petersburg: Izdatel'stvo Rossiiskoi Natsional'noi Biblioteki, 1995), 668.

13. Garros, Korenevskaya, and Lahusen, *Intimacy and Terror,* 352, 359.

14. Harrison Salisbury, *The 900 Days: The Siege of Leningrad* (New York: Da Capo, 1969), 438, 437.

15. Ibid., 478.

16. Ibid., 484.

17. Ibid., 516.

18. "Na Meste Skorbi Ne Mozhet Byt' Rynka," *Metro,* January 28, 1998, 2.

19. In the course of her work, Flige learned that well-known victims were sometimes buried under false names. In 1932 a group of Catholic prisoners in the Solovetsky Islands were accused of creating a Catholic commune and receiving packages from the Polish Red Cross. They were transferred to the Yaroslavl investigative prison and received increased sentences. According to the investigative file in the Arkhangelsk FSB, where the materials on the case were kept, one of the prisoners was lost en route to Yaroslavl. This was Jan Troigo, a Soviet Pole and well-known Catholic priest in Leningrad. He became ill and was put in the prison hospital in Leningrad, where he died. In the correspondence between the prison hospital and the OGPU, it is explained that Troigo died and was buried under the name Selomakhin in the Preobrazhensky cemetery. This apparently meant that he was buried in an existing grave. Irina Flige, interview with the author, November 8, 2003.

20. Victims were also buried in the Leningrad cemeteries. One of the burial places was the Memory of the Victims of January 9 cemetery, formerly the Preobrazhenskoye cemetery. "In December 1937, the cemetery was closed for visitation for three days," wrote eighty-five-year-old Vera Alexeevna Timofeeva, in a letter to the newspaper *Vecherny Peterburg* in 1992. "Those living in nearby buildings were warned about this. We heard how cars arrived on three nights, the 27th, 28th, and 29th of December, but by New Year's everything was finished and cleaned up. The place where they buried those who had been shot was located five minutes' walk from the Church in honor of Alexander Nevsky, where my father, its senior priest, Father Alexei Chuzhbovsky, led his last service on December 3, 1937. He was arrested on December 4."

Vera Alexeevna said that throughout the 1920s, the bodies of executed persons were brought to the cemetery and secretly buried. In December 1937, after the arrest of her father, during one of those pre–New Year's nights when the cemetery was closed for visitation, one of the grave diggers, Ivan Bogomolov, recognized among the corpses brought for burial, the body of Father Alexei. He pulled it to one side and buried it separately. He told Vera Alexeevna's sister and made her promise to remain silent.

The nights when the cemetery was closed remain in the memories of persons who lived nearby because of the brilliant illumination as the darkness was lit up by the fire from burning trees that had been doused with kerosene. Their scorched trunks were removed only after the war. The two sisters held a funeral service for their father in the absence of his grave. They dared to place a tablet with his name on the family tomb only in the beginning of the 1990s. *Leningradskii Martirolog*, vol. 5 (St. Petersburg: Izdatel'stvo Rossiiskoi Natsional'noi Biblioteki, 2002), 605–6.

21. See, e.g., M. Belousov, "Taina levashovskoi Pustoshi," *Trud*, July 2, 1989.

22. *"Nam Ostaetsya Tol'ko Imya . . . ,"* 7.

23. Skhema "Dachi" so srokami i kolichestvom zaxoronenii (map of the "Dacha" with dates and number of burials), UFSB Archive for St. Petersburg and Leningrad Oblast.

24. Oral testimony of witnesses, Memorial files, 1997.

25. Ibid.

26. N. Odintsova, "Taina Koirangakangas," *Vecherny Peterburg*, November 25, 1992.

27. Ibid.

28. *Memorial'noe Kladbishche Sandormokh* (St. Petersburg: Nauchno-informatsionnyi Tsentr Memorial, 1997), 3.

29. Flige interview.

30. Valery Beresnev, "I Na Kostyakh Rastut Derev'ya," *Tainii Sovetnik*, January, 2006

31. The failure to commemorate even minimally the majority of the St. Petersburg victims of Communist terror has left the city with no moral counterweight to the rise of political extremism. The Soviet regime is gone, but those longing for the return of Russian power find tacit support for dangerous nationalism in the indifference of the Russian authorities to Soviet crimes. The result is that many—particularly among the young—are attracted to fascism, with the paradoxical result that St. Petersburg, a city that endured a nine hundred–day siege during the Second World War at the hands of fascists, is now the center in Russia of pro-Nazi youth groups and fascism.

The most visible manifestation of fascism is the skinhead movement. According to Amnesty International, there are fifty thousand skinheads in Russia, about half the skinheads in the world; five thousand are believed to be in St. Petersburg, the highest concentration in Russia. An authoritative figure for many skinheads is Alexander Sukharevsky, the leader of the right-wing National Peoples' Party. The members of the party use the Nazi salute and wear black armbands with a symbol resembling the swastika. Their favorite greeting is "Heil Hitler!" or "Heil Russia!" and their favorite slogans are "Russians, Forward!" and "Russia for Russians!"

On February 9, 2004, at about 9 P.M., Khursheda Sultanova, a nine-year-old Tajik girl; her father, Yusuf Sultanov, thirty-five; and her cousin Alabir, eleven, were returning home from the Yusupov Garden when they were attacked from behind by a gang of a dozen teenagers armed with knives, brass knuckles, chains, and bats. One group began battering Sultanov with baseball bats and brass knuckles. A second turned its attention to Khursheda and her cousin and started striking them with clubs. The boy scrambled under a parked car, but as Khursheda struggled, one of the skinheads took out a long bladed knife and stabbed her eleven times in the chest. The killers shouted "Russia for Russians!" Khursheda, who was in the second grade, died face up in the snow, with her arms outstretched.

Valentina Matvienko, the governor of St. Petersburg, called the killers "underage scum" and demanded that they face harsh and swift justice. The murder made the nightly news program in Russia. But within hours the fervor of the investigating authorities began to wane. A police spokesman told the media that the police were looking into the business activities of Sultanov. He said, "It's very strange that they would choose to stab the little girl to death and only beat the father. It's no secret that immigrants from Tajikistan are often involved in the drug trade."

In a further sign of the ambivalent attitude in the city toward crimes committed by nationalists against foreigners, 20 percent of the residents of St. Petersburg in a poll said that they "understood" the murder of Khursheda. However, arrests were eventually made in the case, and eight defendants between the ages of fifteen and twenty-one were charged with assault and one with murder.

The murder of Khursheda Sultanov was not an isolated incident. Every year, on April 20, Hitler's birthday, tension in St. Petersburg increases as skinheads promise to mark the date with the murder of Africans or Asians. St. Petersburg is Russia's top destination for foreign students, and every third crime committed against a foreign student in Russia is committed in St. Petersburg or the surrounding oblast. In an interview with the newspaper *Moskovsky Komsomolets,* Aliu Tunkara, chairman of St. Petersburg African Unity, an organization of Africans living in Russia, said that extremist groups operate with the assistance of the police and he and his fellow Africans cannot turn to the police for assistance. "Do you know how 'pleasant' it is to chat with our police officers?" he asked. "At each step, you hear such expressions as 'Hey, chief gorilla, come here!'" Tunkara believes that the situation is better in Moscow, where there are embassies. "But in St. Petersburg, no one wants to talk to us in general." Julie A. Corwin, "Russia: Racist Attacks Plague St. Petersburg," Radio Free Europe/Radio Liberty, rferl.org, September 30, 2005, http://www.rferl.org/content/article/1061791.html.

Besides their attacks on foreigners, the fascists have attacked those who have tried to oppose them. The most frightening example was the murder of the St. Petersburg ethnologist Nikolai Girenko, the leading Russian expert on Russian fascism, June 19, 2004. On the morning Girenko was killed, someone rang the doorbell of his apartment and asked for "Nikolai Mikhailovich." When Girenko said, "Who's there?" he was shot through the wooden door.

Girenko headed the Minority Rights Commission at the St. Petersburg Scientific Union and had testified for the prosecution at numerous trials of fascists.

Girenko had most recently assisted the St. Petersburg prosecutor's office in inves-tigating a local skinhead group called Shultz-88 and in prosecuting three skinheads for the murder of the Azeri street vendor Mamed Mamedov. He had also evalu-ated the publications of the Party of Freedom and the Russian Party, two extremist organizations, for incitement to interethnic violence. At the time of his death, he was scheduled to testify at a trial of extremists in Veliky Novgorod.

Girenko was the object of constant abuse in the St. Petersburg fascist press, whose newspapers are easily available on St. Petersburg streets. The prosecutor's office is dilatory in pressing charges against these newspapers, and, when it does, it almost immediately drops them. One of the most glaring examples was the case of *Nashe Obozreniye,* where Yuri Belayev, the leader of the Freedom Party, wrote in part that the "dirty, dumb bloodsucking invaders from the Caucasus must be fought." The newspaper published on its front page a photo of a group of skinheads with their arms raised in the Nazi salute and the slogan "Anti-fascism will not pass."

For two and a half years, the St. Petersburg city councilor Mikhail Amosov pushed for criminal charges to be brought against Belyaev under article 282 of the criminal code, "Incitement of ethnic, racial, or religious hatred," but the prosecutor's office invariably refused. The explanation was that Belyaev suppos-edly did not intend to spread the idea of ethnic or racial superiority. Still, in January 2004 the city prosecutor's office opened a criminal case against Belyaev, only to close it several months later under the "statute of limitations."

Before he was killed, Girenko was the target of many threats. There was an attempt to attack his office in the Academy of Sciences. The attackers tried to break down the iron door and succeeded in dislodging several bricks. They managed to avoid the guard and open the lock in the entryway and to cut off the electricity. They left a note: "This is a warning, now we will kill."

Girenko believed that the death threat was intended for him, but the efforts of the police were perfunctory. An expert gathered material evidence at the scene, but the police investigator forgot it there. The police said that insofar as the attackers did not get into the office and the material damage was insignificant, there was no point in opening a case. As for the death threat, the investigators treated it as a joke.

In fact, a society that cannot take a stand on behalf of its own dead is inclined to tolerate any group that supports the chauvinism of the state. Yuli Rybakov, a former State Duma deputy who also dealt with the question of fascism, said that when he and others were filing draft amendments on the section on national hatred in the criminal code, they faced constant resistance from both the Kremlin and the prosecutor general's office. As matters stand, the law is very difficult to apply. There is no exact definition of nationalism and national hatred. "As for convictions," Rybakov said, "people can be prosecuted only for inciting someone to kill someone, and it has to be shown that the instigation was made to a specific killer.

"But I'm sure that if someone showed up on the street with a poster saying, 'Kill the president," the prosecutor's office would find legal reasons to detain that person immediately." Vladimir Kovalev, "Prosecutors asked to Probe Ultranationalist Newspaper," *St. Petersburg Times,* July 30, 2004.

5. The Appeal of Communism

1. Alexander Zinoviev, *The Reality of Communism* (London: Victor Gollancz, 1984), 127.

2. Felix Serebrov was a member of the Working Commission on the Abuse of Psychiatry, a dissident group that monitored psychiatric abuse during the Brezhnev era. He was arrested in 1981 and sentenced to four years in a labor camp and five years of exile for anti-Soviet agitation.

3. Zinoviev, *The Reality of Communism,* 99.

4. Michael R. Gordon, "Post-Communist Russia Plumbs Its Soul, in Vain, for New Vision," *New York Times,* March 31, 1998.

5. A. Dugin, "Manifesto of the Eurasist Movement," Eurasia Above All, http://www.arctogaia.com/public/eng/Manifesto.html, January 1, 2001.

6. "Russian-style Democracy: Is It Feasible?" *Argumenty i Fakty,* April 19, 2006.

7. John B. Dunlop, "Aleksandr Dugin's Foundations of Geopolitics," *Demokratizatsiya* 11, no. 4 (2004), 48.

8. Nikita Kaledin, "Podpol'e Vykhodit Naruzhu," *Stringer,* May 1, 2003, republished on Kompomat.ru, http://www.compromat.ru/page13068.htm.

9. A. Dugin, "Basic Principles of the Eurasist Doctrinal Platform," Pan-Russian Social-Political Movement EURASIA, http://eurasia.com.ru/eurasist.vision .html.

10. Another proponent of "Eurasianist" ideas is Alexander Prokhanov, the editor of the nationalist newspaper *Zavtra.* Like Dugin, Prokhanov is known to have close ties to the military and intelligence services. In a book published in 2006, *Symphony of the Fifth Empire,* he calls for the creation of a new Eurasian empire; Alexander Prokhanov, *Simfoniya "Pyatoi Imperii"* (Moscow: Eksmo, 2007). "The first Russian empire," he said at the book launch, October 24, 2006, "was Kievan Rus, the second was the Moscow Kingdom, the third was the St. Petersburg empire of the Romanovs, the fourth was the Soviet empire, and now we are witnessing the emergence of the 'fifth empire.' It is still invisible but its inauguration has taken place." In his book, Prokhanov sees signs of emerging empire in events such as the launching of the new Bulova missile . . . or the construction of the North European Gas Pipeline. Referring to Gazprom, the state-controlled gas monopoly, he writes, "It gathers together Russia by merging companies, connecting pipelines, extending its steel tentacles to the terminals of St. Petersburg and Nakhodka, laying [new pipeline] tracks at the bottom of the Baltic Sea and to China and stitching together the tissue of the former Soviet republics." Cited in Victor Yasmann, "Russia: The Fiction and Fact Of Empire," www.rferl.com, November 3, 2006, http://www.rferl.com/featuresarticle/2006/11/ab624837 -fc03-4fbc-8be2-af624bbe20f2.html.

11. Valery Beresnev, "V Peterburge Taino Gotovyat Podkop pod Smol'ny," *Vash Tainii Sovetnik,* February 6, 2006.

12. Viktor Rezunkov, "V Peterburge Sozdan Gosudarstvennyi Institut Nravstvennosti," Radio Svoboda, March 10, 2006.

13. *Zemlya Russkaya,* Special Edition no. 5, 2005.

14. Beresnev, "V Peterburge Taino Gotovyat Podkop pod Smol'ny."

Russian officials have responded to the desire for a new ideology with the idea of "sovereign democracy." The architect of this idea is Vladislav Surkov, a deputy head of the Kremlin administration. Proponents of the principle use democratic rhetoric to justify authoritarianism. On July 28, 2006, on the eve of the G-8 summit meeting in St. Petersburg, Surkov gave an explanation of sovereign democracy to a group of foreign journalists. He said that because of its past, Russia has to build democracy in its own way, from the top down. "The bottom-up model is an ideal which we should all strive to achieve," he said. "But real life is more complicated."

In a political essay in the journal *Expert,* November 26, 2006, Surkov wrote that sovereign democracy in Russia is a factor in preserving international diversity. Russia has parted forever with hegemonic aspirations, he wrote, "but [Russians] don't give anyone else the possibility to acquire them. They are on the side of a community of sovereign democracies (and the free market) and against any global dictatorship (and monopoly)."

15. Quoted in Mikhail Heller, *Cogs in the Wheel* (New York: Knopf, 1988), 5, 23.

16. Sheela Bhatt, "PM to Join World Leaders to Fete Russia," Rediff India Abroad, May 6, 2005, http://www.rediff.com/news/2005/may/06russia.htm. Accessed November 14, 2010.

17. Tatyana Sinitsyna, "War Ages Like a Man: The Passing Years Alter Its Appearance, Leaving Only the Memory," RIA Novosti, April 27, 2005, http://en.rian.ru/analysis/20050427/39749310.html?id=.

18. Serguei Alex. Oushakine, *The Patriotism of Despair: Nation, War and Loss in Russia* (Ithaca, N.Y.: Cornell University Press, 2009), 193–94.

19. Adam Tanner, "Yeltsin Praises Achievements of Soviet-Era KGB," *Reuters,* December 19, 1997. "Looking back on things I think that the exposés on the crimes of the security organs may have just too far," Yeltsin said in his weekly nationwide radio address. "After all, there are some things to be proud of." Citing the recent seizure by the FSB of $25 million in diamonds and 175 pounds of gold that were being traded illegally, Yeltsin said, "As you can see, the economic safety of the country under contemporary conditions is becoming one of the most important tasks of our Chekists."

20. Ibid.

21. Pavel Kanygin, "Dostuchat'sya do Nebes," *Novaya Gazeta,* March 3–9, 2005, 10.

22. C. G. Jung, *The Undiscovered Self,* trans. R. F. C. Hull (New York: New American Library, 1958), 72.

23. Roy Medvedev, *Post-Soviet Russia: A Journey through the Yeltsin Era* (New York: Columbia University Press, 2000), 181.

24. For a discussion of the demographic consequences of the Russian "reforms," see David Satter, *Darkness at Dawn: The Rise of the Russian Criminal State* (New Haven: Yale University Press, 2003), 253–56.

25. The Moscow apartment bombings, including evidence that they were carried out by the FSB, are also discussed in *Darkness at Dawn.*

6. The Responsibility of the State

1. On July 28, Yezhov sent Stalin a list of 138 of the Soviet Union's leading political, diplomatic, political, and cultural figures, asking for permission to execute them. Stalin and Molotov signed, "Shoot all 138." The executions took place on July 27–29 and August 1, 1938.

2. Semen Budenny commanded the First Cavalry Army during the Civil War and was one of the first marshals of the USSR. Kliment Voroshilov was the head of the commissariat of defense in the 1920s and 1930s, and from 1926 to 1960 a member of the politburo. He authorized the arrest of the leading officers of the Red Army during the Great Terror. Lazar Kaganovich, a close associate of Stalin's from the early 1920s, was the party leader in Ukraine and in Moscow. One of the Soviet Union's top economic managers, his approach was characterized by absolute ruthlessness. He played a key role in both collectivization and the Great Terror.

3. William Taubman, *Khrushchev: The Man and His Era* (New York: Norton, 2003), 241.

4. Stephen Cohen, "Vozvrashcheniye iz za cherti zakona," *Novaya Gazeta,* November 24, 2008.

5. Taubman, *Khrushchev,* 246.

6. The Leningrad case took place in 1949–50. About three thousand senior party leaders in Leningrad were arrested and many were shot, including Alexei Kuznetsov, who had played a key role in the wartime defense of besieged Leningrad, and Nikolai Vosznesensky, the chairman of Gosplan, the state planning agency, and a member of the politburo. The affair arose out of an intraparty intrigue organized by Beria and Malenkov to compromise Andrei Zhdanov, the former head of the Leningrad party organization, and eliminate Voznesensky, Kuznetsov, and others.

Georgi Malenkov was head of the top personnel section of the party Central Committee during the Great Terror. He became a member of the politburo after the Second World War and was briefly the Soviet premier after Stalin's death. He was widely assumed to be Stalin's likely successor but was outmaneuvered by Khrushchev.

7. Nanci Adler, *Beyond the Soviet System: The Gulag Survivor* (New Brunswick, N.J.: Transaction, 2002), 23.

8. Cohen, "Vozvrashcheniye."

9. Taubman, *Khrushchev*, 278, 279.

10. Ibid., 279

11. Robert Service, *A History of Twentieth-Century Russia* (Cambridge: Harvard University Press, 1997), 338.

12. Vyacheslav Molotov was the Soviet prime minister from 1930 to 1941 and foreign minister from 1939 to 1949. He was cosigner of the Molotov-Ribbentrop Pact, which divided eastern Europe between Germany and the Soviet Union, and he actively participated in the Great Terror, signing many execution lists and singling out individuals for execution.

13. Aleksandr Yakovlev, *Sumerki* (Moscow: Izdatel'stvo Materik, 2003), 254.

14. Service, *A History of Twentieth-Century Russia*, 341.

15. Andrei Artizov et al., *Reabilitatsiya: Kak Eto Bylo*, ed. Aleksandr Yakovlev, vol. 1 (Moscow: Mezhdunarodnyi Fond Demokratiya, 2003), 6.

16. E. Nosov, "Kostriuma ne Aiova," in *Nikitia Sergeevich Khrushchev: Materialy k biografii* (Moscow: Izdatel'stvo politicheskoi literatury, 1989), 98, cited in Adler, *Beyond the Soviet System*, 172.

17. *Kino: Politika i Liudi* (Moscow: Materik, 1995), 179, cited in Adler, *Beyond the Soviet System*, 200.

18. Vasily Grossman, *Forever Flowing*, trans. Thomas P. Whitney (New York: Harper and Row, 1986), 8–9. In many cases, there was no home to which a prisoner could return. In general, divorce in the Soviet Union cost five hundred rubles, but divorce from a prisoner only cost three rubles. The wives and children of "enemies of the people" were frequently arrested and sometimes shot. One way for a wife to protect herself was to denounce her husband. Arrested husbands sometimes encouraged their wives to file for divorce to protect themselves and their children. In many cases, however, prisoners received letters like the one delivered to the campmate of a memoir writer. It read: "Dear husband, I heard that you miss me. Don't miss me and don't write to me anymore, because I have been living with another man for a year and a daughter was born to us one month ago. I only learned about life after you were in prison . . . I learned about what rights women are given in the USSR, and you concealed these rights from me, and never read me *Vechernyaya Moskva*, [you acted like] a class enemy." Gleb Iosifovich Anfilov, "Materialy k biografii: vyderzhki iz pisem, dnevnikov I drugie dokumenti," Memorial, f. 2, op. 1, d. 4, 1.0001 2909 0327, cited in Adler, *Beyond the Soviet System*, 64.

19. Artizov et al., *Reabilitatsiya*, 1: 6.

20. Quoted in Anne Applebaum, *Gulag: A History* (New York: Doubleday, 2003), 514.

21. Adler, *Beyond the Soviet System*, 122.

22. Arseny Roginsky, "Bez Ukazaniya Prichin Smerti," *Karta*, no. 2 (1993).

23. Artizov et al., *Reabilitatsiya*, 1: 9.

24. Andrei Artizov et al., *Reabilitatsiya: Kak Eto Bylo,* ed. Aleksandr Yakovlev, vol. 2 (Moscow: Mezhdunarodnyi Fond Demokratiya, 2003), 8.

25. Nikolai Bukharin was the chief theoretician in the party after Lenin's death. He was a member of the politburo from 1924 to 1929 and opposed Stalin's policies for the radical collectivization of agriculture. He was shot in 1938 after being convicted in a show trial on false charges of treason and the commission of terrorist acts. Karl Radek was a close associate of Lenin's and a leading party journalist. He became a secretary of the Comintern and helped to write the 1936 Soviet Constitution. He was arrested and charged with treason in 1937 and sentenced to ten years at hard labor. He was murdered in prison on orders of the NKVD. Leonid Serebryakov was a close associate of Lenin's and a member of the Central Committee secretariat during Lenin's lifetime. He was later made head of the chief directorate of roadways and was arrested in 1936 and confessed under torture to preparing terrorist acts against Stalin and Beria. He was executed on January 30, 1937. After Serebryakov's arrest, his dacha in Nikolina Gora was acquired by the Soviet prosecutor Andrei Vyshinsky, who had long coveted it. It was Vyshinsky who demanded the death penalty in Serebryakov's case. Grigory Zinoviev was a member of the Bolshevik leadership that carried out the October Revolution. He was the head of the Petrograd party organization. After Lenin's death, he sided with Stalin and then against him in the intraparty power struggle, only to be outmaneuvered and arrested. In August 1936 he was tried on charges of trying to kill Stalin and other leaders of the Soviet government. He was found guilty and executed on August 25, 1936. Lev Kamenev was also a member of the original Bolshevik leadership. He was an ally of Zinoviev's in the intraparty struggle for power, and with him was convicted on fabricated charges of plotting to kill the Soviet leadership and executed on August 25, 1936.

26. Adler, *Beyond the Soviet System,* 176.

27. Ibid., 39, 34

28. Ibid., 113, 155.

29. *Moskovskiye Novosti,* March 31, 1996, cited ibid., 48.

30. V. Rogovin, *Partiia Rasstreliannikh* (Moscow, 1997), 457, cited in Adler, *The Gulag Survivor,* 48.

31. Adler, *The Gulag Survivor,* 181–82, 179.

32. Ibid., 223.

33. Quoted ibid., 209.

34. Ibid., 29.

35. Ibid., 142, 220.

36. Taubman, *Khrushchev,* 514.

37. Andrei Artizov et al., *Reabilitatsiya: Kak Eto Bylo,* ed. Aleksandr Yakovlev, vol. 3 (Moscow: Mezhdunarodnyi Fond Demokratiya, 2004), 6.

38. Alexei Rykov, a member of Lenin's politburo, was Soviet premier from 1924 to 1930. He supported Stalin against Trotsky as a member of the moderate wing of

the leadership, but he lost power after Stalin adopted more radical policies. In 1937 he was arrested and charged with plotting with Trotsky against Stalin. He was tried in 1938, found guilty of treason, and executed.

39. On May 31, 1962, the Soviet government introduced sharp price increases on food products for urban residents, leading to unrest and calls for strikes in many cities, including Moscow, Kiev, Leningrad, Donetsk, and Chelyabinsk. In Novocherkassk, a city in the North Caucasus, there was already a crisis mood because of poor working conditions and work-norm increases that had caused takehome pay to fall by as much as 30 percent. On June 1 a strike broke out at the giant Budenny Electric Locomotive Factory. The strike spread, and on June 2, thousands of demonstrators gathered in the central square, where they were fired on by Soviet Army units. Twenty-three persons were killed, most of them between the ages of eighteen and twenty-five.

40. Verkhovnyi Sovet Rossiiskoi Federatsii, *Sbornik Zakonodatel'nykh i Norma-tivnykh Aktov o Repressiyakh i Reabilitatsii Zhertv Politicheskikh Repressii* (Moscow: Izdatel'stvo Respublika, 1993), 194–206.

Under Khrushchev, when the process of rehabilitation was getting started, almost all the secretaries of the regional party committees condemned by Stalin were rehabilitated, although they themselves had helped to carry out the repression, signing extrajudicial sentences and participating in the troikas. Pavel Sudoplatov, who organized assassinations for the Stalinist regime, spent years after his 1968 release struggling for rehabilitation. He defended his terrorist acts as "military operations carried out against evil opponents of the Soviet government." He received rehabilitation in 1991.

Opponents of the Stalinist regime fared less well. Lt. Gen. Andrei Vlasov, the Soviet commander who defected to the Germans in World War II and organized an army of Soviet prisoners of war to free Russia from Communism and was convicted of treason and hanged in 1946, was refused rehabilitation, as were eleven of his subordinates. Valery Sablin, who led a revolt aboard the Soviet destroyer *Storozhevoy* in 1975 and was executed, also has not been rehabilitated.

According to the logic of the law on rehabilitation, the Stalin-era executioners, who were tried and convicted not for their real crimes but on trumped-up charges, should have been eligible for rehabilitation. But here the Russian courts were inconsistent. In 1998 the Russian Supreme Court declared that a reevaluation of the cases of Yagoda, Yezhov, Beria, and Abakumov would take place. It was determined, however, that the law on rehabilitation could not be applied to the men because of their crimes. Anatoly Ukolov, a Supreme Court justice, said, in an interview with the radio station Ekho Moskvy, that Beria could not be rehabilitated because he was "a bloody figure on whose conscience lies thousands of murdered people, and there can be no forgiveness for him"; David McHugh, "Russia Won't Overturn 1953 Case," AP Online, May 29, 2000, http://www.highbeam.com/library/doc3.asp?DOCID=1P1:30885264&num=142&ctr1Info=.

In Germany, the victims of Nazi terror were not rehabilitated because the system itself was pronounced criminal. In Russia, this did not happen, which is the reason for the paradoxes of the rehabilitation process.

41. Adler, *Beyond the Soviet System*, 33.

42. Speech of G. F. Vesnovsky, head of the Department of Rehabilitation of the General Prosecutor of the Russian Federation, *Informatsionnii Bulletin Pravleniya obshchestvo "Memorial,"* no. 24, http://www.memo.ru/about/bull/b26/4.htm. Accessed April 1, 2006.

43. The rehabilitated had been enemies according to the media of the time and many had lived lives of shame, constantly aware of a disgrace that they had to conceal. Their survivors now received confirmation that their relatives were not enemies. They sometimes needed to be persuaded that their relatives had done nothing wrong. The new law gave relatives the right for the first time to see the KGB files of their repressed family members. Many people, out of fear, had destroyed photographs of their arrested relatives, so children often did not know what their parents looked like. In some cases, the photograph of a parent in a prison uniform in a KGB file was the only photograph his or her children were destined to see.

Children sometimes did not even know of a parent's existence. Olga Cosorez, a legal consultant to victims of repression, cited the case of a woman who believed she was the daughter of a single mother and learned of the existence of her father only after sixty years. One day, her mother's brother visited her and, after looking at her son, said "how he resembles your father." She asked, "What father?" This forced him to speak. He said her father was a German who had been arrested. After his arrest, her mother had changed her last name and had never spoken of him again, at least to her daughter. The woman went to the local registration office (ZAGS) and found her mother's original married name. This made it possible to obtain her father's KGB file. She learned that he had been arrested and then exiled and had spent his final years in a remote settlement, where he taught German. She went to the settlement. The residents spoke affectionately of her father and showed her his grave. Olga Cosorez, interview with the author, March 18, 2005.

44. Elizaveta Zhirikova and Tatyana Nikoltseva, interviews with the author, March 18, 2005.

45. Some physical ailments were common among Compassion clients. "They all had sick hands and legs," said Zhirikova. "This was labor where there were no provisions for safety. If a prisoner removed mica from coal every day without gloves, he or she was already traumatized. They had arthritis, problems with joints, eyes problems, and tuberculosis. They breathed in dust. They could be cured, but the effects were still felt. They had sores that didn't heal. They had skin problems. They were all diabetics. Those who suffered beatings had impaired hearing. Men had prostate problems."

At the same time, the former prisoners lost family ties. A mother who returned from the camps was often alone. Her husband had been shot, the children had been put in special orphanages where their last names were changed, and now were grown. It was no longer a family. They were people who grew up in different worlds and hoped that someday they would see each other again.

Even where former prisoners returned to their children, it was difficult to re-establish relations. "The former prisoners often were forced to suppress emotions," said Zhirikova, "to react to horrible things without expressing anything. As a result, they were not able to love their own children, or there was a kind of hysterical love. They demanded from their children shows of feeling that were unrealistic.

"Many former prisoners created a labor camp at home. No one was allowed to move or speak. They were cruel to their children and intolerant. It was hard to expect good relations after growing up like that."

7. The Trial of the Communist Party

1. F. Rudinsky, *Delo KPSS v Konstitutsionnom Sude: Zapiski Uchastnika Protsessa* (Moscow: Bylina, 1999), 26–28.

2. Carla Thorson, "The Fate of the Communist Party in Russia," *RFE/RL Research Report* 37 (1992): 3, 29.

3. The Nuremberg trials attempted to deal by judicial means with the "violations of the conventions of civilization" by the Nazis. The charges were preparing for war, waging aggressive wars, violating the traditional rules of warfare through the conduct of a war of annihilation and, most important, "crimes against humanity," a new category that applied to extermination of civilian populations on racial or religious grounds. "The fourth charge," wrote Konrad H. Jarausch, "made clear the Allies attempt to respond not only to Germany's culpability for the outbreak of war and the brutality of its conduct but also to the previously unimaginable quality of the crimes against non-combatants. By avenging these violations through a legal process, the Nuremberg trials sought to reaffirm the principle of human rights for the future." Jarausch, *After Hitler: Recivilizing Germans, 1945–95* (New York: Oxford University Press, 2006), 7.

4. Orlando Figes, *The Whisperers: Private Life in Stalin's Russia* (New York: Metropolitan, 2007), 251.

5. Quoted by Sergei Grigoriants, interview with the author, February 18, 2003.

6. Sergei Grigoriants, "Generaly i Stukachi Pomenyalis' Mestami," *Moskovskiye Novosti,* November 26, 2002.

7. Vadim Bakatin, "Seichas Ne Vremya Beredit' Rany," *Nezavisimaya Gazeta,* August 29, 1991.

8. James Meek, "Russian Patriarch Was KGB Spy," *Guardian,* February 12, 1999; John I. Dunlop, "KGB Subversion of Russian Orthodox Church," *Social Issues* 1, no. 12 (1992): 51–53.

9. Sergei Kovalyev, interview with the author, March 19, 2004.

10. In the end, all of these difficulties could have been dealt with. It would have

been necessary to provide persons exposed as informers with opportunities to explain their connections with the KGB, to clarify them and to apologize. It would also have been important to explain the extent to which many other persons cooperated with the KGB without leaving a documentary trace. But none of these expedients was considered because there was a general feeling that revealing the names of informers would be traumatic for post-Soviet society.

11. Timothy J. Colton, *Yeltsin: A Life* (New York: Basic, 2008), 249.

12. "FSB: Svedeniya o Neglasnykh Sotrudnikakh Spetssluzhb Ne Budut Rassekrecheny Nikogda," Grani.ru, July 8, 2007, http://www.grani.ru/Society/History/p.124449.html. Accessed September 7, 2007

13. Interview with Archepiscop Khristosom, *Moskovsky Komsomolets,* November 30, 1993.

14. Arsenii Roginsky, interview with the author, November 19 and 21, 2004.

15. Thorson, "The Fate of the Communist Party in Russia," 3.

16. "Gospoda! Kogda Zhe Vy Govorili Pravdu? Vchera ili Segodnya?" *Pravda,* July 4, 1992.

17. Rudinsky, *Delo KPSS v Konstitutsionnom Sude,* 30.

18. "Transcript of the Trial," *Pravda,* July 14, 1992, 4.

19. Ibid., 6.

20. "Transcript of the Trial," *Pravda,* July 18, 1992, 3.

21. Ibid., 6.

22. Quoted by Olga Sveridova, interview with the author, July 1, 2009.

23. Russia (Federation), *Konstitutsionnyi Sud, Materialy Dela o Proverke Konstitutsionnosti Ukazov Presidenta RF, kasayuschikhsya deyatel'nosti KPSS I KP RSFSR, a takzhe o proverke konstitutionnosti KPSS I KP RSFSR,* 6 vols. (Moscow: Izdatel'stvo Spartak, 1996–1998), 1: 248, 3: 263.

24. Thorson, "The Fate of the Communist Party in Russia," 4.

25. Ibid.

26. Roy Medvedev, "The Party Is Not Yet Over," *Independent,* July 22, 1992.

27. Rudinsky, *Delo KPSS v Konstitutsionnom Sude,* 138.

28. In addition to seeking a judgment against the Communist Party, the Yeltsin forces had more prosaic motives for wanting a major political trial. The personal antagonism between Yeltsin and Gorbachev that had been demonstrated during their struggle for power was far from over, and many in the Yeltsin camp saw the trial as a way to discredit Gorbachev and put an end to his political ambitions. The idea of putting the Communist Party on trial had been raised in the reformist Soviet media as early as 1988. Some members of the pro-Yeltsin opposition argued that Gorbachev, Eduard Shevarnadze, the former Soviet foreign minister, and Yakovlev should also be tried for the regime's crimes and, by the end of 1991, this was official policy.

On June 5 a press conference was held by the Russian government to mark the forthcoming release of documents from the archives. Some of the documents concerned the Bolshevik seizure of power, the 1921–22 famine, the purge of the

Red Army, the war in Afghanistan, and Soviet support for terrorist activities. There were also, however, documents from Gorbachev's time in power. They included plans for sending KGB agents abroad disguised as correspondents and documents on Soviet support for terrorist groups and the financing of foreign Communist Parties. The earlier documents were discussed in general terms, but the Gorbachev-era documents were discussed in detail. In an interview with the Italian daily *l'Unità,* Mikhail Poltaranin, the minister of information, said the idea was to "bury Gorbachev with one blow" and release information about him that would make the world "tremble with indignation."

As it happened, Yeltsin was vulnerable to the same treatment. In 1980, while he was the first secretary in the Sverdlovsk oblast, at least seven persons were arrested in the region on political grounds. As the regional party leader, Yeltsin had to sanction those arrests. Yeltsin also ordered the destruction in 1977 of the Ipatev mansion, where the last tsar and his family were murdered, after it became a place of pilgrimage. On June 10, 1992, *Komsomolskaya Pravda* reported that Yeltsin had been involved in the coverup of a leak in 1980 at a biological weapons plant in Sverdlovsk that claimed many lives.

29. Russia (Federation), *Konstitutsionnyi Sud, Materialy Dela o Proverke Konstitutsionnosti Ukazov Presidenta RF,* 4: 26; "Transcript of the Trial," *Pravda,* October 17, 1992, 4.

30. Russia (Federation), *Konstitutsionnyi Sud, Materialy Dela o Proverke Konstitutsionnosti Ukazov Presidenta RF,* 5: 308.

31. Y. Golik et al., "Agenti Vliyaniya. Kto and chto skrivaetskya za etimi tainstvennimi slovami," *Sovetskaya Rossiya,* November 21, 1992.

32. Olga Sveridova, interview with the author, December 2, 2008.

33. Ruling of the Constitutional Court on CPSU and CP RSFSR Activities, November 30, 1992, http://www.az-design.ru/Projects/AZLibrCD/Law/Constn/CCrt9296/2r004.shtml. Accessed December 22, 2008.

34. Aleksandr Frolov, "'Nurnberg' Provalilsya," *Sovetskaya Rossiya,* December 3, 1992.

8. Moral Choice under Totalitarianism

1. Alexander Yakovlev, *A Century of Violence in Soviet Russia* (Harrisonburg, Va.: Donnelley, 2002), 224.

2. William Taubman, *Khrushchev: The Man and His Era* (New York: Norton, 2003), 323, 116.

3. Boris Sokolov, "Georgy Zhukov: Narodny marshal ili marshal liudoed?" Grani.ru, February 23, 2001, http://old.grani.ru/symbols/articles/zhukov/priont .html. Accessed July 23, 2005.

4. Ibid.

5. Yakovlev, *A Century of Violence in Soviet Russia,* 225.

6. Taubman, *Khrushchev,* 323.

7. Yakovlev, *A Century of Violence in Soviet Russia,* 224–25. The quotations are from the minutes of the 1957 party plenum.

8. Lt. Col. Danil Kopelyanski, who was still alive well into the 2000s, interrogated Wallenberg. Dmitri Tokarev, the former head of the Kalinin oblast NKVD, organized the executions of the Polish officers from the Ostashkov camp, and Petr Soprunenko, who was in charge of prisoner of war matters for the NKVD, compiled the lists of Polish officers for execution. Georgiy Morozov, the former director of the Serbsky Institute for Social and Forensic Psychiatry, where many political dissenters were incarcerated and tortured, was still practicing psychiatry in 2002. On September 9, 1989, Soviet special forces attacked demonstrators in Tblisi who were demanding the restoration of Georgian independence. Nineteen protestors were killed. On January 13, 1991, Soviet troops attacked peaceful demonstrators outside the television tower in Vilnius. Thirteen persons were killed. In the case of each attack, the commander in chief of the Soviet armed forces was Mikhail Gorbachev.

9. Vladimir Bukovsky, interview with the author, October 10, 2005.

10. Nikita Khrushchev, *Khrushchev Remembers* (Boston: Little, Brown, 1970), 307.

11. "Gruppa Deyatelei Politiki i Kul'tury Predlagayet Uvekovechit' Pamyat' Rukovoditelya Blokadnogo Leningrada Kuznetsova," *Interfax,* February 20, 2005.

12. Oksana Khimich, "Preyemnik Stalina," *Moskovsky Komsomolets,* March 14, 2005.

13. Taubman, *Khrushchev,* 221.

14. Quoted by Vladimir Shnitke, interview with the author, May 20, 2005.

15. Sergo Mikoyan, interviews with the author, September 25–26, 2005.

16. Boris Pustyntsev and Vladimir Shnitke, "Izbiratel'naya Pamyat'," *Novoe Vremya,* 11 (2005): 30–31.

17. F. B. Komal, "Leningrad. Konets 30-kh Godov," *Leningradskaya Panorama,* 1 (1990).

18. Quoted in Nikita Lomagin, *Neizvestnaya Blokada* (St. Petersburg: Izdatel'skii Dom Neva, 2004), 148.

19. Oksana Khimich, "Preemnik Stalina," *Moskovsky Komsomolets,* March 14, 2005.

20. Vladimir Mikoyan, interview with the author, October 1, 2005.

21. Roy Medvedev, *All Stalin's Men: Six Who Carried Out the Bloody Policies* (New York: Anchor/Doubleday, 1984), 38, 37.

22. Inessa Yazhborovskaya, Anatoly Yablokov, and Valentina Parsadanova, *Katynskii Sindrom v Sovetsko-Pol'skikh i Rossiisko-Pol'skikh Otnosheniyakh* (Moscow: Izdatel'stvo Rossiiskaya Politicheskaya Entsiklopedia, 2009), 160–61.

23. Aleksandr Fursenko and Timothy Naftali, *Khrushchev's Cold War: The Inside Story of an American Adversary* (New York: Norton, 2006), 478–80.

24. Stepan Mikoyan, interview with the author, July 10, 2005.

25. Anastas Mikoyan, *Tak Bylo* (Moscow: Vagrius, 1999), 582–83.

26. Ibid., 583.

27. Robert Conquest, *The Great Terror: A Reassessment* (New York: Oxford University Press, 1990), 246.

28. Mikoyan, *Tak Bylo,* 553.

29. Ibid., 568.

30. Ibid.

31. Stepan Mikoyan interview.

32. Mikoyan, *Tak Bylo,* 589.

33. Sergo Mikoyan interview.

34. Mikoyan, *Tak Bylo,* 591.

35. Ibid.

36. Ibid., 557.

37. Sergo Mikoyan interview.

38. Leon Aron, *Yeltsin: A Revolutionary Life* (New York: St. Martin's, 2000), 683.

39. Ibid., 112, 113.

40. Interview with Vladimir Pribylovsky, *Svobodnaya Pressa,* December 31, 2009, http://svpressa.ru/politic/article/19191/. Accessed October 9, 2010.

41. Aron, *Yeltsin,* 113.

42. Boris Yeltsin, *Against the Grain,* trans. Michael Glenny (New York: Summit, 1990), 82.

43. Interview with Vladimir Pribylovsky, *Svobodnaya Pressa,* December 31, 2009.

44. Yeltsin, *Against the Grain,* 82.

45. Ilya Milshteyn, "Alexander Osvoboditel," October 19, 2005, http://www.grani.ru/Society/m.96859.html. Accessed October 19, 2005.

46. Alexander Yakovlev, interview with the author, February 11, 2003.

47. "Secret 2nd Sector 04057, Central Committee of the Communist Party," "Istoriya Inakomisliya," *Karta,* no. 4 (1994), 38.

48. Aleksandr Yakovlev, *Sumerki* (Moscow: Izdatel'stvo Materik, 2003), 300.

49. Ibid., 303.

50. Yuri Lepsky, "Alexander Yakovlev: 'No Need to Look for Ideology. All It Means Is Freedom,'" *Trud,* April 11, 1997.

51. Tom Carver, "General in Exile," *Assignment,* BBC 2, November 16, 1996.

52. Alexandra Samarina, "Pravo na Pamyat," interview with Alexander Yakovlev, *Obshchaya Gazeta,* October 18, 2001.

53. Alexander Podrabinek, "Ideolog Kommunisma Opyat' pri Dele: A. N. Yakovlev Vernulsya k Lyubimoi Rabote," *Ekspress-Khronika,* December 24, 1994.

54. Yakovlev, *A Century of Violence in Soviet Russia,* 8.

55. Alexander Yakovlev, interview with the author, June 23, 2003.

56. Medvedev, *All Stalin's Men,* 136, 137.

57. Ibid., 138.

58. Ibid., 139.

59. Ibid., 161, 162.

60. Ibid., 162.

61. Ibid., 163.

62. Ibid.

63. Ibid., 107, 108.

64. Ivan Stadnyuk, "Ispoved' Stalinista," *Pravda,* November 26, 1992.

65. Medvedev, *All Stalin's Men,* 112.

66. Ibid., 110.

67. Related to the author by Viktor Erofeev, 1981.

68. Natalia Narochnitskaya, *Za Chto i s Kem My Voyevali* (Moscow: Izdatel'stvo Minuvsheye, 2005), 74.

69. Vladimir Tikhomirov, "'Palyenaya' Pravda," *Ogonek,* May 25, 2009.

70. Alexander Podrabinek, "Kak Antisovetchik Antisovetchikam . . . ," *Ezhednevny Zhurnal,* September 21, 2009, http://ej.ru/?a=note_print&id=9467. Accessed September 30, 2009.

71. Alexander Podrabinek, "Situatsiya, Vozmozhno, Khuzhe, chem Eto Kazhetsya na Pervyi Vzglyad . . .," *Ezhednevny Zhurnal,* September 29, 2009, http://ej.ru/?a=note_print&id=9494. Accessed September 30, 2009.

72. Valery Beresnev, "V Peterburge taino gotovyat podkop pod Smolny," *Vash Tainii Sovetnik,* February 6, 2006.

73. Quoted in Orlando Figes, *The Whisperers: Private Life in Stalin's Russia* (New York: Metropolitan, 2007), 270, 266–67.

9. The Roots of the Communist Idea

1. Christian Neef and Matthias Schepp, interview with Alexander Solzhenitsyn, *Der Spiegel,* July 23, 2007, http://www.spiegel.de/international/world/0,1518,druck-496211,00.html. Accessed March 8, 2008.

2. Roy Medvedev, "Andrei Sakharov and Alexander Solzhenitsyn," *Social Sciences* 2 (2002): 11, 14.

3. Ibid., 6.

4. Alexander Solzhenitsyn, "A World Split Apart," text of address, Harvard Class Day, June 8, 1978, http://www.columbia.edu/cu/augustine/arch/solzhenitsyn/harvard1978.

5. "Deklaratsiya o pravakh I dostoinstve cheloveka X Vsemirnogo Russkogo Narodnogo Sobora," official site, Moskovskogo Patriarkhata, Russkaya Pravoslavnaya Tserkov, http://www.mospat.ru/center.php?page=30728&newwin=1&prn=1. Accessed September 7, 2006.

6. Vitaly Tretiakov, "Alexander Solzhenitsyn: Sberezheniye Naroda—Vysshaya izo Vsekh Nashikh Gosudarstvennykh Zadach," *Moskovskiye Novosti,* May 2, 2006, http://www.mn.ru/print.php?2006-15-43.

7. Alexander Solzhenitsyn, *Kak Nam Obustroit' Rossiyu?* (Paris: YMCA Press, 1990), 9.

8. Ibid., 5.

9. Neef and Schepp, interview with Solzhenitsyn.

10. A. I. Solzhenitsyn, *Dvesti Let Vmeste (1795–1995): Issledovaniya Noveishei Russkoi Istorii,* 2 vols. (Moscow: Russkii Put', 2001), 1: 6.

11. Alexander Solzhenitsyn, *Dvesti Let Vmeste,* 2 vols.(Moscow: Russky Put', 2002), 2: 79, 89.

12. Ibid., 2: 132, *Dvesti Let Vmeste,* 129, *Dvesti Let Vmeste,* 130.

13. Cathy Young, "Traditional Prejudices: The Anti-Semitism of Alexander Solzhenitsyn," *Reason,* May 2004, http://reason.com/archives/2004/05/01/traditional-prejudices. Accessed October 28, 2010.

14. Solzhenitsyn, *Dvesti Let Vmeste,* 287.

15. Neef and Schepp, interview with Solzhenitsyn.

16. Igor Shafarevich, *Russkii Vopros* (Moscow: Algoritm-Kniga and Izdatel'stvo Eksmo, 2009), 287.

17. Ibid., 288, 290.

18. Ibid., 290.

19. Ibid., 98.

20. Ibid., 66, 85.

21. Tibor Szamuely, *The Russian Tradition* (London: Secker and Warburg, 1974), 65.

22. Quoted ibid., 69.

23. Ibid.

24. Ibid., 67.

25. Quoted in Richard Pipes, *Russian Conservatism and Its Critics: A Study in Political Culture* (New Haven: Yale University Press, 2005), 97.

26. Ibid.

27. Ibid.

28. Quoted in Ronald Hingley, *The Russian Mind* (London: Bodley Head, 1977), 131.

29. Pipes, *Russian Conservatism and Its Critics,* 107.

30. Nikolai Gogol, *Selected Passages from Correspondence with Friends,* trans. Jesse Zeldin (Nashville: Vanderbilt University Press, 1969), 58.

31. Ibid., 59.

32. Nikolai Gogol, *Vybrannya mesta iz perepiska s druziami* (St. Petersburg: Department Vneshnei Torgovli, 1847), 74.

33. Gogol, *Correspondence with Friends,* 259.

34. Fyodor Dostoevsky, *Dnevnik Pisatelya* (Moscow: Astrel', 2004), 207.

35. Ibid., 207, 208.

36. Ibid., 358.

37. Ibid., 359.

38. Ibid., 357.

39. Ibid., 360.

40. Petr Chaadaev, *Izbranniye. Sochineniya i Pis'ma* (Moscow: Pravda, 1991), 28.

41. Ibid., 30.

42. Ibid., 32.

43. A. Yermichev and A. Zlatopolskaya, "P. Y. Chaadaev v russkoi mysli. Opit istoriografii," introduction to Petr Chaadaev, *Pro et Contra* (St. Petersburg: Izdatel'stvo Russkogo Khristianskogo Gumanitarnogo Instituta, 1998), 13.

44. V. Proskurin, "O Zhizni i Mysli P.Y. Chaadaev," introduction to Chaadaev, *Izbranniye*, 11.

45. M. O. Gershnzon, "P. Y. Chaadaev. Zhizn' I myshleniye," in Chaadaev, *Pro et Contra*, 260.

46. Proskurin, "O Zhizni I Mysli P.Y. Chaadaev," 10-11.

47. Gershnzon, "P. Y. Chaadaev. Zhizn' I myshleniye," 260.

48. Ibid., 260-61.

49. Ibid., 262.

50. Chaadaev, *Izbranniye*, 146.

51. Ibid., 153.

52. M. O. Gershenzon, *Chaadaev* (Moscow: NIMP, 2000), 157.

53. Chaadaev, *Izbranniye*, 153.

54. Gershenzon, *Chaadaev*, 160.

55. Ibid., 155.

56. Nikolai Berdyaev, *The Russian Revolution* (Ann Arbor: University of Michigan Press, 1966), 37.

57. Nikolai Berdyaev, "The Third Way," *Novy Zhurnal* 33 (1952): 274, Hoover Institution Archives.

58. Berdyaev, *Russian Revolution*, 56.

59. Nikolai Berdyaev, *Vyderzhki iz Pisem N. A Berdyaeva k Gospozhe X. (1930–1939)*, B. I. Nikolaevsky Collection (1954), 35: 182, Hoover Institution Archives.

60. Nikolai Berdyaev, "Pravda i Lozh' Kommunizma," *Zarubezh'e*, December 1970, 2, Hoover Institution Archives.

61. "Russians in France, Religion, and Soviet Government" *Manchester Guardian*, December 27, 1944, Hoover Institution Archives.

62. Berdyaev, "The Third Way," 279.

63. Nikolai Berdyaev, "Nuzhno Perezhit' Sud'bu Russkogo Naroda," *Russkiye Novosti*, February 8, 1946, Hoover Institution Archives.

64. Berdyaev, "The Third Way" 276, 277.

65. Nikolai Berdyaev, "O Dvusmyslennosti Svobody," *Russkiye Novosti*, May 23, 1947, Hoover Institution Archives.

66. Berdyaev, "The Third Way" 277, 278.

67. Chaadaev, *Izbrannye*, 170.

10. Symbols of the Past

1. Andrei Zolotov, "Russian Orthodox Church Approves as Putin Decides to Sing to a Soviet Tune," *Christianity Today*, January 1, 2000, http://www.christianity today.com/ct/2000/decemberweb-only/57.0.html. Accessed December 26, 2007.

2. Vladimir Isachnikov, "Parliament Votes to Restore Soviet Anthem," *Moscow Times,* December 8, 2000, http://www.themoscowtimes.com/stories/2000/12/08/162.html. Accessed December 26, 2007.

3. Valeria Korchagina, "Duma Set to Revive the Soviet Anthem," *Moscow Times,* December 6, 2000, http://www.themoscowtimes.com/stories/2000/12/06/013.html. Accessed December 26, 2007.

4. Yevgenia Albats, "Putin Marches to the Beat of the Soviet Anthem," *Moscow Times,* December 7, 2000, http://www.themoscowtimes.com/stories/2000/12/07/00.7-full.html. Accessed December 26, 2007.

5. In 1998 the Communists, who held a majority in the State Duma, proposed a bill to reinstate the Soviet anthem and the Soviet red flag. The motion failed, winning 242 votes, well shy of the 300 required for passage. In response, opponents proposed bringing back the imperial national anthem, "God Save the Tsar." This effort also failed.

6. Maura Reynolds, "National Anthem Is a Time to Hum," *Moscow Times,* September 26, 2000, http://www.themoscowtimes.com/stories/2000/09/26/200.html. Accessed December 26, 2007.

7. Ron Popeski and Tara Fitzgerald, "Parliament Restores Soviet Anthem," *Moscow Times,* December 9, 2000, http://www.themoscowtimes.com/stories/2000/12/09/001.html. Accessed December 26, 2007.

8. Korchagina, "Duma Set to Revive the Soviet Anthem."

9. The decision to restore the Soviet hymn also mandated that it be broadcast on state television at 6 A.M. and midnight every day, inspiring great irritation on the part of persons who suffered under the Soviet regime.

The Orthodox Church supported the restoration of the Soviet anthem. Archpriest Vsevolod Chaplin said, "It is very important that all the symbols of the country are viewed in combination: a prerevolutionary flag and coat of arms, which show the continuity with the prerevolutionary period . . . and, at the same time, Alexandrov's music, which shows continuity with the Soviet era, in which, of course, there were terrible tragedies but there were also a lot of good things. Thus the continuity of all Russian history is restored and demonstrated." This attitude was not shared by everyone. Sergei Kovalyev, a former political prisoner, risked arrest by remaining seated when the anthem was played to mark the inaugural session of the Duma.

10. Nikolai Patrushev, "Taina Andropova," *Rossiyskaya Gazeta,* June 15, 2004.

11. Fedor Burlatsky, "Potaennyi Andropov," *Izvestiya,* June 15, 2004.

12. Petrushev, "Taina Andropova."

13. Burlatsky, "Potaennyi Andropov."

14. Quoted in Igor Minutko, "Putin and Andropov," *Eurasian Politican,* August 2001, http://www.cc.jyu.fi/~aphamala/pe/issue4/putandrop.htm. Accessed December 26, 2007.

15. Ibid. Ironically, there were rumors in Karelia that with regard to the World

War II partisans in the region, Andropov himself had something to hide. Irina Gulyaeva, who taught Russian literature in a high school in Petrozavodsk, said, "There were rumors based on people who had seen the archives that the partisans were organized incompetently and that many of the brigades that were supposed to fight the Finns died of starvation in the forest. It was Andropov who was supposed to organize supplies to them."

16. Ibid.

17. Quoted ibid.

18. Quoted ibid.

19. Maksim Fajtel'berg, *Eliseevskij. Kaznit'. Nel'zya pomilovat'*, documentary film, 2004, shown on RTR television, March 10, 2007.

20. Ilya Zemtsov, *Andropov* (Jerusalem: IRICS, 1983), 176.

21. At the ceremony in Petrozavodsk marking Andropov's ninetieth birthday, Katanandov said, "We pay tribute not only to a countryman but to an outstanding leader who is admired by all the people of our country. We remember his time as a time . . . of positive changes in our society."

The ceremony had almost come to an end when a group of fifteen young people appeared near the monument carrying homemade wreaths with the inscriptions, "From the victims of the NKVD-KGB-FSB," "From the grateful Hungarians — 1956," "From the victims of the war in Afghanistan." The path of the demonstrators was immediately blocked by persons in plainclothes. The demonstrators were told that placing their wreaths would be an act of vandalism. After the ceremony was over, the demonstrators again tried to reach the monument. But they were detained and taken to the local police station, where they were held until the participants in the ceremony had dispersed.

22. Sergei Tataurshchikov, interview with the author, January 17, 2005.

23. *Gorod Orel,* April 7, 2005.

24. "Karaul! Ugroza Vsemirnoj Demokratii!" *Gorod Orel,* April 28, 2005. Shortly after the vote, two reporters for the newspaper *Orlovsky Meridian,* Maria Snitkova and Christina Yurkova, decided to test public opinion on the issue of Stalin. They stood in front of the mayoralty, where Maria held a placard in favor of the monument to Stalin and Christina held one opposing it. They then collected signatures. This provoked a lot of interest as passersby stopped and argued before signing one or the other of the petitions.

One passerby, Vladimir Vershinin, said, "There is a monument to Peter the First. He was a monster but he raised up Russia. Stalin was also a monster, but he ruined Russia. It seems that only monsters can have an effect on Russia. They have enormous strength of will. But we can't create monuments to all of them. And besides, we didn't owe the victory in the war to Stalin. Even without him, the people would have risen up in their own defense, so I'm against."

Sophia Yarigina had just walked out of a casino and seemed to be in a hurry. "Where do I sign so that this monster won't be in the city?" she asked.

"But why are you against the monument to Stalin?" asked one of the reporters.

"It's none of your business," she said. "It would be better to put up a monument to a devil with a tail."

A young man who had been watching silently for ten minutes said, "Sign me up. I'm for it."

When the reporters reminded him about the repressions, he said, "So what? My grandmother and grandfather suffered, but it's better that the money of the taxpayers went for monuments than somewhere else," a hint that otherwise it would be stolen.

The next persons who wanted to express an opinion were two young girls and a young man.

"No, we don't need Stalin," one of the girls said. "My parents said bad things about him, and now in school we're studying the consequences of his repressions."

After this, an old man with a cane who was carrying a cloth bag in his hands offered his opinion.

"The great victory was the achievement of the heroic Russian people. We should put up a monument to the people."

"But if there were a war today no one would go to defend the country," said a passerby.

"What do you mean no one would go. I would go," the old man said, hitting his cane on the asphalt. "And you would go; after all, we're Russians."

The old man said his name was Nikolai Salkov. "You know I'm almost eighty. I was a witness to these events, and nothing can shake my respect for Stalin. Give that to me. I'll sign."

A tall, dark-haired man emerged from the building. "You aren't by any chance a deputy?" the reporters asked.

"No," said Georgy Sarkisian, "I'm a deputy's assistant. I'm against a monument, of course. This was a tyrant."

"I took part in military actions. I saw a lot," said Yuri Sokolov. "And if Russians had as much respect and fear today as they did under Stalin, a lot of things would be different."

The lunch break ended and various members of the city council returned to the mayoralty and signed the petition in favor of the monument.

"How do you do," one of them said. "I'm Nikolai Lazarev, the deputy who suggested putting up the bust. Let's not be petty. Let's put up the monument. . . . Stalin—this is a person before whom even Churchill stood up. And as far as repression is concerned," he said, lowering his voice, "I had the opportunity in my time to talk to many persons who were repressed, and they said that they were punished for real crimes and they obediently accepted their punishment."

After three hours, the test of public opinion was broken up on the grounds that it was an unsanctioned picket. By that time, there were more signatures against than for, but this was only on the strength of young people.

25. Dmitri Krayukhin, interview with the author, May 15, 2005. From August 5

to December 27, 1937, during the initial months of the Great Terror, 17,015 persons were arrested and condemned in the territory of the oblast. Y. N. Balakina, compiler, *Kniga Pamyati Zhertv Politicheskikh Repressii na Orlovshchine*, vol. 1 (Orel, 1994), 5, http://orel.rsl.ru/nettext/memorial/orlov1.htm. Accessed March 7, 2007.

26. Vasily Grossman, *A Writer at War: A Soviet Journalist with the Red Army, 1941–45* (New York: Vintage, 2005), 48.

27. Balakin, *Kniga Pamyati Zhertv Politicheskikh Repressiy na Orlovshchine.*

28. Ibid.

29. Dmitri Krayukhin, interview with the author, May 15, 2005.

30. In early July, Krayukhin received a photocopy of an article in *Izvestiya* about the murder of Nikolai Girenko in St. Petersburg in June. The section of the article about Girenko's planned participation in a trial against RNE activists from Novgorod was highlighted. In September a photograph and contact details for Krayukhin appeared on the website Slavic Union, with the caption "Know your enemy." The website alluded to the court decision that denied Krayukhin witness protection and encouraged readers to contact him.

31. A municipal agency plants red tulips at the monument to the victims of repressions and at the statue of Dzerzhinski in front of FSB headquarters in Orel. Earlier the city ignored the monument and it was overgrown. In 2004, however, Krayukhin mounted a press campaign calling attention to the neglect of the monument, and that fall, the city began to plant tulips at the monument regularly.

32. G. Skiruta, "Ryadovye Velikoy Vojny," *Dal'nij Vostok*, no. 5 (1978): 118.

33. "Opolchentsy Traktornogo," *Molodoj Kommunist*, no. 2 (1973): 18, 16.

34. Catherine Merridale, *Ivan's War: Life and Death in the Red Army, 1939–1945* (New York: Picador, 2006), 157.

35. Antony Beevor, *Stalingrad: The Fateful Siege, 1942–1943.* (New York: Penguin, 1999), 172.

36. Ibid., 106, 177.

37. Vasili I. Chuikov, *The Beginning of the Road* (London: Macginbon and Kee, 1963), 283.

38. "Gryzlov pokhvalil Stalina za neuryadnost'," Lenta.ru, December 21, 2004, http://lenta.ru/russia/2004/12/21/stalin/. Accessed December 23, 2007.

39. Pavel Kostin, "Stalin v natural'nuyu velichinu," *Russkiy Kur'er,* July 24, 2006, http://ruscourier.ru/archive/1593. Accessed January 18, 2008.

40. Irina Ilicheva, "Na Mamaevskom kurgane otkrylsya chastnyj muzej, posvya shennyj Staliny," May 15, 2006, http://www.rian.ru/culture/20060515/481491 20.html. Accessed January 18, 2008.

41. Yelena Silantieva, interview with the author, July 7, 2005.

42. Istoriko-Memorial'nyj Kompleks "Geroyam Stalingradskoj Bitvy" na Mamaevom Kurgane, http://mamayevhill.volgadmin.ru. Accessed January 28, 2008.

43. Galina Kotelnik, "Stalingrad v Ogne. *Mysli po povodu,"* *Donetskij kryazh,* February 18, 2005, http://media.ukr-info.net/smi/view_article.cgi?sid=3&nid=14 94&ai. Accessed January 20, 2008.

11. History

1. Nail Gafutulin, "Pamyat' ne merknet," *Krasnaya Zvezda,* November 8, 2007.

2. Vladimir Putin, phone-in, February 9, 2000, text printed in *Komsomolskaya Pravda,* February 11, 2000.

3. Claire Bigg, "Russia: Romanov Burial May Be Part of Kremlin Image Campaign," Radio Free Europe/Radio Liberty, September 27, 2006, http://www.rferl.org/articleprintview/1071663.html. Accessed February 2, 2007. "Tsarist Spy Catcher Could Be New Symbol for FSB," *St. Petersburg Times,* October 26, 2004.

4. Viktor Cherkesov, "Nevedomstvennye razmyshleniia o proffessii," *Komsomolskaya Pravda,* December 28, 2004.

5. Mike Eckel, "In Remarks, Putin Laments Soviet Fall," *The Boston Globe,* April 26, 2005.

6. I. I. Dolutsky, *Otechestvennaya Istoriya XX vek. V dvukh chastiakh* (Moscow: Mnemozina, 2001).

7. V. Kuznetsov, interview with I. Dolutsky, "Istorya dolzhna byt' strastnoi," *Novoe Vremya,* December 21, 2003.

8. A. V. Filippov, *Noveishaya Istoriya Rossii 1945–2006* (Moscow: Prosveshcheniye, 2007), 6, 93, 88–90, 85–86.

9. Ibid., 333–34.

10. Ibid., 357, 363, 451, 435. The Yukos case involved the arrest in October 2003 on charges of fraud and tax avoidance of Mikhail Khodorkovsky, the president of the Yukos Oil Company and, at the time, Russia's wealthiest man. Khodorkovsky was sentenced to eight years' imprisonment although his business practices had been no different from those of Russian oligarchs who continued to enjoy the favor of the Putin regime. Unlike other oligarchs, however, Khodorkovsky had demonstrated political independence and given financial support to opposition parties. In January 2011 Khodorkovsky was again tried and convicted. He was accused of stealing 200 million tons of oil from Yukos subsidiaries, more than the total annual output of many oil-producing countries. The charges were widely seen as absurd.

11. Peter Finn, "New Manuals Push a Putin's-Eye View in Russian Schools," *Washington Post,* July 20, 2007.

12. Denis MacShane, "Russian Revisionism Is Our Best Guide to Putin's Priorities," *Independent,* September 1, 2009.

13. One such film, which enjoyed wide popularity, was *1612,* about the Polish occupation of Moscow. Another film that was clearly intended to convey lessons for Russia was *The Collapse of an Empire,* by Father Tikhon, the prior of the Sretenska Monastery, who is Putin's spiritual guide. The filmmaker sought to show that the penetration of alien Western values had led to Byzantium's collapse.

14. Mikhail Moshkin, "A Brief Introduction to Vladimir Putin," *Vremya Novostei,* June 22, 2007.

15. Andrei Kolesnikov, "Don't Wait for Favors from History: Russian President Instructs Social Sciences Teachers," *Kommersant,* June 22, 2007.

16. Ibid.

17. Filippov, *Noveishaya Istoriya Rossii,* 423.

18. "Tekst kontseptsii kursa istorii Rossii 1900–1945," *Vremya Novostei,* August 25, 2008.

19. Ibid.

20. Ibid.

21. Sergei Lebedev, "Noveishaia istoriia vtoroi svezhesti," August 30, 2008, http://ps.1september.ru/articlef.php?ID=200801601. Accessed November 10, 2010.

22. Anatoly Bershtein, "Ratsionalnoe upravlenie ubiistvami," *Vremya Novostei,* August 25, 2008.

23. Aleksandr Tsipko, "Neostalinizm i krasnyi patriotism," *Vremya Novostei,* October 27, 2008.

24. Yuri Afanas'ev, "Uchebnaya trevoga," Grani.ru, June 22, 2007, http://grani.ru/Society/History/m.123805.html. Accessed November 10, 2010.

25. Victor Yasmann, "Russia Again Demonstrates Its Past Is Unpredictable," Radio Free Europe/Radio Liberty, October 2, 2008, http://www.rferl.org/content/Russia_Again_Demonstrates_Its_Past_Is_Unpredictable/1293374.html. Alexander Nevsky was the prince of Novgorod and grand prince of Vladimir in the thirteenth century. He achieved an epic victory against the invading Teutonic knights in the "Battle on the Ice." Pyotr Stolypin was the Russian prime minister from 1906 until his assassination in 1911. His efforts to break up the peasant communes and create a class of free landowners was intended to protect Russia from social revolution.

26. Fund of Public Opinion and RTR, Imya Rossiya, www.nameofrussia.ru. Accessed November 10, 2010.

27. Peter Baker, "Russia Rebukes Bush on Remark," *Washington Post,* May 6, 2005, http://www.democraticunderground.com/discuss/duboard.php?az=view_all&address=102x1449334. Accessed November 10, 2010.

28. Valentinas Mite, "Estonia: Russia Opposes Law on Soviet War Memorials," Radio Free Europe/Radio Liberty, January 17, 2007, http://www.rferl.org/content/article/1074094.html.

29. "The Last Soviet in Tallinn: Saga of the 'Bronze Soldier,'" Tallinn-Life.com, date unknown, http://www.tallinn-life.com/tallinn/estonian-russian-relations. Accessed October 19, 2008.

30. Mark Landler, "Digital Fears Emerge after Data Siege in Estonia," *New York Times,* May 29, 2007, http://www.nytimes.com/2007/05/29/technology/29estonia.html. Accessed October 19, 2008.

31. Larry Greenemeier, "Estonian Attacks Concern Over Cyber 'Nuclear Winter,'" InformationWeek, May 24, 2007, http://www.informationweek.com/news/199701774. Accessed October 19, 2008.

32. Ibid.

33. "Estonia Urges Firm EU, NATO Response to New Form of Warfare: Cyber-attacks," *Sydney Morning Herald,* May 16, 2007, http://www.smh.com.au/

news/Technology/Estonia-urges-firm-EU-NATO-response-to-new-form-of-war farecyberattacks/2007/05/16/1178995207414.html. Accessed May 16, 2007.

34. Kairi Leivo, interview with the author, November 28, 2008.

35. "Vozvrashchenie Bronzovogo soldata," Molodezhnoe antifashistskoe dvizhenie NASHI, June 22, 2007, http://www.nashi.su/news/193020. Accessed January 5, 2009.

36. "Konstantin Goloskokov nachal bessrochnuyu golodovku u posol'stva Estonii," Molodezhnoe antifashistskoe dvizhenie NASHI, June 22, 2007, http://www.nashi.su/news/20960. Accessed January 5, 2009.

37. A. Golov, "Druzhestvennye i nedruzhestvennye srtany dlya rossiyan," Levada Center, May 30, 2007, http://www.levada.ru/press/2007053003.html. Accessed November 10, 2010.

38. "Wrap: Kremlin Irked by EU, US Stance on War Memorial Flap with Estonia," May 3, 2007, RIA Novosti, May 3, 2007, http://en.rian.ru/russia/2007 0503/64854682.html. Accessed November 10, 2010.

39. Yaroslav Bilinsky, "Basic Factors of the Foreign Policy of Ukraine: The Impact of the Soviet Experience," in The Legacy of History in Russia and the New States of Eurasia, ed. S. Frederick Starr (New York: M. E. Sharpe, 1994), 179.

40. Viktor Kondrashin, Golod 1932–33 godov: Tragediya rossiskoi derevni. (Moscow: Rossiiskaya politicheskaya entsiklopediya, 2008), 14.

41. Cited ibid., 15.

42. Quoted in Vladimir Vasilenko, "Samoe glavnoe seichas Ukraina," Zerkalo Nedelu, Ukraina, October 19, 2008, translated from Ukrainian and republished by inoSMI.ru, "Golodomor 1932–33 godov v Ukraine: Pravovaya otsenka," October 19, 2008, http://www.inosmi.ru/translation/244745.html.

43. Vladimir Vasilenko, "Golodomor 1932–33 godov v Ukraine: Pravovaya otsenka," inoSMI.ru, October 19, 2008, http://inosmi.ru/translation/244745 .html. Accessed June 20, 2009.

44. Kondrashin, Golod 1932–33 godov, 18, 19.

45. "Gorbachev nazval prichini Golodomora," Korrespondent.net, June 4, 2008, http://korrespondent.net/russia/482915/print. Accessed November 11, 2008.

46. Steve Gutterman, "Russia: 1930s Famine Was Not Genocide," USA Today, February 4, 2008, http://www.usatoday.com/news/world/2008-04-02-8570729 62_x.htm. Accessed November 10, 2010.

47. Jonas Bernstein, "Former Duma Deputy Calls Liberal Promises a Cover for Growing Authoritarianism," Eurasia Daily Monitor, April 14, 2008.

48. "President's Address on the Occasion of Observation of the 75th Anniversary of Holodomor, 1932–1933 in Ukraine," Press Office of President Viktor Yushchenko, November 22, 2008, http://www.ukemonde.com/holodomor/yush chenko_address_2008.html.

49. Interview, Ekho Moskvy, November 11, 2008, http://www.echo.msk.ru /programs/razvorot/553883-echo. Accessed November 10, 2010.

50. Claire Bigg, "Ukraine Marks 75th Anniversary of Great Famine," Radio Free

Europe/Radio Liberty, November 12, 2008, http://www.rferl.org/content/Ukraine_Marks_75th_Anniversary_Of_Great_Famine/1351733.html. Accessed November 10, 2010.

51. Alexander Solzhenitsyn, "Possorit rodniye narodi?" *Izvestiya,* April 2, 2008, http://www.izvestia.ru/opinions/article3114723/. Russian writers with links to the Kremlin went beyond denying the existence of genocide to charging that attention to the Golodomor was really an attempt to justify Nazism. This argument was presented by Yuri Shevtsov, a historian from Belarus, in *New Ideology: Golodomor.* The version of a terror famine, according to Shevtsov, appears to justify those Ukrainians who allied themselves with the Nazis. Since contemporary Europe, he writes, is the product of the joint efforts of Communists and anti-Communists to lay the foundations for a new way of life on an anti-Nazi basis, inspiring doubt in the worth of the Allied victory destabilizes Europe spiritually and culturally, undermining the basis of present-day European civilization. Yuri Shevtsov, *Novaya Ideologiya: Golodomor* (Moscow: Izdatil'stvo "Evropa," 2009).

52. European Parliament resolution of April 2, 2009, on European conscience and totalitarianism, http://www.europarl.europa.eu/sides/getDoc.do?pubRef=-//EP//TEXT+TA+P6-TA-2009-0213+0+DOC+XML+V0//EN.

53. "Gitler = Stalin: OBSE priravniala stalinizm k natsizmu," Kasparov.ru, July 3, 2009, http://www.kasparov.ru/material.php?id=4A4E42EA357CC. Accessed August 13, 2009.

54. Katya Fisher Yoffe, "Stalinism and Nazism: A Perfect Equation?" Russia, the World Affairs Blog Network, July 23, 2009, http://russia.foreignpolicyblogs.com/2009/07/23/Stalinism-and-nazis.

55. "Gitler = Stalin: OBSE priravniala stalinizm k natsizmu," Kasparov.ru. As the Putin-era interpretation of Russian history has become established in Russia, legal steps have been taken to assure its viability. On May 19, 2009, President Dmitri Medvedev issued a decree on the creation of a commission "to counteract the falsification of history." The commission includes professional historians but also representatives of the foreign ministry, the FSB, and the foreign intelligence service. At the same time, a proposed law, "Against the Rehabilitation of Nazism," makes it a crime to criticize Soviet tactics and behavior during the Second World War. Calls for such a law came after the airing of an *NTV* documentary about the Battles of Rzhev, a series of Soviet offensives in 1942 and early 1943 that showed that the Soviet death toll was nearly a million, compared with the half-million for the German side, and that the Germans had been shocked at the way Soviet troops were thrown into battle with little regard for their lives.

56. Anatol Lieven, *Chechnya: Tombstone of Russian Power* (New Haven: Yale University Press, 1998), 46.

57. Anatol Lieven, "Be Ready for Yeltsin's Demise," *The Times,* December 29, 2004.

58. L. N. Tolstoy, "Nikolai Pankin," *Sobranniye Sochienii,* 22 vols. (Moscow: Khudozhestvennaya Literatura, 1984), vol. 17.

12. The Shadow of Katyn

1. There are other sources of disquiet. There is no plaque on the former building of the NKVD in Smolensk on Dzerzhinsky Street. Many of the Polish officers buried at Katyn were murdered in a room in the basement. The yellow, four-story building across the street from the city park and the old Kremlin wall now belongs to the oblast ministry of internal affairs.

Uniformed police stand in the entryway, smoking. The doors are flanked with small Christmas trees. When the subject of a plaque for the building was raised by Memorial, the police said, "We did not kill anyone. We weren't even born. Why should this affect us?"

The Polish officers sent from the Kozelsk prisoner of war camp were unloaded at the small suburban station of Gnezdovo, outside of Smolensk, from which they were taken to be executed. But there is no plaque at Gnezdovo either. When Alexander Beresnev, a journalist for the newspaper *Smolenskiye Novosti*, was a boy, a drunken old woman began shouting in a crowded bus that years earlier prisoners had been brought to the station and the local people had prepared food for them, but by morning they had disappeared.

Nikolai, a railroad worker, was carrying solution to remove the ice on the wagons of incoming trains when I ran into him. He said he had heard somewhere that Polish officers had been unloaded at the station, but he couldn't recall when. "There were some conversations, but now people don't talk about it," he said. On the subject of a plaque at the station to commemorate the murdered officers, he said, "I don't know if there should be one. Whatever the bosses say, that's how it will be."

Yulia, a woman in her twenties who worked as a dispatcher at the station, said the fact that thousands of Polish prisoners were unloaded at the station and taken to be shot was news to her. "I never heard that," she said. "There is so much work keeping track of cargoes that we don't have time for anything else. I had no idea that that happened at this station." On the subject of a memorial plaque, she said, "It would be better to have a plaque. People died. You can't be indifferent to this. I think it makes sense to offer an apology."

Svetlana, a middle-aged woman who worked in a furniture factory nearby, stopped to talk after crossing the tracks. "I never heard that prisoners were brought here," she said. Should there be a plaque? She hesitated. "I think so — so that people know."

2. Anna M. Cienciala, Natalia S. Lebedeva, and Wojciech Materski, eds., *Katyn: A Crime without Punishment* (New Haven: Yale University Press, 2007), 112–13.

3. Ibid., 31.

4. Allen Paul, *Katyn: Stalin's Massacre and the Seeds of Polish Resurrection* (Annapolis: Naval Institute Press, 1996), 70.

5. Ibid., 77.

6. Cienciala, Lebedeva, and Materski, *Katyn*, 179.

7. Ibid., 118.

8. Ibid.

9. Paul, *Katyn,* 108.

10. Ibid., 109–10.

11. Ibid.

12. Ibid.

13. Cienciala, Lebedeva, and Materski, *Katyn,* 124–25.

14. Ibid., 126–27.

15. Paul, *Katyn,* 127–29.

16. Cienciala, Lebedeva, and Materski, *Katyn,* 289–90.

17. Paul, *Katyn,* 204.

18. Cienciala, Lebedeva, and Materski, *Katyn,* 227.

19. Quoted ibid., 230.

20. Ibid., 240–41.

21. A. N. Yakovlev, "K chitateliu," in *Katyn: Plenniki neob'iavlennoi voiny,* ed. N. S. Lebedeva, V. Materski, and N. A. Petrosova (Moscow: Mezhdunarodnyi Fond Demokratiya, 1999), 5.

22. Vladimir Abarinov, *The Murderers of Katyn* (New York: Hippocrene, 1993), 11.

23. Vladimir Abarinov, interview with the author, October 26, 2009.

24. Cienciala, Lebedeva, and Materski, *Katyn,* 338.

25. Yakovlev, "K chitateliu," 6.

26. Cienciala, Lebedeva, and Materski, *Katyn,* 253.

27. Quoted ibid., 255.

28. Inessa Yazhborovskaya, Anatoly Yablokov, and Valentina Parsadanova, *Katynsky Sindrom V Sovetsko-Polskikh i Rossiisko-Polskikh otnosheniakh* (Moscow: Rossiiskaya politicheskaya entsiklopedia, 2009), 371.

29. Ibid., 371.

30. Ibid., 372.

31. Ibid., 374.

32. Ibid.

33. Jerzy Moravsky, "Kto zhe stanet rasstrelivat' dnem?!" *Novoye Russkoye Slovo,* May 26, 1995.

34. Ibid.

35. Ibid.

36. Yazhborovskaya, Yablokov, and Parsadanova, *Katynsky Sindrom V Sovetsko-Polskikh i Rossiisko-Polskikh otnosheniakh,* 410.

37. Ibid., 412.

38. Quoted in Cienciala, Lebedeva, and Materski, *Katyn,* 254.

39. Institut Pamieci Narodowej, http://www.ipn.gov.pl/portal/pl/764/1261 3/1990_2005_r.html. Accessed May 3, 2011.

40. Yazhborovskaya, Yablokov, and Parsadanova, *Katynsky Sindrom V Sovetsko-Polskikh i Rossiisko-Polskikh otnosheniakh,* 456.

41. Jane Perlez, "Yeltsin 'Understands' Polish Bid for a Role in NATO," *New York Times,* August 26, 1993.

42. Quoted in Yazhborovskaya, Yablokov, and Parsadanova, *Katynsky Sindrom V Sovetsko-Polskikh i Rossiisko-Polskikh otnosheniakh,* 459.

43. Benjamin B. Fischer, "The Katyn Controversy: Stalin's Killing Field," CIA .gov, https://www.cia.gov/library/center-for-the-study-of-intelligence/csi-publi cations/csi-studies/studies/winter99-00/art6.html. Accessed November 13, 2009.

44. Vyacheslav Bragin, interview with the author, June 28, 2005.

45. The Trial of German Major War Criminals, Nizkor Project, July 1, 1946, 350, http://www.nizkor.org/hweb/imt/tgmwc/tgmwc-17/tgmwc-17-168-07.shtml.

46. Fischer, "The Katyn Controversy."

47. Inessa Yazhborovskaya, Anatoly Yablokov, Valentina Parsadanova, *Katynsky Sindrom V Sovetsko-Polskikh i Rossiisko-Polskikh otnosheniakh, Moskva, Rossiiskaya politicheskaya entsiklopedia,* 436

48. Tomasz Nalecz, "Prestupleniya ne bylo," *Wprost,* October 20, 2005, re-published in inoSMI.ru, http://www.inosmi.ru/print/223117.html. Accessed April 11, 2005.

49. Speech by the Deputy Prime Minister of the Russian Federation, Viktor Khristenko, at the Opening of the Katyn Memorial Complex, July 28, 2000, Katyn, in Cienciala, Lebedeva, and Materski, *Katyn,* 352.

50. "Senate Pays Tribute to Katyn Victims," Embassy of the Republic of Poland in Rome, Italy, http://www.ambasciatapolonia.it/Files/A/Daily%20News/News 2005.04.htm. Accessed May 3, 2011.

51. Anna M. Cienca, "Sledztwa katynskie," Przegląd Polski on-line, http://www .dziennik.com/www/dziennik/kult/archiwum/01-06-05/pp-04-15-02.html.

52. "Zayavlenie Mezhdunarodnogo Obshchestvo 'Memorial' o Rassledovanii 'Katynskogo Prestupleniya' v Rossii," *30 Oktyabrya,* no. 52 (2005), 4.

53. Lilya Turchenkova, interview with the author, December 24, 2009.

54. Press release, Tsentr obshchestvennikh svyazi, UFSB RF po Smolenskoi Oblast, April 20, 1995.

55. Alexander Bereznev, "Vesti s Nashei Golgofi," *Smolenskiye Novosti,* July 23, 2002.

56. Anatoly Volosenkov, interview with the author, May 18, 2005.

57. Gennady Zhavoronkov, "Secret of Katyn Forest," *Moskovskiye Novosti,* no. 32 (August 6, 1989).

58. Cienciala, Lebedeva, and Materski, *Katyn,* 110.

59. Ibid., 118–20

60. Ibid., 277.

61. Ibid., 208.

13. Vorkuta

1. Mikhail Baitalsky, *Notebooks for the Grandchildren: Recollections of a Trotskyist Who Survived the Stalin Terror,* trans. Marilyn Vogt-Downey (Atlantic Highlands, N.J.: Humanities, 1995), 239–40.

2. R. Mitin, "I Odin v Pole Voin," *Zapolyar'e,* October 5, 1999. A book about Vorkuta published in 1972 described the building of the railroad in these words: "Builders began to compete for the fulfillment of the shift quota by 200 per cent. There appeared the slogan, 'Two kilometers of finished track per day.' . . . There was an exceptionally huge role for communists and komsomols of the project. 'Work for two! Work for yourself and for your comrade who has left for the front!' This call of the paty was seized by the workers of the most northern construction project"; N. Ushik and V. Griner, *Vorkuta* (Syktyvkar: Komi Knizhnoe Izdatel'stvo, 1972), 14–16.

3. Quoted by Evgeniya Khaidarova, interview with the author, June 28, 2004.

4. Joseph Scholmer, *Vorkuta* (New York: Henry Holt, 1955), 63.

5. Anne Applebaum, *Gulag: A History* (New York: Doubleday, 2003), 82.

6. Andrew Osborn, "How Siberia's Dark History Could Be Its Financial Saviour," *Independent,* June 10, 2005. Osborn reports that 200,000 died, and that more than 2million were deported.

7. Baitalsky, *Notebooks for the Grandchildren,* 224.

8. Tamara Roman'kova, "Naideno mesto Kashkentskih rasstrelov," *Zapolyar'e,* September 16, 2005.

9. Mikhail Baitalsky, *Tetradi dlya Vnukov,* Russian version of *Notebooks for the Grandchildren,* 220, manuscript, Hoover Institution Archives.

10. Baitalsky, *Notebooks for the Grandchildren,* 225.

11. Roman'kova, "Naideno mesto Kashketinskikh rasstrelov."

12. N. Morozov, "Istrebitel'no-trudovye gody," in *Pokayaniye: Komi respublikanskii martirolog zhertv massovikh politicheskikh repressii* (Syktyvkar: Komi respublikanskii obshechestvennii fond, 2001), 89, 94.

13. Baitalsky, *Notebooks for the Grandchildren,* 349.

14. Morozov, "Istrebitel'no-trudovye gody," 88.

15. Baitalsky, *Tetradi dlya Vnukov,* 234.

16. Scholmer, *Vorkuta,* 66.

17. Morozov, "Istrebitel'no-trudovye gody," 95.

18. T. Roman'kova "Krovavyi Avgust 53-go," *Zapolyar'e,* September 2, 1995.

19. Ibid.

20. R. Mitin, "Na Starom Nemetskom . . .," *Zapolyar'e,* August 6, 1993.

21. Roman'kova, "Naideno mesto Kashketinskikh rasstrelov."

22. Rima Yakovenko, interview with the author, June 29, 2004.

23. Igor Shpector, "Ya mechtaiu postroit' Gulag," *Tribuna,* March 11, 2005.

14. The Odyssey of Andrei Poleshchuk

1. Pete Earley, *Confessions of a Spy: The Real Story of Aldrich Ames* (New York: Putnam, 1997), 192.

2. Ibid.

3. Vladimir Nadein, "Eti Liudi Rasstreliany KGB: O nikh znayut v Amerike, no ne znayut v Rossii," *Izvestiya,* June 15, 1995.

4. Boris Piliatskin and Gennadiy Charodeyev, "Ames prigovoril k rasstrelu 14 sovetskih agentov," *Izvestiya,* April 11, 1998.

5. Ibid.

6. Ibid.

7. Ibid.

8. Andrei Poleshchuk, "Prosvetlenie na Lubianke," *Nezavisimoye Voyennoye Oboz-renie,* March 19, 1999.

9. "Putevoditel' po 'Lubianke, 2,'" *Nezavisimaya Gazeta,* April 23, 1999.

10. Ibid.

11. Earley, *Confessions of a Spy,* 12.

12. Ibid., 345.

13. Ibid., 347.

Conclusion

1. Patrick Cockburn, "Putin Set to Win Despite Suspicions about Bombs," *Independent,* March 25, 2000. In 2002 a poll of Russians by the Public Opinion Studies Center (VTSIOM) showed that 42 percent of those surveyed believed that participation of the FSB in the bombings of the apartment buildings could not be ruled out. Thirty-eight percent of those polled firmly denied the possibility of FSB involvement, and 19 percent were undecided. Yuri Zarakhovich, "A French Documentary Alleges Kremlin Involvement in Russia's 1999 Apartment Bomb-ings," *Time,* April 19, 2002. Zarakhovich wrote that allegations of FSB involve-ment "have been the talk of the country ever since the tragedy."

2. "Likhoimstvo militsii v 'Domodedovo' bylo 'postavleno na potok', obnaru-zhil SKR," NEWS.ru.com, January 26, 2011, http://newsru.com/russia/26jan 2011/liho.html.

3. "Moskvichi propadayut s kontsami," gazeta.ru, October 9, 2008, http://www.gazeta.ru/social/2008/10/07/2850900.shtml.

4. In the immediate aftermath of the terrorist act, estimates for the number of dead ranged from 125 to 130, with 129 the figure that was cited most frequently. Nord Ost, an organization of victims of the terrorist act, released a statement on October 23, 2005, the third anniversary of the attack, declaring that on the basis of materials from the investigation of the incident made available to the members of the organization, the death toll was at least 174. "It is not clear," the statement said, "who erred in arithmetic and why for three years 45 deaths were hidden." "Spravka: Zayavlenie regionalnoi obshchestvennoi organizazatsiya 'Nord-Ost,'" Grani.ru, October 23, 2005, http://www.grani.ru/Events/Terror/m.97107.html.

The nature of the rescue effort suggested that saving the lives of the hostages was a low priority. Doctors arriving at the scene were not told that the hostages had been gassed and were not provided with an antidote which would have had to be injected immediately. The order to ambulances to proceed to the theater came forty-five minutes after the beginning of the operation, with the result that many hostages were taken to hospitals in buses, microbuses, and cars. In one case, thirty hostages were put in a twelve-seat military microbus, some on the floor. A thirteen-year-old girl was crushed under other bodies and died en route. It was estimated that one hundred persons who died from gas poisoning or other causes could have been saved if the rescue effort had been properly organized. David Satter, "Death in Moscow: The Chechnya Problem," *National Review Online,* October 29, 2002, http://old.nationalreview. Com/comment/comment-satter102 902.asp. Also see Galina Mursalieva, interview with Alexander Shabalov, director, Moskovsky Sluzhbi Spasenie, *Novaya Gazeta,* November 4, 2002, and Yelena Vrantseva, "Sortirovali po printsipu zhivoi—ne zhivoi," gazeta.ru, October 29, 2002, http://www.gazeta.ru/2002/10/29/sortirovalip.shtml.

5. John B. Dunlop, *The 2002 Dubrovak and 2004 Beslan Hostage Crises: A Critique of Russian Counter Terrorism,* Soviet and Post-Soviet Politics and Society 26 (Stuttgart: Ibidem-Verlag, 2006), 145–46. On October 27, the day after the theater in Dubrovka was "liberated," Putin invited the commandos from the Alfa and Vympel units that had conducted the operation to a reception at the Kremlin. In his remarks, Putin praised the units for professionalism and joined them in a silent, standing toast. In January, Putin signed a secret decree to confer six Hero of Russia awards to persons who participated in the operation, including three FSB officers, two soldiers from Alfa and Vympel, and the chemist who flooded the hall with gas.

The Russian special forces appear to have executed all of the terrorists, including many who were unconscious as a result of the gas. Nonetheless, there are questions about the number killed in the raid. In June 2003 the Moscow city prosecutor Mikhail Avdyukov said that forty terrorists had been killed and none had escaped. At 9:44 A.M. on October 26, 2002, almost three hours after the building was secured, however, *Interfax* reported that thirty-two terrorists had been killed and an unspecified number arrested. On October 28 gazeta.ru reported that fifty terrorists—thirty-two men and eighteen women—had been killed and three others taken into custody. There is also doubt as to whether "Abubakar"—Ruslan Abu-Khasanovich Elmurzaev, the leader of the terrorists—was killed. In June 2003 Avdyukov insisted that his body had been found and identified, but attempts to confirm this independently were unsuccessful. In October 2003 the film director Sergei Govorukhin, who was one of the volunteer negotiators during the crisis and spoke at length with Abubakar, said that despite his persistent requests, Russian prosecutors had been unable to show him Abubakar's body, and he was told by Russian intelligence officers in Chechnya that Abubakar was alive. Dunlop, *The 2002 Dubrovka and 2004 Beslan Hostage Crises,* 148–50.

Under any circumstances, the fact of the mass execution of incapacitated terrorists who could have been a priceless source of information led to speculation that the authorities had killed the terrorists in order to silence them. Boris Sokolov, in an article November 4, 2002, on the website Grani.ru, wrote, "It's possible to assume that those attacking the hall had orders to finish off all the unconscious terrorists in order to prevent any kind of public trial. After all, in a court of law, it would have been necessary to discuss the mistakes of the security services but also the motives that guided the terrorists in their inhuman action. Dead terrorists are very easy to connect, if there is a wish to, either with [Aslan] Maskhadov [the former Chechen president] or Al Qaeda or with any of the Chechens living in Moscow." Boris Sokolov, "Pochemu ne Vzorvalsya 'Nord-Ost,'" Grani.ru, November 4, 2002, http://www.grani.ru/Events/Terror/m.13642.html. Accessed September 22, 2007.

6. In the aftermath of the tragedy, questions began to be raised about the high death toll among the hostages. Russian officials denied that hostages had died from gas poisoning. On September 30, 2003, in answer to questions from journalists, Putin sought to put the blame for the deaths exclusively on the terrorists. He said that the hostages did not die from the gas because "this gas was harmless and could not have done any damage to people. The victims died as a result of a set of circumstances — immobility, chronic diseases, and the fact that they had to remain in this building." The conclusion of medical experts from the Center for Catastrophic Medicine, however, was very different. Their report said, "The high concentration of a chemical substance . . . led to an immediate fatal outcome." Svetlana Gubareva, Karina Moskalenko, and Olga Mikhailova, "'Nord-Ost,' Gaz ne spasal ot vzriva," *Novaya Gazeta,* March 21, 2005, http://www.novgaz.ru/data/2005/20/01.html.

When the victims filed suit against the Moscow city government, in an attempt to learn the full truth about the theater siege, they suffered harassment at the hands of the authorities.

7. Svetlana Gubareva, "Vystuplenie no press konferentsii k tretei godovshchine, 'Nord Osta,'" "Tragediya no Dubrovke," www. zalozhniki.ru/, October 25, 2005, www.zalozhniki.ru/comment/97181.html.

8. There are also indications that the attack on the school stemmed from a provocation organized by the Russian secret services that went awry. In August 2004, according to police documents obtained by *Novaya Gazeta,* Kazbek Mamaev, the head of security of the North Ossetian police, received a report from an informant that a group of Chechens were planning an act of terror that would involve children. This report, however, was never acted upon. Nor was that warning unique. Other reports about preparations for a terrorist act in North Ossetia were being received at the time with unnerving regularity.

The last warning of an impending attack came on September 1, 2004. At 5 A.M., the Chechen police passed along to the Russian Internal Affairs Ministry information provided by a man named Arsamikov, who had just been arrested in Chechnya, about plans by terrorists to seize a school in Beslan on that day. This gave the police four hours to avert the seizure. However, no action was taken. Moreover, all roadblocks on the route to the school were removed, giving the terrorists unhindered access.

There were many known terrorists in the North Caucasus at the time, but the Russian authorities made no effort to arrest them. Many of the terrorists who would participate in the school seizure were wanted criminals but had been walking around freely in their home villages for months before the attack. The terrorists' second in command, Vladimir Khodov, a Ukrainian convert to Islam, had been involved in two terrorist attacks in North Ossetia, a car bombing in Vladikavkaz in February 2004 and a train derailment in May near Elkhotovo, his hometown. After the bombing in Vladikavkaz, he was made the subject of a federal search, and his photograph was hung up all over the republic. Nonetheless, during the spring and summer, Khodov lived openly in Elkhotovo. His presence was reported to the republican FSB and the police organized crime division, but for some reason he was not apprehended.

An explanation of why warnings were ignored, roadblocks were removed, and known terrorists were not apprehended came from Shamil Basaev, the Chechen terrorist leader who planned the Beslan attack and was killed on July 10, 2006. In an open letter entitled "We Have a Lot to Tell about Beslan," published on the separatist website Kavkaz Center on August 31, 2005, Basaev wrote that the attackers had been pushed toward the seizure of the school by the leadership of the secret services of North Ossetia with the help of their agent Abdulla (Vladimir) Khodov.

According to Basaev, Khodov confessed to being an agent, and Basaev persuaded him to become a double agent. In that capacity, he led the Russians to believe that the terrorists were preparing to seize the North Ossetian government and parliament on September 6, the anniversary of Chechen independence. The Russian secret services, Basaev wrote, "intended [on September 6] to meet the group as they entered Vladikavkaz and destroy them. On August 31 they opened a corridor for us for the active collection of intelligence, but we used it to enter Beslan [and seize the school], changing the date and objective of the attack."

In fact, there was considerable evidence in police files that Khodov was indeed an agent of the North Ossetia secret services. In October 2004, a month after the tragedy, A. A. Bigulov, the North Ossetian prosecutor, said in a report to the Russian ministry of internal affairs that despite repeated requests for the whereabouts of Khodov sent to the police in his hometown, no steps had been taken to determine his location and no effort made to detain him. He called for a check on whether Khodov was a police agent and punishment of those responsible for carelessness and inaction in the search for him. See Dunlop, *The 2002 Dubrovak and 2004 Beslan Hostage Crises,* 23–25, 31, and Yelena Milashina, "Agentura vyshla iz-pod kontrolya i doshla do Beslana: Kak melkaya operativnaya igra s boevikami zakonchilas samim krovavim teraktom v istorii Rossii," *Novaya Gazeta,* August 31, 2009.

9. Yelena Milashina, "Est Liudi kotorim izvestno vse," *Novaya Gazeta,* in special supplement, "Beslan: Resultati Rassledovaniya," no. 65, 8/28–30, 2006. Maskhadov did not even ask for a guarantee of his own safety. He asked only to be allowed to enter the school.

10. Ibid. According to Saveliev, the first explosion was the result of a shot from a

flamethrower fired from the fifth floor of a building near the school at 1:03 P.M. The second explosion, which came twenty-two seconds later, was caused by a fragmentation grenade with a dynamite equivalent of thirteen pounds shot from a different five-story building on the same street.

Saveliev was the only specialist on the commission. Nonetheless, when he presented his conclusions, he was accused by the chairman, Alexander Torshin, of "deliberate falsification." In July 2007 members of the group Mothers of Beslan received copies of a videotape of the events in the mail that had been made by an employee of the prosecutor of North Ossetia and had been reported lost for three years. It contained an interview with two sappers who entered the gymnasium at 3 P.M. on their own initiative to try to save lives. In the interview, which took place at roughly 4 P.M., the sappers said that the homemade explosive devices of the rebels had not exploded and were incapable of exploding and that there were no fragments in the walls. The interview confirmed Saveliev's conclusion that there were no explosions inside the gymnasium.

BIBLIOGRAPHY

∎

Abarinov, Vladimir. Interview with the author, October 26, 2009.

——. *The Murderers of Katyn*. New York: Hippocrene, 1993.

——. "Tainoye Stanovitsya Yavnim," new chapter 7 of *Katynski Labirint,* for the Polish edition, *Oprawcy z Katynia* (Warsaw: Znak, 2007), "Pravda o Katyne: Nezavisimoye Rassledovaniye," http://www.katyn.ru/index.php?go=Pages&in=view&id=908&page=1.

Abdullaev, Nabi. "The Bronze Chekist." *Transitions Online,* October 4, 2002. http://www.tol.org/client/article/7395-the-bronze-chekist.html.

——. "Luzhkov Wants to Restore Iron Felix." *Moscow Times,* September 16, 2002.

Adler, Nanci. *Beyond the Soviet System: The Gulag Survivor.* New Brunswick, N.J.: Transaction, 2002.

Albats, Yevgenia. "Putin Marches to the Beat of the Soviet Anthem." *Moscow Times,* December 7, 2000, http://www.themoscowtimes.com/opinion/article/putin-marches-to-the-beat-of-soviet-anthem/256829.html. Accessed December 26, 2007. Access to this site requires a subscription.

Analiticheskii, Tsentr Yuriya Levady. Survey on the Role of Stalin in the History of USSR conducted on February 22–25, 2008. http://www.levada.ru/press/2008030506.html. Accessed October 19, 2010.

Andrew, Christopher, and Oleg Gordievsky. *KGB: The Inside Story.* New York: HarperCollins, 1990.

Antonov, Andrei. "'Kholodnye Golovy' Dzerzhinskogo i Luzhkova." *primanews.ru,* September 16, 2002, http://prima-news/news/articles/2202/9/16/16826.html. Accessed September 27, 2005.

Aron, Leon. *Yeltsin: A Revolutionary Life.* New York: St. Martin's, 2000.

Artizov, Andrei, Yri Sigachev, I. Shevchuk, and V. Khlopov. *Reabilitatsiya: Kak Eto Bylo.* 3 vols. Ed. Alexander Yakovlev. Moscow: Mezhdunarodny Fond Demokratiya, 2003.

Atlantov, Ivan. "Gosduma Reshit Sud'bu Pamyatnika Dzerzhinskomu." *Izvestiya,* September 27, 2002.

Bagritskii, Eduard. "TVS," 1929. Trans. in Sinyavsky, *Soviet Civilization,* 131.

Baitalsky, Mikhail. *Notebooks for the Grandchildren: Recollections of a Trotskyist Who Survived the Stalin Terror.* Trans. Marilyn Vogt-Downey. Atlantic Highlands, N.J.: Humanities, 1995.

Balakin, Yu. N. *Kniga Pamyati Zhertv Politicheskikh Repressiy na Orlovshchine.* http://orthedu.ru/ch_hist/hist/knigi-pamja-/11840rlov1-.html.

Beevor, Antony. *Stalingrad: The Fateful Siege, 1942–1943.* New York: Penguin, 1999.

Belomestnov, Dmitri. "Schastlivoy Lustratsii!" *Internet Gazeta Garri Kasparova,* December 11, 2207. http://www.kasparov.ru/material.php?id=475E8A9F7 8E05. Accessed December 15, 2007.

Berdyaev, Nikolai. "Nuzhno Perezhit' Sud'bu Russkogo Naroda." *Russkiye Novosti,* February 8, 1946. Hoover Institution Archives.

——. "O Dvukhsmyslennosti Svobody." *Russkiye Novosti,* May 23, 1947. Hoover Institution Archives.

——. "Pravda I Lozh' Kommunizma." *Zarubezh'e,* December 1970, 2. Hoover Institution Archives.

——. *The Russian Revolution.* Ann Arbor: University of Michigan Press, 1966.

——. *Samopoznanie.* Moscow: Mysl', 1991.

——. "The Third Way," *Novy Zhurnal* 33 (1952): 274. Hoover Institution Archives.

——. "Vyderzhki iz Pisem N. A. Berdyaeva k Gospozhe X. (1930–1939)." *B. I. Nikolaevsky Collection* 35 (1954): 182. Hoover Institution Archives.

Bereznev, Alexander. "U polyakov—chelovek, u nas, kak vsegda, 'massy.'" *Smolenskiye Novosti,* June 7, 2000.

——. "Vesti s Nashei Golgofi." *Smolenskiye Novosti,* July 23, 2002.

Bragin, Vyacheslav. Interview with the author, June 28, 2005.

Burlatsky, Fedor. "Potaennyi Andropov," *Izvestiya,* June 15, 2004.

Carver, Tom. "General in Exile." *Assignment,* BBC 2. November 16, 1996.

Cherepova, Olga. "Katynskoe prestuplenie." *30 Octyabrya,* no. 5 (2000).

Chuikov, Vasili I. *The Beginning of the Road.* London: Macginbon and Kee, 1963.

Cienciala, Anna M., Natalia S. Lebedeva, and Wojciech Materski, eds. *Katyn: A Crime without Punishment.* New Haven: Yale University Press, 2007.

Conquest, Robert. *The Great Terror: A Reassessment.* New York: Oxford University Press, 1990.

Cosorez, Olga. Interview with the author, March 18, 2005.

Dobrovolsky, Alexander. "Slezy Edmundovicha." *Moskovskii Komsomolets,* October 21, 2002.

Dunlop, John I. "KGB Subversion of Russian Orthodox Church." *Social Issues* 1, no. 12 (1992): 51–53.

Embassy of the Republic of Poland in Canada. "Senate Pays Tribute to Katyn Victims." March 31, 2005.

Erofeev, Viktor. Conversation with the author, 1981.

"56% Rossiyan Podderzhivayut Ideyu Vozvrashcheniya Feliksa." Grani.ru, September 28, 2002. http://www.grani.ru/Society/m.20304.html.

Figes, Orlando. *A People's Tragedy: A History of the Russian Revolution.* New York: Viking, 1997.

———. *The Whisperers: Private Life in Stalin's Russia.* New York: Metropolitan, 2007.

Fischer, Benjamin B. "The Katyn Controversy: Stalin's Killing Field." Central Intelligence Agency, https://www.cia.gov/library/center-for-the-study-of-intelligence/csi-publications/csi-studies/studies/winter99-00/art6.html. Accessed November 13, 2009.

"FSB: Svedeniya o Neglasnykx Sotrudnikakh Spetssluzhb Ne Budut Rassekre cheny Nikogda." Grani.ru, July 8, 2007. http://www.grani.ru/Society/His tory/p.124449.html. Accessed September 7, 2007.

Fursenko, Aleksandr, and Timothy Naftali. *Khrushchev's Cold War: The Inside Story of an American Adversary.* New York: Norton, 2006.

German, Yuri. *Rasskazy o Felikse Dzerzhinskom.* Leningrad: Lenizdat, 1974.

"Gospoda! Kogda Zhe Vy Govorili Pravdu? Vchera ili Segodnya?" *Pravda,* July 4, 1992.

Grechnevsky, Oleg. "Smert' Shchekochikhina — Kremlevskaya Mafia Ubrala Eshhe Odnogo Cheloveka, Kotoryi Ei Meshal." Rosich.ru, July 5, 2003. http://rocich.ru/article.php?sid=287. Accessed October 14, 2010.

Grigoriants, Sergei. "Generaly i Stukachi Pomenyalis' Mestami," *Moskovskie Novosti,* November 26, 2002.

Grossman, Vasily. *A Writer at War: A Soviet Journalist with the Red Army, 1941–45.* New York: Vintage, 2005.

"Gruppa Deyatelei Politiki i Kul'tury Predlagayet Uvekovechit' Pamyat' Rukovoditelya Blokadnogo Leningrada Kuznetsova." Rol.ru, December 21, 2004, http://www.rol.ru/news/misc/news/04/12/21 064.htm.

"Gryzlov pokhvalil Stalina za neuryadnost." Lenta.ru, December 24, 2004. http://lenta.ru/russia/2004/12/21/stalin/24.12.2007. Accessed December 23, 2007.

Isachnikov, Vladimir. "Parliament Votes to Restore Soviet Anthem." *Moscow Times,* December 8, 2000. http://www.themoscowtimes.com/stories/2000/12/08/162.html. Accessed December 26, 2007.

Istoriko-Memorial'nyj Kompleks. "Geroyam Stalingradskoj Bitvy." Mamaevom Kurgane, http://mamayevhill.volgadmin.ru. Accessed January 28, 2008.

Ivanov, Yuri. "The Tragedy of the Polish Camps." *Nevazisimaya Gazeta,* 16 July 1998.

Jaspers, Karl. *The Question of German Guilt.* New York: Capricorn, 1961.

Kagarlitsky, Boris. "'Iron Felix' and Fetishism." *Moscow Times,* October 1, 2002.

"Karaul! Ugroza Vsemirnoj Demokratii!" *Gorod Orel,* April 28, 2005.

"Keep Iron Felix on Scrapheap of History." Editorial. *Moscow Times,* September 18, 2002.

Khimich, Oksana. "Preyemnik Stalina." *Moskovskii Komsomolets,* March 14, 2005.

Khristosom, Archepiscop. Interview. *Moskovskii Komsomolets,* November 30, 1993.

Khrushchev, Nikita. *Khrushchev Remembers*. Boston: Little, Brown, 1970.

Komal, F. B. "Leningrad. Konets 30-kh Godov." *Leningradskaya Panorama* 1 (1990).

Korchagina, Valeria. "Duma Set to Revive the Soviet Anthem." *Moscow Times,* December 6, 2000. http://www.themoscowtimes.com/stories/2000/12/06/013.html. Accessed December 26, 2007.

Kostin, Pavel. "Stalin v natural'nuyu velichinu." *Russkiy Kur'er,* July 24, 2006. http://ruscourier.ru/archive/1593. Accessed January 18, 2008.

Kotel'nik, Galina. "Stalingrad v Ogne. Mysli po povodu." *Donetskij kryazh,* February 18, 2005. http://media.ukr-info.net/smi/view_article.cgi?sid=3&nid=1494&aid=. Accessed January 20, 2008.

Kozakov, Mikhail. *Tretii Zvonok.* Moscow: Izdatel'stvo Nezavisimaya Gazeta, 2004.

Krayukhin, Dmitri. Interview with the author, May 15, 2005.

Kremlev, Vladimir. "ROAR: Stalin's Portraits Appear and Disappear in Russian Cities." *Russia Today,* May 6, 2010. http://rt.com/politics/roar-stalin-portraits-russia/.

"Krovavy Avgust." *Zapolyar'e,* September 2, 1995.

Latkovskis, Leonards. *Baltic Prisoners in the Gulag Revolts of 1953.* Rpt. from *Lituanus* 51, nos. 3, 4 (2005).

Leong, Albert. *Centaur: The Life and Art of Ernst Neizvestny.* Lanham, Md.: Rowman and Littlefield, 2002.

Lepsky, Yuri. "Alexander Yakovlev: 'No Need to Look for Ideology. All It Means Is Freedom.'" *Trud,* April 11, 1997.

Levchenko, Alexei. "Stalin Vstaet iz-pod Zemli." *Gazeta.ru,* August 26, 2009, http.//gazeta.ru/politics/2009/08/26 a 3240785.shtml.

Lomagin, Nikita. *Neizvestnaya Blokada.* St. Petersburg: Izdatel'skii Dom Neva, 2004.

Lozhkin, Viktor. "Abez'sky Lager." *30 Oktyabrya,* no. 45 (2004).

"Luzhkov Predlagaet Vosstanovit' Pamyatnik Dzerzhinskomu kak Pamyatnik Vuchetichu." Polit.ru, September 13, 2002, http://old.polit.ru/singlenews/503713.html.

Mayakovsky, Vladimir. "Khorosho!" 1927. Trans. in Sinyavsky, *Soviet Civilization,* 130.

Medvedev, Roy. *All Stalin's Men: Six Who Carried Out the Bloody Policies.* New York: Anchor/Doubleday, 1984.

———. "Andrei Sakharov and Alexander Solzhenitsyn." *Social Sciences* 2 (2002): 3–18.

Meek, James. "Russian Patriarch Was KGB Spy." *Guardian,* February 12, 1999.

Melgunov, S. P. *Krasny Terror v Rossii.* Moscow: PUICO, 1990.

Merridale, Catherine. *Ivan's War: Life and Death in the Red Army, 1939–1945.* New York: Picador, 2006.

"Mikhail Kozakov priznalsya, chto byl agentom KGB." NEWSru.com, August 2,

2002, http://newsru.com/cinema/02aug2002/kozakov.html. *Butovskiy Poligon*. Moscow: Al'zo, 1997.

Mikoyan, Anastas. *Tak Bylo*. Moscow: Izdatel'stvo Vagrius, 1999.

Mikoyan, Sergo. Interview with the author, September 26, 2005.

Mikoyan, Stepan. Interview with the author, July 10, 2005.

Milshteyn, Ilya. "Alexander Osvoboditel." Grani.ru, October 19, 2005. http:// www.grani.ru/Society/m.96859.html. Accessed October 19, 2005.

Minutko, Igor. "Putin and Andropov." *Eurasian Politican,* August 2001. http:// www.cc.jyu.fi/~aphamala/pe/issue4/putandrop.htm. Accessed December 26, 2007.

Mitin, R. "I Odin v Polye Voin." *Zapolyar'e,* October 5, 1999.

Moravsky, Jerzy. "Kto zhe stanet rasstrelivat' dnem?!" *Novoye Russkoye Slovo,* May 26, 1995.

Murphy, Kim. "Soviet Spy Chief Is Back—on a Pedestal." *Los Angeles Times,* November 10, 2005.

Nalecz, Tomasz. "Prestuplenuya ne bylo." *Wprost,* October 20, 2005, http://www .wprost.pl/ar/82085/Nalecz-Zbrodni-nie-bylo/?|=1194, republished in ino-SMI.ru, http://www.inosmi.ru/print/223117.html. Accessed April 11, 2005.

Narochnitskaya, Natalia. *Za Chto i s Kem My Voyevali*. Moscow: Izdatel'stvo Minuvsheye, 2005.

Neef, Christian, and Matthias Schepp. Interview with Alexander Solzhenitsyn. *Der Spiegel,* July 23, 2007. http://www.spiegel.de/international/world/o ,1518,druck-496211,00.html. Accessed March 8, 2008.

Negretov, Pavel. *Vsye Dorogi Vedut Na Vorkutu*. Benson, Vt.: Chalidze, 1985.

Nikonov, Vyacheslav. Interview with the author. November 10, 2003.

Noble, John. *I Was a Slave in Russia: An American Tells His Story*. New York: Devin-Adair, 1958.

Novaya Gazeta. Special edition 48, July 7, 2007. http://ys.novayagazeta.ru/text/ 2003-07-07-03. Accessed October 14, 2010.

O'Flynn, Kevin. "City Rejects Return of Dzerzhinsky." *Moscow Times,* January 22, 2003.

"Opolchentsy Traktornogo." *Molodoj Kommunist,* no. 2 (1973), 18.

Pankin, Alexei. "A Debt of Gratitude to Dzerzhinsky." *Moscow Times,* October 1, 2002.

Paul, Allen. *Katyn: Stalin's Massacre and the Seeds of Polish Resurrection*. Annapolis, Md.: Naval Institute Press, 1996.

Perlez, Jane. "Yeltsin 'Understands' Polish Bid for a Role in NATO." *New York Times,* August 26, 1993.

Petrushev, Nikolai. "Taina Andropova." *Rossiyskaya Gazeta,* June 15, 2004.

Piontkovsky, Andrei. "The Hubris of Russia's Governing Elite." *Insight on the News,* April 8–21, 2008. www.insight-mag.com.

Pipes, Richard. *Russian Conservatism and Its Critics: A Study in Political Culture*. New Haven: Yale University Press, 2005.

Podrabinek, Alexander. "Ideolog Kommunisma Opyat' pri Dele: A. N. Yakovlev Vernulsya k Lyubimoi Rabote." *Ekspress-Khronika,* December 24, 1994.

———. "Kak Antisovetchik Antisovetchikam . . ." *Ezhednevny Zhurnal,* September 21, 2009. http://ej.ru/?a=note_print&id=9467. Accessed September 30, 2009.

———. "Situatsiya, Vozmozhno, Khuzhe, chem Eto Kazhetsya na Pervyi Vzglyad . . ." *Ezhednevny Zhurnal,* September 29, 2009. http://ej.ru/?a=note_print&id=9494. Accessed September 30, 2009.

Poleshchikov, V. M. *Za Semyu Pechatyami: Iz arkhiva KGB.* Syktyvkar: Komi knizhnoe izd-vo, 1995.

Poltavchenko, Georgy. "Pamyatnik Dzerzhinskomu Vosstanovlen Ne Budet." *Leningradskaya Pravda,* September 23, 2002.

Popeski, Ron, and Fitzgerald, Tara. "Parliament Restores Soviet Anthem." *Moscow Times,* December 9, 2000. http://www.themoscowtimes.com/stories/2000/12/09/001.html. Accessed December 26, 2007.

Popov, Gavriil. "Vokrug Pamyatnika Dzerzhinskomu." *Moskovskiy Komsomolets,* October 11, 2002.

Potapkin, Petr. "Glukhie Telefony." *Novaya Gazeta,* January 24, 2002.

"Pravoslavnaya obschestvennost' protive vosstanovleniya pamyatnika Dzerzhinskomu, no predlagaet sdelat' Aleksandra Nevskogo pokrovitelem FSB." NEWSru.com, September 22, 2008, http://www.newsru.com/religy/22sep2008/fsb.html.

Pribylovsky, Vladimir. Interview. *Svobodnaya Pressa,* December 31, 2009. http://svpressa.ru/politic/article/19191/. Accessed October 9, 2010.

Pustyntsev, Boris, and Vladimir Shnitke. "Izbiratel'naya Pamyat'?" *Novoye Vremya,* March 20, 2005, 11.

Rakhmatullin, Rustam. "Rasstrel'nyi Dom' pod Pritselom." *Izvestiya,* January 20, 2006.

Razrushennye i Oskvernennye Khramy. Frankfurt: Posev-Verlag, 1980.

Reynolds, Maura. "National Anthem Is a Time to Hum." *Moscow Times,* September 26, 2000. http://www.themoscowtimes.com/stories/2000/09/26/200.html. Accessed December 26, 2007.

Roginsky, Arseny. "Bez Ukazaniya Prichin Smerti." Fond Pokayanie. Received by fax on June 24, 2004.

———. Interview with the author. November 19 and 21, 2004.

Rudinsky, F. *"Delo KPSS" v Konstitutsionnom Sude: Zapiski Uchastnika Protsessa.* Moscow: Bylina, 1999.

Ruling of the Constitutional Court on CPSU and CP RSFSR Activities. November 30, 1992. http://www.az-design.ru/Projects/AZLibrCD/Law/Constn/CCrt9296/2r004.shtml. Accessed December 22, 2008.

Russia (Federation), Konstitutsionnyi Sud. *Materialy Dela o Proverke Konstitutsionnosti Ukazov Presidenta.* Vols. 3–5. Moscow: Izdatel'stvo Spartak, 1997.

"Russians in France, Religion, and Soviet Government." *Manchester Guardian,* December 27, 1944. Hoover Institution Archives.

Ryzhkov, Vladimir. "Privivka ot Terrora." *Novaya Gazeta,* February 21–27, 2008.

Samarina, Alexandra. "Pravo na Pamyat." Interview with Alexander Yakovlev. *Obshchaya Gazeta,* October 18, 2001.

Saradzhyan, Simon. "Iron Felix Panned by Kremlin, Patriach." *Moscow Times,* September 23, 2002.

"Secret 2nd Sector 04057 of Central Committee of the Communist Party." *Karta,* 1994.

Service, Robert. *A History of Twentieth-Century Russia.* Cambridge: Harvard University Press, 1998.

Shafarevich, Igor. *Russkii Vopros.* Moscow: Algoritm-Kniga and Izdatel'stvo Eksmo, 2009.

Shentalinsky, Vitaly. "Filosofskiy Parokhod," from "Oskolki Serebryanogo Veka." *Novyi Mir,* nos. 5–6 (1998).

Shevtsov, Yuri. *Novaya Ideologiya: Golodomor.* Moscow: Izdatil'stvo "Evropa," 2009.

Shiryaev, Valery. "283 Shaga." *Novaya Gazeta,* February 21–27, 2008.

Shnitke, Vladimir. Interview with the author, May 20, 2005.

Silantieva, Yelena. Interview with the author, July 7, 2005.

Sinyavsky, Andrei. *Soviet Civilization.* New York: Arcade, 1990.

Skiruta, G. "Ryadovye Velikoy Vojny." *Dal'nij Vostok,* no. 5 (1978): 118.

Sokolov, Boris. "Nerzhaveyushchiy Feliks." Grani.ru, September 11, 2002, http://www.grani.ru/Politics/Russia/FSB/m.9142.html.

Solzhenitsyn, Alexander. *Kak Nam Obustroit' Rossiyu?* Paris: YMCA Press, 1990.

"SPS protiv Dzerzhinskogo." Dni.ru, September 16, 2002.

Stavitskaya, Anna. Interview with the author, December 20, 2009.

Svanidze, Nikolai. Interview with Boris Nemtsov. *Zerkalo* television program, October 5, 2002.

Sveridova, Olga. Interview with the author, July 1, 2009.

Svetova, Zoya. "Muzei ili 'Diskoteka na Kladbishche'?" *Novye Izvestiya,* April 26, 2006.

Szamuely, Tibor. *The Russian Tradition.* London: Secker and Warburg, 1974.

Taubman, William. *Khrushchev: The Man and His Era.* New York: Norton, 2003.

Thorson, Carla. "The Fate of the Communist Party in Russia." *RFE/RL Research Report* 37 (1992): 1–6.

Tikhomirov, Vladimir. "'Palyenaya' Pravda." *Ogonek,* May 25, 2009.

Tolz, Vera. "The Katyn Documents and the CPSU Hearing." *RFE/RL Research Report* 44 (1992): 27–33.

Tolz, Vera, and Julia Wishnevsky. "The Russian Government Declassifies CPSU Documents." *RFE/RL Research Report* 26 (1992): 8–11.

Transcript of the Trial of the Communist Party. *Pravda,* July 14, July 18, and October 17, 1992.

Tretiakov, Vitaly. "Alexander Solzhenitsyn: Sberezheniye Naroda — Vysshaya izo Vsekh Nashikh Gosudarstvennykh Zadach." *Moskovskiye Novosti,* April 28, 2006. http://www.mn.ru/print.php?2006-15-43. Accessed March 5, 2006. Republished in Rodina, http://www.rodina-nps.ru/point/show/?id=160.

Tsentr obshchestvennikh svyazi, UFSB RF po Smolenskoi Oblast. Press Release, April 20, 1995.

Turrou, Leon. "An Unwritten Chapter." Manuscript, 1926. Furnished by the Hoover Institution.

Ushik, N., and V. Griner. *Vorkuta*. Syktyvkar: Komi Knizhnoe Izdatel'stvo, 1972.

Varfolomeev, Vladimir. Interview with Nikolai Kharitonov. Ekho Moskvy, July 6, 2000.

Verkhovnyi Sovet Rossiiskoi Federatsii. *Sbornik Zakonodatel'nykh i Normativnykh Aktov o Repressiyakh i Reabilitatsii Zhertv Politicheskikh Repressii*. Moscow: Izdatel'stvo Respublika, 1993.

Vilert, Arnold. *Eshelon Idet na Vorkuta: Vospominaniya Uznika GULAGa*. Latvia (?): 1998.

Vlasova, Irina. "Feniks v Kozhanom Pal'to." *Novye Izvestiya*, November 9, 2005.

Volosenkov, Anatoly. Interview with the author, May 18, 2005.

Vorsobin, Vladimir. " 'Pomogite, Menya Razdavit Press v Musorovoze!' " *Komsomolskaya Pravda*, January 22, 2002.

Yakovlev, Alexander. *A Century of Violence in Soviet Russia*. Harrisonburg: Donnelley and Sons, 2002.

———. Interviews with the author. February 11 and June 23, 2003.

———. "K chitateliu." In *Katyn: Plenniki neob'iavlennoi voiny*. Ed. N. S. Lebedeva, V. Materski, and N. A. Petrosova. Moscow: Mezhdunarodnyi Fond Demokratiya, 1999.

———. *Sumerki*. Moscow: Izdatel'stvo Materik, 2003.

Yazhborovskaya, Inessa, Anatoly Yablokov, and Valentina Parsadanova. *Katynskii Sindrom v Sovetsko-Pol'skikh i Rossiisko-Pol'skikh Otnosheniyakh*. Moscow: Izdatel'stvo Rossiiskaya Politicheskaya Entsiklopedia, 2009.

Yeltsin, Boris. *Against the Grain*. Trans. Michael Glenny. New York: Summit, 1990.

Young, Cathy. "Traditional Prejudices: The Anti-Semitism of Alexander Solzhenitsyn." *Reason,* May 2004. http://reason.com/archives/2004/05/01/traditional-prejudices. Accessed October 28, 2010.

http://www.zaprava.ru/hronica/krayhin.htm. Accessed September 28, 2007.

"Zayavlenie Mezhdunarodnogo Obshchestvo 'Memorial' o Rassledovanii 'Katynskogo Prestupleniya' v Rossii." *30 Oktyabrya*, no. 52 (2005).

Zemtsov, Ilya. *Andropov*. Jerusalem: IRICS, 1983.

Zhavoronkov, Gennady. "Secret of Katyn Forest." *Moscow News,* no. 32 (1989).

Zolotov, Andrei. "Russian Orthodox Church Approves as Putin Decides to Sing to a Soviet Tune." *Christianity Today,* January 1, 2000. http://www.christianity today.com/ct/2000/decemberweb-only/57.0.html. Accessed December 26, 2007.

INDEX

■